INSPIRE / PLAN / DISCOVER / EXPERIENCE

# SOUTH AFRICA

DK EYEWITNESS

# SOUTH AFRICA

# CONTENTS

# DISCOVER 6

# FIELD GUIDE 66

# EXPERIENCE 114

# NEED TO KNOW 362

Left: Traditional Zulu beadwork
Previous page: Cape Town and Table Mountain
Front cover: Scenic view of Table Mountain,
as seen from the beach at Bloubergstrand

# DISCOVER

The skyline of Johannesburg at night

# WELCOME TO SOUTH AFRICA

Abundant wildlife, spectacular scenery and vibrant city life: South Africa has it all. Whatever your dream trip to this captivating country includes, this DK Eyewitness Travel Guide is your perfect companion.

1 The City Hall building in central Durban.

2 A lion in Kgalagadi Transfrontier Park.

3 Traditional baskets for sale at a crafts market.

4 Picturesque Camps Bay, just outside Cape Town.

Nestled at the southern tip of Africa, this vast land is a natural paradise of rugged vistas, beautiful beaches, and kaleidoscopic flora and fauna. From the curvaceous, rust-coloured dunes of the Kalahari to the verdant plateau of Table Mountain, the pull of the outdoors is impossible to resist. Whether it's coming eye to eye with an elephant in Kruger National Park, standing amid a colourful carpet of spring wildflowers in Namaqualand, or hiking across the craggy peaks of the uKhahlamba-Drakensberg, you'll find plenty of experiences worthy of any bucket list.

Peppered throughout this landscape is an endlessly appealing assortment of cities and towns, infused with a unique blend of colonial and Indigenous influences. Cosmopolitan Cape Town exudes coastal cool, while glittering Johannesburg pulsates with entrepreneurial energy. An old-world charm endures in smaller towns, like Stellenbosch and Franschhoek, many of which are unexpected havens of world-class wine and gourmet cuisine. A strong sense of history is palpable throughout, from the prehistoric origins of our earliest ancestors to the inspirational legacy of Nelson Mandela.

With so many things to see and do, any visit to South Africa packs a punch. We've broken the country down into easily navigable chapters, with detailed itineraries and comprehensive maps to help plan the perfect visit. Add insider tips, a Field Guide and a Need To Know section with all the practical essentials to be aware of, and you've got an indispensable guidebook. Enjoy the book, and enjoy South Africa.

# REASONS TO LOVE
# SOUTH AFRICA

Immense swathes of savannah teeming with fearsome beasts and colourful birds. A coastline as varied as it is beautiful. Ancient rock-art sites and world-class vineyards. Here are just some of the reasons why we love South Africa.

## 1 SPECTACULAR SAFARIS

Lions lazing in the sun, a family of elephants parading through the bush, vivid sunbirds flitting between branches: enjoy close encounters with some of nature's most majestic animals.

## NATURAL WONDERS 2

Whether it's the rolling dunes of the Kalahari *(p194)*, chasmic Blyde River Canyon *(p348)* or the Drakensberg's jagged peaks *(p278)*, South Africa's scenery is truly unforgettable.

## 3 CITY LIFE

South Africa's vibrant cities not only house an appealing array of cultural attractions, but thrive with buzzing markets, trendy restaurants and lively nightlife.

## DIVERSE COASTLINE 4
From family-friendly beaches to land-based whale-watching, South Africa's epic coastline – spanning the warm Indian Ocean and chillier Atlantic – has something for everyone.

## ADVENTURE ACTIVITIES 5
Get an adrenaline fix by leaping the world's highest bungee-jump at Bloukrans Bridge *(p232)*, scaling the heights of Table Mountain *(p126)* or rafting the mighty Orange River *(p203)*.

## THE WINELANDS 6
Soak up the summer sunshine of the scenic Winelands while savouring a mouthwatering array of world-class wines and fine dining in Stellenbosch *(p172)* and Franschhoek *(p178)*.

### FOOTING IT 7
From the lofty peaks of uKhahlamba-Drakensberg Park *(p278)* to the coastal cliffscapes of Robberg *(p242)*, the country's network of walking trails is seemingly limitless.

### CAPE PENINSULA 8
A mountainous sliver of land that stretches south from Cape Town, the Cape Peninsula is a haven of sandy beaches, pretty seaside towns and rugged natural beauty *(p142)*.

### 9 TRADITIONAL CULTURE
South Africa's cultural tapestry is a rich blend of traditions. Learn to throw a Zulu spear at Shakaland *(p290)* or attend the sensational Umhlanga (Reed Dance) *(p361)* in Eswatini.

## 10 SPECTATOR SPORTS

Sport is a national obsession in South Africa. Soak up the atmosphere at a rugby or soccer match, where the passion of the unabashedly partisan crowds is palpable *(p54)*.

## ANCIENT PREHISTORY 11

Uncover the lives of our earliest ancestors: go fossil-hunting at the Cradle of Humankind *(p314)* and marvel at the rock art of uKhahlamba-Drakensberg Park *(p278)*.

## THE MANDELA LEGACY 12

The iconic political leader died in 2013, but his legacy lives on in the country's soul. Learn about his life at Robben Island *(p129)* and Mthatha *(p257)*, near his childhood home in Qunu.

# EXPLORE
# SOUTH
# AFRICA

This guide divides South Africa, Eswatini and Lesotho into 11 colour-coded sightseeing areas, as shown on the map here. Find out more about each area on the following pages.

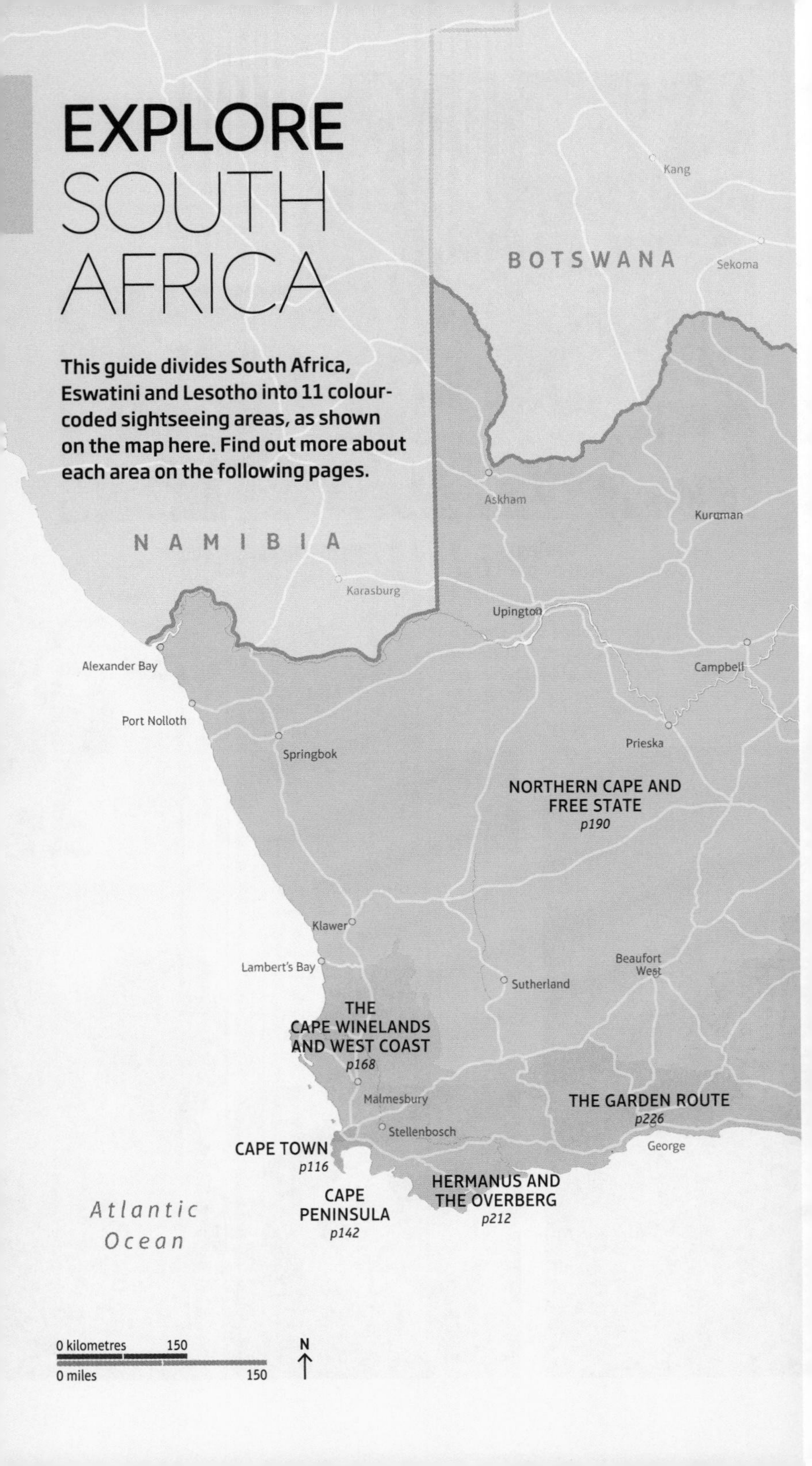

BOTSWANA

Kang

Sekoma

NAMIBIA

Askham

Kuruman

Karasburg

Upington

Alexander Bay

Campbell

Port Nolloth

Prieska

Springbok

**NORTHERN CAPE AND FREE STATE**
*p190*

Klawer

Beaufort West

Lambert's Bay

Sutherland

**THE CAPE WINELANDS AND WEST COAST**
*p168*

Malmesbury

**THE GARDEN ROUTE**
*p226*

Stellenbosch

George

**CAPE TOWN**
*p116*

*Atlantic Ocean*

**CAPE PENINSULA**
*p142*

**HERMANUS AND THE OVERBERG**
*p212*

0 kilometres       150

0 miles              150

N
↑

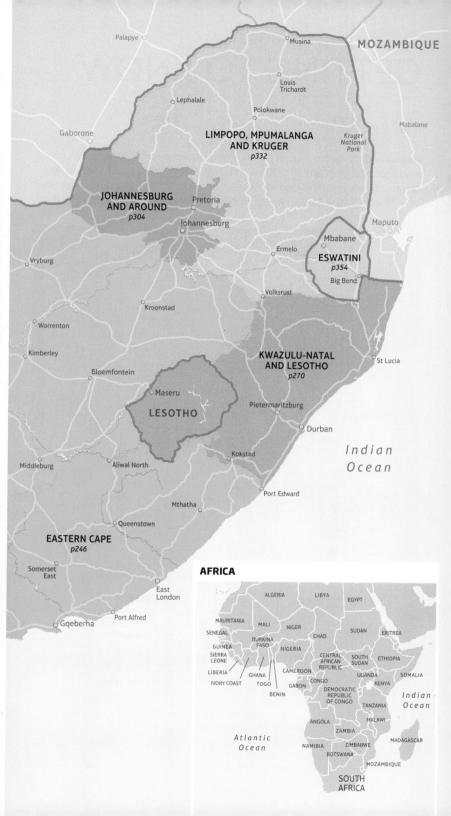

# GETTING TO KNOW
# SOUTH AFRICA

Renowned for its biodiversity and superb safari opportunities, South Africa also boasts a spectacular 2,800-km (1,740-mile) coastline. Elsewhere, the terrain ranges from the jagged peaks of the uKhahlamba-Drakensberg to the lush forests of the Garden Route to the parched dunescapes of the Kalahari.

## CAPE TOWN

PAGE 116

Scenically sandwiched between the sparkling blue waters of Table Bay and the imperious heights of Table Mountain, Cape Town is one of the world's most beautiful cities. Its central streets are steeped in history, lined with centuries-old landmarks and illuminating museums dedicated to every aspect of the city's past. The vibe here is laid-back coastal chic, with an abundance of cosmopolitan restaurants, lively bars, pan-African crafts markets and quirky shops centred around the bright V&A Waterfront and more down-to-earth Long Street.

**Best for**
*Museums, shopping, eating out, families*

**Home to**
*District Six Museum, the V&A Waterfront, Table Mountain, Robben Island*

**Experience**
*Ascending from the city bowl to the summit of Table Mountain on the sensational revolving cable car*

# CAPE PENINSULA

PAGE 142

A flinty mountainous spine that extends 50 km (30 miles) south from Cape Town, the Cape Peninsula is flanked to the west by the tempestuous Atlantic Ocean and to the east by the calmer waters of False Bay. Lined with scenic swimming beaches, its changing coastline offers great opportunities for whale-watching, sea kayaking and surfing, and also provides supplies for the area's fine seafood restaurants. On terra firma, wine lovers flock to the venerable estates of Constantia, while outdoor enthusiasts enjoy spectacular hikes and the delightful Kirstenbosch Botanical Garden.

**Best for**
*Suburban beaches, marine wildlife, scenic seaside walks*

**Home to**
*Kirstenbosch National Botanical Garden, Groot Constantia, Cape of Good Hope, Boulders Penguin Colony*

**Experience**
*The windswept end-of-the-continent aura that permeates the wave-battered cliffs of the Cape of Good Hope*

PAGE 168

# THE CAPE WINELANDS AND WEST COAST

This is the scenic heart of the country's wine industry, with verdant, vine-covered valleys overlooked by striking sandstone mountains. The appealing town of Stellenbosch has an old-world feel, with its distinctive architecture, while nearby Franschhoek is a foodie's paradise. You'll also find plenty of natural delights here, in the sweeping marine landscapes, rich birdlife and seasonal flowers of the West Coast National Park.

**Best for**
*Wine tasting, fine dining, marine birds*

**Home to**
*Stellenbosch, Franschhoek, West Coast National Park*

**Experience**
*A picnic lunch on the lawns of Boschendal with a bottle of the estate's world-class bubbly*

→

PAGE 190

# NORTHERN CAPE AND FREE STATE

Nature reigns supreme in this thinly populated region, where the ground is carpeted with diverse flora. It's best explored from August to October when the spring wildflowers are in bloom. Augrabies Falls is an awe-inspiring demonstration of the power of Mother Earth, Kimberley's "Big Hole" provides an insight into the country's diamond mining industry, and on the dunefields of Kgalagadi Transfrontier Park, a fascinating array of wildlife can be found.

**Best for**
*Wide open spaces, spring wildflowers, arid-country wildlife*

**Home to**
*Kgalagadi Transfrontier Park, Kimberley*

**Experience**
*The incredible force of Augrabies Falls as it explodes into the world's largest granite gorge*

PAGE 212

# HERMANUS AND THE OVERBERG

This quiet corner of the Western Cape is often bypassed by visitors, most of whom tend to congregate around the quaint seaside town of Hermanus. Set atop magnificent rocky cliffs, the town offers the world's best land-based whale-watching from July to November. Elsewhere, the Overberg harbours an array of lesser-known treasures that include Cape Agulhas (the most southerly point in Africa), several top notch wineries and a clutch of fine pedestrian-friendly nature reserves.

**Best for**
*Whale watching, fynbos-associated wildlife*

**Home to**
*Hermanus*

**Experience**
*A gull's-eye view of southern right whales and their newborn calves from the cliffs of Walker Bay*

# THE GARDEN ROUTE

PAGE 226

Gentler in feel than the Atlantic coastline to its west, the aptly named Garden Route follows the Indian Ocean coastline for 200 km (125 miles) between Mossel Bay and Tsitsikamma. Partially protected within the Garden Route National Park, its natural mosaic of pretty swimming beaches, tranquil lakes, sheltered lagoons and forested mountain slopes supports a kaleidoscopic variety of birdlife and marine fauna. You'll find a warm welcome at the region's string of small seaside towns, where individuality trumps chains and franchises.

**Best for**
*Coastal scenery, forest hikes, adventure activities, ostrich farms*

**Home to**
*Cango Caves, Tsitsikamma*

**Experience**
*Plunging over the Bloukrans Bridge on the world's tallest commercial bungee jump*

PAGE 246

# EASTERN CAPE

It might not boast the big-name attractions of other regions, but the unassuming Eastern Cape is an underrated treasure trove of stellar sights. The rugged Wild Coast is no less scenic than the more feted and touristy Garden Route, while Addo Elephant National Park and its neighbouring private reserves offer some of the best Big Five viewing in the country. Off-the-beaten-track historical sites include Nelson Mandela's birthplace at Qunu and the time-warped Victoriana of Makhanda (formerly Grahamstown).

**Best for**
*Elephant encounters, the Mandela legacy*

**Home to**
*Addo Elephant National Park, the Wild Coast, Graaff-Reinet*

**Experience**
*Being immersed in contemporary culture at Makhanda's annual National Arts Festival*

$\rightarrow$

# KWAZULU-NATAL AND LESOTHO

The most biodiverse of South Africa's nine provinces, KwaZulu-Natal has a varied landscape, ranging from the towering peaks of uKhahlamba-Drakensberg Park to the pristine coastal wetlands of iSimangaliso. Sun-seekers are drawn to the beach resorts that flank the seaside city of Durban, while wildlife lovers are delighted by the province's excellent game reserves. This is also a great place to explore Indigenous culture, with Zulu dances at Shakaland and ancient rock art across the Drakensberg.

**Best for**
*Zulu culture, prehistoric rock art, mountain hikes, subtropical beaches*

**Home to**
*Durban, uKhahlamba-Drakensberg Park, Hluhluwe-Imfolozi Game Reserve, iSimangaliso Wetland Park*

**Experience**
*A face-to-face encounter with a wild rhino on a guided walk in Hluhluwe-Imfolozi*

# JOHANNESBURG AND AROUND

Founded on the world's richest gold seams, the sprawling economic powerhouse of Gauteng encompasses the country's largest city (Johannesburg), the national capital (Pretoria) and the most populous and well-known of the townships established under apartheid (Soweto). Urban attractions abound, but their brash modernity is placed in perspective by the Cradle of Humankind, with its wealth of early hominin fossils, and the wild game reserves of Madikwe and Pilanesberg.

**Best for**
*City life, museums, safaris, paleontological sites*

**Home to**
*Apartheid Museum, Gold Reef City, Soweto, Cradle of Humankind, Pilanesberg Game Reserve and Sun City, Madikwe Game Reserve*

**Experience**
*Visiting the restored Soweto home where Nelson Mandela once lived*

PAGE 332

# LIMPOPO, MPUMALANGA AND KRUGER

This wild region is prime safari country, with large numbers of the Big Five roaming the vast Kruger National Park. Kruger is hugely popular with self-drivers and those on a tight budget, thanks to its excellent amenities, but you can also safari in style at the cluster of legendary private reserves that border the park. Elsewhere, you'll find yet more natural wonders in the form of the more westerly escarpment and the breathtaking Blyde River Canyon.

**Best for**
*Self-drive safaris, five-star luxury safaris, birding, escaping the winter chill*

**Home to**
*Kruger National Park, Pilgrim's Rest*

**Experience**
*Self-driving at your leisure through Kruger, a protected wilderness the size of Wales*

PAGE 354

# ESWATINI

Bordered by South Africa on three sides, the diminutive country of Eswatini (formerly Swaziland) is Africa's only remaining autonomous kingdom. Most visitors simply pass through here on their way between Kruger and KwaZulu-Natal, but it's well deserving of a more extended stay. There's plenty of scope for game viewing, as well as trying your hand at adventure activities such as white-water rafting or rock climbing. For full immersion in Swazi tradition, time your visit to coincide with the annual Umhlanga Reed Dance.

**Best for**
*Traditional African culture, rafting*

**Home to**
*Sibebe Rock, Malolotja Nature Reserve*

**Experience**
*Seeing 40,000 traditionally attired Swazi women paying tribute to the Queen Mother at the Umhlanga Reed Dance*

←

1 Admiring the view of Cape Town from Table Mountain.

2 The V&A Waterfront.

3 Penguins at Boulders Beach.

4 A bottle of Groot Constantia's acclaimed wine.

Vast and varied, South Africa brims with travel possibilities. These suggested itineraries pick out the highlights of each region, to help you plan your time in this beautiful country.

# 3 DAYS

## *in Cape Town and the Cape Peninsula*

### Day 1

**Morning** Start with an early breakfast before catching the first cable car for the breathtaking ascent up Table Mountain (*p126*). Work up an appetite exploring the plateau's gentle network of self-guided trails – with plenty of stops to admire the spectacular views – then grab lunch at the self-service Table Mountain Café.

**Afternoon** Back in the city centre, take a tour of Cape Town's past with a leisurely stroll from the shady Company's Garden to the Castle of Good Hope (*p131*). On the way, call in at the thought-provoking District Six Museum (*p120*).

**Evening** Relax over a drink at one of the many bars that line bohemian Long Street, then sample the pan-African menu (and, with luck, live music) at the legendary Mama Africa restaurant (*p134*).

### Day 2

**Morning** After breakfast at the V&A Waterfront (*p122*), take the 9am or 11am guided tour to Robben Island (*p129*). Keep an eye out for dolphins on the crossing to this African Alcatraz, where Nelson Mandela and other political prisoners were incarcerated under apartheid.

**Afternoon** Enjoy a light lunch at Makers Landing (*p123*) at the V&A Waterfront, then dedicate the rest of the afternoon to

exploring this vast harbourfront complex. Dive into the deep at the Two Oceans Aquarium, soak up some culture at the dazzling Zeitz Museum of Contemporary Art Africa or indulge in a spot of retail therapy at the hundreds of shops.

**Evening** Settle in for a relaxed evening at Quay Four (*p123*), enjoying the scenery with a sundowner from the extensive craft beer and wine menu, followed by a delicious seafood dinner.

### Day 3

**Morning** Embark on a day tour of the Cape Peninsula by following the cliff-hugging Chapman's Peak toll road to the Cape of Good Hope (*p150*). Catch the funicular to Cape Point Lighthouse to enjoy dramatic cliff-top views over the Peninsula's southern tip.

**Afternoon** After a leisurely lunch in Simon's Town (*p158*), pay a visit to the penguins at Boulders Beach (*p152*), then take a fascinating heritage walking tour of Kalk Bay (*p159*).

**Evening** End the afternoon at Groot Constantia (*p148*), South Africa's oldest wine-producing estate. After admiring the Winelands scenery and lovely Cape Dutch architecture, enjoy fine dining and the estate's superb wine in the historic Jonkerhuis Restaurant.

→

1 The charming Village Museum in Stellenbosch.

2 Betty's Bay at sunset.

3 The historic lighthouse at Cape Agulhas.

4 Ostriches in Oudtshoorn.

# 9 DAYS

## *along the Western Cape and Garden Route*

### Day 1

Start in Stellenbosch (p172), South Africa's second-oldest town. Dedicate your first morning to exploring its oak-lined roads, making sure to visit Oom Samie Se Winkel and the Village Museum. Once you've finished soaking up the old-world atmosphere, drive to the lovely small town of Franschhoek (p178), stopping en route for a scenic picnic lunch on the lawns of the Boschendal Wine Estate (p177). After visits to Franschhoek's Huguenot Monument and Museum, drop in for a wine-tasting session at Tokara (p176), a modern winery with a sensational setting on Helshoogte Pass. Return to Stellenbosch and wind down with dinner at Oude Werf, the country's oldest hotel.

### Day 2

Explore more of the Stellenbosch Winelands (p176), calling in at the historic Neethlingshof and Saxenburg estates and fun-for-all-the-family Spier, with its raptor centre and spa. Lunch at Vergelegen, a beautifully located wine estate on the slopes of the Helderberg outside Somerset West, then follow the coastal road southwest to Hermanus (p216), stopping en route at Betty's Bay's penguin colony (p223). Make the most of the coastal setting with a seafood dinner and chilled white wine at one of Hermanus's ocean-facing restaurants.

### Day 3

Enjoy a hearty breakfast before embarking on a bracing morning walk along the cliff paths around Hermanus, keeping a sharp eye out for whales in calving season (September to October). Drive southeast to the pretty 19th-century Moravian mission at Elim (p223), then on to windswept Cape Agulhas (p222), the most southerly point in Africa. Admire its forbidding coastline from the top of the century-old lighthouse, then kick back with sand between your toes over an al-fresco beachfront dinner at the unpretentious Struisbaai Sea Shack (seashackstruisbaai.co.za), 8 km (5 miles) east of Agulhas.

### Day 4

Set off early on the four- to five-hour drive to Oudtshoorn (p234), breaking up the journey with a coffee stop at picturesque Swellendam (p225), South Africa's third-oldest town. After settling in at Oudtshoorn, take a guided tour of the mind-blowing Cango Caves (p230), adorned with striking dripstone formations. If there's time afterwards, you could pay a visit to one of the local ostrich farms. In the evening, dine on locally sourced ostrich steak or burgers – free range and almost totally cholesterol-free, these are the must-try speciality at most of Oudtshoorn's restaurants.

→

1

2    3

## Day 5

A two-hour drive through George *(p235)* brings you to the lovely coastal village of Wilderness *(p236)*. Shortly before arriving here, take a quick detour to the well-signposted Dolphin Point for a photo opportunity with some stunning ocean views. After an early lunch, hire a canoe and paddle into Garden Route National Park's spectacular Touw River Gorge to enjoy the wonderful forest scenery and birdlife. For dinner, treat yourself to the best pizza along the Garden Route at Pomodoro *(p237)*, watching the world go by from its wide terrace.

## Day 6

After a relaxed morning stroll along Wilderness's stunning beach, drive 45 km (30 miles) east to Knysna *(p238)*. There, enjoy a snack or light lunch at the legendary Île de Païn bakery and café *(iledepain.co.za)* on Thesen Island. Spend the afternoon exploring Knysna's lively town centre and the pretty lagoon shore by foot, making sure to climb the short but vertiginous footpath that traverses the more easterly of the rocky "heads"

that guard the lagoon entrance. Reward yourself with a sundowner session of chilled Mitchell's beer (produced nearby at South Africa's oldest craft brewery) and freshly shucked oysters – no visit to Knysna would be complete without experiencing a taste of these local delicacies.

## Day 7

Drive north of Knysna to Diepwalle Forestry Station *(p238)*, where an easy 9-km (6-mile) circular walking trail leads through a lush evergreen forest known for its ancient giant yellowwood trees and small and elusive population of free-ranging elephants. Return to Knysna for lunch, then drive the 30 km (20 miles) to Plettenberg Bay *(p240)*, optionally stopping en route at the family-friendly Knysna Elephant Park. Spend the rest of the day relaxing on the Garden Route's best-loved swimming beach, which runs south from the town centre to Robberg Peninsula. When evening arrives, hit the beachfront for yummy cocktails, and fresh Mediterranean-style seafood or sushi at the attractively positioned Fat Fish *(thefatfish.co.za)*.

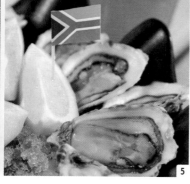

① The town of Wilderness.

② A Knysna lourie, or turaco.

③ The suspension bridge at Storms River Mouth.

④ Knysna Elephant Park.

⑤ Fresh oysters in Knysna.

⑥ Kerubooms Beach.

## Day 8

Get up early to make the most of the magnificent coastal scenery and marine wildlife-viewing along Robberg Nature Reserve's trio of self-guided circular walking trails (p242). Afterwards, stop in at Global Village (p241) for a light lunch and Plett's best handicraft shopping, then head 10 km (6 miles) east to Keurbooms Beach, which is even wilder and more beautiful than its counterpart in town. After an afternoon relaxing on the beach, grab a table at Keurbooms's wide terraced beachfront Ristorante Enrico (enricorestaurant.co.za) for a sundowner and dinner before heading back to town.

## Day 9

It's only 60 km (37 miles) from Plett to the Tsitsikamma sector of Garden Route National Park (p232), but there's plenty to see and do along the way. Enjoy a scenic stroll along the wide, forest-lined beach at Nature's Valley (p241), go on a guided tour to meet the tame primate inhabitants of Monkeyland (p240) or make the gut-churning bungee jump off the 216-m- (709-ft-) high Bloukrans Bridge

(faceadrenalin.com). At Tsitsikamma, embark on the short but sensational self-guided hike that incorporates the suspension bridge over the chasmic Storms River Mouth. Spend the night at The Rest Camp at Storms River, which has arguably the most spectacular setting of any national park accommodation in South Africa. Soak up the views while relaxing over a self-catering barbecue. The next day, either retrace your route 150 km (95 miles) back west to George Airport or continue 180 km (110 miles) east to Gqeberha (p260), depending on your onward plans.

← 
1 Table Mountain, viewed from the beach at Bloubergstrand.

2 Cape gannets, Lambert's Bay.

3 Rock art in the Cederberg.

4 The rocky landscape of the Cederberg, with Wolfberg Arch.

# 9 DAYS
## *Cape Town to Johannesburg*

### Day 1

Drive two hours from Cape Town to West Coast National Park *(p180)*, making a stop at Bloubergstrand *(p186)* on the way – the view back across Table Bay to Table Mountain is unmissable. Lunch within the national park at Geelbek Homestead *(sanparks.org)*, which serves traditional Cape cuisine and also houses a natural history museum. In spring-flower season (August to October), continue to the park's Postberg sector, where multihued floral displays are complemented by striking rock formations and plentiful wildlife. At other times of year, you can explore the two bird hides and several short trails around Geelbek. Follow the east shore of Langebaan Lagoon to the characterful coastal village of Paternoster *(p186)*, where you can dine in one of the renowned local crayfish restaurants before spending the night in a converted fisherman's cottage.

### Day 2

Take a short pre-breakfast stroll through the peninsular Columbine Nature Reserve bordering Paternoster, then follow the scenic, little-used coast road north for 130 km (80 miles) to Lambert's Bay *(p188)*. Make the acquaintance of the local wildlife at Bird Island, which can be reached from Lambert's Bay harbour along a 100-m (330-ft) breakwater. The main attraction is a noisy breeding colony of colourful Cape gannets, but Cape cormorants and African penguins also breed here – you might see Cape fur seals, too. As the day draws to a close, make your way to Muisbosskerm *(muisbosskerm.co.za)*, a beachfront restaurant 5 km (3 miles) south of Lambert's Bay. Enjoy the superb sunset views while savouring a great selection of inexpensive West Coast wine and mouthwatering seafood and traditional Cape fare.

### Day 3

Join a guided motorboat excursion from Lambert's Bay to look for Heaviside's dolphin, a west coast endemic that often swims playfully in the boat's wake. After an early lunch, drive 95 km (60 miles) east into the Cederberg *(p189)* to walk the undemanding Sevilla Trail. It offers a fine introduction to the region's superb prehistoric paintings, passing nine different rock art sites in the space of 5 km (3 miles). Spend the night in the Cederberg area, or – if it's spring-flower season – journey 120 km (75 miles) north to Nieuwoudtville *(p200)* for the night.

### Day 4

In the Cederberg, start with a hearty breakfast to energize you for a day of exploring by foot. Fit walkers should try the steep in-and-out hike to the sensational 30-m- (100-ft-) high Wolfberg Arch, which takes the best part of a full day but is well worth the effort. For a more sedate alternative, follow the easy footpath through the stunning and highly photogenic Stadsaal (Town Hall) Caves, an ancient cave complex that houses several excellent examples of rock art. In Nieuwoudtville, ask local advice about the best places to see floral displays, as they can be unpredictable – if in doubt, give the the Nieuwoudtville Wildflower Reserve or Hantam National Botanical Garden a try. Spend the night in whichever location you've passed the rest of the day.

→

## Day 5

Allow three to four hours for the northward drive to Springbok *(p203)*, or longer if you stop to check out wildflower displays on the way. After a quick lunch, take a relaxed walk or drive through the out-of-town Goegap Nature Reserve. Characterized by granite peaks and sandy plains, it's home to a large number of endemic succulents, as well as plenty of dry country birds and other wildlife – including South Africa's only population of Hartmann's mountain zebra. In spring-flower season, the reserve comes alive with colourful floral displays. Have dinner at Tauren Steak Ranch *(027 712 2717)*, which has undergone several name changes since it opened in 1986 but remains consistently good. The menu is primarily aimed at meat lovers, but it does include some veggie options.

## Day 6

Get the earliest possible start for the long 310-km (190-mile) drive northeast to Augrabies Falls National Park *(p202)*, pausing for a coffee break at the sleepy small town of Pofadder. Upon arrival at Augrabies Falls, settle yourself in at the park's rest camp, making sure to check out the stunning main viewpoint over the falls. Once the midday heat has died down, allow two hours of daylight to explore the scenic circular 5-km (3-mile) Dassie Trail. Admire the views at Arrow Point, and look out along the way for dassies (rock hyrax), Broadley's flat lizard, Verreaux's eagle and mountain zebra. For dinner, sample the house speciality venison at the rest camp's Quiver Tree Restaurant – its wide terrace is within earshot of the surging waterfall.

## Day 7

Enjoy a change of pace this morning on the thrilling Augrabies Rush *(p203)*, a four-hour rafting trip on the Orange River that starts at 8am. Once you've dried off, it's a 370-km (230-mile) drive to your next destination: Kgalagadi Transfrontier Park *(p194)*. The road is excellent, so it's not as bad as it sounds – it takes only four hours

1 The spectacular Augrabies Falls.

2 A springbok in a field of wild-flowers near its namesake town.

3 A lizard in Goegap Nature Reserve.

4 On safari in Kgalagadi Transfrontier Park.

5 Rafting the Augrabies Rush.

6 Hartmann's zebra in Goegap.

to get to Kgalagadi's Twee Rivieren Entrance Gate and Rest Camp. Break up the drive with lunch at Upington (p205), 125 km (75 miles) from Augrabies. After a long day's rafting and driving, unwind under the glittering night skies at Twee Rivieren, eating dinner at the camp's excellent restaurant.

## Day 8

Get up with the sun for a game drive in Kgalagadi, following the Nossob Road north out of camp. Not only is dawn the coolest time of day in this searing region, but predators are most active in the early morning, so there's a chance of spotting big cats like lion and leopard. Escape the heat with a long lunchtime break, cooling off as needed at the rest camp swimming pool. Head out for an afternoon drive about three hours before the gate closes, to see what wildlife you can spot as the temperature starts to cool – the park is famous for its gemsbok and birds of prey. Spend a relaxed evening enjoying a self-catering barbecue under the stars.

## Day 9

Rise early again and head off in search of more wildlife, possibly varying the routine by trying the Mata-Mata road that runs northeast towards the border with Namibia. Take a long midday break, enjoying the plentiful small wildlife – mongoose, ground squirrel and dry-county birds – that becomes more active around camp in the late afternoon. Join one of the camp's guided Sunset Drives, which offer a great chance of spotting rare nocturnal wildlife as you return. Treat yourself to dinner at the camp restaurant for your final night, before embarking on the 1,000-km (600-mile) drive to Johannesburg the next day – the journey is feasible in one long day, but if you've got time then a more relaxed option is to have an overnight stop at Kuruman (p204).

1

2

# 7 DAYS

## *in KwaZulu-Natal*

### Day 1

Start by exploring central Durban *(p274)*, stopping in at the Old Court House Museum and City Hall, home to the Natural Science Museum and Durban Art Gallery. When hunger pangs start to hit, make your way to the Victoria Street Market for a snack lunch of Indian-influenced Durban specialities. Spend the rest of the day relaxing at the beach on the Golden Mile, or head a short distance inland to enjoy the tranquility and tropical vegetation of Durban Botanic Garden. Sip an early-evening cocktail at one of the Golden Mile's many bars, then ascend to the 32nd-floor Roma Revolving Restaurant for a meal with a view.

### Day 2

Allow three hours to make the 240-km (150-mile) drive from Durban to St Lucia village, where you'll arrive in time for lunch at the quaint Thyme Square Coffee Shop *(035 590 1692)*. St Lucia is the gateway to iSimangaliso Wetland Park *(p284)*, and a guided boat trip on the St Lucia Estuary, with its hippos, crocodiles

and waterbirds, provides the perfect introduction to the area. For dinner, eat al fresco overlooking the estuary mouth at the St Lucia Ski Boat Club *(035 5901376)*.

### Day 3

Head deeper into the wetland park on a half-day excursion to the stunning Cape Vidal, with a stop at the St Lucia Crocodile Centre on the way out. Allow up to two hours for the drive to Hluhluwe-Imfolozi's Memorial Gate *(p282)*, then enjoy a slow afternoon game drive in search of the Big Five. Pass a lazy evening at the reserve's Hilltop Camp or at one of the lodges outside the gates, soaking up the atmosphere of the African bush over a sundowner.

### Day 4

Rise at dawn for another game drive – early morning is the best time to look for big cats – and be ready to set off towards Shakaland *(p290)*, two hours to the south-west, by 11am. After an African-style buffet lunch, relax for an hour or two before taking part in the enjoyable and

1 The winding Sani Pass.
2 A traditional Basotho house.
3 Hluhluwe-Imfolozi Game Reserve.
4 Durban's Golden Mile.
5 iSimangaliso Wetland Park.

informative Zulu cultural programme, which starts at 4pm for overnight guests. After dinner, enjoy a visceral display of energetic Zulu dancing, singing and drumming.

## Day 5

It's just 20 km (12 miles) from Shakaland to Eshowe (p290), where you can explore the aerial boardwalk through the mist forest of Dlinza, and Zulu artifacts in the Vukani Museum. Have brunch in Eshowe, then make the three-hour drive east to Howick (p297) using the back road through Greytown. Don't miss the Nelson Mandela Capture Site outside Howick before heading into town to see the Howick Falls. Have dinner at nearby Little Mozambique (littlemozambique.com).

## Day 6

Pick up some snacks and supplies for a picnic lunch then allow two hours to travel 80 km (50 miles) west to Kamberg Nature Reserve (p280). There, join the 11am guided excursion to Game Pass Shelter, a three-hour round walk that leads to one of the finest of uKhahlamba-Drakensberg's rock art sites. After a late lunch, take a leisurely drive south along the 80 km (50 miles) of scenic roads that run through the Drakensberg foothills to Himeville. Dine at Moorcroft Manor (moor croft.co.za), a converted farmhouse whose cosy country feel befits the rather chilly setting at an altitude of 1,500 m (4,920 ft).

## Day 7

Join a full-day 4WD guided tour up the spectacular Sani Pass (p300), the only road to breach the Drakensberg's imperious eastern escarpment. Lunch at a gasping altitude of 2,874 m (9,429 ft) at Sani Mountain Lodge (p300), then pay a visit to a rural Basotho village before returning to Himeville in the late afternoon. Stop the night in Himeville before returning to Durban the next day along the 210-km (130-mile) road through Pietermaritzburg.

# 7 DAYS
## *in Mpumalanga and Kruger*

### Day 1

Drive from Gauteng to Pilgrim's Rest *(p344)*, allowing four to five hours for the journey – plus one more if you break for an early lunch at the pretty highland town of Dullstroom *(p346)*. Dedicate a full afternoon to exploring the restored highlands gold rush village of Pilgrim's Rest – highlights include the Victorian House Museum, Diggings Site Museum and Robber's Grave. Dine on hearty fare such as oxtail *potjie* (a slow-cooked stew) at the Victorian-styled restaurant at the Royal Hotel *(royalhotelpilgrims.co.za)*.

### Day 2

Spend today exploring the Mpumalanga Escarpment. A good morning route leads through Graskop north to God's Window viewpoint, Lisbon Falls, Bourke's Luck Potholes and the Three Rondawels viewpoint over the Blyde River Canyon *(p348)*. Return to Graskop for a sweet or savoury lunch at Harrie's Pancakes *(p347)*, then head south to explore the half-dozen waterfalls in the vicinity of Sabie

*(p346)*. Return to Pilgrims Rest, stopping for a typical South African dinner at Graskop's Glass House *(013 7671316)*.

### Day 3

Allow an hour to drive the 80 km (50 miles) via Graskop and Hazyview to Kruger National Park's Phabeni Gate *(p336)*. Stretch your legs at the Albasini Ruins, then enjoy a relaxed two-hour game drive to Skukuza Rest Camp. This is Kruger's largest rest camp and makes a good spot for lunch. Allow at least three hours for the 45-km (30-mile) drive from here to Lower Sabie, along a road that follows the Sabi River – it usually offers excellent Big Five viewing, so keep your eyes peeled. Overnight at Lower Sabie, admiring the sparkling African night sky over a barbecue.

### Day 4

Rise early for a morning game drive to Crocodile Bridge, keeping a careful lookout for lion activity. The best loop follows the main surfaced road south

1 Looking for wildlife at Olifants River.

2 Animals crossing in Satara.

3 One of Kruger's majestic lions.

4 Bourke's Luck Potholes at Blyde River Canyon.

(stop at Crocodile Bridge for coffee) then returns via one of the unsurfaced tracks to its east. Be on the watch for rhinos, which are renowned in this part of the park. An excellent short afternoon drive is the scenic loop to Mlondozi Dam and Picnic Site. After an early dinner at Lower Sabie's cafeteria-like restaurant, join an organized night drive in search of genet, bushbaby and other nocturnal creatures.

## Day 5

With the earliest possible start, allow at least five hours to cover the 100-km (60-mile) road from Lower Sabie to Satara, stopping to look for wildlife at Eileen Orpen Dam, and for breakfast or brunch at Tshokwane Picnic Site. The plains around Satara attract large herds of wildebeest and zebra, and are also good for cheetah and lion. Look out for them during a four-hour afternoon game drive to Nwanetsi, looping out along the main surfaced road and back on the dirt S100. Listen out for lion and hyena as you barbecue outside your hut at the Satara rest camp.

## Day 6

Drive north to Olifants Camp, following an untrammelled and mostly unsurfaced 70-km (45-mile) back road via Nsemani Dam, with stops at Timbavati Picnic Site (a great breakfast spot) and Nwamanzi Viewpoint. Have lunch at Olifants Camp, enjoying its spectacular views over the Olifants River – a major wildlife magnet. Once the heat of the day dissipates, allow three hours for the 55-km (35-mile) drive back to Satara on the main surfaced road. Wind down with an alfresco dinner at Satara's restaurant.

## Day 7

Make your way out of the park along the 50-km (30-mile) road west to Orpen Gate – it's best taken at game drive speed, as there's a fair chance of spotting lion, cheetah and rhino. Allow another two hours to get to Graskop for lunch. Drive the 400 km (250 miles) to Johannesburg, or fly there from Mbombela. Relax after a long day of travelling with dinner at one of the city's many excellent restaurants.

### The Little Five
In addition to ticking off the Big Five, enrich your safari experience by seeking out their lesser-known cousins. The "Little Five" are the ant lion (a small predatorial larva), the gold-and-black leopard tortoise, the nocturnal elephant-shrew, the noisy red-billed buffalo-weaver and the armour-plated rhinoceros beetle.

The leopard tortoise, named for the decorative markings on its shell

# SOUTH AFRICA FOR
# WILDLIFE

**South Africa's wildlife is legendary. For first-time visitors, the so-called Big Five tend to hog the limelight, but an African safari provides an opportunity to see a menagerie of other wonderful creatures, from stretch-necked giraffes to bug-eyed nocturnal bushbabies.**

### The Big Five
A term coined in the colonial era to describe the quintet of animals most feared and sought by trophy hunters, the Big Five – lion, leopard, elephant, buffalo and rhino – has now become the most desired quarry on any African photographic safari. Top Big Five destinations include Addo Elephant *(p250)* and Kruger *(p336)* national parks.

## One-Off Wonders

South Africa's location at the continent's southern extremity means that it hosts a high proportion of animals found nowhere else. These endemics are concentrated in three areas: the unique *fynbos* of the southwest Cape, the succulent-rich badlands inland of the west coast and the high Drakensberg (p278). Go searching for Cape mountain zebra, distinguished by their narrow stripes and white bellies; black wildebeest, differentiated from their blue cousins by their white tails; and bontebok, dark brown antelopes with striking white markings.

→

Cape mountain zebra in the Eastern Cape's Mountain Zebra National Park

## Brilliant Birding

With 850 species recorded, from outsized ostriches to dazzling bee-eaters, birds are a conspicuous presence throughout South Africa. While any protected area will offer plenty, Kruger National Park (p336) is recommended for eagles and other raptors, and Isimangaliso Wetland Park (p284) for aquatic birds.

←

A little bee-eater, one of South Africa's many bird species

## Marine Marvels

South Africa's sensational terrestrial wildlife is almost matched by the fauna living along and off its coasts. Enjoy land-based whale-watching at Hermanus (p216), meet the characterful colony of African penguins on Boulders Beach (p152) and look out for the Cape fur seals that breed on numerous offshore islands.

↑ A leopard basking in the sunlight in Kruger National Park

→

African penguins on Boulders Beach

### Local Cuisine

South Africa's cities are a foodie's delight, with an abundance of inviting restaurants and alfresco dining options. Most global cuisines are represented, but be sure to seek out fresh seafood in Cape Town and sample the excellent Indian fare on offer in Durban. Whatever your mood or budget, you'll find a host of appealing eateries in Cape Town's V&A Waterfront (p122), in the atmospheric Johannesburg suburb of Melville and along Durban's seafront Golden Mile (p274).

$\rightarrow$

Restaurants at Cape Town's V&A Waterfront, where seafood (inset) is a speciality

# SOUTH AFRICA FOR
# CITY LIFE

**Blending European colonial influences with contemporary African style, South Africa's cities offer a captivating introduction to local culture. Cape Town is undoubtedly the country's leading metropolitan destination, but Johannesburg, Pretoria and Durban all have much to offer urban explorers.**

### Retail Therapy

To shop till you drop, look no further than Cape Town: its stylish stores sell a wealth of original treasures. Bohemian Long Street is lined with enticing boutiques, while the city's hip Woodstock district (p165) is a hotbed of shops dedicated to art, fashion and design. For handicrafts, try the Watershed (p125) or Greenmarket Square (p133); other top markets around the country include Rosebank Sunday Market in Johannesburg and Durban's Victoria Street Market (p276).

$\leftarrow$

The pan-African crafts and clothing market in Cape Town's Greenmarket Square

↑ A performance at Cape Town's International Jazz Festival

## Live Music

The music scene is diversity personified. Good live venues for South African specialities such as *kwaito* (slow-tempo house beats with vocals in local vernacular), electro-punky *zef* and BPM-giddy Shangaan Electro include Johannesburg's Bassline *(bassline.co.za)*, Cape Town's Crypt Jazz *(cryptjazz.co.za)* and Durban's Beach Bums *(beachbumsdurban.co.za)*.

### TOWNSHIP TOURS

A guided tour of Soweto *(p312)* or the Cape Flats *(p163)* shows a different side to urban life in South Africa in comparison to suburban Johannesburg or central Cape Town. Designated as Black-only residential areas under apartheid, both areas have historically been marked by high levels of poverty and crime. However, these townships – where the infamous Soweto Uprising and Sharpeville Massacre took place – also have uplifting landmarks that commemorate their residents' resistance to apartheid and ultimate victory over oppression.

## Marvellous Museums

Cape Town is the country's museum capital: don't miss the District Six Museum *(p120)* and the superb cluster of institutions around Company's Garden *(p138)*. Johannesburg runs a close second, with the excellent Apartheid Museum *(p308)* and Maropeng Visitors Centre *(p314)*.

↑ The Iziko South African Museum and Planetarium in Company's Garden in Cape Town

### Ancient Rock Art

Attributed to ancient hunter-gatherer cultures, South Africa's rich portfolio of prehistoric rock art is exhibited in situ at myriad alfresco galleries. uKhahlamba-Drakensberg Park *(p278)* alone contains around 50,000 individual images across 500 panels. Other sites are more scattered, but you'll find rich pickings in the Cederberg *(p189)* and Northern Cape.

←

A rock painting of elands and human figures in uKhahlamba-Drakensberg

# SOUTH AFRICA FOR
# ART LOVERS

South Africa's many thousands of prehistoric paintings and engravings are some of the world's most ancient artworks. This creative tradition continues to flourish in the country today, with one of the most vibrant contemporary art scenes anywhere on the African continent.

### Striking Street Art

Street art has flourished in the post-apartheid era, and you'll find vibrant examples – often political in nature – peppered throughout most large towns. A high concentration of creative designs decorate Johannesburg's hip Maboneng Precinct and the bohemian Cape Town suburb of Woodstock – both can be explored independently, but guided street-art tours are available too.

### IRMA STERN

Irma Stern (1894–1966) studied art in Europe but was heavily influenced by her travels in Africa. Her distinctive portraits initially went unappreciated in her home country, but were feted in Europe; posthumous sales of her pieces have set record prices for South African artworks. The Irma Stern Museum *(p164)* has a fabulous display of her work.

## At the Cutting Edge

The thriving art scene fuses South Africa's diverse ethnic roots with international influences. Cape Town's Zeitz Museum of Contemporary Art Africa *(p125)* has a wonderful pan-African collection; its closest counterpart in Johannesburg is Gallery MOMO *(gallerymomo.com)*. It's also worth checking out the KZNSA Gallery in Durban *(kznsagallery.co.za)* and Stellenbosch's Modern and Contemporary Art Gallery *(contemporaryand.com)*.

→

A Mary Sibande exhibit at the Zeitz Museum of Contemporary Art Africa

## Traditional Arts and Crafts

South Africa has a rich tradition of rural handicrafts, many of which you can find at Cape Town and Durban's crafts markets. Intricate Zulu beadwork and Swazi basketry embrace bright colours and geometric patterns, while other specialities include Venda pottery and woodcarvings, as well as woven Basotho hats.

←

Colourful Zulu-style beaded bracelets for sale at a local crafts market

## Classical Paintings

For aficionados of more conventional historic artworks, the Iziko South African National Gallery *(p135)* holds the country's largest collection of canvasses by old masters of South African, British, French, Flemish and Dutch origin. Johannesburg Art Gallery *(p324)* has a similarly impressive display, featuring works by artists such as Rembrandt and Monet.

→

A portrait by Antonio Mancini at the Johannesburg Art Gallery

↑ Eye-catching street art in Johannesburg

### Fine Dining

You'll find a cosmopolitan selection of high-end restaurants in larger cities such as Johannesburg, Cape Town and Durban, and prices tend to be very reasonable. The mecca for serious foodies, however, is the tiny Winelands town of Franschhoek *(p178)* – regarded as the country's culinary capital, it's home to a number of award-winning restaurants that also serve a great selection of local wine. Try Le Quartier Français or Haute Cabrière for a treat.

→
An elegant dish at one of Franschhoek's many fine-dining restaurants

# SOUTH AFRICA FOR
# FOODIES

Exceptional quality and even better value are the hallmarks of South Africa's thriving wining and dining scene. Wherever you eat, you'll be spoilt for choice when it comes to locally sourced wine and craft beer.

### THE BRAAI

If any meal transcends social barriers in South Africa, it's the *braai*, or *shisa nyama* (barbecue), an outdoor ritual that enlivens many a weekend afternoon. Steak, chicken, lamb or *sosaties* might all end up on the grill, but no *braai* is complete without a generous roll of *boerewors* (spicy "farmers sausage"). A variation is *potjiekos*, a meat and vegetable stew cooked slowly over a fire in the small black pot *(potjie)* for which it is named.

### Wonderful Wines

What could be better than sipping a glass of world-class wine in a sunshine-soaked vineyard? The Winelands of the Western Cape are packed with scenic estates offering tasting sessions to visitors – perennial favourites include Boschendal *(p177)*, Lanzerac *(p175)*, Vergelegen *(p177)*, Neethlingshof *(p177)* and Spier *(p176)*.

→
A sumptuous lunch accompanied by local wine in the Winelands

## A Taste of Africa

The local African staple is a stiff maize meal porridge called *mealiepap*, usually eaten with a plain stew. You can try it at many African restaurants, along with the Western Cape fusion cuisine known as Cape Malay. Bursting with flavour, this includes curries, a lamb-based *waterblommetjiebredie* (water-flower stew), *sosaties* (kebab in a fruity marinade) and *bobotie* (a baked minced-meat dish). Biltong, a dried strip of salted and spiced beef or game meat, is so popular that most malls have at least one shop devoted to it.

← A serving of biltong, one of South Africa's most popular snacks

# EAT

Sample pan-African dishes from Morocco, Ethiopia, Zanzibar and Senegal, as well as from South Africa, at these restaurants.

**Marco's African Place**
📍15 Rose Lane, Bo-Kaap, Cape Town
🌐marcosafrican place.com
Ⓡ Ⓡ Ⓡ

**Moyo Restaurant**
📍Kirstenbosch Botanical Garden, 99 Rhodes Dr, Cape Town
🌐moyo.co.za
Ⓡ Ⓡ Ⓡ

**Yeoville Dinner Club**
📍24 Rockey St, Yeoville, Johannesburg 📞083 447 4235
Ⓡ Ⓡ Ⓡ

## Craft Beers

South Africa's beer scene is blossoming, thanks to a proliferation of small independent breweries. Roughly half of the country's 150 or so craft breweries are concentrated in the Western Cape, where most self-respecting bars and restaurants now stock a few different options, bottled or on tap. Top picks include the Cape Brewing Company, Darling Brewery and Devil's Peak Brewing Company.

↑ A bartender dispensing beer at the Darling Brewery

# SOUTH AFRICA'S
# POLITICAL
# HISTORY

For most visitors to South Africa, it's the recent past - the iniquity of apartheid and its resolution under the guidance of Nelson Mandela - that holds the most resonance, but sites reflecting the country's colonial legacy and the battles that helped shape its present also repay exploration.

### Battlefields Route

Northern KwaZulu-Natal was the site of several key battles in the 19th century. Learn about these campaigns on the Battlefields Route, whose sites include Blood River, where heavily armed Boers felled 3,000 Zulus; Isandlwana, where Britain suffered its most humiliating defeat by an African foe; and Rorke's Drift, a British victory immortalized in the film *Zulu* (1964).

A memorial to the Zulus killed in the Battle of Rorke's Drift

## Colonial Architecture

The Western Cape has the country's longest history of European settlement, making it a natural starting place for exploring South Africa's colonial legacy. Visit Cape Town's Castle of Good Hope *(p131)* or take a tour of the attractive Cape Dutch homesteads sprinkled throughout Stellenbosch *(p172)* and the Winelands. Elsewhere, you can admire the simple 1820 Settlers architecture in Makhanda *(p264)* or explore Pretoria's grandiose late 19th-century landmarks *(p330)*.

←

The Cape Dutch Manor House at the Groot Constantia wine estate

## Remembering Apartheid

"Today, apartheid is exactly where it belongs: in a museum." This is the motto of the superb Apartheid Museum *(p308)* in Johannesburg, which randomly allocates visitors a "white" or "non-white" ticket to determine where they enter. Other museums reflecting on this dark period include Cape Town's District Six Museum *(p120)* and Soweto's Hector Pieterson Museum *(p312)*.

→

The segregated entrance gates at Johannesburg's Apartheid Museum

## The Mandela Legacy

One of the 20th century's most inspirational leaders, Nelson Mandela left an enduring legacy. Visit his birthplace in Qunu *(p257)*, stand at the site near Howick where he was captured by police in 1962 *(p297)*, see inside his cramped cell on Robben Island *(p129)* and commemorate his presidential inauguration at Pretoria's Union Buildings *(p330)*.

←

Sculpture by Marco Cianfanelli at the Nelson Mandela Capture Site near Howick

### Diverse Coastlines

Lapped by the chilly Atlantic to the west and more sultry Indian Ocean to the east, South Africa's coastline supplies drama and beauty in equal measure. There are pretty beaches aplenty, but for unforgettable natural spectacles head for the wave-battered headland at the Cape of Good Hope (p150), the forested dunes and lush estuaries of iSimangaliso Wetland Park (p284) or the sheer cliffs of the Robberg Peninsula near Plettenberg Bay (p242).

↑ The towering cliff of Cape Point at the Cape of Good Hope

# SOUTH AFRICA FOR
# NATURAL
# WONDERS

From the "Barrier of Spears" formed by the Drakensberg escarpment to the gorgeous beaches that line the Garden Route, South Africa's landscape is unfailingly beautiful. Immerse yourself in a wonderland of spectacular waterfalls, mysterious cave systems and vast, flowering deserts.

### Magnificent Mountains

It's hard to top the stunning view of Table Mountain (p126) towering above Cape Town and Table Bay. But the Amphitheatre – a precipitous 5-km- (3-mile-) long, 1.2-km- (0.75-mile-) high cliff of burnished sandstone in the uKhahlamba-Drakensberg Park (p278) – arguably does just that. Less celebrated but no less spectacular, the Cederberg Mountains north of Cape Town are studded with gobsmacking rock formations (p189).

## Roaring Rivers

For a dry country, South Africa has some impressive riverine features. Be awed by the cacophonous eruption of the Orange River at Augrabies Falls *(p202)* and marvel at the five-tiered Tugela Falls. Elsewhere, enjoy the scenic splendour of the Blyde River, punctuated by the bizarre Bourke's Luck Potholes *(p348)*.

---

💬 INSIDER TIP
**Once Upon a Star**

Night time in South Africa's wilderness is magical anywhere, but the most spectacular night skies are found in the Northern Cape.

---

↑ The powerful waters of the dramatic Augrabies Falls

## Stunning Desert

The desertscapes of the Northern Cape possess a stark but singular beauty, particularly in the golden light of dawn or dusk. Don't miss the curvaceous apricot dunes of the Kalahari *(p194)* and the sensational spring flower displays that blanket the rocky plains of Namaqualand *(p201)*.

Spring wildflowers in bloom in the plains of Namaqualand

## Otherworldly Caves

Take a tour through Oudtshoorn's Cango Caves *(p230)* to uncover a stunning underground world of wriggly-tight labyrinths and cathedralesque chambers adorned with eerily lit limestone formations. Equally compelling in its own historic way, fossil-rich Sterkfontein Cave is the subterranean showpiece of the Cradle of Humankind UNESCO World Heritage Site *(p314)*.

→ Unusual dripstone formations at Cango Caves

↑ Table Mountain, with the city of Cape Town nestled below

### Secluded Safaris

Escape the crowds and enjoy a self-drive safari through the huge tract of Kruger National Park *(p336)* that lies north of the Letaba River – only three rest camps service the area and they are seldom visited by organized tours. You might not see as many of the Big Five as in the south, but the mesmerizing wilderness feel more than makes up for it.

←

One of the numerous giraffes that inhabit Kruger National Park

# SOUTH AFRICA
# OFF THE BEATEN TRACK

Not only is South Africa vast, but every corner of the country holds something of scenic, natural or cultural interest – meaning that the opportunities for off-the-beaten-track exploration are practically limitless.

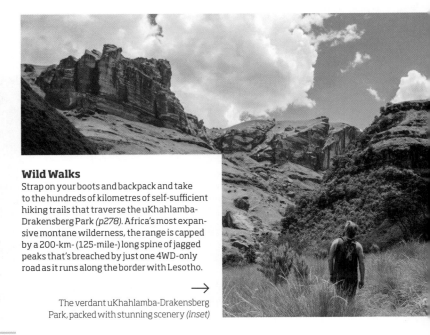

### Wild Walks

Strap on your boots and backpack and take to the hundreds of kilometres of self-sufficient hiking trails that traverse the uKhahlamba-Drakensberg Park *(p278)*. Africa's most expansive montane wilderness, the range is capped by a 200-km- (125-mile-) long spine of jagged peaks that's breached by just one 4WD-only road as it runs along the border with Lesotho.

→

The verdant uKhahlamba-Drakensberg Park, packed with stunning scenery *(inset)*

**TOP 4**

**LITTLE-VISITED RESERVES**

**Tembe Elephant Park**
Home to all the Big Five, this park is like a budget private reserve (p295).

**Oribi Gorge Nature Reserve**
A scenic slow road snakes through this stunning gorge (p286).

**Nylsvley Nature Reserve**
The seasonal floodplain here attracts an array of aquatic birds (p349).

**Mapungubwe National Park**
This park houses the ruins of a major medieval citadel (p351).

## Desert Adventures

Legendary among 4WD enthusiasts, the Richtersveld forms part of South Africa's most remote national park (p202), snuggled up against the Orange River on the border with Namibia. Immerse yourself in arid landscapes of austere beauty, surrounded by bizarre flora – most notably the striking halfmens (half-human) tree – and a range of dry-country antelope and birds.

The remote wilderness of the arid Richtersveld ↓

## Coastal Paradise

For a beach break with a difference, head to iSimangaliso Wetland Park (p284). Lined with breathtaking swathes of sun-drenched sand flanked by turquoise estuaries, subtropical jungles and forested dunes, it's totally unpopulated bar a handful of isolated boutique lodges and small fishing villages.

→

A secluded beach in iSimangaliso Wetland Park

## Letting Off Steam

Thrills and spills aplenty can be had at Gold Reef City *(p310)*, which combines a re-creation of prospector-era Johannesburg with a dozen roller-coasters and other exciting rides. Alternatively, cool off by shooting down giant waterslides at uShaka Wet 'n' Wild in Durban *(p274)* or splashing around at Sun City's Valley of Waves water park *(p318)*.

The Anaconda roller-coaster at Gold Reef City near Johannesburg

# SOUTH AFRICA FOR
# FAMILIES

**With its warm weather, family-friendly beaches and eclectic array of outdoor activities, South Africa is a veritable children's playground. Even the odd rainy day won't detract from the fun, with museums and aquariums providing ample opportunity for indoor adventure.**

## Buckets and Spades

Within easy distance of Cape Town, the Cape Peninsula is flecked with sandy beaches that offer calm, safe swimming conditions for children (though local advice should be sought on the day). Top choices include Muizenberg *(p161)*, with its trademark row of colourfully painted Victorian bathing huts, Fish Hoek *(p159)* and Hout Bay *(p156)*. For dedicated beach holidays, however, your best bet is the warmer Indian Ocean; firm family-friendly favourites here include Plettenberg Bay *(p240)* and the long line of resorts along the KwaZulu-Natal coast flanking Durban *(p274)*.

→

The row of colourful bathing huts that line Muizenberg beach

## Child-Friendly Wine Estates

It may sound like a contradiction in terms, but several estates in the Cape Winelands provide great family-friendly experiences. Make a whole day of it at Spier *(p176)*: visit the fascinating raptor centre, take a two-hour Segway tour through the vineyards, and enjoy tandem tastings of grape juice for kids and wine for adults. Top children's play areas can also be found in the grounds of the Vergelegen *(p177)*, Tokara *(p176)* and Laborie *(p183)* estates.

→

Enjoying a family picnic in the grounds of the Spier Wine Estate

## Rainy Days

Rainy days are rare in South Africa, but it's always worth having a Plan B. Captivating indoor activities include the theme-park-like Maropeng Visitor Centre in Gauteng's Cradle of Humankind *(p314)* or a visit to one of the country's excellent oceanariums, such as Two Oceans in Cape Town *(p123)*.

←

Exploring the underwater world on show at Two Oceans Aquarium

## Malaria-Free Safaris

The risk of malaria can often be a deterrent to young families planning a safari, but South Africa is exceptional in this regard – many of its top game reserves are entirely free of the mosquito-borne disease. There are also several safe safari spots within easy driving distance of Gauteng. These include Madikwe *(p320)*, with several all-inclusive packages, and Pilanesberg *(p316)*, an excellent option for self-drivers.

→

Wild elephants at the Pilanesberg National Park

### Exploring the Ocean

Protected within the marine sector of iSimangaliso Wetland Park *(p284)*, Sodwana Bay's spectacular coral reefs are a magnet for snorkellers and scuba divers. You're guaranteed to see plenty of colourful reef fish, and if you're lucky you might also encounter turtles, rays, moray eels, ragged-toothed sharks and other marine giants. Caged shark dives in Gansbaai *(p223)* and elsewhere off the Western Cape coast offer heart-stopping encounters with toothsome great whites.

$\rightarrow$

A scuba diver swimming with a school of yellow french grunts

# SOUTH AFRICA FOR
# OUTDOOR
# ADVENTURES

Year-round sunny skies and a relatively temperate climate make it hard to resist the lure of South Africa's great outdoors. Whatever your predilection – be it leisurely hikes, deep-sea diving or the rush of white-water rafting – the country's adventure activities are guaranteed to get your blood pumping.

### Hiking the Wilds

It's easy to explore South Africa's scenic wild places on foot, thanks to the extensive network of walking trails. An almost limitless choice of day trails is available to families and moderately active travellers, while specialized destinations for overnight hikers include the uKhahlamba-Drakensberg *(p278)*, Garden Route *(p226)* and Cederberg *(p189)*. Try one of the guided wilderness trails in Kruger *(p336)* or Hluhluwe-Imfolozi *(p282)* for a walk on the wild side in Big Five territory.

$\rightarrow$

Hiking through the scenic surrounds of the uKhahlamba-Drakensberg

A diver exploring one of the colourful reefs along the Indian Ocean coast

**TOP 3 ADRENALINE RUSHES**

**Bloukrans Bridge Bungee**
The world's highest commercial bungee jump (p232), with a stomach-churning drop of 216 m (709 ft).

**Abseiling from Table Mountain**
A giddying descent from the 1,000-m- (3,280-ft-) tall plateau of Table Mountain (p126) towering above Camps Bay.

**Tugela Falls Hike**
This challenging day hike in uKhahlamba-Drakensberg Park (p278) includes a vertiginous ascent of two long chain ladders.

## Riding the Rivers

The most established rafting venue is the Orange River, where options range from mellow overnight camping trips to the short but frantic Augrabies Rush (p203). Elsewhere, you can glide through a valley of volcanic outcrops on Eswatini's Usutu (p360) and traverse Grade IV rapids at Mpumalanga's Blyde (p348). For a more sedate option, try canoeing through the forested gorge carved by the Touws River in Wilderness (p236).

↑ Rafting the white-water rapids at Hells Gate on the Orange River

### Did You Know?

South Africa is one of two countries to have hosted the football, cricket and rugby world cups.

SOUTH AFRICA FOR
# SPORTS FANS

Sports-mad South Africa punches above its weight in the global arena, particularly in the disciplines of rugby, cricket, golf, swimming and running. Behind this international success is a vibrant domestic sports scene, and there's no better way to experience it than from the thick of the crowds.

## TOP 5 INDIGENOUS SPORTS AND GAMES

**Morabaraba**
This two-player board game tests problem-solving skills.

**Iintonga**
A stick-fighting game with two combatants.

**Jukskei**
Players try to knock down a peg by throwing a wooden yoke-pin.

**Kgati**
A rope-skipping game played by three people.

**Diketo**
This game is played with pebbles and a *ghoen* (a bigger stone).

### Tee Time

Follow in the footsteps of South African golfing legends such as Ernie Els and play a round on one of the country's world-class golf courses. For a challenging game in scenic surrounds, try the Fancourt Estate in George or Rondebosch on the slopes of Table Mountain. At Phalaborwa's Hans Merensky Golf Course, you might even encounter big game.

## The Beautiful Game

Soccer is South Africa's favourite sport, whether it's watching Bafana Bafana (the men's national team) or taking part in a local kickabout. Join the excitable fans at a Premier Soccer League match – local derbys such as Soweto's Kaizer Chiefs vs Orlando Pirates are particularly lively. If you can't make a game, you can take a tour of the "Calabash", Soweto's iconic FNB Stadium (p313).

←

Kaizer Chiefs fans cheering their team on during a match at Soweto's FNB Stadium

## Bowled Over

There are few more appealing ways to enjoy South Africa's sporting prowess than by soaking in the sunshine at a game of cricket. The national team is consistently strong, while the domestic first-class competition is contested by 15 teams split across two divisions.

←

A member of South Africa's cricket team

## Join the Scrum

South Africa is a rugby superpower, with a trophy cabinet that includes three World Cups. You can catch the country's best in action at fixtures in the annual Rugby Championship (a competition between South Africa, Australia, Argentina and New Zealand), which invariably attract a passionate crowd.

↑ The lush surrounds of the renowned golf course at Fancourt Estate

↑ Nelson Mandela congratulates François Pienaar on South Africa's 1995 World Cup victory

### Glide Through the Skies

It's hard to beat floating above a sensational landscape on a serene dawn ride in a hot air balloon. The Pilanesberg *(p317)* offers your best chance of getting an eagle's-eye view over the Big Five, but you'll find equally spectacular sights at the Cape Winelands *(p168)*, Magaliesberg *(p328)* and the KwaZulu-Natal Midlands *(p296)*.

→

Floating peacefully above Pilanesberg National Park in a hot air balloon

# SOUTH AFRICA FOR
# SCENIC
# JOURNEYS

With spectacular scenery wherever you travel, journeying through South Africa is as much of a delight as arriving at your destination. The only difficult part is deciding which mode of transport to take – with a variety of options by air, road and rail, the whole country is open to exploration.

### All Aboard!

Travel in unfettered style on one of the country's two long-haul five-star luxury train services. Crisp linens, marble-clad bathrooms and faultless service set the tone for the magnificent Blue Train *(p367)*, which takes 27 hours to cover the 1,600 km (995 miles) between Cape Town and Johannesburg, while Rovos Rail *(p367)* – "the most luxurious train in the world" – operates a number of routes connecting Cape Town to the likes of Victoria Falls and Dar es Salaam.

A Rovos Rail train snaking through the lush countryside ↑

## Get Behind the Wheel

The call of the open road is strong in South Africa, with a plethora of epic landscapes and an excellent system of surfaced highways making a compelling case for taking an extended road trip. Out of season, there's usually an abundance of accommodation available at short notice, which means that self-drivers can easily explore the country at their whim. Crack open the car window, crank up the stereo and follow whatever side road takes your fancy.

 Driving past Lion's Head on the outskirts of Cape Town

**TOP 5** **SCENIC DRIVES**

**Sani Pass**
Navigable only in a 4WD, Sani Pass *(p300)* leads to the highest-altitude pub in Africa.

**Namaqualand**
Renowned for its spring wildflower displays, Namaqualand *(p201)* is best explored between August and October.

**Chapman's Peak Drive**
A cliff-hugging toll road on the west side of the Cape Peninsula *(p166)*.

**Four Passes**
Allocate a full day to drive this sensational route *(p244)* as a round trip from Oudtshoorn.

**Blyde River Canyon**
The nippy road running west of the Blyde River Canyon *(p348)* features some of the country's most expansive views.

**INSIDER TIP**
**Full Steam Ahead**

Ceres Rail Company *(ceresrail.co.za)* operates one of South Africa's last steam trains, running regular weekend return trips from Cape Town to Ceres or Elgin.

## Venture into the Bush

A guided game drive *(p372)* in an open 4WD is full of thrills, as you bump through the bush with very little separating you from the surrounding wildlife. Day drives provide a good chance of spotting rhino, elephant, buffalo, giraffe and, to a lesser extent, lion, but night drives have an electric atmosphere as you search in the dark for leopard and other secretive nocturnal creatures.

→ A lucky daytime leopard sighting on a game drive in Kruger National Park

# A YEAR IN
# SOUTH AFRICA

**South Africa is more than just safaris and beautiful scenery. A range of festivities takes place across the country all year round, celebrating the wonderful array of local music, food, wildlife and culture found here.**

## *Spring*

All across the country, but especially noticeable in the semiarid Western and Northern Cape regions, the onset of warmer weather from September raises colourful fields of wildflowers. Unsteady newborns join the herds in South Africa's many wildlife reserves, while whales congregate offshore around Hermanus for the breeding season – an event celebrated by the town's annual Whale Festival.

*1 Colourful wildflowers in the Northern Cape*

## *Summer*

Summer is a season spent outdoors. With the local school holidays extending from December to January, this is when many South African families head for the seaside and wildlife reserves – as do the majority of visitors. Christmas lunch is

---

**COMRADES MARATHON**

First held in 1921, the 89-km (55-mile) Comrades Marathon was established as a tribute to South African soldiers who lost their lives during World War I. Today, this taxing race between Durban and Pietermaritzburg is one of the world's best known ultramarathons.

more likely to be celebrated around an informal *braai* (barbecue) than at a dining table, and open-air music concerts carry the festive atmosphere well into the new year.

*2 A close encounter with a lion on a morning safari*

## Autumn

When deciduous trees and grapevines begin to shed their leaves, a new round of country fairs is ushered in. The harvest festivals of many small towns celebrate crops such as olives and potatoes – even sheep and gems are cause for cheerful gatherings. A number of wine festivals are held, from Paarl in the fertile Western Cape to Kuruman in the arid Northern Cape.

*3 Sampling local wines at Paarl's Ommiberg Harvest Festival*

## Winter

This is the dry season for most of the country; only the winter rainfall area along the southwestern and southern Cape coast is lush and green at this time. Inland, days are typically warm, although nightly frosts are common in high-lying areas and mountains even get snow. Cultural events continue with the National Arts Festival in Makhanda, while endurance athletes amaze at the ultra-long-distance Comrades Marathon.

*4 Snowy peaks in the Drakensberg mountain range and (inset) performers at the National Arts Festival*

**TOP 4**

## FOOD AND DRINK FESTIVALS

**Stellenbosch Wine Festival**
Taking place in late February, this fun event gathers vinophiles in the Winelands.

**Prince Albert Olive Festival**
A celebration of the olive in the arid Klein Karoo region, held in late April or early May.

**Knysna Oyster Festival**
A hugely popular event in late June, honouring Knysna's local delicacy.

**Cherry Festival**
A quirky mid-November festival marking cherry-picking season in Ficksburg.

3

4

# A BRIEF
# HISTORY

Inhabited since prehistoric times, South Africa has experienced tensions between settlers and Indigenous Africans ever since the establishment of a Dutch colony there in 1652. Following the dismantling of apartheid in the 1990s, the country is now on a course to reconciliation.

## Prehistoric South Africa

Although hominins most probably evolved in East Africa, a wealth of fossils unearthed at the Cradle of Humankind near Johannesburg indicates that they inhabited South Africa at least three million years ago. The Northern Cape's Wonderwerk Cave contains the oldest evidence of the controlled use of fire, around one million years ago, probably by *Homo erectus*. The 260,000-year-old Florisbad Skull, discovered in the Free State in 1932, is assigned by some experts to *Homo sapiens*, which would make it one of the oldest specimens of our species in the world.

1 A 17th-century map of South Africa.

2 Ancient rock art by the Khoe or San.

3 The first European voyage to South Africa.

4 Portuguese explorer Bartolomeu Dias facing down a mutiny by his crew in 1488.

## Timeline of events

**1.75 million years BC**
The genus *Homo* first appears on the fossil record at the Cradle of Humankind.

**3.3 million years BC**
Likely date of South Africa's oldest hominin fossil.

**115,000 BC**
Eve's Footprints is the country's earliest relic of modern humans.

**500 BC**
The Khoe adopt a pastoral lifestyle of sheep-, goat- and cattle-herding.

**42,000 BC**
The date of the oldest unambiguous evidence of modern human behaviour: a suite of hunting tools.

## Early Inhabitants

The country's oldest nameable inhabitants were the San and Khoe; the former were hunter-gatherers while the latter were mainly pastoralists. DNA markers indicate that both communities' ancestors have lived in the region for at least 150,000 years. The primary ancestral group of most modern South African peoples are Bantu-speaking migrants of West African origin who arrived in the region via East Africa 1,500 years ago. They introduced iron-age technology and slash-and-burn agriculture to South Africa, and gradually displaced the San and Khoe in the country's relatively fertile eastern half.

## Explorers and Colonizers

The first European expedition to reach South Africa was led by the Portuguese navigator Bartolomeu Dias, who sailed around the Cape and continued as far as the Bushman's River Mouth before turning back. From then on, European ships bound for East Africa and Asia frequently stopped on South African shores, often trading with the local Khoekhoe for fresh produce, but also occasionally skirmishing with them.

### EVOLUTIONARY LANDMARKS

The border area of South Africa and Swaziland is rich in behavioural firsts. Border Cave, in the Lebombo Mountains, contains the world's oldest evidence of ritual burials, religious worship and counting tools. Close by, in Swaziland, the world's oldest known mine, dating back more than 40,000 years, is on Ngwenya Mountain.

*500 AD*

Probable arrival of the first Bantu-speaking farmers and ironworkers in South Africa.

*1100*

The gold-exporting Kingdom of Mapungubwe is established alongside the Limpopo River.

*1488*

Bartolomeu Dias lands at Mossel Bay on 3 February.

*1498*

Dias's compatriot Vasco da Gama pioneers a mercantile sea route from Europe to India via the Cape.

1

2

## Dutch Colonization

In 1652, the Dutch East India Company established a fort on the site of present-day Cape Town. Initially, the Khoe welcomed this opportunity to trade, but as more land was granted to settlers, rivalry over water and grazing turned into open hostility. The impact of these wars, combined with the effects of smallpox, left the Indigenous Khoe population completely decimated by the late 18th century. By then, settlers comprised around 15,000 free citizens, alongside an even greater number of enslaved people – some partially descended from the Khoe, others imported from elsewhere in Africa and the Dutch East Indies – who eventually evolved into the so-called Cape Coloured community.

## Colonial Expansion

As Dutch power faded, Britain seized the Cape Colony, assuming permanent control in 1814. The Great Fish River was proclaimed as the colony's eastern boundary, and plots of land in the border region were assigned to government-sponsored British immigrants dubbed the 1820 Settlers. This move deprived the local Xhosa herdsmen already established there of their pastures, and a century of bitter "frontier wars" ensued. Further

### THE MFECANE

Inspired by the tactics of the Zulu king Shaka, the Mfecane (Crushing) was a 20-year period of mass killing by rival leaders that rippled as far afield as Tanzania and claimed at least one million lives.

## Timeline of events

**1652**
The Dutch East India Company establish a station at present-day Cape Town, commanded by Jan Van Riebeeck.

**1814**
The Dutch Colony at the Cape is formally ceded to Britain.

**1816**
King Shaka seizes the Zulu throne and starts expanding his fiefdom to become a militant unified kingdom.

**1820**
The 1820 Settlers arrive at Port Elizabeth (now Gqeberha) to start farming the eastern frontier of the Cape Colony.

disruption was created by the foundation of Zulu king Shaka's empire during 1816–27, and the inland exodus of more than 12,000 Boers (Dutch farmers) in the Great Trek. The short-lived Natalia Republic was established by the first wave of trekkers in 1839 and annexed by Britain in 1843. By 1857, two independent Boer states, Transvaal and Orange Free State, had been consolidated north of the Orange and Vaal rivers.

## Diamonds and Gold

The discovery of diamonds at Kimberley and gold in the Witwatersrand in the late 19th century laid the foundation for the modern South African economy. Both deposits lay under Boer soil, but were coveted by the British, who initiated a series of skirmishes that culminated in the Anglo-Boer War of 1899–1902. In the aftermath, the British colonies at the Cape and Natal were merged with the Boer states to become a self-governing colony called the Union of South Africa. The South African Act, negotiated in advance of the union, granted few political rights to people of non-European descent – a deliberate oversight that led to the founding of the South African Native National Congress (later the African National Congress/ANC).

1 The landing of Dutch colonial administrator Jan van Riebeeck in Cape Town in 1652.

2 The arrival of British forces in Cape Town in 1814.

3 Diamond mining in Kimberley at the De Beers Diamond Mine.

**1886**

The discovery of gold in the Witwatersrand leads to a gold rush and the foundation of Johannesburg.

**1835–46**

The Great Trek causes huge social upheaval to Indigenous populations in South Africa's interior.

**1899**

The start of the Anglo-Boer War, which is won by the British in 1902.

**1912**

Foundation of the South African Native National Congress (SANNC), which became the African National Congress (ANC) in 1923.

## Early 20th Century

Afrikaner hopes for self-determination were revived in 1938 by the centenary of their ancestors' Great Trek. Black political protest, led by the ANC, gained momentum after World War II, and came to the forefront of public awareness after August 1946, when police waded into a peaceful miners' strike, killing nine people. As the 1948 election drew close, the incumbent United Party (UP) responded to the changing mood by proposing a relatively progressive policy of limited racial integration, which was countered by the right-wing Nationalist Party's (NP) race-based policy of apartheid ("separateness"). With much of the population excluded from voting on the grounds of their skin colour, a predominantly Afrikaner electorate swept the NP into power.

## The Apartheid Era

Protest against apartheid was peaceful until March 1960, when 69 protesters were shot dead by police in Sharpeville. In the aftermath, a state of emergency was declared and the ANC and other anti-apartheid organizations were banned. The ANC responded by forming a military wing led by Nelson Mandela, who was sentenced to life imprisonment in 1963 for acts of

### CREATING APARTHEID

The Population Registration Act classified all citizens as White, Coloured, Black or Indian, with each group designated a specific living area by the Group Areas Act. Adults classified as Black were legally required to carry internal passports at all times, and the Immorality and Mixed Marriages Acts outlawed interracial sex and romance.

## Timeline of events

### 1948
The NP comes to power to implement a policy of systematic racial discrimination called apartheid.

### 1960
Police open fire on anti-apartheid protesters, killing 69 people, in the Sharpeville Massacre.

### 1963
Several ANC leaders, including Nelson Mandela, are sentenced to life imprisonment for terrorism.

### 1976
During the months-long Soweto Revolt, 700 people die at the hands of the police.

terrorism. The decree that Afrikaans should be the language of instruction at Black schools sparked the 1976 Soweto Revolt. In 1990, cowed by ungovernability, as well as international economic sanctions, the NP lifted the ban on the ANC and entered into multiparty negotiations, which led to the 1994 election that swept the ANC and the now freed Nelson Mandela into power.

## South Africa Today

Since 1994, the ANC has convincingly won all parliamentary elections, and while these results undoubtedly reflect their popularity, the lack of credible opposition has allowed internal party politics to overshadow national interests. Mandela retired in 1999, and his successor Thabo Mbeki resigned as a result of party infighting in 2008, to be replaced by Jacob Zuma. Under Zuma, government corruption reached economically damaging proportions, leading to his replacement by businessman Cyril Ramaphosa in 2018. The biggest challenge faced by Ramaphosa is the COVID-19 pandemic, which claimed over 50,000 lives in its first year and led to a 7 per cent decrease in GDP. Despite this, South Africa is likely to remain the busiest tourist destination in sub-Saharan Africa for the foreseeable future.

1 Mine workers on strike in 1946.

2 Nelson Mandela on his release from prison.

3 Jacob Zuma facing corruption charges.

4 Cyril Ramaphosa making an address.

### Did You Know?

The world's first heart transplant was carried out in South Africa in 1967.

*1990*
The NP unbans the ANC and releases Nelson Mandela from prison.

*1994*
Nelson Mandela becomes the country's first Black president.

*1977*
The prominent Black Consciousness leader Steve Biko is killed while in police custody.

*2013*
Nelson Mandela dies aged 95; ten days of national mourning follow.

*2018*
The ANC forces the scandal-hit President Jacob Zuma to resign.

# FIELD GUIDE

Two mountain zebra, with their distinctive stripes

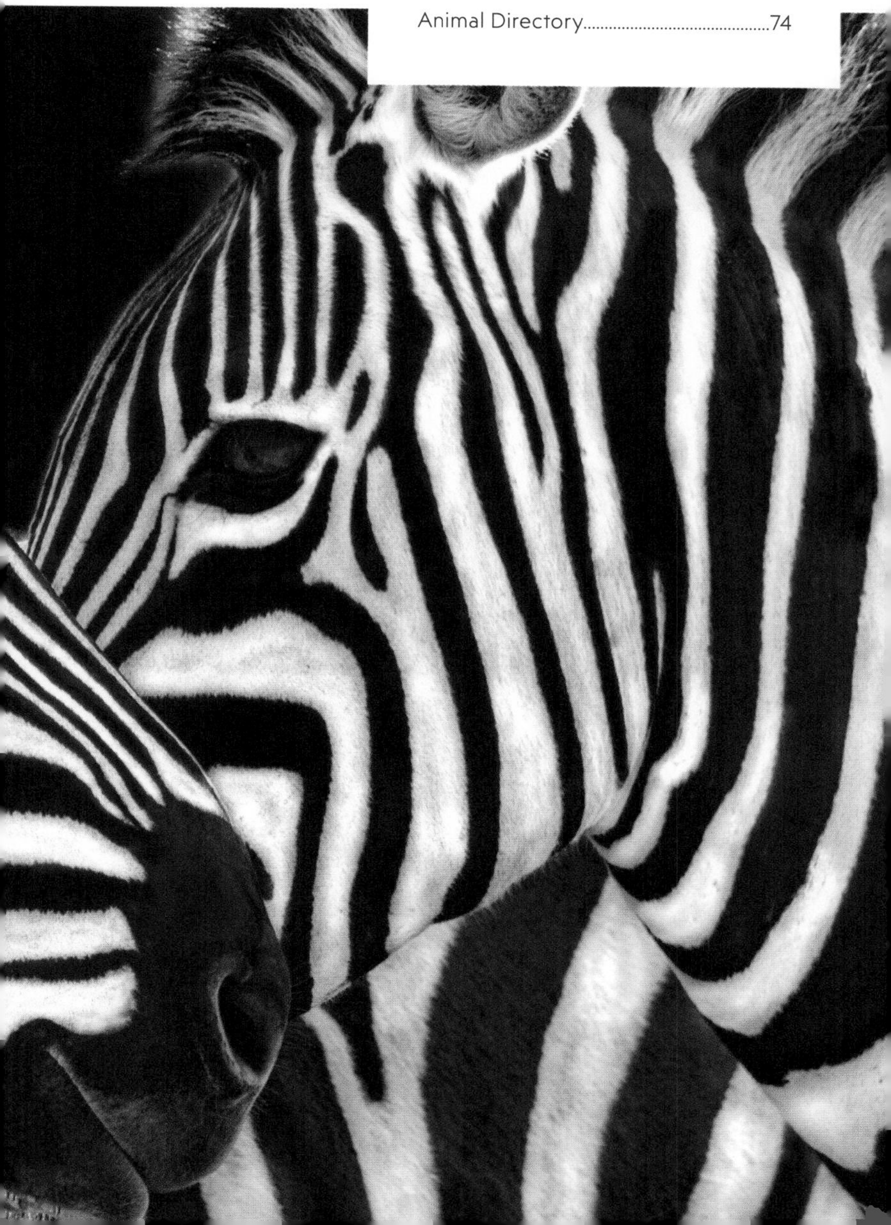

# SOUTH AFRICA'S
# HABITATS

Habitat types are determined by a variety of factors, including climate, vegetation and geology. In South Africa, the most important of these factors are rainfall, soil type, altitude and latitude. Broadly speaking, rainfall is significantly higher in the east, while soil is sandiest in the west, altitude is highest in the central highveld area and temperatures tend to be highest at more northerly latitudes.

*The western part of South Africa mostly consists of thinly populated **semiarid** plains and mountains, from the tall red dunes of the Kalahari to Namaqualand with its dazzling spring wildflower displays.*

*The Cape Floral Kingdom supports a remarkably diverse cover known as **fynbos** (fine bush), comprising 9,600 plant species, most of which occur only here. Much of the wildlife is unique to the region.*

*Closed-canopy **forest**, although scarce in South Africa, is highly biodiverse. It is particularly attractive to bird-watchers as it hosts many species of limited range.*

Vryburg

Kuruman

Upington

Campbell

Kimberley

Port Nolloth

Springbok

Kleinsee

Clanwilliam

Sutherland

Graaff-Reinet

Beaufort West

Langebaan

Worcester

George

Cape Town

Stellenbosch

Riversdale

Hermanus

Orange

0 km    100
0 miles          100

N
↑

The largely high-lying central region of South Africa, rising to 3,480 m (11,420 ft) in the Drakensberg range, is dominated by **highveld grassland**. In the past century much of it has been lost to agriculture or urban development.

Much of the north and east is covered in **savannah woodland**, mostly dominated by thorny acacia trees. In terms of viewing game, this is the most important habitat in South Africa.

South Africa is generally a dry country but it does have some **wetland** areas, including several natural lakes in the iSimangaliso Wetland Park. Most other freshwater bodies are artificially dammed.

The **intertidal** zone is the stretch of coast dividing the permanent tree line from the open sea. The northeast coastal belt features lush mangrove swamps and off-shore coral reefs teeming with fish.

Musina

Louis Trichardt

Polokwane

Baphalaborwa

Rustenburg

Pretoria

Johannesburg

Ermelo

Mbabane

ESWATINI

Klerksdorp

Vereeniging

Vaal

Newcastle

Vryheid

Clarens

Ladysmith

Bloemfontein

Maseru

LESOTHO

KwaDukuza

Durban

Kokstad

Port Edward

Lusikisiki

Cradock

East London

Grahamstown

Port Elizabeth

Limpopo

Lusutfu

Phongolo

Tugela

Orange

HABITATS OF
SOUTH AFRICA

- Semiarid
- Forest
- Fynbos
- Intertidal
- Wetland
- Savannah woodland
- Highveld grassland

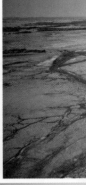

# TERRAIN AND FLORA

South Africa's flora has charmed visitors and intrigued botanists for years. Many species are widely distributed, but each region has produced distinct characteristics. In the more arid west, plants tend to be small and low-growing, flowering briefly after the winter rains, while further east, open grassland and bushveld dominate. Lush subtropical coastal forests grow along the East Coast.

## Savannah Woodland

Large tracts of the interior are covered with tall grasses and low trees, most of them deciduous, fine-leaved and thorny. The Kruger National Park (p336) is an excellent example of several transitional types occurring between sparse shrub and savannah; here shrubs grow densely and larger tree types include marula, mopane and baobab. The many acacia species are characterized by podbearing trees and shrubs with clusters of small, yellow flowers.

## Semiarid

In southern Africa, true desert is confined to the Namib. The semi-desert Great Karoo region covers about one-third of South Africa, and its flora has evolved to withstand aridity and extreme temperatures. Many succulents, including the aloes, mesembryanthemums, euphorbias and stapelias, store water in their thick leaves or roots. The seeds of daisy-like ephemeral plants may lie dormant for years, only to germinate and flower briefly when the conditions are favourable (p201). Trees tend to grow along seasonal river courses.

## Forest

Dense evergreen forests thrive in the high-rainfall area around Knysna (p238). They produce lovely rare hardwoods such as stinkwood and yellowwood, two types that also occur along the subtropical coastal belt of KwaZulu-Natal.

[4]

[5]

1 Savannah woodland at Kruger National Park.
2 Intertidal vegetation at Kosi Bay.
3 The semiarid Great Karoo.
4 Wetlands at iSimangaliso.
5 King protea, a *fynbos* flower.

Knysna's temperate forests have a characteristic undergrowth of shrubs, ferns, fungi and creepers such as the wispy "old man's beard". Mature trees may reach a height of 60 m (195 ft), with a girth of 7 m (23 ft).

## Highveld Grassland

Mountain flora, zoned according to altitude and increasing severity of the environment, rises from dense heath to mixed scrub and grasses. A relatively small subalpine belt, 2,800 m (9,000 ft) above sea level, is confined to the Drakensberg region (p278). Characteristic flowering plants here are helichrysum ("everlastings"), sedges and ericas. In many areas, annuals make brief, colourful spring appearances. Among the proteas growing in this region is the rare snow protea on the high peaks of the Cederberg (p189).

## Wetland

The term wetlands embraces all freshwater and most saline aquatic habitats other then open sea. This watery environment creates very harsh conditions for plants to grow in, and those that flourish – such as water lilies, rushes and common reeds – have cleverly adapted to cope with waterlogged soil.

## Intertidal

Brackish swamps, saline estuaries and lush plant growth are characteristic of the KwaZulu-Natal coast. Mangroves anchor themselves to their unstable habitat with stiltlike roots, while higher up on the banks grow palms and the broadleaved wild banana of the Strelitzia genus. A good example of typical East Coast vegetation can be seen at Kosi Bay (p285), where swamps surround lakes that are over-grown with water lilies and reeds. Dune forests and grasslands are dotted with wild palms.

## Fynbos

The comparatively small Southwestern Cape is one of the world's six floral kingdoms. Its so-called *fynbos* includes some 350 species of protea, as well as pelargoniums, ericas, reeds and irises. Most are endemic to the area, and are well represented in the Kirstenbosch National Botanical Garden (p146).

# CONSERVATION

Despite the relative profligacy of wildlife in South Africa's national parks and other protected areas, a considerable portion of the country's bio-diversity was lost during three centuries of European settlement. A series of conservation measures introduced since the turn of the 20th century have brought about an amazing recovery, and today South Africa's wildlife reserves are among the finest in the world.

Before the arrival of the white colonists, the nomadic Khoe and San hunted wild animals for food, while to the east, Zulu and Venda traded in ivory and organized ceremonial hunts – but their spears and pitfall traps had little impact. When Europeans arrived on the scene in the 17th century, South Africa's wildlife seemed inexhaustible. By the mid-19th century, however, the settlers – with their deadly weapons – had seen to it that the vast herds had disappeared. The sable-like blue-buck and zebra-like quagga that once roamed the *fynbos*-strewn slopes of the Western Cape were hunted to extinction, as was the Cape lion, a subspecies of lion with a distinctive black mane. Populations of big game were decimated, and many animal species were in danger of dying out.

### The First Wildlife Reserves

As towns expanded, people began to view wildlife as an asset, and in 1889, the Natal Volksraad (people's council) agreed to establish a wildlife reserve. In 1894, a strip of land between KwaZulu-Natal and Swaziland became the Pongola Game Reserve, Africa's first conservation area. In 1898, President Paul Kruger signed a proclamation establishing the forerunner of a sanctuary that was later named Kruger National Park in his honour.

1 Elephants in Kruger National Park.
2 A radio-tracked crocodile.
3 Kruger National Park.
4 The helicopter crew of an anti-poaching force.
5 Protected bontebok.

## Conservation Today

The conservation ethic that now prevails in South Africa is generally well-managed and forward-thinking, but the scourge of poaching and inevitable habitat loss caused by an expanding human population remain real concerns. Nonetheless, there have been several success stories, including the resurgence of once-dwindling populations of bontebok, Cape Mountain zebra and white rhino following these species' protection within national parks and game reserves.

A key aspect of conservation work in national parks such as Kruger is managing for diversity. Scientists are only now beginning to understand the complicated ecosystem of the African savannah, and are making careful efforts to manage it in a way that maintains the habitat's diversity – such as closing artificial water points, which caused habitat-modifiers such as elephants to flourish (to the detriment of other species). Additionally, radio tracking enables scientists to monitor endangered predators, providing important data about factors that affect their survival.

### IUCN RED LIST

The International Union for Conservation of Nature (IUCN) Red List of Threatened Species assesses the extinction risk of a plant or animal. The categories are:

**Extinct** (EX) - No individuals known to survive eg bluebuck.
**Extinct in the Wild** (EW) - Survives only in captivity or as an introduced population outside its natural range.
**Critically Endangered** (CE) - Extremely high risk of extinction in the immediate future eg black rhino.
**Endangered** (EN) - Very high risk of extinction within the foreseeable future eg African wild dog.
**Vulnerable** (VU) - Significant medium-term risk of extinction eg lion.
**Least Concern** (LC) - No significant risk of extinction at present eg impala.
**Data Deficient** (DD) - Insufficient information available for assessment.

# CATS

Secretive and solitary, cats belong to the family Felidae and are the most efficient killers among carnivores. Also the most strictly carnivorous, they feed exclusively on other warm-blooded creatures, from sparrows and mice to buffaloes and giraffes. Although they differ greatly in coloration and size, all cats have a similar body plan to their domestic counterpart, with an elongated body, long tail, small head, sensitive whiskers, prominent canine teeth and keen, bifocal vision. Much wild felid behaviour will be familiar to the average cat owner.

## TAXONOMY

*Most of South Africa's felid species are small to medium-sized cats of the genera Felis, Caracal and Leptailurus. Big cats of the genus Panthera, including lion and leopard, have a larynx modification that enables them to roar, while the cheetah, of the genus Acinonyx, is the only felid with claws that are not fully retractable – a characteristic tailored to its specialist pursuit of sprinting.*

### Cheetah (VU)
**Species** *Acinonyx jubatus* **Seen** *Phinda, Kruger (central region), Sabi Sands*

This large spotted felid has a streamlined build, small head and unique non-retractable claws. The world's fastest runner, it is capable of accelerating from standstill to a speed of 115 km/h (72 mph) in 4 seconds. Where most feline predators combine hunting with scavenging, the cheetah feeds exclusively on fresh meat. It is also unusual in that it hunts by day as well as at dusk. Less solitary than most cats, the cheetah is often seen in pairs or small groups – either male coalitions of up to three brothers, or a female with cubs. Unlike the true big cats, it cannot roar. Instead, its most common vocalization is a high-pitched, bird-like twitter known as "yipping". The cheetah has suffered a massive range retraction, and is now practically restricted to sub-Saharan Africa and parts of Iran.

## African Wild Cat (LC)
**Species** *Felis silvestris* **Seen** *Sabi Sands, Kgalagadi, Kruger*

This small, elusive felid is closely related to its much rarer European counterpart. DNA evidence suggests that it is the sole wild ancestor of the domestic cat – and indeed it looks much like a domestic tabby, but with longer legs. A versatile hunter of rodents, birds and insects, it is the most widely distributed of all African predators, absent only from rainforest interiors and deserts. Its genetic integrity is under increasing threat as a result of interbreeding with feral domestic cats.

## Black-Footed Cat (VU)
**Species** *Felis nigripes* **Seen** *Kgalagadi, Pilanesberg*

Endemic to southern Africa, this tiny cat is associated with sandy, semiarid habitats, where it is very seldom seen. At a glance, it could be confused with the African wild cat, but the black-footed cat is much smaller, has shorter legs, and is heavily spotted as opposed to faintly striped (it is also known as the small spotted cat). A nocturnal hunter, it preys mainly on small mammals such as gerbils, mice and elephant shrews.

## Caracal (LC)
**Species** *Caracal caracal* **Seen** *Kgalagadi, Augrabies Falls*

The largest of Africa's "small cats", the caracal resembles the Eurasian lynx. It has a fairly uniform tan coat, with a paler belly, and long tufted ears whose dark coloration is referred to in Turkish as *karakulak* (black ear), from which the cat gets its name. Because of this tufting, the caracal is exceptionally sharp of hearing, even by felid standards. Active at night, this agile carnivore is a versatile hunter and is particularly skilled at taking birds in flight.

## Serval (LC)
**Species** *Leptailurus serval* **Seen** *Kruger, uKhahlamba-Drakensberg, Ithala*

A sleek cat with streaky (as opposed to circular) black-on-gold spots, the serval has the longest legs in relation to body size of any felid, and very large ears – adaptations that help it to locate prey in its preferred habitat of tall grassland. It feeds mainly on small mammals and birds, pouncing with a spectacular high spring. The serval is the most readily seen of the smaller felids, especially during the first 30 minutes after sunrise.

# LION

Africa's largest terrestrial predator, the charismatic "king of the jungle" is the ultimate safari icon. Today, South Africa's lions are confined to a few protected areas and the continental population has plunged by an estimated 75 per cent since 1990.

---

**KEY FACTS**

**Species**
*Panthera leo. Local names: Mbube (Zulu), Shumba (Shangaan), Leeu (Afrikaans).*

**Size**
*Shoulder height: 100–130 cm (40–50 inches); Weight: up to 280 kg (617 lb).*

**Population in South Africa**
*2,100.*

**Conservation Status**
*VU.*

**Reproduction**
*Females reach sexual maturity at 3 years and give birth to litters of two to six cubs every 18 months.*

**Habitat**
*Most often in savannah, but range into all except desert and rainforest.*

**Seen**
*Kruger, Sabi Sands, Kgalagadi, Madikwe, Pilanesberg.*

---

## Family and Breeding

The most sociable of the world's 37 cat species, the lion generally lives in prides of five to ten animals, including an adult male, a few adult females and their offspring. Larger prides also occur, often involving male coalitions; one such grouping, active in Sabi Sands in 2010, had five adult males, four of them siblings. Prides defend their territories, which cover anything from 20 to 200 sq km (8–77 sq miles). Takeover battles are often fought to the death and result in the usurper killing all cubs, thereby encouraging the females back into oestrus sooner. Lions undergo an extraordinary mating ritual.

A male and female pair off, mating briefly but violently at gradually increasing intervals of 12–25 minutes for up to 3 days, after which they return to their pride.

## Feeding

Hunting is normally a team effort undertaken by females, who rely on stealth more than speed. A common strategy is for one or two lionesses to herd their prey in the direction of other pride members hidden in tall grass. Males seldom take part in a hunt but are quick to exercise their feeding rights once a kill is made. Favoured prey includes antelope, and large prides can even bring down a buffalo. Although not usually thought of as scavengers, lions are not above stealing a carcass from hyenas.

## Communication and Voice

Adult lions are most active around dusk and dawn, but cubs interact throughout the day. Subordinate individuals frequently stop to greet or groom dominant pride members, especially when they reunite after a period apart. Although lions are famous for their roar, the most common call, made by females as well as males, is a series of far-carrying moaning grunts that increase in volume, then fade away. As dominant males often move separately from the main pride (regrouping after a kill), this characteristic sound of the African night has the dual purpose of advertising the caller's presence to the pride and warning rivals off its territory.

### Did You Know?

Unusually among felids, lions seldom take to the trees.

# LEOPARD

The most abundant yet most elusive of Africa's large predators, the leopard is distinguishable by its rosette-patterned coat and powerful physique. This nocturnal cat is the supreme solitary hunter, capable of creeping to within a metre of its prey before pouncing.

## KEY FACTS

### Species
*Panthera pardus. Local names: Ingwe (Zulu), Nkwe (Sotho), Luiperd (Afrikaans).*

### Size
*Shoulder height: 70–80 cm (28–32 inches); Weight: up to 60 kg (132 lb).*

### Population in South Africa
*4,500 and declining.*

### Conservation status
*VU.*

### Reproduction
*Females reach sexual maturity at 2–4 years, when they come into oestrus.*

### Habitat
*Might occur anywhere.*

### Seen
*Sabi Sands, Kruger, Phinda.*

## Family and Breeding

The leopard is among the most solitary and territorial of cats. Adults live alone in well-marked territories that are never shared with individuals of the same sex, although males and females frequently have partial territorial overlap. Even so, a chance meeting between two individuals is usually accompanied by real or feigned aggression. Far smaller than males, female leopards come into oestrus every 6–7 weeks. At this time, males from bordering or overlapping territories will often fight to the death for coupling rights. Mating itself is an ill-tempered affair, and the male has no involvement in rearing the cubs. Females give birth to litters of two to three cubs in a sheltered cave or thicket, and keep a close watch over them for the next 10–14 days, when the cubs' eyes open. Infant mortality is high; it is unusual for more than one cub to survive to adulthood. Cubs can fend for themselves at around one year, but usually stay close to their mother for another 6–12 months before becoming fully independent.

## Feeding

An opportunistic hunter, the leopard feeds on anything from medium-sized antelopes down to hares, birds, baboons and even insects. It depends almost entirely on stealth, stalking silently through thick vegetation before emerging at the last moment to pounce and strangle its prey with its powerful jaws. A leopard will frequently carry a large kill high into the canopy, where it is safely out of the reach of less arboreal scavengers such as lions, hyenas and jackals. This furtive behaviour has been a key factor in ensuring the persistence of the species in ranchland and numerous other unprotected areas throughout Africa.

## Communication and Voice

As might be expected of such a stealthy creature, the leopard is not given to extensive vocalization. Males in particular advertise their presence with a repetitive rasping cough that sounds not dissimilar to wood being sawed. Purring has also been recorded, probably indicating contentment during feeding. Territorial clashes between males are accompanied by snarling and hissing.

## Did You Know?

The leopard's name reflects an old belief that it is a lion *(leo)* and panther *(pardos)* hybrid.

# DOGS AND HYENAS

Two other major families of large carnivore in South Africa are Canidae (dogs) and Hyaenidae (hyenas). Spotted hyenas are socially complex animals, and wild dogs are riveting to watch, especially while denning.

### Black-Backed Jackal (LC)
**Species** *Canis mesomelas* **Seen** *Kruger, Kgalagadi, Madikwe*

The black-backed jackal is most active at dusk and dawn, and its shrill yelping is a typical sound of the African night. It has a shoulder height of 40 cm (16 inches) and an ochre coat offset by a silver-flecked black saddle. An opportunistic feeder, it subsists on small mammals, birds and carrion, and is often seen lurking near lion kills.

### Side-Striped Jackal (LC)
**Species** *Canis adustus* **Seen** *Kruger*

Associated with brachystegia woodland, the side-striped jackal is more strictly nocturnal and less vocal than other jackals. It is similar in general coloration to the black-backed jackal, but with a pale stripe along the flanks. An adaptable omnivore seen singly or in pairs, it supplements a meat-based diet with fruit, grain and carrion.

### Cape Fox (LC)
**Species** *Vulpes chama* **Seen** *Kgalagadi, Pilanesberg*

The Cape fox is a nocturnal species whose range runs from southern Angola to the Western Cape. With a grizzled grey back and browner underparts, its general coloration is jackal-like, but its long bushy tail precludes confusion with any other canid in the region. It has an exclamatory yap and is heard more often than it is seen.

### Bat-Eared Fox (LC)
**Species** *Otocyon megalotis* **Seen** *Kgalagadi, Augrabies Falls*

With huge ears and a black eye-mask, this canid is not a true fox. A number of peculiarities – up to 50 sharp teeth, for instance – have led to it being placed in its own genus. Exclusively insectivorous, it tends to be nocturnal in the hot months and diurnal in the cooler ones. Small family groups can be seen throughout the year.

### Spotted Hyena (LC)
**Species** *Crocuta crocuta* **Seen** *Kruger, Sabi Sands, Pilanesberg*

Africa's second-largest predator after the lion stands 1-m (3-ft) high at the shoulder. Powerfully built, it has a characteristic sloping back, bone-crushingly powerful jaws and a dog-like face and snout. Routinely portrayed as a scavenger, it is actually an adept hunter, capable of killing an animal as large as a wildebeest.

### African Wild Dog (EN)
**Species** *Lycaon pictus* **Seen** *Kruger, Hluhluwe-Imfolozi, Madikwe*

Africa's largest canid has a distinctive black, brown and cream coat. It lives in packs of five to 50 animals that hunt cooperatively. Once so common that it was treated as vermin, it is now Africa's second-most endangered large carnivore, with a total wild population of around 5,000. Of these, around 500 are in South Africa.

### Aardwolf (LC)
**Species** *Proteles cristatus*
**Seen** *Pilanesberg, Madikwe, Kgalagadi*

Lightly built and strictly nocturnal, the aardwolf (literally meaning "earth wolf") has a soft creamy striped coat and a dorsal mane. It is exclusively insectivorous, feeding almost entirely on two specific termite genera, and its distribution is linked strongly to the presence of suitable nests, into which it burrows nose-first to feed.

### Brown Hyena (NT)
**Species** *Parahyaena brunnea*
**Seen** *Pilanesberg, Kgalagadi, Madikwe*

Endemic to the dry west of southern Africa, the brown hyena is a more solitary creature than its spotted counterpart and a more dedicated scavenger, though it will hunt opportunistically. It is relatively lightly built, and has a pale mane and shaggy dark brown coat offset by creamy vertical stripes on its side and flanks.

# SMALL CARNIVORES

South Africa's small carnivorous mammals range from the mongooses of the family Herpestidae, which are likely to be seen on any safari, to the nocturnal – and less likely to be spotted – viverrids and mustelids.

**TAXONOMY**

*Genets and civets belong to the carnivore Viverridae family, which is confined to Africa and Asia; their closest relatives are cats. By contrast, Mustelidae is the most diverse carnivore family, represented by 57 species in 22 genera worldwide.*

### Cape Clawless Otter (LC)
**Species** *Aonyx capensis*
**Seen** *False Bay, Kruger*

Arguably the largest of the "small" carnivores, weighing as much as 35 kg (77 lb), the Cape clawless otter is most common in waters where it can evade crocodiles.

### Honey Badger (LC)
**Species** *Mellivora capensis*
**Seen** *Kruger*

The honey-badger has a pugilistic build, with a black body bisected by an off-white stripe down its back, and heavy, bear-like claws. An opportunistic feeder, its diet includes snakes and scorpions.

### Striped Weasel (LC)
**Species** *Poecilogale albincha*
**Seen** *Kgalagadi*

A widespread but uncommon resident of open grassland, the striped weasel is mostly black below and white on top, with an all-white tail and very short legs. It preys almost exclusively on small rodents.

### African Civet (LC)
**Species** *Civettictis civetta*
**Seen** *Kruger*

An omnivore with a black, white and gold coat, the African civet feeds on small animals but will also eat fruits and roots. It is seen on night drives, pacing with its nose to the ground as if following a scent.

### Common Genet (LC)
**Species** *Genetta genetta*
**Seen** *Addo Elephant, Karoo*

Also known as the small-spotted genet, this is the most familiar member of a genus of cat-like predators represented by some eight species in sub-Saharan Africa. It is quite often seen on night drives.

### Blotched Genet (LC)
**Species** *Genetta tigrina*
**Seen** *Addo Elephant, Kruger*

Similar to the common genet but with a black-tipped rather than a white-tipped tail, the blotched genet has a spotted black-on-gold coat. It is seen on night drives or scavenging around lodges after dark.

### Banded Mongoose (LC)
**Species** *Mungos mungo*
**Seen** *Kruger*

The banded mongoose is a slender, cat-sized carnivore whose dark brown coat bears faint black stripes along the back. Diurnally active, it is typically seen in family bands of 10 to 20 members.

### Dwarf Mongoose (LC)
**Species** *Helogale parvula*
**Seen** *Kruger, Marakele*

The highly social dwarf mongoose has a shoulder height of 7 cm (2 inches). It is a light brown predator often seen by the termite mounds and hollowed dead branches that it uses as a home.

### Slender Mongoose (LC)
**Species** *Herpestes sanguineus* **Seen** *Kruger*

The slender mongoose forages both terrestrially and arboreally. Though quite variable in shade, it is usually uniform grey or brown in colour, with an elongated body and a black-tipped tail.

### White-Tailed Mongoose (LC)
**Species** *Ichneumia albicauda* **Seen** *Kruger*

About the size of a badger, this is the largest African mongoose. One of the most strictly nocturnal and solitary species, it is often observed by spotlight on night drives.

### Yellow Mongoose (LC)
**Species** *Cynictis pencillata*
**Seen** *Kgalagadi*

This mongoose with a bushy orange-yellow coat has a habit of standing alertly on its hind legs. It favours sandy environments, where it lives in sprawling burrows with dozens of entrance holes.

### Meerkat (LC)
**Species** *Suricata suricata*
**Seen** *Kgalagadi*

Intelligent and playful, the meerkat lives underground in closely knit gangs of 20 or so individuals. It has monkey-like fingers with long claws and often stands on its hind legs, particularly when disturbed.

# PRIMATES

Intelligent, hyperactive and graceful, monkeys are among the most entertaining of creatures. They are well represented in equatorial Africa, but less so in South Africa, where only three species are present. This lack of diversity is due to the scarcity of suitably forested habitats. All of South Africa's monkeys are Cercopithecids (cheek-pouched monkeys), an adaptable family of omnivores that fills many ecological niches from swamp forests to semiarid plains, and is named for its inner cheek pouch, which can hold as much food as a full stomach.

**TAXONOMY**

*The three species of diurnal primate that inhabit South Africa are all classified as Old World Monkeys (family Cercopithecidae) and placed in the sub-family Cercopithecinae (cheek-pouched monkeys).*

### Blue Monkey (LC)
**Species** *Cercopithecus mitis* **Seen** *iSimangaliso, Hluhluwe-Imfolozi, Kruger (far north only)*

The most widespread of African forest monkeys and the only one whose distribution extends south of the Limpopo River, the blue monkey lives in troops of up to 10 animals that travel riparian corridors through savannah habitats. It has a very limited distribution in South Africa, where it is confined to the northeast corner of the country – the KwaZulu-Natal coast, the Mpumalanga escarpment forests, and the riparian forest along the Limpopo and its tributaries bordering Zimbabwe. The blue monkey can be distinguished from other South African monkeys by its more arboreal behaviour and retiring nature, its dark grey-blue coat with flecks of orange-brown on the back and its white throat.

## Bushbaby (Variable depending on species)
**Family** *Galagonidae* **Seen** *Kruger, Sabi Sands, Pilanesberg*

More closely related to the lemurs of Madagascar than to the diurnal monkeys of the African mainland, bushbabies (or galagos) have wide round eyes and agile bodies that enable them to leap between trees. Formerly, only two species were recognized – greater and lesser bushbaby – but a pioneering study used calls and genital patterns to identify around a dozen species in East Africa alone. Pending a similar study in South Africa, the taxonomy of bushbabies in the region remains indeterminate. Seldom seen in daylight, bushbabies become very active after dark and are often seen on night drives in reserves with suitable wooded savannah habitats.

## Vervet Monkey (LC)
**Species** *Chlorocebus pygerythrus*
**Seen** *Kruger, Hluhluwe-Imfolozi, Durban*

The vervet monkey lives in troops of 30–75 animals that are constantly engaged in interaction of one kind or another, whether fighting, grooming, carrying their young on their chest or raiding the nearest lodge's buffet. Thought to be the world's most numerous primate species apart from humans, it is predominantly terrestrial, though it seldom strays too far from the trees in which it shelters when threatened. It is highly intelligent, boasting an array of different alarm calls that some scientists have likened to a rudimentary language. The vervet has a grizzled light olive or grey coat, a black face, white ruff and pale belly, though this rather dull coloration is offset in the male by a gaudy blue scrotum.

## Chacma Baboon (LC)
**Species** *Papio ursinus* **Seen** *uKhahlamba-Drakensberg, Kruger, Cape Peninsula*

Weighing up to 45 kg (99 lb), the chacma baboon is the largest primate in South Africa and likely the most widespread. Dark grey-brown in coloration, it has a pugilistic build, dog-like head and long fangs. An adaptable omnivore, the baboon is at home in almost any habitat but is particularly fond of well-wooded savannah and mountains. Although mainly terrestrial, baboons feel safest when close to trees – their first path of retreat when predators are in the vicinity. Baboons ordinarily steer clear of people, but they can become very aggressive in places where they have come to see humans as a source of food. If encountered, be extremely cautious, as they can inflict a nasty bite.

# LARGE MAMMALS

Many of South Africa's large mammals are herbivores and for the most part they fall into one of two broad categories: grazers (grass eaters), such as zebras and buffalos, and browsers (leaf eaters), such as giraffes. A few animals, including elephants, fall into both categories, depending on the availability of food.

## TAXONOMY

*Many of South Africa's large mammals are ungulates, or hoofed mammals. They are split into two main groups: Artiodactyla (even-toed ungulates), such as giraffe, hippopotamus and African buffalo, and Perissodactyla (odd-toed ungulates), such as zebra and rhinoceros. Elephants (and other species) without true hooves are "near-ungulates".*

### Common Hippopotamus (VU)
**Species** *Hippopotamus amphibius* **Seen** *iSimangaliso, Kruger, Pilanesberg*

The most characteristic resident of Africa's rivers and freshwater lakes is the common hippo, with its purple-grey hairless hide, barrel-like torso and stumpy legs. Ears, eyes and nostrils are placed high on the skull, allowing it to spend most of its time submerged in the shallows. It feeds terrestrially, however, emerging between dusk and dawn to crop grass with its wide mouth. The hippo is highly gregarious, living in pods of up to 30 members, and very territorial, with fights for dominance between males often resulting in serious injury or death. Contrary to appearance, the hippo is highly mobile on land and can easily attain a speed of above 32 km/h (20 mph). It can be very dangerous to humans, as it typically heads straight to the safety of the water when disturbed, mowing down anything in its path.

### Giraffe (VU)
**Species** *Giraffa camelopardalis*
**Seen** *Kruger, Hluhluwe-Imfolozi,
Pilanesberg*

As the world's tallest land mammal, the giraffe
is a specialized canopy-feeder, browsing on
high-grade leaf foliage at heights of up to 6 m
(20 ft), though it will occasionally eat grass too.
Giraffes typically move in groups of up to 15
animals, with individuals often leaving or joining
at will; a herd may be all-male, all-female or
mixed in composition. Males are significantly
larger than females and often engage in a form
of behaviour called necking – intertwining their
necks and heads and occasionally dealing out
heavy blows. Females normally have one calf
and give birth standing, with the newborn
dropping up to 2 m (7 ft) to the ground, then
standing up and suckling within 30 minutes.

### Mountain Zebra (VU)
**Species** *Equus zebra* **Seen** *Goegap,
Table Mountain*

The mountain zebra is a southern African
endemic associated with dryish mountainous
habitats up to 2,000 m (6,562 ft) above sea
level. Two races are recognized. The Cape
mountain zebra is a fynbos endemic that was
hunted close to extinction. In the early 1900s
the population bottlenecked at below 100
individuals, but it has since risen to between
1,700 and 3,250. Hartmann's mountain zebra is
near-endemic to Namibia, though a small South
African population is protected within the
Goegap Nature Reserve. The mountain zebra
is very similar to the plains zebra, from which it
can be distinguished by the absence of shadow
stripes, but it lives in smaller core herds that
never form larger temporary groups.

### Plains Zebra (NT)
**Species** *Equus quagga* **Seen** *Kruger,
Hluhluwe-Imfolozi, Sabi Sands*

The plains zebra is a grazer whose natural
distribution ranges from Ethiopia to the Cape.
It is often seen in large ephemeral herds, but
its core social unit is an aggressively defended
non-territorial herd comprising one stallion, up
to five mares and their respective foals. The
purpose of the zebra's stripes is often cited as
camouflage, breaking up the animal's outline in
long grass, but it is more likely that the striping
is visually confusing to predators when the
herd scatters. The quagga, a partially striped
Western Cape endemic that was hunted to
extinction in the early years of colonialism, is
thought to have been a race of plains zebra
(hence the Latin name *Equus quagga*).

# AFRICAN ELEPHANT

The world's largest land animal, the African elephant is notable for two unique adaptations – a long trunk that combines immense strength with great sensitivity and outsized tusks that grow throughout its life, sometimes reaching lengths in excess of 3 m (10 ft).

## KEY FACTS

**Species**
*Loxodonta africana. Local names: Ndlovu (Zulu), Tlou (Tswana), Olifant (Afrikaans).*

**Size**
*Shoulder height: 2.5–4 m (8–13 ft); Weight: up to 6,300 kg (13,890 lb).*

**Population in South Africa**
*18,800.*

**Conservation status**
*VU.*

**Reproduction**
*Females first conceive in their early teens and give birth every 5–10 year until their late 50s.*

**Habitat**
*All except desert.*

**Seen**
*Addo Elephant, Tembe Elephant, Madikwe, Pilanesberg, Kruger.*

## Family and Breeding

Elephants are intensely sociable creatures. Females and youngsters move around in close-knit matriarchal clans. Females typically come into oestrus between one and five years after giving birth. Once impregnated, they give birth about 22 months later. Unlike their female kin, males are generally booted out of their birth group in their early teens, after which they roam around singly or form bachelor herds, often tailing the larger breeding herds with which they share a territory. Males periodically come into musth, a sexually related state characterized by a fifty-fold increase in testosterone levels. Such elephants are unpredictable and best treated with caution by other elephants and humans alike. A female gives birth to a 100-kg (220-lb) calf every 5 to 10 years. Adult females maintain a vigilant watch over their young until they are old enough to deter predators. Each calf represents a major genetic investment for the matriarchal herd and is raised communally. Matriarchal herds typically comprise up to four generations of sisters, daughters and granddaughters, who are dominated by the oldest female.

## Feeding

A versatile feeder, the African elephant is a mixed grazer-browser that spends up to 15 hours daily chomping 200 kg (440 lb) of vegetable matter. It drinks up to 200 litres (44 gallons) daily, arriving at a waterhole a few hours after sunrise and often staying on until late afternoon to play in the water or spray itself. Herds range widely in search of food, but concentrated populations in protected areas often cause serious environmental degradation by uprooting trees.

## Communication and Voice

In 1987, it was discovered that the elephant's main means of communication are not bouts of trumpeting, but subsonic rumblings that can travel through the earth for several miles. These are picked up by the skin on the trunk and feet, allowing dispersed herds to coordinate their movements over a vast area. Elephants also have an exceptional sense of smell and good eyesight.

### Did You Know?

Elephants are able to swim, using their trunks like snorkels to breathe when underwater.

# RHINOCEROS

With their armoured hide, massive bulk and fearsome horns, the world's five rhino species represent one of the most ancient branches of the ungulate line. Some 75 per cent of the world's surviving rhinos are protected within South Africa's borders.

## KEY FACTS

### Species
*Diceros bicornis (black); Ceratotherium simum (white). Local names: Tshukudu (Sotho), Ubhejane (Zulu), Renoster (Afrikaans)*

### Size
*Shoulder height: 1.4–1.7 m (4½– 5½ ft) (black); 1.5–1.8 m (5–6 ft) (white).*

### Weight
*Up to 1,300 kg (2,866 lb) (black); up to 3,500 kg (7,716 lb) (white).*

### Population in South Africa
*1,900 (black); 18,800 (white).*

### Conservation status
*CE (black); NT (white).*

### Reproduction
*Females mature sexually at 5 years and give birth to a calf every 3–4 years.*

### Habitat
*Dense woodland, thicket (black); open woodland, grassland (white).*

### Seen
*Hluhluwe-Imfolozi, Kruger, Pilanesberg, Ithala.*

## Family and Breeding

Adult rhinos are essentially solitary creatures, though not especially territorial. Both sexes are aggressive towards unfamiliar individuals but equable towards rhinos with neighbouring or over-lapping territories, sometimes even pairing off temporarily. Courtship between rhinos is a protracted affair. In the case of the black rhino, the female scrapes her territorial dung piles vigorously, and the first male to pick up the scent trails behind her, trying to cover it up with his own faeces. Prior to mating, the pair often indulge in noisy mock-sparring. Once the male is accepted, the two stay together for days or even weeks. A single calf weighing up to 50 kg (110 lb) is born 15–16 months later and is fully mobile within days. The bond between mother and calf is generally strong and lasts for 3–4 years. The female will eventually terminate the relationship once another birth is imminent.

## Feeding

The black rhino is a dedicated browser, utilizing the leaves, branches and fruits of at least 200 plant species, while the white rhino subsists mainly as a grazer. Rhinos feed mostly in the early morning and late afternoon, ideally retiring to a wallow or waterhole at midday, though the black rhino can go almost a week without drinking water if need be.

## Communication and Voice

Vocalizations, though complex and varied, are seldom observed during a casual rhino encounter. When two individuals meet, they may growl or trumpet to signal aggression, but will more likely snort in amicable greeting. Rhinos give a high-pitched alarm call when moderately threatened and emit a loud, piglike squeal when seriously alarmed. Indirect communication between neighbours includes the sharing of common dung heaps at waterholes and feeding places, which allows every individual to know which other rhinos have passed by recently.

# AFRICAN BUFFALO

Africa's only wild ox, the powerfully built African buffalo is famed for its unpredictable temperament. Indeed, the hunters who coined the term Big Five regarded it as the most dangerous of foes. Buffaloes are the most numerous of the Big Five, but numbers are in decline.

## KEY FACTS

**Species**
*Syncerus caffer. Local names: Inyathi (Zulu), Nare (Tswana), Buffel (Afrikaans).*

**Size**
*Shoulder height: 1.2–1.7 m (4–6 ft); Weight: 500–800 kg (1,102–1,764 lb)*

**Population in South Africa**
*30,000–60,000.*

**Conservation status**
*NT*

**Reproduction**
*Females mature at the age of 4–5 years and give birth to a single calf at the start of the rainy season.*

**Habitat**
*Mostly non-arid environments.*

**Seen**
*Kruger, Hluhluwe-Imfolozi, Pilanesberg.*

## Family and Breeding

The African buffalo is highly gregarious and non-territorial, generally moving in mixed-sex herds of 10 to 50 animals, with one dominant male and a hierarchical structure binding the adult females and non-dominant males. Females come into oestrus at the start of the rainy season and give birth to a single calf, or more infrequently twins, almost exactly a year later. Tensions between males run high during the mating season, with dominant bulls trying to pull rank and subordinate males fighting to challenge their breeding rights. The imposing bulk of an adult buffalo ensures that it has few natural enemies and a strongly bonded herd will

cooperate to chase away predators. Nevertheless, buffaloes are sometimes preyed upon by lions, with the predator occasionally coming off second best in the confrontation.

## Feeding

Primarily a grazer, the African buffalo requires a significant proportion of grass in its diet, although it can supplement this by feeding on low trees and shrubs. Large herds are common in most grassland habitats, while forests support smaller herds. The buffalo feeds throughout the day, but will adopt a nocturnal feeding pattern in areas where it is repeatedly disturbed. It must drink at least once every 24 hours and also enjoys wallowing. Herds rarely stray more than 10–15 km (6–9 miles) away from a reliable water source. Cattle egrets flock around herds of buffalo to feed on insects that are disturbed as the mammals move through the grass.

## Communication and Voice

The African buffalo is generally far quieter than its mooing domestic counterpart when it comes to day-to-day communication. However, upon sighting a predator it makes an explosive snorting alarm call that swiftly mobilizes the rest of the herd into defensive mode. A threatened animal may also grunt aggressively. The buffalo has an acute sense of smell and exceptional hearing, but poor eyesight, which may cause a herd to stand and stare myopically at a perceived intruder.

## Did You Know?

Buffalo herds are democratic - individuals vote on the direction of travel by orienting their bodies.

# SMALL MAMMALS

South Africa's smaller mammals range from rodents and bats, which you are likely to spot on a daily basis, to the more elusive aardvark and pangolin, both of which feature high on the wish list of seasoned safari-goers.

> ### TAXONOMY
>
> *Many of these smaller animals are evolutionary one-offs. For instance, the aardvark is the only living member of the order Tubulidentata. By contrast, pigs belong to the same order as giraffes, camels and antelopes.*

### Ground Pangolin (VU, EN or CR)
**Family** *Manidae* **Seen** *Kgalagadi*

Also known as scaly anteaters, pangolins are unobtrusive nocturnal insectivores who curl into a tight ball when disturbed. The savannah-dwelling ground pangolin is the only species found in South Africa, where it is more or less confined to the northern border regions. Weighing up to 18 kg (40 lb), it is very unlikely to be seen in the wild.

### Hyrax (Most species LC)
**Order** *Hyracoidea* **Seen** *Table Mountain, Mapungubwe, uKhahlamba-Drakensberg*

Hyraxes are dwarfish relicts of a once-prolific near-ungulate order more closely related to elephants than to any other living creature. The Cape rock hyrax (or dassie) *Procavia capensis* is a conspicuous resident of rocky slopes, where it lives in territorial family groups of up to 20 individuals.

### Aardvark (LC)
**Species** *Orycteropus afer*
**Seen** *Sabi Sands, Kruger, Pilanesberg*

The aardvark – a Dutch name meaning earth pig – weighs up to 80 kg (176 lb). It is a shy, strictly nocturnal insectivore with a stout body, pinkish skin, a heavy, kangaroo-like tail and long, upright ears. It uses its elongated snout and long, retractable sticky tongue to snaffle up as many as 50,000 termites in one night.

### Cape Porcupine (LC)
**Species** *Hystrix africaeaustralis*
**Seen** *Sabi Sands*

Porcupines are the largest of the African rodents, though the species found in South Africa is not quite so bulky as its 27-kg (60-lb) East African counterpart. The porcupine is coated in long black-and-white quills, which occasionally betray its presence by rattling as it walks.

### Bats (Variable depending on species)
**Order** *Chiroptera* **Seen** *Common in most non-urban environments*

The Chiroptera order numbers 1,000-plus species globally. Bats play a vital ecological role in controlling flying insect populations, and small, insect-eating bats are often seen hawking at dusk throughout South Africa, most commonly in game reserves and other relatively unspoiled habitats.

### Springhare (LC)
**Species** *Pedetes capensis* **Seen** *Kgalagadi, Augrabies Falls, Mapungubwe*

With powerful hind legs that enable it to cover up to 2 m (6 ft) in one bound, the sandy brown springhare weighs up to 4 kg (9 lb) and is most likely to be seen after dark. By day, it rests up in deep burrows in sandy soils. The springhare is particularly common in the semiarid savannah of the Kalahari region.

### Bushpig (LC)
**Species** *Potamochoerus larvatus*
**Seen** *Sabi Sands, Kruger, Hluhluwe-Imfolozi*

Larger, more hirsute and shorter-legged than the warthog, the nocturnal bushpig has small eyes, a blunt snout, pointed, tufted ears, buckled toes and small tusks. It can be quite aggressive when cornered. Bushpigs are often seen after dark at the rest camp in Hluhluwe-Imfolozi Game Reserve.

### Common Warthog (LC)
**Species** *Phacochoerus africanus*
**Seen** *Kruger, Hluhluwe-Imfolozi, Pilanesberg*

The warthog is a long-legged, slender-bodied swine that stands 80 cm (32 inches) high at the shoulder. It has upward-curving tusks and a trio of callus-like "warts" on its face. The warthog is an unfussy omnivore whose favoured food consists of roots and bulbs.

# ANTELOPES

A constant of South Africa's wild places, antelopes thrive in every habitat from rainforest to desert. They range from the tiny blue duiker, which weighs about the same as a domestic cat, to the cattle-sized eland. Otherwise similar in appearance to deer, antelopes sport permanent horns rather than seasonal antlers. The family has its very own photogenic "Big Five": eland, kudu, gemsbok, sable antelope and roan antelope.

> ### TAXONOMY
>
> *Antelopes split into two groups. The eland, greater kudu, nyala and bushbuck belong to the tribe Tragelaphini, more closely related to buffaloes than to other antelopes, which are split across nine tribes.*

## Common Eland (LC)
**Species** *Taurotragus oryx*
**Seen** *uKhahlamba-Drakensberg, Pilanesberg, Kgalagadi*

Also known as the Cape eland, Africa's largest antelope has a maximum shoulder height of 1.8 m (6 ft) and can weigh almost 950 kg (2,094 lb). Light tan in colour, with faint white vertical stripes, small unisex horns and a hefty dewlap, it moves in groups of about 10 animals, but larger parties are also seen. The eland was revered by the San – hunter-gatherers who have long inhabited South Africa – and is the animal most commonly depicted in their rock art.

## Greater Kudu (LC)
**Species:** *Tragelaphus strepsiceros*
**Seen** *Kruger, Pilanesberg, Mapungubwe*

Second in stature only to the eland, the greater kudu stands up to 1.5 m (5 ft) high and has a greyish coat with up to 10 vertical white stripes on each side. Males have large double-spiralled horns. Small family parties are seen in dense woodland along dry-country watercourses. An accomplished jumper, the greater kudu can clear fences twice its shoulder height. It is the most common large antelope in unprotected parts of South Africa.

### Gemsbok (Common Oryx) (LC)
**Species** *Oryx gazella* **Seen** *Kgalagadi, Augrabies Falls, Pilanesberg*

This dry-country antelope has a shoulder height of 1.2 m (4 ft), a cleanly marked grey, black and white coat, a long black tail and long straight horns that sweep back from the skull at the same angle as the forehead and muzzle. Seen in nomadic herds of up to 10 animals, it can survive without water for almost as long as a camel. Naturally restricted to the more arid northwest of South Africa, it has also been introduced to the Pilanesberg National Park and other reserves outside that range.

### Sable Antelope (LC)
**Species** *Hippotragus niger*
**Seen** *Pilanesberg, Sabi Sands, Kruger (Around Pretoriuskop and Letaba)*

The male sable stands up to 1.4 m (4 ft 7 inches) at the shoulder and weighs up to 270 kg (595 lb). It has a jet-black coat offset by a white face, underbelly and rump, and splendid decurved horns. The female is less striking, with a chestnut-brown coat and shorter horns. Common elsewhere on the continent, in South Africa the sable is confined to the far northeast. Sightings are quite frequent in Pilanesberg.

### Roan Antelope (LC)
**Species** *Hippotragus equinus* **Seen** *Kruger (Letaba area), Pilanesberg*

Similar in size to the sable antelope, the roan has short, decurved horns and a fawn-grey coat with a pale belly and light mane. The Pilanesberg National Park offers perhaps the best opportunity for a sighting in the wild. Captive populations of roan are also held on some private ranches in the north of the country. Roan form groups of five to 15 animals, with a dominant male. Fighting among males for control of the herd is not uncommon.

### Common Waterbuck (LC)
**Species** *Kobus ellipsiprymnus*
**Seen** *Kruger, iSimangaliso, Hluhluwe-Imfolozi*

The largest member of the kob tribe, the common waterbuck stands up to 1.3 m (4 ft 3 inches) at the shoulder, and weighs up to 240 kg (529 lb). It has a shaggy grey-brown to chestnut coat and a white inverted U-mark on its rump; the male has large, lyre-shaped horns. Waterbuck are usually found in open grassland or woodland. Herds comprise up to 10 individuals lorded over by a dominant male.

### Impala (LC)
**Species** *Aepyceros melampus*
**Seen** *Kruger, Hluhluwe-Imfolozi, Madikwe*

This medium-sized antelope has a chestnut coat with black-and-white stripes on the rump and tail. Males have magnificent black-ringed horns. Impalas are usually seen in herds of over 100, dominated numerically by females and young. They are agile jumpers and herds often leap in all directions to confuse predators. The commonest antelope in the Kruger National Park, impalas are also prolific in bush habitats elsewhere in the northeast, although they don't occur naturally in the rest of the country.

### Red Hartebeest (LC)
**Species** *Alcelaphus buselaphus*
**Seen** *Kgalagadi, Madikwe, Pilanesberg*

Similar in height to the related wildebeests, the hartebeest has large shoulders, a slender torso, pale yellow-brown coat and smallish, heart-shaped unisex horns. Males frequently climb on termite hills to scan, as a display of territorial dominance. Half a dozen races are recognized, the one present in South Africa being the red hartebeest. It occurs naturally only in the north, on the border with Botswana, but is farmed in other parts of the country.

### Tsessebe (LC)
**Species** *Damaliscus lunatus*
**Seen** *Kruger (north only)*

Also known as topi or tiang, the tsessebe comes across as a darker, glossier variation of the red hartebeest, with which it shares similar habits and a preference for open grassland. It is dark brown in coloration, with some black on the flanks and snout, and striking yellow lower legs. In South Africa, its natural range is more or less confined to the Kruger National Park, where it is most likely to be seen on the eastern basaltic plains, north of the Olifants River.

### Blesbok/Bontebok (LC)
**Species** *Damaliscus pygargus*
**Seen** *Bontebok, Table Mountain, Golden Gate*

Endemic to South Africa, the blesbok and bontebok are smaller relatives of the tsessebe that freely interbreed where their ranges overlap and are thus regarded as races of the same species. The bontebok is a *fynbos* endemic that was hunted close to extinction prior to the creation of the eponymous national park in the 1930s, but since then the population has recovered. The blesbok is a resident of highveld grassland in the centre of the country.

## Blue Wildebeest (LC)
**Species** *Connochaetes taurinus*
**Seen** *Kruger, Hluhluwe-Imfolozi, Sabi Sands*

Although common in southern-hemisphere grassland habitats from the Serengeti-Mara to KwaZulu-Natal, the blue wildebeest is totally absent north of the equator. It is highly gregarious, particularly in areas where it follows an annual migration, often assembling in groups of several hundred. Its dark grey-brown coat precludes confusion with other antelopes, but at a distance it could be mistaken for a buffalo, although its slighter build and shaggy beard are distinguishing features.

## Black Wildebeest (LC)
**Species** *Connochaetes gnou*
**Seen** *Golden Gate*

Another South African endemic hunted close to extinction by early European settlers is the black wildebeest or white-tailed gnu. Some authorities regard it as extinct in the wild, since the only surviving herds are farmed or semi-captive, but the population of several thousand is high enough for it to be IUCN-listed in the "Least Concern" category. It might be seen from the roadside on farmland anywhere in the central highveld northwest of Lesotho.

## Bushbuck (LC)
**Species** *Tragelaphus scriptus*
**Seen** *Kruger, Hluhluwe-Imfolozi, uKhahlamba-Drakensberg*

The bushbuck is a widespread medium-sized antelope of forest and riparian woodland. The male is usually dark brown or chestnut in colour, while the smaller female is generally pale red-brown. Both sexes have white throat patches and a variable combination of white spots, and sometimes stripes, on the coat. The bushbuck usually moves singly or in pairs and tends to be rather furtive in its behaviour.

## Nyala (LC)
**Species** *Nyala angasii* **Seen** *Hluhluwe-Imfolozi, Kruger, iSimangaliso*

Hunted to near-extinction in most of its former range, the nyala would be listed as endangered were it not for the population of 25,000 animals in northern KwaZulu-Natal. The nyala typically occurs in small family groups in thicketed habitats close to water. The male is dark chestnut-grey in coloration, with a grey-black mane, light white stripes along the sides, yellow leg stockings and lyre-shaped horns that can grow to a length of 80 cm (2 ft 8 inches).

**Springbok** (LC)
**Species** *Antidorcas marsupialis* **Seen** *Kgalagadi, Augrabies Falls, Goegap*

South Africa's national animal, the springbok resembles the East African Thomson's gazelle, with fawn upperparts and creamy belly separated by a black side-stripe. Despite its iconic status, it is far rarer than it was in the 18th century; today it is largely confined to the extreme northwest of the country.

**Suni** (LC)
**Species** *Neotragus moschatus* **Seen** *Phinda, iSimangaliso, Ndumo*

A small antelope that lives in coastal forests and thickets, the suni may be confused with the duiker. However, it has a more freckled coat. It can also be distinguished by its backward-sweeping horns (only on rams), large, rounded and almost rabbit-like ears, and its habit of flicking its tail from side to side, rather than up and down.

**Common Duiker** (LC)
**Species** *Sylvicapra grimmia* **Seen** *Kruger, Pilanesberg, uKhahlamba-Drakensberg*

The most widespread and conspicuous of Africa's 30+ duiker species, the common or grey duiker favours wooded savannah habitats. Most often seen in pairs, it could be confused with steenbok, but it is generally greyer. The duiker has a unique identifier in the form of a black tuft of hair that divides its horns.

**Blue Duiker** (LC)
**Species** *Philantomba monticola* **Seen** *Eshowe, Phinda, iSimangaliso*

A widespread but shy resident of coastal forests, the blue duiker is the smallest South African antelope, with a height of about 35 cm (14 inches) and a weight of 5 kg (11 lb). One of a group of hunch-backed forest-dwellers, it can be distinguished by its white under-tail, which it flicks regularly. Both sexes have short sharp horns.

**Natal Red Duiker** (LC)
**Species** *Cephalophus natalensis* **Seen** *Phinda, Hluhluwe-Imfolozi, iSimangaliso*

A forest-dweller confined to the eastern coastal littoral, the 46-cm- (18-inch-) tall Natal red duiker is among the South African representatives of a cluster of red duiker species, most of which are chestnut in colour with a black snout patch. Its rich coloration distinguishes it from the blue duiker and the suni.

**Klipspringer** (LC)
**Species** *Oreotragus oreotragus* **Seen** *Mapungubwe, uKhahlamba-Drakensberg, Augrabies Falls*

The klipspringer (Afrikaans for "rock jumper") has several unusual adaptations to its mountainous habitat. Bin-ocular vision enables it to gauge jumping distances accurately and its hollow fur insulates at high altitude. Both sexes have a grizzled grey-brown coat and forward-curving horns.

### Reedbuck (Southern: LC; Mountain: EN)
**Species** *Redunca spp.*
**Seen** *iSimangaliso, Kruger, uKhahlamba-Drakensberg*

Two species of reedbuck occur in South Africa – the southern and the mountain. The former is exceptionally common in iSimangaliso, while the latter can be seen in uKhahlamba-Drakensberg. Both are pale, skittish and lightly built grassland-dwellers characterized by white underbellies and small horns.

### Oribi (LC)
**Species** *Ourebia ourebi*
**Seen** *uKhahlamba-Drakensberg, Kwazulu-Natal (Midlands)*

Patchily distributed, the oribi has a shoulder height of about 50 cm (20 inches) and small, straight unisex horns. It has a sandy coat with a white belly and a round black glandular patch below its ears. Typically seen in pairs or small herds in tall open grass, the oribi gives a trademark sneezing alarm call before rapidly fleeing.

### Steenbok (LC)
**Species** *Raphicerus campestris* **Seen** *Kruger, Pilanesberg, Hluhluwe-Imfolizi*

Resembling a scaled-down version of the oribi, the steenbok is a small antelope with tan upperparts, white underbelly and short straight horns. However, it tends to prefer thicker vegetation than the oribi. The name steenbok is Afrikaans for stone buck and it refers to its habit of "freezing" when disturbed.

### Cape Grysbok (LC)
**Species** *Raphicerus malanotus* **Seen** *Table Mountain, De Hoop, Cedarberg Mountains*

Endemic to *fynbos* and other thicket habitats in the Western and Eastern Cape, the Cape grysbok can be distinguished from other small antelope in its geographic range by its larger size, chunky build, tailless appearance, and the combination of a flecked russet coat and white circles around the eyes.

### Sharpe's Grysbok (LC)
**Species** *Raphicerus sharpei*
**Seen** *Kruger (Central and Northern Regions), Mapungubwe*

Sharpe's grysbok is the tropical counterpart to the Cape grysbok. The reddish, white-flecked coat and unusual grazing posture, with white rump tilted skywards, preclude confusion with other antelope in its range. Very timid, it sometimes retreats into aardvark burrows when threatened.

### Grey Rhebok (NT)
**Species** *Pelea capreolus*
**Seen** *uKhahlamba-Drakensberg, Mountain Zebra, Bontebok*

This South African endemic is superficially similar to the mountain reedbuck, but it has a woollier grey coat, a longer neck and snout, and distinctive hare-like ears. Around 20 per cent of the global population lives in the uKhahlamba-Drakensberg and it is commonly depicted in that park's ancient rock art.

# AMPHIBIANS AND REPTILES

Amphibians and reptiles – particularly crocodiles and snakes – tend to get bad press, but most are generally harmless to people and are of great ecological value. Both maintain their body heat using external sources, for instance by basking in the sun, meaning they are prolific in warm climates and tend to be poorly represented at high altitudes.

### TAXONOMY

*Reptiles and amphibians share several similar characteristics (such as being cold-blooded), for which reason amphibians were once classified as reptiles (Reptilia). Today, however, they are classified separately as Amphibia.*

## Nile Crocodile (LC)
**Species** *Crocodylus niloticus* **Seen** *Kruger, iSimangaliso, Ndumo*

Crocodiles have lurked in the lakes and rivers of Africa for at least 150 million years. South Africa is home to the Nile crocodile, which grows to a maximum recorded length of 8 m (26 ft), weighs up to 1,000 kg (2,205 lb) and has a lifespan similar to that of humans. It occurs naturally in freshwater habitats, basking open-mouthed on the sandbanks before it slips, silently, into the water. A female lays up to 100 hard-shelled eggs in a small hole, covers them to protect them from predators, then returns three months later to carry the hatchlings to the water, where she leaves them to fend for themselves. The Nile crocodile feeds mainly on fish, but occasionally drags a mammal as large as a lion into the water.

## Terrapin
(Variable depending on species)
**Family** *Pelomedusidae* **Seen** *iSimangaliso, Kruger, Ndumo*

South Africa is home to several freshwater terrapin species, most of which are flatter and a plainer brown than any of the region's tortoises. They are usually seen in or close to water, sunning on partially submerged rocks or dead logs, or peering out from roadside puddles. The most common and widespread species is the marsh terrapin, which inhabits waterholes, puddles and other stagnant water bodies in savannah habitats, but often wanders considerable distances on land in rainy weather. During the dry season, it buries itself deep in mud to re-emerge only after the first rains – hence the local legend that terrapins drop from the sky during storms.

## Tortoise
(Variable depending on species)
**Family** *Testudinidae* **Seen** *Kruger, Addo Elephant, Pilanesberg*

The term tortoise is used to describe any terrestrial chelonian, an order of shelled reptiles that also includes freshwater terrapins and marine turtles. The leopard tortoise, which is South Africa's largest terrestrial chelonian, can weigh as much as 40 kg (88 lb) and is recognized by its tall, domed, gold-and-black-mottled shell. It has a lifespan of over 50 years and few natural enemies, but its lack of mobility makes it susceptible to fast-spreading bush fires. Another dozen species are recognized in South Africa, all but one of them endemic to the country. At up to 9 cm (3½ inches) long, the speckled padloper, a Karoo endemic, is the world's smallest chelonian.

## Marine Turtle
(Variable depending on species)
**Family** *Chelonidae* **Seen** *iSimangaliso*

Five of the world's seven marine turtle species occur along the South African coast and all are much larger than any indigenous tortoises or terrapins. Two species, the leatherback and loggerhead, breed on the beaches of northern KwaZulu-Natal, while the other three (olive ridley, hawksbill and green turtle) are visitors that breed further to the north. An individual turtle lays hundreds of eggs in the sand every season. After two months of incubation, the hatchlings make their way towards the sea. In the late 1800s, marine turtles were common throughout their natural habitat. Today, as a result of poaching and pollution, most species are classed as either endangered or critically endangered.

### African Bullfrog (LC)
**Species** *Pyxicephalus adspersus*

South Africa's largest frog species is an aggressive carnivore that weighs up to 2 kg (4 lb) and goes after prey as large as rats. During the rains, it emits a memorable medley of lusty bellows and grunts, whereas in the dry season it estivates, burying itself in a subterranean cocoon for months on end.

### Reed Frog (Variable depending on species)
**Family** *Hyperoliidae*

One of Africa's most diverse frog families, found in moist woodland habitats, reed frogs are small and brightly coloured, with long broad-tipped toes used to climb trees and reeds. A common species is the bubbling kassina, whose popping chorus is among the most wondrous of sounds heard in the African bush.

### Skink (Variable depending on species)
**Family** *Scincidae*

Represented in South Africa by more than a dozen species, skinks are small, fleet-footed lizards with slender bodies, long (and usually tapering) tails and dark scaling. Among the more visible species in South Africa are the variable, striped and rainbow skinks of the genus *Mabuya*, most of which are associated with rocky environments.

### Gecko (Variable depending on species)
**Family** *Gekkonidae*

The most diverse African lizard family, geckoes have lidless bug-eyes that are adapted for nocturnal hunting and adhesive toes that allow them to run upside-down on smooth surfaces. Most familiar is the common house gecko, a translucent white lizard that can be seen in safari lodges in the Kruger area.

### Chameleon (Variable depending on species)
**Family** *Chamaeleonidae*

These charismatic lizards are known for their colour changes (caused by mood rather than background), independently swivelling eyes and long sticky tongues that uncoil to lunge at insects. The most commonly sighted species is the flap-necked chameleon, but South Africa also has several endemic dwarf chameleons.

### Agama (Variable depending on species)
**Family** *Agamidae*

Agamas are medium to large lizards with bright plastic-looking scales – blue, purple, red or orange, depending on the species. The flattened head is generally differently coloured from the torso. Often observed basking on rocks, the male red-headed agama is particularly eye-catching with its striking blue-and-red colouring.

### African Rock Python (NE)
**Species** *Python sebae*

As the continent's largest snake, the African rock python can reach lengths of 6 m (20 ft) and is very likely to be seen on safari. It is non-venomous, wrapping its body around its prey and killing it by constriction. It then swallows it whole, slumbering for weeks or months while the digestive juices do their work.

### Mamba (LC Western green and black mambas)
**Genus** *Dendroaspis spp*

Mambas are fast-moving and widely feared snakes that generally attack only when cornered. The 4-m (12-ft) black mamba, Africa's largest venomous snake, features a distinctive coffin-shaped head. The green mamba is smaller and shyer. Bites are rare but the venom is fatal.

### Cobra (Variable depending on species)
**Genus** *Naja spp*

Cobras are long snakes – up to 3 m (10 ft) – whose trademark hoods open in warning when they raise their head to strike or, as some species do, spit venom into the target's eye. Bites are fatal, but spitting, though it can result in temporary blindness, causes little long-term damage if the venom is diluted with water.

### Boomslang (NE)
**Species** *Dispholidus typus*

As its Afrikaans name suggests, the boomslang (tree snake) is almost exclusively arboreal. It is generally green in colour, but may also be brown or olive. Theoretically the most toxic of African snakes, it is back-fanged and passive, and, except on snake handlers, it has never inflicted a fatal bite.

### Puff Adder (NE)
**Family** *Bitis arietans*

The puff adder's notoriously sluggish disposition means that it is more frequently disturbed than any other venomous snake – and is thus responsible for more bites than other species. Thickset and cryptically marked, with a triangular head, it is widespread over much of South Africa, particularly in rocky areas, but also in most bush habitats.

### Monitor (Variable depending on species)
**Family** *Varanidae*

Africa's largest lizard, the Nile monitor can grow to be 3 m (10 ft) long and is often seen along river margins. The closely related savannah monitor is a little smaller in size. Both species feed on meat and carrion and, though not normally dangerous, can inflict a rather nasty bite if they are feeling under threat.

# BIRDS

With more than 860 species, South Africa supports an exceptionally varied avifauna. The best areas for birding are in the northeast (especially the Kruger National Park, Ndumo Game Reserve and iSimangaliso Wetland Park). Avian diversity is greatest from September to April, when migrants arrive and residents shed their drab plumage to emerge in brilliant breeding colours.

**TAXONOMY**

*A considerable body of genetic and fossil evidence has helped establish that birds are most properly placed with crocodiles as the only living members of the Archosauria, a group that also includes the extinct dinosaurs.*

### Marabou Stork (LC)
**Species** *Leptoptilos crumeniferus*
**Relatives** *Saddle-Billed Stork, Yellow-Billed Stork, Open-Billed Stork*

An ungainly omnivore standing 1.5 m (5 ft) tall, the marabou is identified by its inflatable neck pouch. It may be seen near water, alongside vultures at a kill, or in urban environments. Its South African range is largely confined to the Kruger National Park and surrounds.

### Hadada Ibis (LC)
**Species** *Bostrychia hagedash*
**Relatives** *Sacred Ibis, Glossy Ibis, Southern Bald Ibis*

A bird of hotel gardens and grassy wetlands, the hadada is best known for its onomatopoeic cackle. It is a robustly built bird that uses its long, decurved bill to probe for snails and other invertebrates. Also common is the sacred ibis, which was revered in ancient Egypt.

### Egyptian Goose (LC)
**Species** *Alopochen aegyptiacus*
**Relatives** *Spur-Winged Goose, Yellow-Billed Duck, White-Faced Whistling Duck*

South Africa supports 19 species of resident and migrant waterfowl. The most conspicuous is the Egyptian goose – a large reddish-brown bird that is perpetually honking. Waterfowl populations tend to increase in the European winter, when the Palaearctic migrants arrive.

### African Darter (LC)
**Species** *Anhinga rufa*
**Relatives** *White-Breasted Cormorant, Long-Tailed Cormorant*

Frequently seen perching on bare branches overhanging rivers and lakes, the African darter or snakebird looks like a distended cormorant, with a kinked serpentine neck almost as long as its torso and striking russet patches that glow off-gold in the right light.

## Great White Pelican (LC)
**Species** *Pelecanus onocrotalus*
**Relatives** *Pink-Backed Pelican*

Easily recognized by their enormous wingspan and larder-like bills, South Africa's two pelican species are its largest water-associated birds. Most common is the great white pelican, an almost all-white bird with a large yellow pouch hanging from its long bill and black underwings that are clearly visible in flight.

## Greater Flamingo (LC)
**Species** *Phoenicopterus roseus*
**Relatives** *Lesser Flamingo*

Associated with flat, shallow pans, flamingoes are pink-tinged birds that feed on algae and microscopic fauna, which are sifted through filters in their down-turned bills. The greater flamingo is the larger of the two species in South Africa, but it is outnumbered by the lesser flamingo, which is much pinker.

## Goliath Heron (LC)
**Species** *Ardea goliath* **Relatives** *Grey Heron, Black-Headed Heron, Great White Egret, Cattle Egret*

Tall and long-necked, herons use their sharp, elongated bills to spear fish, frogs and other prey. The goliath heron stands up to 1.5 m (5 ft) tall and is commonest in the north and east. More prevalent, however, are the familiar Eurasian grey heron and black-headed heron.

## Blue Crane (LC)
**Species** *Anthropoides paradisea*
**Relatives** *Grey Crowned Crane, Wattled Crane*

South Africa's national bird stands up to 1.2 m (4 ft) tall and has a silvery-blue plumage broken only by its white forehead and black tail plumes. This near-endemic, with a declining population currently estimated at 17,000, is most often seen in the uKhahlamba-Drakensberg foothills.

### Lappet-Faced Vulture (EN)
**Species** *Torgos tracheliotos*
**Relatives** *White-Backed Vulture, Hooded Vulture, Cape Vulture*

Africa's largest raptor has a bald pink head, a massive blue-and-ivory bill and black wings that spread open like a cape. It often shares kills with the region's five other carrion-eating vulture species. Capable of soaring on thermals for hours on end, this vulture ranks among the world's most powerful fliers and its vision is practically unmatched in the animal kingdom. It is also unexpectedly fastidious and will spend hours preening itself after feeding.

### African Fish Eagle (LC)
**Species** *Haliaeetus vocifer*
**Relatives** *Martial Eagle, Bateleur, Verreaux's Eagle*

Among the most evocative sounds of the bush is the call of two African fish eagles, a piercing wail delivered in duet. This monogamous eagle is visually striking, with a hooked yellow bill and black-and-white feathering against a rich chestnut belly. It is a resident of rivers and lakes, perching high in the branches of tall fringing trees, or soaring above the water, sweeping down occasionally to scoop a fish into its talons.

### Jackal Buzzard (LC)
**Species** *Buteo rufofuscus*
**Relatives** *Yellow-Billed Kite, Chanting Goshawk, Harrier Hawk*

Named for its jackal-like call, this medium to large raptor has a black back and head, a striking chestnut breast and a distinctive bright orange-red tail. Like other buzzards, it has long, broad wings, a relatively short tail and a stocky build. Probably the commonest large resident raptor in and around the uKhahlamba-Drakensberg, it is outnumbered by the duller migrant steppe buzzard in the northern winter.

### Verreaux's Eagle-Owl (LC)
**Species** *Bubo lacteus* **Relatives** *Barn Owl, Spotted Eagle-Owl, Scops Owl*

Also known as the giant eagle-owl, Africa's largest nocturnal bird is most often seen near the large acacia trees in which it likes to breed. It is identified by its black eyes with pinkish eyelids that it closes during diurnal rest, grey-brown feathering, crested ears and bold black facial disk marks. Usually unobtrusive, it is sometimes heard hooting at night. As with other owls, it is feared as a harbinger of death in many South African cultures.

### Secretary Bird (VU)
**Species** *Sagittarius serpentarius*
**Relatives** *No close relatives, affinities uncertain*

A grassland bird with long skinny legs, a slender grey torso, long black tail and bare red face-mask, the 1.5-m- (5-ft-) tall secretary bird may have been named for its flaccid crest, which recalls the quills used by Victorian secretaries. Its name might also be a corruption of the Arabic *saqr-et-tair* (hunting bird). A terrestrial hunter, it feeds on snakes and lizards, which it stamps to death in a flailing dance ritual. It roosts in trees, but flies only when disturbed.

### Southern Ground Hornbill (VU)
**Species** *Bucorvus leadbeateri*
**Relatives** *Trumpeter Hornbill, Silvery-Cheeked Hornbill, Crowned Hornbill*

With black feathers, white underwings, large casqued bills, and red throat and eye wattles, ground hornbills are often seen marching along in small family parties in open habitats, probing the ground for insects. Despite their terrestrial habits, they are strong fliers. The southern ground hornbill is confined to the eastern part of the country, in particular the Kruger National Park and Sabi Sands.

### Common Ostrich (LC)
**Species** *Struthio camelus*
**Relatives** *No close relatives in South Africa*

At a height of 2 m (7 ft 6 inches) and weighing more than 100 kg (220 lb), ostriches are the world's largest birds. There are two species, but the common ostrich (which has pink legs, as opposed to the Somali ostrich's blue legs) is the only one to occur in South Africa. A resident of protected grassland areas, the larger male has a handsome black-and-white plumage, while the female is duller. Ostriches are farmed for their feathers, eggs and low-cholesterol meat.

### Kori Bustard (NT)
**Species** *Ardeotis kori* **Relatives** *Stanley's Bustard, Black-Bellied Korhaan, Black Korhaan*

Bustards and korhaans are medium to large ground birds associated with open habitats. The most conspicuous species is the kori bustard, the world's heaviest flying bird, weighing up to 12.5 kg (28 lb) and standing about 1.3 m (4 ft 3 inches) tall. Usually rather stately in demeanour, it performs a manic courtship dance, raising and fanning its tail and flapping its wings up and down in apparent agitation.

### Helmeted Guineafowl (LC)
**Species** *Numida meleagris*
**Relatives** *Crested Guineafowl, Swainson's Francolin, Coqui Francolin*

Guineafowl are large, gregarious ground birds with spotted white-on-grey feathers and blue heads. The distinctive helmeted guineafowl is commonly seen everywhere from Kirstenbosch Botanical Garden to the Kruger National Park.

### Hamerkop (LC)
**Species** *Scopus umbretta*
**Relatives** *No close relatives, affinities uncertain*

The sole member of its family, the hamerkop is a rusty brown, rook-sized bird with a long, flattened bill and angular crest. This bird's proverbially massive nest is normally constructed untidily over several months in a tree fork close to the water, and is made of litter, branches, mud, and other natural and artificial objects.

### African Jacana (LC)
**Species** *Actophilornis africanus* **Relatives** *Blacksmith Plover, Pied Avocet, Crowned Plover*

The African jacana is a waterbird associated with lily pads and other floating vegetation, on which it is able to walk, thanks to its far-spreading toes. An attractive bird, it has a rich chestnut torso and wings, white neck, black cap, and blue bill and frontal shield.

### Yellow-Billed Hornbill (LC)
**Species** *Tockus flavirostris*
**Relatives** *African Grey Hornbill, Red-Billed Hornbill*

Savannah hornbills are clownish birds with heavy, decurved bills. One of the more common species is the yellow-billed hornbill. Most nest in holes in tree trunks. During the incubation period, the female plasters the entrance to seal herself in and the male feeds her through a slit until the eggs hatch.

### Cape Sugarbird (LC)
**Species** *Promerops cafer*
**Relatives** *Gurney's Sugarbird*

The larger of two species in the family Promeropidae, the Cape sugarbird is a striking nectar-eater with a sunbird-like bill, yellow vent and a tail that can be almost three times longer than the torso in the male. The similar but shorter-tailed Gurney's sugarbird inhabits the uKhahlamba-Drakensberg and escarpment region.

### Common Hoopoe (LC)
**Species** *Upupa epops*
**Relatives** *Green Woodhoopoe, Common Scimitar-Bill*

The common hoopoe is a handsome bird with orange, black and white coloration and a crest that is very striking when held erect. Seen singly or in pairs, it is most common in park-like habitats and hotel gardens, where it feeds on the lawn, poking around for insects with its long, curved bill.

### Grey Go-Away Bird (LC)
**Species** *Corythaixoides concolor* **Relatives** *Knysna Loerie, Purple-Crested Loerie*

Endemic to Africa, grey go-away birds (so named for their onomatopoeic call) and loeries are vocal frugivores with elongated bodies, long tails and prominent crests. The related knysna loerie inhabits eastern coastal and montane forests, while the purple-crested loerie is associated more with riparian woodland.

### Lilac-Breasted Roller (LC)
**Species** *Coracius caudata* **Relatives** *Broad-Billed Roller, Eurasian Roller, Racket-Tailed Roller*

A jay-like bird with a lilac chest, sky-blue underparts and gold back, the lilac-breasted roller is often seen perching on an acacia branch. Four similar roller species occur in bush habitats in South Africa, all indulging in the agile aerial displays to which their name refers.

### Long-Tailed Widowbird (LC)
**Species** *Euplectes progne* **Relatives** *White-Winged Widow, Red Bishop, Golden Bishop*

This black bird with red-and-white shoulder markings has an extraordinary long, droopy tail that gives it a total length of up to 80 cm (32 inches) during the breeding season. It is often seen from the roadside, flying low over reedy marshes and highveld grassland.

---

### White-Fronted Bee-Eater (LC)
**Species** *Merops bullockoides* **Relatives** *Little Bee-Eater, Southern Carmine Bee-Eater, Eurasian Bee-eater*

A common resident of the Kruger National Park and other bushveld reserves, this bright-green bird has a red neck and chest, cobalt vent and white head with a black eye-stripe. Its sleek profile is determined by an upright stance, long wings and tail, and long, decurved bill.

### Fork-Tailed Drongo (LC)
**Species** *Discrurus adsimilis* **Relatives** *Square-Tailed Drongo*

A savannah and woodland passerine, the fork-tailed drongo is an insectivore that tends to hawk its prey from an open perch below the canopy. It is sometimes confused with black cuckoos, male black cuckoo-shrikes and black flycatchers, but none of these have the drongo's comparably deep fork in their tail.

### White-Browed Coucal (LC)
**Species** *Centropus superciliosus* **Relatives** *Red-Chested Cuckoo, Yellowbill, Diederick's Cuckoo*

The white-browed coucal is a large, clumsy bird seen in rank grassland, marsh and lake margins. It has a white eye-stripe and streaked underparts. It is most visible before rainstorms, which it tends to predict with a dove-like bubbling.

### African Firefinch (LC)
**Species** *Lagonosticta rubricata* **Relatives** *Common Waxbill, Pin-Tailed Wydah, Blue Waxbill*

Bright red with light spotting on the flanks, this ubiquitous but unobtrusive small bird frequents gardens and lodge grounds. It is one of several small, colourful seed-eaters in the family Estrildidae, most of which have conical bills whose waxen sheen gives them the common name of waxbill.

### Common Bulbul (LC)
**Species** *Pycnonotus barbatus* **Relatives** *Cape Bulbul, Red-Eyed Bulbul, Spotted Nicator*

The common bulbul is one of the most prevalent birds in the northeast. Its counterparts in the southwest and northwest respectively are the Cape bulbul, with white eyes, and the red-eyed bulbul. All three are cheerful, habitat-tolerant garden birds with a bright tuneful song, slight crest and yellow vent.

### Malachite Sunbird (LC)
**Species** *Nectarinia famosa* **Relatives** *Collared Sunbird, Scarlet-Chested Sunbird, Orange-Breasted Sunbird*

Sunbirds are small nectar-eaters with long, decurved bills. In most species, the females are less conspicuous than the iridescent males. The widespread malachite sunbird, long-tailed and metallic green in colour, is arguably the most beautiful, and is associated with aloes and other flowering shrubs.

---

### Lesser Masked Weaver (LC)
**Species** *Ploceus intermedius* **Relatives** *Red-Billed Quelea, Spotted-Backed Weaver, White-Browed Sparrow-Weaver*

The lesser masked weaver is probably the commonest species in South Africa. The male builds an intricate, ball-shaped nest at the end of a thin hanging branch, which is inspected by the female, who deconstructs it ruthlessly if she deems it unsatisfactory.

### Cape Wagtail (LC)
**Species** *Motacilla capensis* **Relatives** *African Pied Wagtail, Long-Tailed Wagtail, Orange-Throated Longclaw*

Frequently seen at the edge of rivers, lakes and swimming pools, the boldly marked grey-and-white Cape wagtail is the most common and widespread wagtail in South Africa. It is outnumbered in the northeast by the African pied wagtail and seasonally in some areas by the migrant yellow wagtail.

### Speckled Mousebird (LC)
**Species** *Colius striatus* **Relatives** *White-Backed Mousebird, Red-Faced Mousebird*

This scruffy frugivore is the most widespread member of the order Coliidae, which is endemic to Africa and consists of half-a-dozen species. It is generally seen in flocks of around five to eight birds. The name mousebird may refer to its habit of shuffling nimbly along branches.

### Olive Thrush (LC)
**Species** *Turdus olivaceous*
**Relatives** *Cape Robin-Chat, Common Rock Thrush, Stonechat*

The Turdidae is a family of medium to small insectivores, which is represented by about 40 species in South Africa. Among the most recognizable is the olive thrush, often seen hopping around hotel lawns. The family also includes robin-chats, a group of orange, blue, black and white birds that are also common in gardens.

### African Paradise (LC) Flycatcher
**Species** *Terpsiphone viridis*
**Relatives** *Vanga Flycatcher, Chin Spot Batis, Common Wattle-Eye*

This leaf-gleaning flycatcher might be seen anywhere, although local abundance is affected by complex seasonal intra-African movements. Usually bluish with an orange tail, it also has black-and-white and intermediate morphs. The male's tail can be up to three times its body length.

### Pied Kingfisher (LC)
**Species** *Ceryle rudis*
**Relatives** *Malachite Kingfisher, Giant Kingfisher*

Probably the most visible of South Africa's water-associated kingfishers, this black-and-white bird hunts by hovering above open water then diving down sharply to spear a fish with its dagger-like bill. Other water-associated species include the finch-sized malachite kingfisher and the giant kingfisher.

### Crested Barbet (LC)
**Species** *Trachyphonus vaillantii* **Relatives** *Black-Collared Barbet, Red-Fronted Tinker-Barbet, Cardinal Woodpecker*

The repetitive trilling of the crested barbet is one of the most distinctive sounds in Kruger National Park. The bird is mainly yellow, with a black-and-white back and bib, and red streaking on the face and belly. The black-collared barbet has a red head and performs a haunting whirring duet.

### Cape Glossy Starling (LC)
**Species** *Lamprotornis nitens*
**Relatives** *Red-Winged Starling, Plum-Coloured Starling, Red-Billed Oxpecker*

With glossy green-blue feathering, red eyes and a faint black eye-stripe, this is the most widespread and visible of several beautiful South African starlings. Even more stunning is the plum-coloured starling, which occurs in riverine woodland and acacia bush.

### Common Fiscal (LC)
**Species** *Lanius collaris*
**Relatives** *Long-Tailed Shrike, Crimson-Breasted Shrike, Southern Boubou*

This handsome resident of the highveld, usually seen perching on acacia trees or fences, is sometimes referred to as the butcher-bird, for its habit of impaling its prey on thorns or barbs to eat later. The related southern boubou and spectacular crimson-breasted shrike are more furtive bush-shrikes.

# EXPERIENCE

Surfers on the beach at Sedgefield

# CAPE TOWN

Now known as Cape Town, the settlement's origins date back to 1652, when Commander Jan van Riebeeck of the Dutch East India Company landed at Table Bay to found a victualling station for merchant ships travelling to India. The central park known as the Company's Garden started life under van Riebeeck, as did the rudimentary precursor of the imposing Castle of Good Hope. A century later, Cape Town was home to 5,500 European settlers, plus 7,000 enslaved people of local and Asian origin. In 1814, Cape Town was ceded to the British, who freed all enslaved people in 1834, a legislation that led to the inland exodus known as the Great Trek *(p63)*. Historically, with a demographic dominated by European settlers and mixed-race inhabitants, referred to then as "Coloureds", Cape Town was more liberal than other parts of South Africa. Under apartheid, however, many civil rights enjoyed by mixed-race people were revoked, and integrated suburbs such as District Six were rezoned as "White" only; communities and families were broken up as they were forcibly removed and had to go live in areas on the outskirts of town known as the Cape Flats. Apartheid was abolished in the 1990s, and Cape Town today is a gracious and progressive city with a vibrant economy in which tourism plays a significant role.

# CAPE TOWN

## Must Sees

1. District Six Museum
2. The V&A Waterfront
3. Table Mountain
4. Robben Island

## Experience More

5. Grand Parade and City Hall
6. Lutheran Church
7. Castle of Good Hope
8. Iziko Koopmans-De Wet House
9. St George's Cathedral
10. Iziko Michaelis Collection
11. Iziko Slave Lodge
12. Greenmarket Square
13. Iziko South African Museum and Planetarium
14. South African Jewish Museum
15. Iziko Bo-Kaap Museum
16. Iziko South African National Gallery
17. Groote Kerk
18. Green Point and Sea Point
19. Cape Town Stadium
20. Greenpoint Park and Biodiversity Garden

## Eat

1. Biesmiellah
2. Mama Africa
3. Gold Restaurant
4. Addis in Cape
5. Manna Epicure Restaurant

## Stay

6. Derwent House
7. Mount Nelson Hotel
8. Victoria & Alfred Hotel
9. President Hotel
10. Daddy Long Legs

## Shop

11. Clarke's Books
12. Pan-African Market
13. Tribal Trends
14. Long Street Antique Arcade
15. WAG Fashion

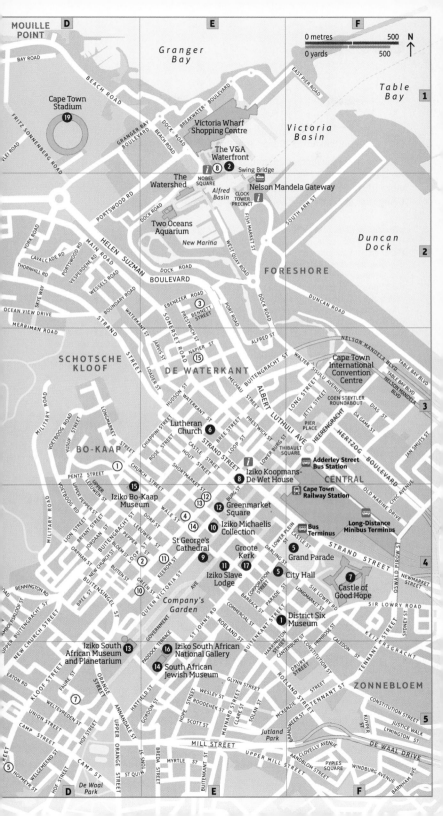

❶ 🏷️ 🅜 🗨️ 🛍️

# DISTRICT SIX MUSEUM

📍 E4  🏠 25a Buitenkant St  🕐 9am–4pm Mon–Sat  🌐 districtsix.co.za

This evocative museum is an unmissable stop for history buffs. Housed in a former Methodist church, it pays tribute to the vibrantly diverse community that once lived in this area, before being torn apart by apartheid.

Up until the 1970s, the sixth municipal district of Cape Town was home to almost a tenth of the city's population. In 1965, the apartheid government declared the area "white", under the Group Areas Act of 1950. Removals began in 1968, and by 1982, more than 60,000 people had been forcibly uprooted from their homes and relocated 25 km (16 miles) away on the barren plains of the Cape Flats (p163).

The District Six Museum was inaugurated in 1994 to commemorate the events of the apartheid era and to preserve the memory of District Six as it was before the removals. It does so through a fascinating collection that includes historical documents, photographs, audiovisual recordings and physical remains of the area such as street signs. Visitors can explore the museum alone, or take a guided tour with a former resident of the destroyed District Six.

💬 INSIDER TIP
**Little Wonder Store**

The museum's bookshop is a reincarnation of a once-thriving hub of the District Six community. The store stocks a wide selection of titles about the district and the many other mass evictions of the apartheid era.

① The museum's photography collection comprises a large part of its permanent exhibits.

② In 1965, the area was declared "white" by the government, who erected signs such as this one.

③ The façade of the District Six Museum is covered in colourful murals.

↑ Visitors exploring the exhibition space of the District Six Museum

**2**

# THE V&A WATERFRONT

**Q** E1 **⌂** Cape Town harbour **🚌🚗 ⏱** Shops: most open 9am–9pm; restaurants: most open until midnight **W** waterfront.co.za

The V&A Waterfront is one of Cape Town's most visited attractions. Easily accessible from the city centre, it's a shopper's and foodie's paradise, with a huge choice of boutiques and eateries. It also houses numerous sights and leisure activities, and several luxury hotels.

→

Looking out over the V&A Waterfront from one of its many restaurants

### Did You Know?

Playful Cape fur seals can often be seen swimming between boats or sunning on the dock here.

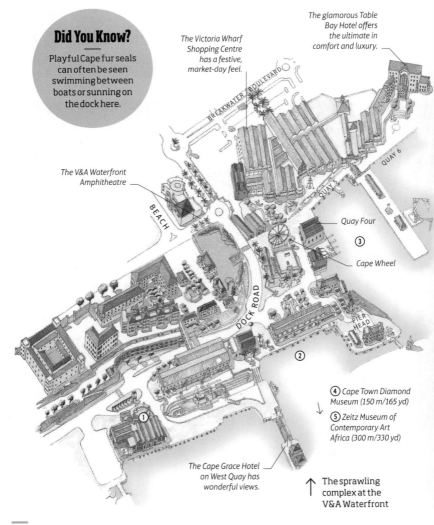

The Victoria Wharf Shopping Centre has a festive, market-day feel.

The glamorous Table Bay Hotel offers the ultimate in comfort and luxury.

The V&A Waterfront Amphitheatre

BREAKWATER BOULEVARD

BEACH

QUAY 5

QUAY 6

Quay Four

③

Cape Wheel

DOCK ROAD

PIER HEAD

②

④ Cape Town Diamond Museum (150 m/165 yd)

↓

⑤ Zeitz Museum of Contemporary Art Africa (300 m/330 yd)

①

The Cape Grace Hotel on West Quay has wonderful views.

↑ The sprawling complex at the V&A Waterfront

# EAT

### Quay Four
Lively restaurant with good seafood and beer.

📍 West Quay Rd
🌐 quay4.co.za

®®®

### Den Anker
Authentic Belgian cuisine and beers.

📍 Pierhead
🌐 denanker.co.za

®®®

### Baia Seafood Restaurant
Superb classic-contemporary seafood.

📍 Victoria Wharf
🌐 baiarestaurant.co.za

®®®

### Makers Landing
A food market with farm-to-table restaurants serving local food.

📍 The Cruise Terminal
🌐 makerslanding.co.za

®®®

### Sevruga
Sophisticated Asian fusion cuisine.

📍 Quay 5
🌐 sevruga.co.za

®®®

# Two Oceans Aquarium

📍 Dock Rd  🕐 9:30am–6pm daily  🌐 aquarium.co.za

One of the top attractions in Cape Town, this complex aims to introduce visitors to the incredible diversity of sealife that exists in the ocean around the Cape coast. A world first is the interesting exhibit of a complete river ecosystem that traces the course of a stream from its mountain source down to the open sea. One of the most fascinating features is the kelp forest, housed in a ceiling-high glass tank that holds various shoals of line fish swimming among the waving fronds. Along with waterbirds such as oystercatchers, there is a resident colony of African penguins and a children's touch pool.

An innovative approach to education has assured the popularity and success of this venture. The complex is constantly upgraded to accommodate new exhibits, such as a fun gallery dedicated to frogs. The wholesome Children's Play Centre offers an interesting programme, including daily puppet shows and supervised arts and crafts. Novel "sleep-overs" in front of the Predator Tank are also a hit with families. Adventurous visitors in possession of a valid scuba licence may book dives with sharks or turtles and stingrays during the day.

↑ A family enjoying a close encounter with a shark at the Two Oceans Aquarium

## ②
### Alfred Basin (West Quay)

The first docks to be built for the Port of Cape Town, Alfred Basin still forms a crucial part of the working harbour, as fishing boats chug to the Robinson Graving Dock for repair and maintenance. Alongside the dry dock is The Watershed crafts market, one of South Africa's largest indoor markets.

The **Iziko Maritime Centre** traces the history of shipping in Table Bay, with exhibits including model ships. The museum also encompasses the John H Marsh Maritime Research Centre, an important archive of photos of ships from the 1920s to the 1960s, and the SAS *Somerset*, a former naval defence vessel.

## 1860

Prince Alfred (son of Queen Victoria) began contruction of the docks by tipping a load of stones into the sea.

### Iziko Maritime Centre
 Union Castle Building, Dock Rd Hours vary, check website 1 May, 25 Dec iziko.org.za

## ③
### Victoria Basin

Completed in 1905, Victoria Basin was once one of the main piers of the original Cape Town Harbour. Today it is home to the Victoria Wharf Shopping Mall. One of the largest malls in South Africa, it houses numerous shops and restaurants, as well as two cinemas.

Visitors can take harbour tours, seal-watching trips and sunset cruises in Table Bay with one of the boat operators located here; the Quay Four tavern at the edge of the basin *(p123)* offers superb views of the harbour and its constant boat traffic.

Also in this area is the iconic **Cape Wheel**, a 40-m- (131-ft-) high Ferris wheel with 30 air-conditioned cabins. The four-revolution ride lasts between 12 and 15 minutes; at the top, impressive views across the Waterfront and Table Mountain stretch out before you.

↑ One of the exhibition galleries at the Iziko Maritime Centre

### Cape Wheel
 V&A Waterfront 10:30am-9:30pm daily capewheel.co.za

## ④
### Cape Town Diamond Museum

Clock Tower Centre 9am-9pm daily cape towndiamondmuseum.org

Gifted to the city by Shimansky, one of South Africa's leading diamond jewellers, this museum traces the evolution of diamonds from their under-ground formation to sparkling gems. Exhibits document the Orange River diamond rush that started in 1867, as well as the history of local rivalries. There are replicas of famous South African diamonds, such as the Cullinan, the biggest ever found, and the Taylor-Burton, a pear-shaped jewel worn by actress Elizabeth Taylor. Visitors can also watch stones being cut and polished in the workshop.

⑤

### INSIDER TIP

**Live Music**

The V&A Waterfront Amphitheatre offers a vast array of musical and other events. Free jazz, rock and classical concerts regularly take place here, along with rhythmic displays of traditional drumming.

## Zeitz Museum of Contemporary Art Africa

🄰 Southern Arm Rd
🄲 10am-6pm Thu-Sun
🄲 Occasional private events; check website for details
🄦 zeitzmocaa.museum

Opened in 2017, the Zeitz Museum of Contemporary Art Africa (MOCAA) is an award-winning non-profit installation that holds the world's largest collection of 21st-century African and Diaspora-related art. Housed in a grain silo originally constructed in 1921, this stunning 57-m- (187-ft-) high building has been converted to a beautiful nine-storey architectural gem that comprises 100 individual galleries and requires an entire morning or afternoon of exploration to fully appreciate. The permanent collections display the work of more than 100 contemporary artists hailing from all over Africa and further afield. They also host a dozen or so temporary exhibitions, not only embracing fine art but also photography, film and costume design. A well thought through audio tour is included in the entrance fee.

On the upper floors above the museum, with huge pillowed glass windows, is the luxurious Silo Hotel.

# SHOP

**Lindt Chocolate Studio**
Operated by Lindt, this shop sells delicious chocolates and offers regular lessons in making sugary goods.

🄰 Silo 2
🄦 chocolatestudio.co.za

**Cape Union Mart**
South Africa's premier outdoor shop, selling good quality hiking and climbing gear.

🄰 Quay 4
🄦 capeunionmart.co.za

**Oranjezicht City Farm**
This Saturday-only market specializes in artisanal and healthy foodstuffs made by independent local farmers and producers.

🄰 Granger Bay Blvd
🄦 ozcf.co.za

**Uwe Koetter**
Cape Town is renowned for its gold and jewellery, and this shop has plenty on offer.

🄰 Alfred Mall
🄦 uwekoetter.com

**The Watershed**
Clothing, jewellery, mosaics and an array of textiles and artwork are among the miscellany of items sold at the 150-odd stalls in this covered daily market.

🄰 V&A Waterfront
🄦 waterfront.co.za/area/watershed

The Zeitz Museum of Contemporary Art Africa, lit up at dusk

**3** ⊘ 🖥 🛍

# TABLE MOUNTAIN

📍B3 🚠Lower Cable Station: Tafelberg Road 🚌 🕐Cableway: hours vary, check website for details 🚫In bad weather; for annual maintenance (2 weeks in Jul) 🌐tablemountain.net

Cape Town's most iconic landmark, this flat-topped mountain – known as Hoerikwaggo (sea mountain) by the Khoe – climbs 1,086 m (3,560 ft) and offers superb views of the city laid out below. Most visitors are whisked to the summit via a cable car, which has been in operation since 1929.

The Cape Peninsula mountain chain is a mass of sedimentary sandstone lying above ancient shales deposited some 700 million years ago, and large areas of granite dating back some 540 million years. The sandstone sediment that forms the main block of the mountain was deposited about 450 million years ago, when the peninsula – then a part of the ancient supercontinent Gondwana – lay below sea level. After the subsidence of the primeval ocean, the effects of wind, rain, ice and extreme temperatures caused erosion of the softer layers, leaving behind the characteristic mesa of Table Mountain.

The mountain lies in the northern section of Table Mountain National Park, part of UNESCO's Cape Floral Region World Heritage Site. Other areas of the park include the Cape of Good Hope (*p150*) and the Boulders Penguin Colony (*p152*).

## TABLE MOUNTAIN FAUNA AND FLORA

More than 1,500 plant species of the 2,285 that make up the Cape Floral Kingdom of the peninsula can be found in the protected natural habitat of Table Mountain. They include *Disa uniflora* (also called Pride of Table Mountain), which mostly grows near streams and waterfalls, and several members of the regal protea family. Wildlife, consisting mostly of small mammals, reptiles and birds, includes the rare and secretive ghost frog, which is found in a few perennial streams on the plateau.

← The vibrant, vein-laced petals of *Disa uniflora*

Views from the summit and *(inset)* towards the mountain from the V&A Waterfront ↑

① Table Mountain's plateau and Lion's Head are the range's most popular peaks.

② Reinforced viewing platforms are located at strategic vantage points.

③ Six shrines, or *kramats*, mark the graves of Muslim holy men who died at the Cape.

💬 **INSIDER TIP**
**Walking Up**

Several well-marked trails of varying difficulty lead to the summit. Weather conditions may deteriorate quickly; hiking on windy or misty days is not advised. For safety, do not hike alone.

The starkly furnished interior
of Nelson Mandela's cell,
within the island prison ↑

**4** 🗺️ 🎬 📷

# ROBBEN ISLAND

📍 A2  🕐 Only by tour; boats depart (weather permitting): Apr–Sep: 9am, 11am, 1pm daily (also 3pm Oct–Mar)  🌐 robben-island.org.za

Located in Table Bay, this island is best known as the place where Nelson Mandela spent 18 of the 27 years for which he was imprisoned. Today it is a UNESCO World Heritage Site and a museum, and boatloads of visitors make the journey daily to experience a little of South Africa's political past in this hauntingly evocative place.

This flat, rocky island lies 11 km (7 miles) north of Cape Town in the icy Atlantic Ocean. Composed mainly of blue slate, it is only 30 m (98 ft) above sea level at its highest point. Named "Robben Eiland" – seal island – by the Dutch in the mid-17th century, Robben Island has seen much human suffering. As early as 1636 it served as a penal settlement, and it was taken over by the South African Prisons Service in 1960. There is a lime quarry on the island, and political prisoners were required to work in it for at least six hours a day. Prisoners suffered damage to their eyesight as a result, due to the constant dust and the glare of the sunlight on the stark white lime cliffs.

↑ The bleak stone entryway to Robben Island Prison

The island's most famous inmate was Nelson Mandela; tours of the island end with a viewing of his cell (tours must be booked in advance). In 1991, the South African Natural Heritage Programme nominated the island for its significance as a seabird breeding colony; it hosts more than 130 bird species, including the endangered Caspian tern. In 1997 the island was designated a museum, and in 1999 it was declared a UNESCO World Heritage Site.

> **Named "Robben Eiland" - seal island - by the Dutch in the mid-17th century, Robben Island has seen much human suffering.**

↑ Seagulls and a lone African penguin on the shores of the island

### POLITICAL PRISONERS

In the 18th century, high-ranking princes and sheikhs from India, Malaysia and Indonesia were sent to Robben Island by the Dutch East India Company for inciting resistance against their European overlords. The British banished rebellious Xhosa rulers to the island in the early 1800s. In 1963, Nelson Mandela and seven other political activists were charged with conspiracy against the state for their political beliefs and were condemned to life imprisonment. Mandela spent 18 of his 27 years in prison on Robben Island; the last political prisoners there were released in 1991.

# EXPERIENCE MORE

## 5

### Grand Parade and City Hall

**⊙ E4  ⌂ Darling St**

The Grand Parade was the site Cape Town's founder Jan van Riebeeck selected for his first fort in 1652. The structure was levelled in 1674 and until 1821 the area was used as a parade and exercise ground for the troops. As buildings went up around the perimeter, greengrocers established fruit stalls, precursors of today's weekday flea market. The site is now used as a car park and as an events venue.

Overlooking the Grand Parade is Cape Town's imposing City Hall. Built in 1905 in the elaborate Italian Renaissance style, it presents its elegant façades on four different streets. A 39-bell carillon tower was added in 1923,

which is a half-sized replica of London's Big Ben. It was from the balcony here that Nelson Mandela addressed the world in 1990 after spending 27 years in prison. On that day, 250,000 people streamed to the Grand Parade to celebrate the release of the country's future president. Today, the City Hall is home to the Cape Philharmonic Orchestra.

## 6

### Lutheran Church

**⊙ E3  ⌂ 99 Strand St**
**⊙ 10am–2pm Mon–Fri and for Sun services**
**ⓦ lutheranchurch.org.za**

Since the ruling authority was intolerant of any religion other than that of the Dutch Reformed Church, the Lutheran Church began life as a hall that had to be officially

 City Hall, and *(inset)* iron dials of the Turret Clock atop the hall's tower

described as a "warehouse". Wealthy Lutheran business-man Martin Melck built it with the intention of modifying it into a place of worship once the religious laws were relaxed, and the first service was held there in 1776. A few years later, the sexton's house was added.

The German-born sculptor Anton Anreith embellished the church from 1787 to 1792, designing a more fitting front elevation and adding a tower. Today, both the church and the sexton's house are national monuments.

Next door is the 1781 Martin Melck House, declared a national monument in 1936. It is a fine example of an 18th-century Cape townhouse.

> **It was from the balcony of City Hall that Nelson Mandela addressed the world in 1990 after spending 27 years in prison.**

**7**

## Castle of Good Hope

📍 F4  🏠 Cnr Buitenkant & Darling sts  🕐 9am–5pm daily  🚫 1 Jan, 25 Dec  🌐 castleof goodhope.co.za

The oldest functional building in South Africa, the pentagonal Castle of Good Hope was built during 1666–79 with slate quarried on Robben Island and sandstone from Lion's Head. Back then it stood sentinel over Table Bay but an extensive programme of land reclamation started in the 1930s has left it stranded inland. Its imposing walls enclose a military museum displaying artifacts dating to the Dutch and British occupations, and the William Fehr Collection of old paintings, period furniture and other colonial relics. Notable features include the 17th-century staircase that leads to

---

**INSIDER TIP**
**Pomp and Ceremony**

A stately Key Ceremony and the firing of the Signal Cannon take place at the Castle of Good Hope at 10am and noon on weekdays; make sure to arrive early for a good spot.

---

the exquisite De Kat Balcony and a bell cast in Amsterdam in 1697.

---

**8**

## Iziko Koopmans-De Wet House

📍 E3  🏠 35 Strand St  🕐 9am–5pm daily  🚫 1 May, 25 Dec  🌐 iziko.org.za

This Neo-Classical home was built in 1701 when Strand Street, then close to the shore, was the most fashionable part of Cape Town. The building was enlarged in subsequent centuries; a second storey was added, and renowned French architect Louis Michel Thibault remodelled the façade around 1795 in Louis XVI style. The De Wet family was the last to own the house. After the death of her husband in 1880, Maria De Wet lived here with her sister until her death in 1906.

Over the years, the sisters assembled the fine antiques that can still be seen in the museum today. Maria De Wet, apart from being a renowned society hostess, also took the first steps to protect Cape Town's historic buildings. It was due to her intervention that the destruction of part of the Castle of Good Hope was prevented when the new railway lines for the city were being planned.

# STAY

### Derwent House

A boutique hotel tucked below Table Mountain, with excellent service and Afro-chic decor.

📍 C5  🏠 14 Derwent Rd  🌐 derwenthouse.co.za

---

### Mount Nelson Hotel

Head here for 19th-century architecture combined with 21st-century luxury.

📍 D5  🏠 76 Orange St  🌐 belmond.com

---

### Victoria & Alfred Hotel

Set on the V&A Waterfront, this hotel offers unbeatable views of the harbour.

📍 E2  🏠 19 Dock Rd  🌐 newmarkhotels.com

---

### President Hotel

Expect four-star amenities at budget-friendly prices.

📍 A3  🏠 4 Alexander Rd, Bantry Bay  🌐 presi denthotel.co.za

---

### Daddy Long Legs

Quirky hotel in the city's nightlife hub. Each room is decorated by a different local artist.

📍 D4  🏠 134 Long St  🌐 daddylonglegs.co.za

---

←
Sculptures guarding the entrance to the Castle of Good Hope

## 9

### St George's Cathedral

📍 E4 🏛 Wale St
🕐 9am-1pm Tue-Fri
🌐 sgcathedral.co.za

South Africa's oldest cathedral began life as a relatively modest church that opened its doors on Christmas Day of 1834. The grander cruciform cathedral seen today is a Neo-Gothic masterpiece designed by Sir Herbert Baker, with the foundation stone laid by the future King George V in 1901. It is sometimes referred to as the People's Cathedral, in recognition of its contribution to the anti-apartheid struggle under Archbishop Desmond Tutu of Cape Town, whose 1986 appointment to that rank led many white Anglicans to abscond in protest. A museum near the main entrance evokes this period.

The cathedral's magnificent Hill Organ, which first stood in London's Church of St Margaret (next to Westminster Abbey) in 1675, was donated to St George's by an English businessman in 1909.

> **South Africa's oldest cathedral began life as a relatively modest church that opened its doors on Christmas Day of 1834.**

**Did You Know?**

Siyahamba Labyrinth in St George's courtyard is a replica of Chartres Cathedral's iconic 13th-century original.

## 10

### Iziko Michaelis Collection

📍 E4 🏛 Greenmarket Sq
🕐 9am-4pm Mon-Sat
📅 1 May, 25 Dec
🌐 iziko.org.za

Located in the Old Town House, this national monument was built in 1755 in the Cape Rococo style. It initially served as the "Burgherwacht Huys" (house of the night patrol) and the magistrate's court. In 1839, it was claimed as a town hall by the newly formed municipality. After renovations in 1915, the building was handed over to the Union Government for use as an art gallery.

The original collection was donated to the city in 1914 by the wealthy financier Sir Max Michaelis. It was added to by Lady Michaelis after the death of her husband in 1932. The collection consists of a world-renowned selection of Dutch and Flemish art from the 17th-century Golden Age.

→

A collection of bright market stalls lining Greenmarket Square

The portraits are particularly interesting, offering an insight into Dutch society at the time.

In addition to the permanent collection, the gallery holds a series of temporary exhibitions that have been designed to appeal to both locals and visitors alike. After hours, the gallery becomes a cultural centre, hosting chamber-music concerts and lectures.

## 11

### Iziko Slave Lodge

📍 E4 🏛 Cnr Adderley & Wale sts 🕐 9am-5pm Mon-Sat 📅 1 May, 25 Dec
🌐 iziko.org.za

The first building on this site was a lodge that housed the enslaved people who worked in the Company's Garden (p138). One of the oldest buildings in Cape Town, it was built around 1679 on land that originally formed part of the garden. It is thought that up to 9,000 enslaved people – along with convicts and those with mental illnesses – lived in the building during its time as a slave lodge.

↑ Stained-glass window by master glassmaker Gabriel Loire in St George's Cathedral

**12**

## Greenmarket Square

**♀ E4 🏠 Cnr Longmarket & Burg sts**

By 1807, new premises from which to administer the Cape colony were needed, and the Slave Lodge suited most requirements. Many enslaved inhabitants of the lodge were sold, while others were moved to the west wing of the building. The vacated area was turned into offices, and in 1811, the west wing followed suit. The people responsible for the conversion were the builder Herman Schutte, the sculptor Anton Anreith and the architect Louis Michel Thibault. As well as government offices, the lodge also housed the Supreme Court, the post office and the public library. The present building once extended into Adderley Street, but this portion had to be demolished when the road was widened. However, the original façade, designed by Thibault, has been restored to its former splendour.

Iziko Museums of Cape Town have transformed the Slave Lodge into a major site that increases public awareness of slavery, cultural diversity and the struggle for human rights in South Africa. The history of slavery at the Cape is illustrated with 3D and audiovisual displays, alongside exhibits of text, images and maps that trace the hardships suffered. A section about life at the lodge is based on archaeological and archival sources, as well as on the memories of people who trace their roots to the time of slavery in the Cape.

The museum also hosts regularly changing temporary exhibitions, on subjects ranging from the experience of individual colonial subjects to life in ancient Egypt.

Surrounded by historic buildings and terrace cafés, pedestrianised Greenmarket Square hosts a vibrant pan-African crafts and clothing market, whose vendors are often more comfortable speaking French or Swahili than they are English or any Indigenous tongue. The square also attracts an ever-changing cast of street performers.

Yet it was not always like this. Established in 1696 as Burgher Watch Square, it served as the city's main slave market from 1710 until the era of abolition. It then became a vegetable market, before being converted into a car park.

### MALAY CULTURE IN CAPE TOWN

The original Malays were brought to the Cape from 1658 onwards by the Dutch East India Company. Most were Muslims from Sri Lanka, the Indonesian islands and India. Many were enslaved, while others were political exiles of considerable stature. After slavery's abolition in the 1830s, the Cape Malays (also referred to as Cape Muslims) settled in an area called Bo-Kaap to be near the mosques that had been built there. The Malays had a significant influence on the Afrikaans tongue and other aspects of local culture. Today, the muezzins' calls, ringing out to summon the faithful, are an innate part of Cape Town life.

# EAT

### Biesmiellah

Set in the atmospheric Bo-Kaap, this no-frills café serves authentic Cape Malay specialities and excellent *braai* (barbecue) at weekends.

**◊ D3 ◊ 2 Wale St**
**w biesmiellah.co.za**

®®®

### Mama Africa

A funky institution with a well-priced pan-African menu and regular live music.

**◊ E4 ◊ 178 Long St**
**w mamaafrica restaurant.co.za**

®®®

### Gold Restaurant

A thoroughly African experience, complete with 14-course tasting menu and an optional *djembe* drumming session beforehand.

**◊ E2 ◊ 15 Bennett St**
**w goldrestaurant.co.za**

®®®

### Addis in Cape

The ideal place to sample a wide variety of Ethiopia's deliciously spicy cuisine.

**◊ E4 ◊ 41 Church St**
**w addisincape.co.za**

®®®

### Manna Epicure Restaurant

Head to this chic, trendsetting venue for a meat-heavy fusion of South African and French dishes.

**◊ D5 ◊ 151 Kloof St**
**w mannaepicure.com**

®®®

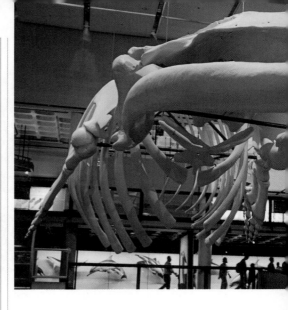

**13**

## Iziko South African Museum and Planetarium

**◊ D5 ◊ 25 Queen Victoria St ◊ 9am–5pm daily ◊ 1 May, 25 Dec w iziko.org.za**

This natural history museum is both a research and education institution. Of special interest in the collection are the coelacanth, reptile fossils from the Karoo, and the Shark World exhibition. There are also exceptional examples of rock art, including whole sections from caves.

The planetarium presents a diverse programme on the wonders of the universe.

**14**

## South African Jewish Museum

**◊ E5 ◊ 88 Hatfield St ◊ 10am–5pm Mon–Thu & Sun, 10am–2pm Fri ◊ Jewish hols w sajewishmuseum. co.za**

This museum, housed in a building opened in 2000 by Nelson Mandela, narrates the story of South African Jewry from its beginnings, setting it against the backdrop of the country's history. The interactive exhibits celebrate the pioneering spirit of South Africa's early Jewish immigrants and their descendants.

**15**

## Iziko Bo-Kaap Museum

**◊ D4 ◊ 71 Wale St ◊ 9am–4pm Mon–Sat ◊ Eid-ul-Fitr, Eid-ul-Adha, Good Fri, 25 Dec, 2 Jan w iziko.org.za**

The Iziko Bo-Kaap Museum is housed in the oldest house in the area (1763), still in its original form. Bo-Kaap has traditionally been associated with the Muslim community, and the building's characteristic *voorstoep* (front terrace) and courtyard both emphasize the social aspects of Cape Muslim culture. The museum focuses on the history of Islam in the Cape of Good Hope, highlighting its local cultural expressions.

→

The Iziko South African National Gallery, located by the Company's Garden

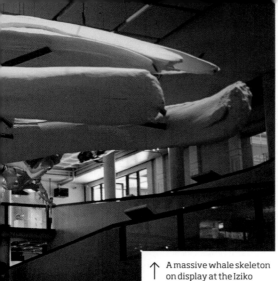

↑ A massive whale skeleton on display at the Iziko South African Museum

### Iziko South African National Gallery

📍 E5 🏛 Government Ave, Company's Garden ⏰ 9am–5pm daily 🚫 1 May, 25 Dec 🌐 iziko.org.za

South Africa's premier gallery houses outstanding collections of British, French, Dutch, Flemish and South African paintings. Selections from the permanent collection change regularly to allow for a full programme of temporary exhibitions of contemporary photography, sculpture, beadwork and textiles. These rotating exhibits provide a great insight into the range of artworks produced in this country, the African continent and further afield.

### Groote Kerk

📍 E4 🏛 43 Adderley St ⏰ 10am–2pm Mon–Fri 🌐 grootekerk.org.za

Across the road from the Slave Lodge (p132) is the Groote Kerk (big church), one of the best known buildings in Cape Town. Upon their arrival at the Cape, the Dutch held religious services on board Jan van Riebeeck's ship, *Drommedaris*. Later, they switched to a small room at the Castle Good of Hope, but quickly realized the need for a permanent site. A first, temporary structure at the northeast end of the Company's Garden was replaced by a thatched church on the same site in 1700, on the orders of Governor Willem Adriaan van der Stel. The church was completely rebuilt in the 19th century, and the new building was dedicated in 1841. All that remains of the original church now is the Baroque belfry, which, unfortunately, is almost obscured by tall modern buildings.

Of interest inside the church is the splendid pulpit supported by carved lions, which replaced the original podium in 1789. It is believed that sculptor Anton Anreith's original concept included the symbolic images of Hope, Faith and Charity, but this was rejected as being too papist.

The façade of the church has high Gothic-style windows divided by bold pilasters. In front of the building stands a statue of Andrew Murray, who was minister of the Dutch Reformed Church in Cape Town from 1864–71. For tours, visitors need to book ahead online.

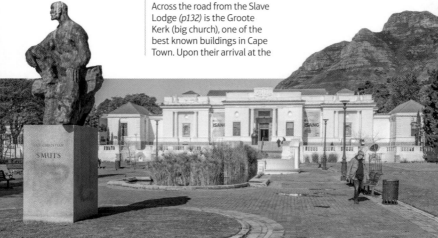

**18**

# Green Point and Sea Point

C1/A3  Main or Beach rds

Since the development of the V&A Waterfront began in 1995, the property value in neighbouring seaside suburbs such as Green Point and Mouille Point has soared. Beach Road, only a stone's throw from the sea, is today lined with expensive high-rise apartments, trendy restaurants and upmarket office blocks.

GREAT VIEW
**Lion's Head and Signal Hill**

A gentle climb to the top of Lion's Head in Sea Point affords views of the City Bowl and the Atlantic coastline. Climbers can park their cars along Signal Hill Road. This spot is popular for its night views, but be aware that there is a risk of crime after dark.

Green Point Common backs the residential strip. It started in 1657 as a farm granted to Jan van Riebeeck, but the soil proved unfit for cultivation. The sports complexes and clubs now on the common have athletics, rugby and cricket fields and tennis and squash courts, while the Cape Town Stadium borders the Green Point Urban Park. Nearby, Green Point's red and white candy-striped lighthouse, which was built back in 1824, is still functional. Its resonant foghorn is notorious for keeping Mouille Point's residents awake when mist rolls in from the sea.

Further along Beach Road lies the suburb of Sea Point. It, too, has undergone intensive development over the years and today sports towering apartment blocks, hotels and offices. Sea Point is one of

Cape Town's most popular entertainment districts beyond the V&A Waterfront, and its Main Road teems with restaurants, bars, malls and night spots. In the afternoon, the 3-km (2-mile) Sea Point promenade is abuzz with joggers, rollerbladers, children, people-watchers and residents walking their dogs.

The full 10-km (6-mile) Prom, as locals call it, actually starts at Mouille Point near the V&A Waterfront, and ends with a large parking area and the open-air **Sea Point Swimming Pool**, which is filled with filtered seawater and has an impressive diving pool.

Small sandy coves that are packed with sunbathers in summer dot the rocky shoreline. The tidal pools here are always a source of amazement, particularly for children, who enjoy scrambling around looking for tiny sea creatures. Other amenities along the promenade include a maze, a mini-golf course, outdoor gyms and children's playgrounds.

> Sea Point is one of Cape Town's most popular entertainment districts beyond the V&A Waterfront, and its Main Road teems with restaurants, bars, malls and night spots.

The cheerful striped exterior of Green Point lighthouse, which dates from the 19th century

↑ Cape Town Stadium, during a 2010 FIFA World Cup match

### Sea Point Swimming Pool

 🅰Beach Rd 📞(021) 434-3341 🕐Oct–Apr: 7am–6:45pm daily; May–Sep: 9am–5pm daily 🔒Only in bad weather

---

**19**

### Cape Town Stadium

📍D1 🅰Fritz Sonnenberg Rd 🕐Tours: 12pm Tue & Thu 🌐capetownstadium.co.za

Probably the city's most distinctive landmark when viewed from the lofty heights of Table Mountain, the 55,000-seater Cape Town Stadium was custom built for the 2010 FIFA World Cup and hosted eight games in the tournament, including the semi-final between Uruguay and the Netherlands. Today, the stadium is the home ground of two sides in the South Africa premier football league, Ajax Cape Town and Cape Town City, and has also hosted the South African leg of the annual rugby Sevens World Series. It is also the city's top concert venue, with previous performers including the likes of Lady Gaga and U2. Despite this, the stadium has run at a massive loss ever since its construction, and is regarded by many Capetonians as a burden on the taxpayer that should be torn down.

---

**20**

### Greenpoint Park and Biodiversity Garden

📍C1 🅰Fritz Sonnenberg Rd 📞021 444 4258 🕐7am–7pm daily

Offering fine views skywards to Signal Hill and Lion's Head, Greenpoint Park and Biodiversity Garden occupies 12.5 ha (31 acres) of common land that King George V donated to the people of Cape Town for recreational purposes in 1923. The area was redeveloped as a biodiversity garden in conjunction with the neighbouring Cape Town Stadium, and now attracts picnicking families, puffing joggers and nature lovers.

Centred on a lily-covered artificial lake fed by the same springs that encouraged Jan Van Riebeeck to establish Cape Town in 1652, the park is planted with habitats indigenous to the Western Cape, including renosterveld, strandveld and various types of *fynbos*. Other features include a menagerie of bird and other animal sculptures made from cut-out steel, a fun family-oriented garden, beads and wire, and a well-labelled section dedicated to medicinal plants and their uses.

# SHOP

Long Street is renowned for its mosaic of quirky shops. Here are a few of our favorites.

### Clarke's Books

This second-hand bookshop is a paradise for Africana collectors.

📍E4 🅰199 Long St 🌐clarkesbooks.co.za

---

### Pan-African Market

A large market spilling over with knick-knacks.

📍E4 🅰76 Long St 🌐panafrican.co.za

---

### Tribal Trends

Sells a superb selection of African crafts, artworks and antiques.

📍E4 🅰72–74 Long St 🌐tribaltrends.com

---

### Long Street Antique Arcade

A cluster of eight antiques shops.

📍E4 🅰127 Long St 🌐theantique arcade.co.za

---

### WAG Fashion

This shop specializes in modern garments made with colourful African fabrics.

📍E4 🅰62 Long St 🌐wagfashion.co.za

# A SHORT WALK
# AROUND THE
# COMPANY'S GARDEN

**Distance** 1.5 km (1 mile)  **Nearest bus station** Upper Long  **Time** 25 minutes

Jan van Riebeeck's famous vegetable garden, established in 1652 to provide ships rounding the Cape of Good Hope with fresh supplies, is still known as the "Company's Garden". It is a leafy, tranquil area that makes a delightful place for a stroll. The garden contains an array of exotic shrubs and trees, an aviary, a conservatory and a sundial dating back to 1787. There is also an open-air restaurant, nearby which is a Saffron pear tree, planted soon after the arrival of Jan van Riebeeck, which makes it the oldest cultivated tree in South Africa. Look out for the disused old well, and the tap that protrudes from the gnarled tree nearby.

↑ One of the pleasant leafy avenues in the Company's Garden

The **garden** is a quiet haven in the city with water features, lawns and benches under tall, old trees.

The **Iziko South African Museum and Planetarium** contains exhibits on natural history, archaeology, entomology and palaeontology, and reconstructs the southern night skies (p134).

Temporary exhibitions of the work of local artists augment the **Iziko South African National Gallery**'s permanent collection of 6,500 paintings (p135).

The entrance to the **South African Jewish Museum** is situated in the Old Synagogue, which was the first synagogue built in South Africa, in 1863 (p134).

BLOEM STREET

GREEN ST

VICTORIA STREET

PERTH ST

QUEEN

EXPERIENCE Cape Town

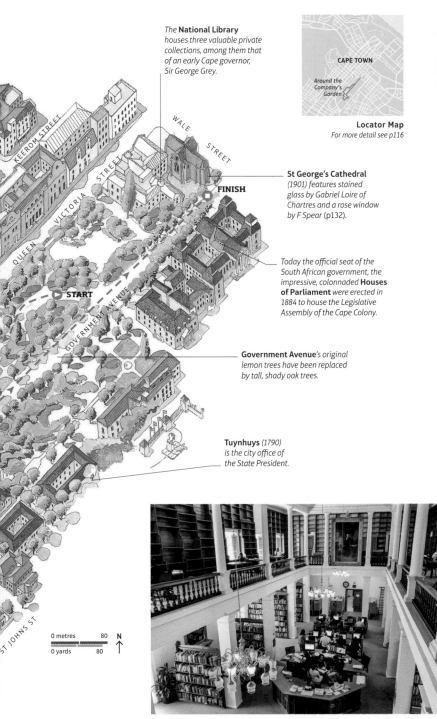

The **National Library** houses three valuable private collections, among them that of an early Cape governor, Sir George Grey.

**Locator Map**
*For more detail see p116*

CAPE TOWN

Around the Company's Garden

FINISH

**St George's Cathedral** *(1901) features stained glass by Gabriel Loire of Chartres and a rose window by F Spear (p132).*

Today the official seat of the South African government, the impressive, colonnaded **Houses of Parliament** *were erected in 1884 to house the Legislative Assembly of the Cape Colony.*

START

**Government Avenue**'s *original lemon trees have been replaced by tall, shady oak trees.*

**Tuynhuys** *(1790) is the city office of the State President.*

KEEROM STREET

VICTORIA STREET

QUEEN

WALE STREET

GOVERNMENT AVENUE

ST JOHNS ST

0 metres    80
0 yards     80    N ↑

↑ The elegant 19th-century interior of the National Library

# A SHORT WALK
# AROUND THE CITY CENTRE

**Distance** 1 km (0.5 miles) **Nearest bus station** Adderly **Time** 20 minutes

The compact city centre lends itself to walking, with most of its major sights easily accessible. Cape Town is dissected by a number of thoroughfares, one of which is Adderley Street. The parallel St George's Mall is a lively pedestrian zone where street musicians and dancers entertain the crowds, while Greenmarket Square, the focal point of the city, is lined with many historically significant buildings. One block west of here, towards Signal Hill, is Long Street. Some beautiful examples of elaborate Victorian buildings with balconies and intricate ironwork – now housing shops, bars and hostels – can be seen here.

A produce market since 1806, and now a national monument, the cobbled **Greenmarket Square** supports a colourful, daily open-air crafts market (p133). Among the historic buildings surrounding it is the Old Town House.

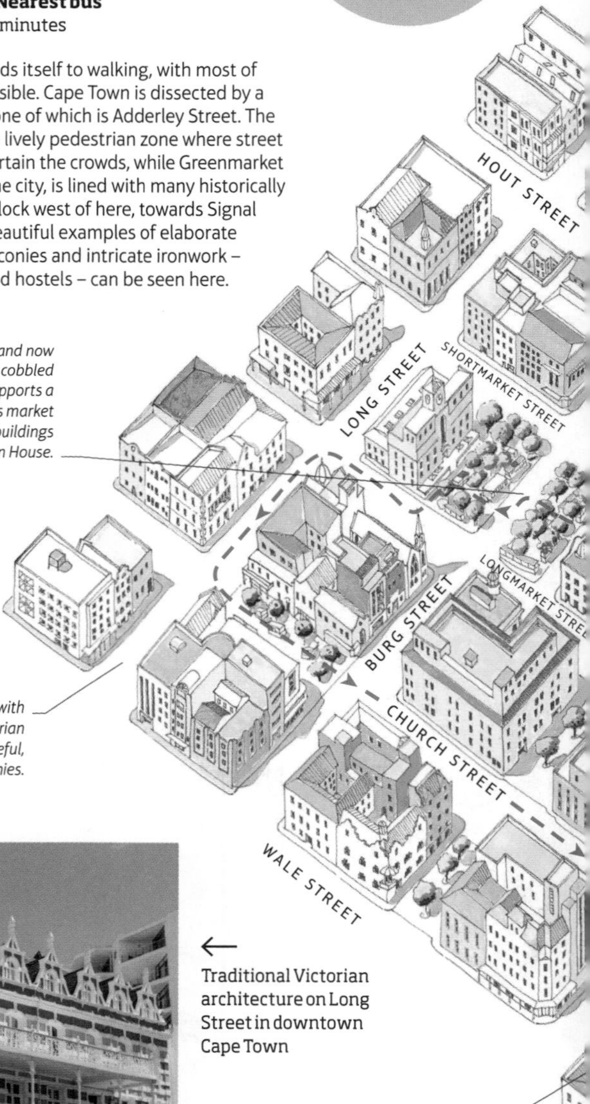

```
0 metres    50    N
0 yards     50    ↑
```

Historic **Long Street** is lined with well-preserved elegant Victorian buildings complete with graceful, delicate wrought-iron balconies.

HOUT STREET

LONG STREET

SHORTMARKET STREET

LONGMARKET STREET

BURG STREET

CHURCH STREET

WALE STREET

← Traditional Victorian architecture on Long Street in downtown Cape Town

The exhibits at **Iziko Slave Lodge** illustrate the history of the site, the second-oldest colonial building in Cape Town (p132).

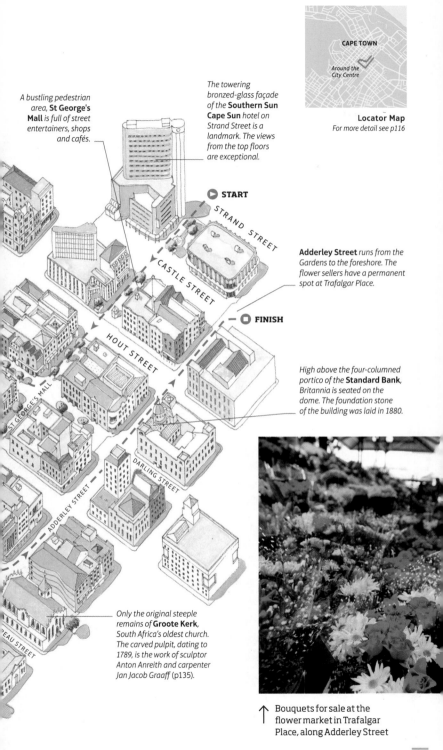

A bustling pedestrian area, **St George's Mall** is full of street entertainers, shops and cafés.

The towering bronzed-glass façade of the **Southern Sun Cape Sun** hotel on Strand Street is a landmark. The views from the top floors are exceptional.

**Locator Map**
For more detail see p116

CAPE TOWN

Around the City Centre

▶ START

STRAND STREET

CASTLE STREET

HOUT STREET

ST GEORGE'S MALL

ADDERLEY STREET

DARLING STREET

BEAU STREET

**Adderley Street** runs from the Gardens to the foreshore. The flower sellers have a permanent spot at Trafalgar Place.

— ◯ FINISH

High above the four-columned portico of the **Standard Bank**, Britannia is seated on the dome. The foundation stone of the building was laid in 1880.

Only the original steeple remains of **Groote Kerk**, South Africa's oldest church. The carved pulpit, dating to 1789, is the work of sculptor Anton Anreith and carpenter Jan Jacob Graaff (p135).

↑ Bouquets for sale at the flower market in Trafalgar Place, along Adderley Street

# CAPE PENINSULA

A mountainous sliver that extends 50 km
(30 miles) south from Cape Town, the Cape
Peninsula has been inhabited by hominins for
at least 1.4 million years. San hunter-gatherers
arrived 30,000 years ago, to be joined by KhoeKhoe
pastoralists around the start of the 1st century AD.
There is little historical record of the region until
1488, when a Portuguese expedition led by
Bartolomeu Dias was blown around the peninsula's
southernmost landfall. King John II of Portugal
named the area the Cape of Good Hope, recog-
nizing it as a key breakthrough in the quest for
a maritime trade route to India. In the 1680s,
three decades after the foundation of Cape Town,
Governor Simon van der Stel established Simon's
Town and Groot Constantia wine estate. Under
apartheid, topographic restrictions on urban
development led to the creation of several
Coloured and Black townships on the more
easterly Cape Flats. These were the setting for
several pivotal events in the struggle, notably
the massacre of 69 peaceful protestors at
Sharpeville in 1960 and the formation of the
United Democratic Front in 1983. Even today, the
contrast between the genteel Cape Peninsula and
densely populated Cape Flats remains striking.

Milnerton   Century City

Ratanga
Junction

Table Bay

**Akasiapark**

N1

Cape Town

R102

**WOODSTOCK**

**21**

**HEART OF CAPE TOWN MUSEUM**

**20**

**SOUTH AFRICAN
ASTRONOMICAL
OBSERVATORY**

**19**

M7

**CAPE TOWN**

*p116*

**22**

**17**   **MOSTERT'S MILL**

**15**

Camps Bay

*Table
Mountain*

**18**   **IRMA STERN
MUSEUM**

**LANGA**

**RHODES
MEMORIAL**

Bridgetown

Surrey

**NEWLANDS**   **16**

Rondebosch

**KIRSTENBOSCH NATIONAL
BOTANICAL GARDEN**   **1**

**Harfield Road**

M7

Kenilworth

**Landsdowne**

Llandudno

M6

Wynberg

M5

**Wetton**

**WORLD OF BIRDS**   **5**

M63

M41

Constantia

Ottery

**2**

M3

**Plumstead**

M17

**GROOT
CONSTANTIA**

*Buitenverwachting
Wine Estate*

Bergvliet

**Southfield**

**HOUT BAY**   **7**

*Tokai Plantation &
Arboretum*

M42

Retreat

M4

**Heathfield**

Grassy Park

*Duiker Island*

*Hout Bay*

*Steenberg
Estate*

Steenberg

M5

**12**

**Steenberg**

**ATLANTIC SEABOARD**   **6**

*Chapman's
Point*

*Chapman's Peak
590 m (1,935 ft)*

**NOORDHOEK**

**Lakeside**

**FALSE BAY
NATURE
RESERVE**

Pelikan Park

*Chapman's
Bay*

Noordhoek

**8**

M310

*Noordhoek
Beach*

*Imhoff
Farm*

San Michel

*Silvermine
Nature Reserve*

**14**   **MUIZENBERG**

*Sun Valley*

M65

**FISH HOEK**   **10**   **Fish Hoek**

**Muizenberg**

**Kalk Bay**

Kommetjie

*Ocean View*

M6

*Fish Hoek Bay*

Da Gama Park

Glencairn

**Glencairn**

**Simon's Town**

**SIMON'S TOWN**

*Schuster's Bay*

**9**

**BOULDERS PENGUIN COLONY**

Scarborough

M66

**4**

*Simonsberg
571 m (1,873 ft)*

*Swartkop
678 m (2,224 ft)*

*Stoney Beach*

*Bonteberg
227 m (745 ft)*

*Klaas Jagersberg
576 m (1,890 ft)*

*Swartkopberge*

A t l a n t i c
O c e a n

*Cape Point
Ostrich Farm*

*Olifantsbos
Bay*

*Smitswinkel
Bay*

*Table
Mountain
National
Park*

M65

*Judas Peak
328 m (1,076 ft)*

*Mast Bay*

*Paulsberg
367 m (1,204 ft)*

*Bordjiesdrif*

*i*

*Buffels Bay*

*Muishond Bay*

**Buffelsfontein
Visitor Centre**

*Rooikrans*

*Platboom
Beach*

*Cape Point
Lighthouse*

**3**

**CAPE OF GOOD HOPE**

0 kilometres        5

0 miles        5

N
↑

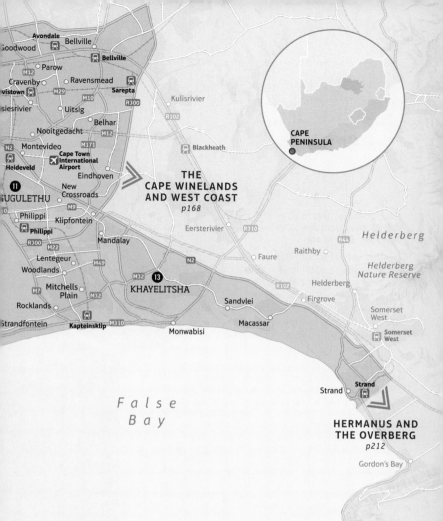

# CAPE PENINSULA

## Must Sees

**1** Kirstenbosch National Botanical Garden
**2** Groot Constantia
**3** Cape of Good Hope
**4** Boulders Penguin Colony

## Experience More

**5** World of Birds
**6** Atlantic Seaboard
**7** Hout Bay
**8** Noordhoek
**9** Simon's Town
**10** Fish Hoek
**11** Gugulethu
**12** False Bay Nature Reserve
**13** Khayelitsha
**14** Muizenberg
**15** Langa
**16** Newlands
**17** Mostert's Mill
**18** Irma Stern Museum
**19** Heart of Cape Town Museum
**20** South African Astronomical Observatory
**21** Woodstock
**22** Rhodes Memorial

**①** 🏃 Ⓜ️ 🍴 💻 👜

# KIRSTENBOSCH NATIONAL BOTANICAL GARDEN

🅰 B7 🅝 Rhodes Dr turn-off on M3
🚌 🚐 🕙 8am-6pm daily (to 7pm
Sep-Mar) 🆆 sanbi.org

Nestled at the foot of Table Mountain, these botanical gardens are among the most beautiful in the world. Attractions include the shady Dell, a Braille trail for visually impaired visitors, and the popular "Boomslang" walkway, added in 2013.

In July 1913, the South African government handed over the running of Kirstenbosch estate (which had been bequeathed to the state by Cecil John Rhodes in 1902) to a board of trustees. The board established a botanical garden that preserves and propagates rare indigenous plant species. Today, the world-renowned garden covers an area of 5.3 sq km (2 sq miles), of which 7 per cent is cultivated and 90 per cent is covered by natural *fynbos* and forest. Kirstenbosch is especially spectacular from August to October, when it is ablaze with spring daisies and gazanias. After the winter rains, carpets of indigenous Namaqualand daisies and gazanias echo the flower display found along the West Coast *(p201)*. Guided tours of the garden run every day apart from Sunday.

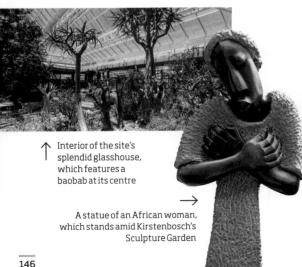

↑ Interior of the site's splendid glasshouse, which features a baobab at its centre

→ A statue of an African woman, which stands amid Kirstenbosch's Sculpture Garden

### Did You Know?

Kirstenbosch is home to a resident Spotted Eagle Owl, which can often be seen near the Dell.

↑ Visitors exploring the garden's "Boomslang" walkway and *(inset)* shady, tree-lined paths

❷ 🦪 🎭 🍴 🖥 🛍

EXPERIENCE Cape Peninsula

# GROOT CONSTANTIA

**🅰B7** 🅾 Off Old Constantia Main Road, Constantia
🕐 Tastings: 9am–6pm daily; cellar tours: 10am–5pm daily;
Manor House: 10am–5pm daily 🚫 Good Friday, 25 Dec 🌐 Winery:
grootconstantia.co.za; Manor House: iziko.org.za

**The oldest wine estate in South Africa, Groot Constantia has a wonderful scenic setting and is home to some of the country's most interesting Cape Dutch architecture.**

The estate was built on land granted in 1685 to Simon van der Stel, Commander of the Cape. On his death in 1712, the farm was subdivided into three parts and sold. After several changes of ownership, the portion with the Manor House was bought in 1778 by Hendrik Cloete, whose family owned it for three generations thereafter and was responsible for the present appearance of the buildings. As well as being an operational farm, Groot Constantia today is also a popular tourist attraction, incorporating a history museum that belongs to the Iziko Museums group.

*The Cloete Wine Cellar houses a display of drinking vessels and wine-making equipment.*

*The façade of the Cloete Wine Cellar, built in 1791, is attributed to architect Louis Thibault.*

*The Manor House contains an authentic representation of a wealthy 19th-century farming household.*

*The sculpted figure of Abundance that decorates the cape Dutch gable's lofty niche is the work of Anton Anreith.*

## SIMON VAN DER STEL

Simon van der Stel was the first non-European and the first person born of mixed parentage to be appointed Governor of the Cape. He was born on a ship in Mauritius, where his father had been posted by the United Dutch East India Company as Commander. His mother was the daughter of an enslaved woman. Van der Stel played a key role in the foundation of Stellenbosch and Simon's Town, both named after him.

# EAT

**Jonkershuis**
Once the abode of the estate owner's bachelor sons, the quaint Jonkershuis is now a charming restaurant that serves traditional Cape dishes with a Cape Malay influence.

⌂ **Groot Constantia**
ⓦ **jonkershuis constantia.co.za**

ⓇⓇⓇ

Groot Constantia's vineyards, which have been producing wine for over three centuries ↑

The historic Manor House and surrounding buildings and gardens ↓

### Did You Know?

The estate's Grand Constance wine was one of Napoleon's favourite tipples.

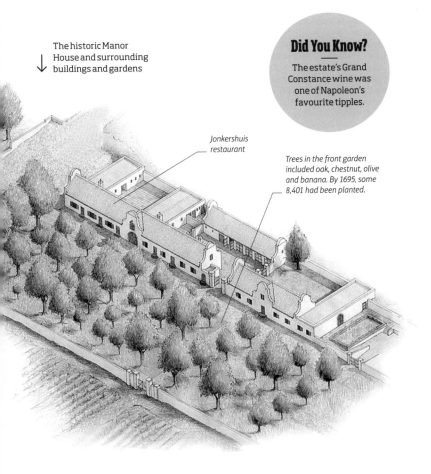

*Jonkershuis restaurant*

*Trees in the front garden included oak, chestnut, olive and banana. By 1695, some 8,401 had been planted.*

# CAPE OF GOOD HOPE

🅰 B7  🚌 M4 via Simon's Town  🕐 Main gate: sunrise–sunset daily; funicular: 9am–4pm daily  🌐 capepoint.co.za

This craggy promontory, often mistaken for the most southerly point of Africa, is home to a sprawling nature reserve. The area is renowned for its dramatic scenery and stormy, changeable weather.

Strictly speaking, the Cape of Good Hope is the rocky headland that marks the most southwesterly point of the Cape Peninsula. Originally named Cape of Storms by the Portuguese explorer Bartolomeu Dias in 1488, the promontory was given its more optimistic title by King John of Portugal, who saw it as a positive omen for a new route to India.

Cape of Good Hope is also the name given to the southernmost sector (formerly referred to as the Cape of Good Hope Nature Reserve) of the wider Table Mountain National Park, which encompasses the whole of the Table Mountain chain from the southernmost point of the peninsula to Signal Hill in the north. Unlike most other parts of Table Mountain National Park, which are freely accessible to the public, conservation fees are payable to enter here.

Not surprisingly, the Cape of Good Hope is exposed to gale-force winds, so the vegetation is limited to hardy milkwood trees and *fynbos*. Small antelopes live here, as do Cape mountain zebras. Visitors may also encounter troops of chacma baboons, which can sometimes be aggressive. For stunning views from the Cape Point promontory, take the Flying Dutchman funicular up to the old lighthouse, 238 m (781 ft) above the crashing ocean waves. From here, a path leads down to the new lighthouse at Dias Point.

Along the sector's east coast, the tidal pools at Venus Pool, Bordjiesrif and Buffels Bay attract hordes of tourists. There are a number of scenic walking trails along the west coast, including the Thomas T Tucker shipwreck trail and the path to Sirkelsvlei; maps are available at the park's entrance gate.

① Rocky Cape Point is one of the most scenic spots in the area.

② Bontebok roam the landscapes within the Cape of Good Hope sector.

③ Steps lead up to Cape Point Lighthouse, which overlooks the coastline at Dias Point.

HIDDEN GEM
**Cape Point Ostrich Farm**

This child-friendly ostrich farm *(capepoint ostrichfarm.com)* is located close to the entrance to the Cape of Good Hope, and offers the best opportunity in the vicinity of Cape Town to hang out with the world's largest bird. A gift shop sells ostrich-derived souvenirs such as hollowed-out eggs and leatherware.

↑ Rolling sea fog and golden dunes on Platboom Beach, Cape of Good Hope

**THE FLYING DUTCHMAN**

This legend originated in 1641, when Dutch sea captain Hendrick van der Decken was battling wild seas off Cape Point while sailing home. No match for the storm, van der Decken's battered ship started sinking, but he swore that he would round the Cape, even if it took him until Judgement Day. Since then, many sightings of a phantom ship, its masts smashed and sails in shreds, have been reported in bad weather. The most significant was recorded in July 1881 in the diary of a certain midshipman sailing on HMS *Bacchante*. The sailor was crowned King George V of England in 1910.

151

**4**

# BOULDERS PENGUIN COLONY

**B7** **Kleintuin Rd, SE of Simon's Town** **Feb-Mar & Oct-Nov: 8am-6:30pm daily; Apr-Sep: 8am-5pm daily; Dec-Jan: 7am-7:30pm daily** **sanparks.org**

**One of the Cape Peninsula's most popular wildlife spectacles, this effortlessly entertaining colony of African penguins is protected as a small isolated enclave of Table Mountain National Park.**

Established by just two breeding pairs in 1982, today Boulders Penguin Colony numbers around 3,000 individuals. The visitor's centre provides a fascinating introduction to these delightful birds, then the colony itself is reached via a wooden boardwalk that leads down to the sandy sweep of Foxy Beach. This forms the main penguin breeding site, and is overlooked by a network of observation platforms that offer close-up views of these comically charismatic creatures as they sunbathe, surf, strut and squabble below.

Willis Walk, a wheelchair-friendly 600-m (2,000-ft) footpath, offers good opportunities to see nesting penguins and their downy offspring. The walk emerges at the main Boulders Beach, a secluded spot named for the ancient granite rocks whose rounded slopes shelter the beach from winds sweeping across False Bay. Boulders supports far fewer birds than Foxy Beach, so sunbathing and swimming is therefore permitted here. There's still a high probability of being joined by a few stray penguins as they propel themselves through the clear water or waddle between the rocks.

### ENDANGERED PENGUINS

The African penguin *Spheniscus demersus* once bred only on off-shore islands. Mainland colonies have now been established in South Africa and in Namibia, but despite this the global population has plummeted to just 50,000. Monitored mainland sites such as Boulders offer the species' best long-term chance of survival.

[1] The African penguins that make up Boulders' colony have been listed as an endangered species since 2010.

[2] A boardwalk overlooks the charming inlets of sheltered Boulders Beach.

[3] Other wildlife, such as the rock hyrax, can be glimpsed from Willis Walk.

**Did You Know?**

The African penguin used to be known as the "jackass penguin", due to its donkey-like call.

A group of African penguins gathering along the sandy shore of Boulders Beach ↑

# EXPERIENCE MORE

EXPERIENCE Cape Peninsula

**⑤** 🖉 🖵 🛍

## World of Birds

🅰 B7  🏠 Valley Rd
🕘 9am–5pm daily
🌐 worldofbirds.co.za

Just north of Hout Bay (p156), World of Birds has high, landscaped, walk-through aviaries that are home to 400 bird species. Around 3,000 birds are kept in the sanctuary for rehabilitation purposes, many of them brought in injured. Others are endangered species that are here for captive breeding. Wherever possible, birds are released into their natural habitat as soon as they are fit enough to survive.

Visitors can watch the site's residents feed, build nests and incubate their eggs. Among the endangered bird species that have benefited from special breeding projects are the blue crane, the citron-crested cockatoo and the Egyptian vulture, extinct in South Africa.

Rare primates can also be seen at the sanctuary, such as the endangered pygmy marmoset and Geoffrey's tufted-ear marmoset. There are also terrapins, skinks and iguanas. The Robin's Nest café offers drinks and light meals and there is a picnic spot next to the flamingo enclosure.

---

**⑥**

## Atlantic Seaboard

🅰 B7

Shortly after the Sea Point Swimming Pool (p136), Beach Road runs via Queens into Victoria Road, which winds southwards along Cape Town's Atlantic Seaboard. Bantry Bay, Clifton, Camps Bay and Llandudno are the desirable addresses along this steep stretch of coast, which is

↑ Two rare crowned cranes, glimpsed at the World of Birds

flanked by luxurious million-dollar homes that boast spacious terraces and glittering swimming pools. With incomparable views and beautiful beaches right on

their doorsteps, this is the haunt of the wealthy.

The coastal route extends all the way to idyllic Hout Bay, which lies over the saddle that separates the Twelve Apostles mountain range from the peak of the mountain known as Little Lion's Head. These 12 impressive sandstone buttresses, named after the biblical apostles by Sir Rufane Donkin, one-time governor of the British Cape Colony, flank the Riviera's suburbs. First is Bantry Bay, whose luxury apartments, many of which are supported on concrete stilts, are built into the steep mountain slope.

Trendy Clifton follows, with its four famous small beaches separated by granite boulders. Fourth Beach is

especially popular among families, as it has a car park nearby, while the other three are accessible only from the road via steep flights of stairs. The Atlantic's waters are icy, but the beaches are sheltered from the strong southeasterly gales by Lion's Head, so during the summer months all of the four beaches are tremendously popular with sunseekers, and the resulting

INSIDER TIP
**Llandudno Beach**

Huddled by the southwestern slopes of Table Mountain, Llandudno is a gorgeous sweep of white sand studded with boulders. The water is too rough for bathing, but it's a perfect spot for sundowners.

traffic congestion is enormous. Victoria Road continues along the shore past Maiden's Cove, which has a tidal pool, good public facilities and is famed as a free diving spot. Further along is Glen Beach, which has no amenities but is frequented nonetheless by surfers and sunbathers. At Camps Bay, the broad sweep of beach, lined with tall, stately palms, is another very popular spot, although the southeaster tends to bluster through here quite strongly, especially during the summer months. Backed by Lion's Head and the Twelve Apostles, Camps Bay's lovely setting has been the inspiration for the establishment of a number of luxurious hotels and a string of good restaurants.

Llandudno arguably has the city's most beautiful little beach, about 10 km (6 miles) east of Camps Bay. The small

### Did You Know?

Llandudno was named after a town of the same name in Wales as both have similar bays.

residential area, settled on a rocky promontory at the foot of Little Lion's Head, is first spotted from the cliff top. Despite being home to some of the most expensive properties in South Africa, this picturesque suburb has the relaxed atmosphere of a tiny coastal town, with no street lamps or shops. A 20-minute walk to the west over the rocky shore leads to secluded Sandy Bay, Cape Town's nudist beach. The inaccessible location ensures plenty of privacy.

← A deserted bay in Clifton at dusk, edged by clusters of houses with spectacular seascape views

## 7 Hout Bay

🅰B7 🚌 𝑖 www.capetown.travel

The green valleys of Hout Bay are threaded with oak-lined roads. Horse paddocks and stables abound, and many local riding centres offer instruction and recreational horse riding. Residents walk their dogs on Hout Bay beach in the early mornings. The beach is also frequented by swimmers, paddlesurfers and, at its west end, by windsurfers and Hobie Cat sailors. From the harbour, tour operators launch regular cruises that take visitors out to watch seabirds and see the Cape fur seal colony on Duiker

 **INSIDER TIP**
**Weather Watch**

Always check the weather when planning a trip to Duiker Island. Conditions are highly changeable and some of the most exciting marine activities may be cancelled if the sea is too choppy.

Hout Bay, home to a healthy seal population *(inset)*, as viewed from the scenic Chapman's Peak Drive ↑

Island. Boat trips last for about 45 minutes. The vessels have large portholes or glass bottoms so seals can be viewed frolicking underwater among giant wavy kelp forests. Sunset cruises are also available, as are fishing trips, organized by local companies to catch a variety of gamefish such as yellowfin and longfin tuna, broadbill swordfish and marlin.

At the bay's eastern edge, a 1.4-m (4.5-ft) bronze statue of a leopard is perched on a rock pinnacle. It was cast in 1963 by the late Ivan Mitford-Barberton, a local artist.

The suburb of Hout Bay itself offers a great variety of small coffee shops, restaurants, and clothing and curio shops. Closer to the harbour there are pubs, such as the popular Dunes, which overlooks the beach and harbour.

At the start of the scenic Chapman's Peak coastal drive is the well-positioned

Chapmans Peak Hotel, which has beautiful views across the bay. Its terrace is popular for lunch and sundowners in summer.

Lying sandwiched between Hout Bay's beach and the busy little fishing harbour is **Mariner's Wharf**. It was built by a local family, the Dormans, whose predecessors farmed in the Hout Bay valley during the 20th century, and offers an open-air bistro, a seafood restaurant and a shop that sells marine-related curios. Visitors can also enjoy a leisurely stroll along the pier, which is usually flanked by moored fishing boats.

At weekends, the **Bay Harbour Market** is held in one of the area's old fishing factories. It features more than

> **Residents walk their dogs on Hout Bay beach in the early mornings. The beach is also frequented by swimmers, paddlesurfers, and, at its west end, by windsurfers and Hobie Cat sailors.**

100 crafts and food stalls and is popular for brunch and lunch, which is enjoyed at communal tables and accompanied by live music. Traders here are mostly small local producers, organic farmers and artisans supporting a sustainable lifestyle.

Inaugurated in 1979, the **Hout Bay Museum** has many interesting displays on the colourful history of the Hout Bay valley and its people, focusing on forestry, mining and the fishing industry. Alongside these exhibits, the museum also organizes weekly guided nature walks into the spectacular surrounding mountains.

Located on the fringes of Hout Bay are the townships of Hangberg and Imizamo Yethu. Hangberg was created in the 1940s to house workers in the lumber (and later fishing) industries and was historically a so-called Coloured area. Today, Hangberg's views of the bay and Chapman's Peak offer

the community another income stream through tourism. Hangberg is best visited on a walking tour with a local guide, who can provide an insider's view of the neighbourhood and its stories, history, culture and food. Imizamo Yethu, created in the 1990s, has grown into a bustling neighbourhood with mostly Xhosa-speaking residents. It can similarly be explored with a township tour.

### Mariner's Wharf

🍴😊🛍 📍Harbour Rd
🕐Daily 🌐mariners wharf.com

### Bay Harbour Market

😊🛍 📍31 Harbour Rd
🕐5–9pm Fri, 9:30am–4pm Sat & Sun 🌐bay harbour.co.za

### Hout Bay Museum

♿ 📍4 Andrews Rd
📞021 790 3270
🕐10am–4pm Mon–Fri 🚫Sat, Sun & public hols

## Noordhoek

📍B7 ℹ️www.noordhoek tourism.co.za

The best feature of this little coastal settlement is its pristine stretch of white-sand beach. The water is unsafe for swimming but it is popular with surfers and paddleskiers. The shore is good for horse riding and long walks (tourists are advised to walk in groups for safety), while along its length lies the wreck of the *Kakapo*, which was beached during a storm in 1900. Part of the 1970 movie *Ryan's Daughter* was filmed here.

Another coastal hamlet, Kommetjie, adjoins a tidal lagoon inland from Noordhoek Beach. Long Beach, which stretches north as far as Klein Slangkop Point, is a venue for surfing championships and is very popular with board-sailors. Scarborough, at the mouth of the Schuster's River, is a sought-after residential area. In summer, the seasonal lagoon is very popular.

→ Visitors dining in the shade at one of the many restaurants at Mariner's Wharf

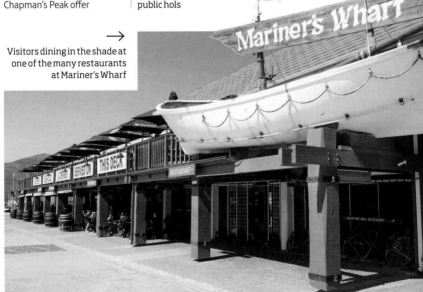

## ❾

# Simon's Town

🅰B7 🚉 From Cape Town station, Adderley St
ℹ www.simonstown.com

Simon's Town in False Bay has been the base of the South African navy since 1957. It was named after Simon van der Stel *(p148)*, who visited this sheltered little spot around 1687. In 1743, the Dutch East India Company decided to make Simon's Bay its fleet's winter anchorage and from 1814 until the handover to South Africa, the bay served as the British Navy's base in the South Atlantic. Thanks to its role as a port, Simon's Town drew diverse inhabitants, but much of its multicultural heritage was erased during the apartheid era by forced removals of the Black, Indian and Coloured populations to Ocean View, Gugulethu and Rylands.

Simon's Town's naval history is best absorbed by walking the "historical mile" that begins near the railway station and ends at the Martello Tower, taking in the **Simon's Town Museum**, the South African Naval Museum and the Warrior Toy Museum along the way. The Simon's Town Museum was established in 1977 and is

↑ Clear blue skies above the charming wide streets of Simon's Town

housed in The Residency, believed to be the town's oldest building. It was built in 1777 as a weekend retreat for Governor Joachim van Plettenberg. Later, it also served as a naval hospital. Among the museum's exhibits is a replica of a World War II royal naval pub and the quarters of the original slave lodge. Martello Tower, the walk's endpoint, was built in 1796 as a defence against the French, and has since been used as a navigational point for ships entering the bay. Guided walks can be arranged at the museum on request.

Between Simon's Town and the Cape of Good Hope sector of Table Mountain National

## Did You Know?

South Africa's iconic Mrs H S Ball's chutney was first produced in Fish Hoek.

Park, the M4 passes through charming settlements that offer safe swimming and snorkelling in protected bays such as Froggy Pond, Boulders and Seaforth. The big granite rocks after which Boulders is named provide shelter when the southeaster blows. Another major attraction is the Boulders Penguin Colony *(p152)*, a land-based colony of around 3,000 African penguins.

Further south, Miller's Point has picnic areas and tidal rock pools. The Black Marlin Restaurant here is popular for its fresh seafood. At Smitswinkel Bay, a lovely cove lies at the foot of a steep path.

**Simon's Town Museum**
🕉 ♿ 🏛 Court Rd 🕙10am-4pm Mon-Fri, 10am-1pm Sat 🚫Sun & public hols 🖥 simons townmuseum.org.za

## ABLE SEAMAN JUST NUISANCE

In Jubilee Square, overlooking Simon's Town's naval harbour, stands the statue of a Great Dane called Just Nuisance. During World War II this dog was the much-loved mascot of British sailors based in Simon's Town. The animal, the only canine ever to be formally enrolled in the Royal Navy, was given the title Able Seaman. When he died in a Simon's Town naval hospital, he was honoured with a full military funeral, which was attended by 200 members of the British Royal Navy. An entire room at the Simon's Town Museum is filled with memorabilia relating to the unusual cadet.

→ A statue of Just Nuisance standing in Jubilee Square

→ Colourful bathing huts lining Kalk Bay beach, near Fish Hoek

## Fish Hoek

**A B7** www.capetown.travel

Only recently was liquor allowed to be sold in Fish Hoek; until then it was a "dry" municipality – the only remaining one in South Africa other than the suburb of Pinelands. This condition had been written into a property grant made by Governor Lord Charles Somerset in 1818, and was repealed only in the 1990s. Since then the sale of alcohol has been allowed in restaurants, and after a prolonged legal battle the town's first "bottle store" opened in 2019.

The broad stretch of Fish Hoek beach is lined with changing rooms, cafés and a yacht club, and is popular with families and the sailing fraternity. Regattas are held regularly, and catamarans and Hobie Cats often line the beach. Jager's Walk, a pleasant pathway overlooking the sea and the beach, runs along the edge of the bay.

Past Fish Hoek itself, the M4 continues northwards, staying close to the shore. It passes through the seaside suburb of St James, which has a small, safe family beach and is characterized by a row of wooden bathing huts that have all been painted in bright primary colours.

At the picturesque little fishing harbour of Kalk Bay, the daily catches of fresh fish, particularly snoek, are sold directly from the boats. The height of the snoek season varies, but usually extends from June to July. The Brass Bell restaurant, sandwiched between the railway station and the rocky shore, has a popular pub and good seafood; at high tide, waves crash against the breakwater between the restaurant and the sea. Kalk Bay is also popular for the many fine antiques and art shops that line Main Road.

>  INSIDER TIP
> ### Hidden History
> Learn about the history of Kalk Bay's mixed-heritage community of fishermen on a two-hour walking tour with local artist and teacher Traci Kwaai *(www.awehkaapstad.co.za)*.

## Gugulethu

**A B7** www.capetown.travel

A contraction of an isiXhosa phrase meaning "Our Pride", Gugulethu – a bustling township that was established in the late 1950s – became a focus of anti-apartheid activity in the 1980s. It retains a reputation as a crime hotspot, though this is no obstacle to visiting by day in the company of a guide. The township's most poignant landmark is the Gugulethu Seven Monument, a line of seven tombstone-like slabs with human outlines carved out of their centres, marking the place where seven young men from Gugulethu were shot dead by police in 1986. The nearby Amy Biehl Memorial commemorates a 26-year-old American anti-apartheid activist who was stoned by an angry mob in 1993. With a healthy tourist industry, Gugulethu is home to a wealth of restaurants, B&Bs and jazz clubs.

### 12

## False Bay Nature Reserve

🄰B7 🄰Entrances on Perth and Zeekooivlei Road 🄲7:30am–6pm daily (to 7:30pm Sat & Sun Dec–Feb) 🅆capetown.gov.za

The largest remaining swathe of green on the Cape Flats, False Bay Nature Reserve protects a rich biodiversity of fragile habitats including several perennial lakes and marshes, and relict patches of Cape Flats Dune Strandveld and Sand Fynbos (both critically endangered types of vegetation). Extending over 2,300 ha (5,684 acres) north-east of Muizenberg, the reserve was recognized as a Ramsar (internationally important) wetland in 2015, and it is also listed as an IBA (Important Bird Area), with more than 240 bird species recorded. The reserve has existed only in its present form since 2011, but the Rondevlei Sector – the oldest of its six parts and the best developed for tourists – was designated as a bird sanctuary in 1952.

The finest aquatic bird-watching site in the vicinity of Cape Town, Rondevlei is serviced by a short walking trail and six hides, from where species including great crested grebe, purple swamp-hen, great white pelican, greater flamingo, African spoonbill and a profusion of waterfowl and waders can be observed. Look out, too, for the hippos that were introduced in 1982 to help to prevent the wetland from being choked by vegetation, and the herd of eland – Africa's largest antelope – that joined them in 2015. Other wildlife ranges from small predators such as the Cape clawless otter and large-spotted genet, to endangered endemics such as the Cape dwarf chameleon and western leopard toad. Rondevlei aside, the most frequently visited of the other five sectors are Strandfontein – which might lack the aesthetic appeal of Rondevlei due to its sewer-age works but often offers even better birding – and Zeekooivlei ("Hippo Pan"), a large lake primarily used for local recreation activities.

---

### 13

## Khayelitsha

🄰B7 🄳www.capetown. travel

Created in 1983, Khayelitsha – an isiXhosa name meaning "new home" – was one of the apartheid regime's final bids to enforce the Group Areas Act.

As South Africa's second-largest township (after Soweto), it is also the country's fastest-growing settlement, with

a predominantly Xhosa population that has soared from 30,000 in the late 1980s to an estimated 400,000 today.

Khayelitsha is conspicuously poorer than Langa (p162), its neighbouring township. Unemployment stands at more than 50 per cent, and more than half of the township's residents live in makeshift shacks, despite the construction of more than 25,000 government houses since the millennium.

An overview of Khayelitsha can be obtained from a board-walk and viewing platform on the Cape Flats' tallest sand dune (reached via 164 steps) at the **Lookout Hill Tourism Centre**. Framed by the False Bay coastline, it also offers a different westwards view of Table Mountain. Khayelitsha is best visited as part of a town-ship day tour with an operator.

Just beyond Khayelitsha, at the township of Lwandle, stands the grim **Lwandle Migrant Labour Museum**: a former hostel where migrant labourers were crammed six to a room into a block with rudimentary bathroom facilities. Today it serves as a memorial to the control of Black workers through the infamous identity document known as the passbook.

↑ Rowers paddling gently across one of the lakes within False Bay Nature Reserve

↑ Surfers and swimmers dotting the waves at Muizenberg's popular white-sand beach

### Lookout Hill Tourism Centre

🏠 Cnr Mew Way & Spine Rd
📞 021 361 7098 🕐 8am–4:30pm Mon–Fri

### Lwandle Migrant Labour Museum

🏠 Vulindlela St, Lwandle
🕐 8:30am–4:30pm Mon–Thu, 8:30am–4pm Fri
🌐 lwandle.com

---

### Muizenberg

🅱 B7 🚉 🚆 www.capetown.travel

The name Muizenberg comes from the Dutch phrase *Muijs zijn berg*, meaning "Muijs's mountain". Wynand Willem Muijs was a sergeant who, from 1743, commanded a military post on the mountain overlooking the beach.

Muizenberg's white sands rightly earned the town its status as the country's premier holiday retreat in the 19th century. Traces of this early popularity are still visible in the shabby façades of once-grand beach mansions. Today, a fast-food pavilion, seawater pool and wide lawns attract young and old alike. One curve of the bay is known as Surfer's Corner, due to its popularity among watersports fans. There are several surf shops here that offer beginner lessons.

Cecil John Rhodes, prime minister of the Cape Colony from 1890 to 1895, started a trend when he bought Barkly Cottage here in 1899. Soon, holiday mansions began to mushroom at the resort, although most were in stark contrast to his simple, stone-walled cottage. Today it serves as a museum and has been renamed **Rhodes Cottage Museum**. It contains photographs and memorabilia of the controversial empire builder and statesman *(p165)*.

### Rhodes Cottage Museum

♿ 🏠 246 Main Rd 📞 021 788 1816 🕐 10am–2pm Mon–Sat

> **Muizenberg's white sands rightly earned the town its status as the country's premier holiday retreat in the 19th century.**

# STAY

The Cape Peninsula is studded with boutique hotels suited to those who prefer to stay away from the city centre.

### Tintswalo at Boulders Boutique Villa

With nine luxurious suites, this villa offers excellent service and food in a prime location overlooking a penguin colony at Boulders.

🏠 7 Gay Rd, Simons Town 🌐 tintswalo.com

Ⓡ Ⓡ Ⓡ

---

### Glen Avon Lodge

Situated in the Constantia winelands, this five-star lodge serves superb meals in its 200-year-old Cape Dutch homestead.

🏠 1 Strawberry Ln, Constantia 🌐 glenavon.co.za

Ⓡ Ⓡ Ⓡ

# EAT

### Cape to Cuba

A laid-back beach shack with great cocktails and Cuban-inspired snacks.

🏠 165 Main Rd, Kalk Bay
📞 021 788 1566

Ⓡ Ⓡ Ⓡ

### Blue Bird Garage

Local artisans, cooks and designers gather at this weekly foods and goods market located in an old plane hangar.

🏠 39 Albertyn Rd, Muizenberg ⏰ 4–10pm Fri 🌐 bluebird garage.co.za

Ⓡ Ⓡ Ⓡ

### La Colombe

Located on the organic Silvermist Wine Estate and offering a dazzling French-African fusion menu.

🏠 Main Rd, Constantia Nek 🌐 lacolombe.co.za

Ⓡ Ⓡ Ⓡ

---

**The township's name – which means "Sun" in isiXhosa and several other Nguni languages – is a contraction of Kwa-Langa-libalele (Place of Langalibalele).**

## ⑮

## Langa

🅰 B7 ℹ www.capetown.
travel

Cape Town's first planned township, Langa was established in 1927 for migrant labourers from the Eastern Cape, and it remains relatively homogenous in cultural terms, with a predominantly Xhosa population. The township's name – which means "Sun" in isiXhosa and several other Nguni languages – is a contraction of Kwa-Langa-libalele (Place of Langalibalele). Its a reference to the eponymous Hlubi chief, who in 1874 became one of the first Black African dissidents to be incarcerated on Robben Island, and was subsequently held under house arrest at the site of present-day Langa for 13 years.

The Langa-Sharpeville Massacre Memorial was unveiled in 2010 to commemorate the 50th anniversary of the police opening fire on protesters in Langa (at least two were killed, but some accounts suggest the death toll was higher) on the same day as the Sharpeville Massacre near Johannesburg. These 1960 protests were a reaction to the Pass Law, which required Black South Africans to carry a passbook – also known as a *Dompas* (literally "stupid pass") – when they travelled outside designated areas.

A local landmark is the **Guga S'thebe Arts & Culture Centre**, which is decorated with a riot of colourful ceramic murals, and is a community centre offering arts-based activities from dance classes to crafts workshops. The complex was expanded in 2015 following the completion of the Guga S'thebe Theatre, an innovative construction built with recycled shipping containers, wooden fruit crates and local materials such as straw and clay. The shop here sells locally made textiles, pottery, and mosaic arts and crafts.

**Guga S'thebe Arts & Culture Centre**

🏠 Washington St 📞 021 695 3493 ⏰ 8am–5pm Mon–Fri, 9am–3pm Sat & Sun

A colourful mural gracing the walls of the Guga S'thebe Arts & Culture Centre in Langa ↑

↑ The South African Springboks taking on New Zealand's rugby team in a 2017 clash at the vast Newlands stadium

 **Newlands**

Ⓐ**B7** 🅿️🚌 *i* **www. capetown.travel**

An exclusive suburb nestled at the foot of Table Mountain's southern slopes, Newlands is the headquarters for the Western Province rugby and cricket unions. The large Newlands sports grounds have served as the venue for many international matches. The rugby stadium can hold up to 50,000 spectators, and hosted the opening game of the 1995 Rugby World Cup.

Newlands Forest runs along the edge of the M3, a major route that links Muizenberg (p161) with the southern suburbs and the city centre. Local residents love to take long walks and exercise their dogs through the forest's tall blue gum, pine and silver trees, which are watered by the Newlands stream.

A little further on stands a beautifully restored national monument, **Josephine Mill**. With its cast-iron wheel, the mill was built in 1840 by a Swede, Jacob Letterstedt, on the bank of the Liesbeeck River, to grind wheat. It was

named after the Swedish Crown Princess of that period, Josephine. Today, this fine example of 19th-century architecture is managed by Cape Town's Historical Society, and is Cape Town's only surviving operational mill. Milling demonstrations take place from Monday to Friday (at 11am and 3pm), and fresh biscuits, bread and flour are available to buy from the site. There is also a pleasant restaurant in the grounds, which has outside tables next to the river.

**Josephine Mill**
🍴♿🎟️ Ⓐ**13 Boundary Rd** 🕐**10am–1pm Mon–Fri** 🌐**josephinemill.co.za**

🔟  **Mostert's Mill**

Ⓐ**B7** Ⓐ**Rhodes Drive** 🚌 ⏰**Currently closed until further notice** 🌐**mosterts mill.co.za**

This old-fashioned windmill dates to 1796 and stands on part of the Groote Schuur estate gifted to the country's people by financier Cecil John Rhodes. Prior to being damaged in a wildfire in April 2021, it was the only working windmill in South Africa and was operated once a month on a Saturday. It remains to be seen whether and when it will be operational again.

---

**THE CAPE FLATS**

The unyielding flatlands east of Cape Town saw little permanent settlement until the 1920s, when an influx of migrant labour led to the creation of the area's first "township" (a residential suburb reserved for individuals classified as Black, Coloured or Indian by the government of the time). The 1950 implementation of the Group Areas Act led to an easterly sprawl of such townships, which were crowded and often lacked basic amenities. They later became a hotbed of anti-apartheid activism. While living conditions have vastly improved, poverty remains rife in this part of Cape Town. The townships of the Cape Flats are best visited on an organized tour or with a local guide.

**18**

## Irma Stern Museum

🅰B7 🏠21 Cecil Rd 🕐10am-5pm Tue-Fri, 10am-2pm Sat 🌐irmasternmuseum.co.za

One of Cape Town's lesser known gems, this under-publicized museum comprises the house where the controversial artist Irma Stern (1894–1966) lived from 1927 until her death. On display is a selection of Stern's striking portraits, whose bold styling and decidedly modernistic sensibility were more widely appreciated in Europe than they were in more conservative South African art circles. The museum also houses a collection of ethnic artifacts accumulated on the artist's extensive African travels, most famously an early 20th-century stool carved by the Congolese craftsman known as the Master of Buli.

---

# EAT

**Tapi Tapi**
A café that serves handcrafted ice cream celebrating African cultures and cuisines.

🇶B7 🏠76 Lower Main Rd, Observatory 🌐tapitapi.co.za

---

**19**

## Heart of Cape Town Museum

🅰B7 🏠Main Rd, Observatory 🕐Tours only, check website for hours 🌐heartofcapetown.co.za

Probably the most famous hospital in South Africa, Groote Schuur was established in 1938 on an estate that dates back to 1657, when the Dutch East India Company built a large granary there. The hospital made international headlines on 3 December 1967 when the world's first heart transplant was performed there by the Cape Town-trained surgeon Dr Christiaan Barnard. The drama of this landmark moment in medical history can be experienced on a guided tour of the interactive Heart of Cape Town Museum, which is housed in the original hospital building.

**20**

## South African Astronomical Observatory

🅰B7 🏠1 Observatory Rd, off Liesbeeck Pkwy 🕐Show: 8pm on 2nd and 4th Sat of every month 🌐saao.ac.za

The site for the Royal Observatory was selected in 1821 by the first Astronomer

↑ Remarkable paintings lining the walls of the Irma Stern Museum

Royal stationed at the Cape, the Reverend Fearon Fellows. Today, as the national headquarters for astronomy in South Africa, the observatory controls the Sutherland laboratory in the Great Karoo and is responsible for transmitting the electronic impulse that triggers the daily Noon Day Gun on Signal Hill (p136), thus setting standard time for the entire country. The world-class observatory is the oldest permanent observatory in the southern hemisphere and was declared a National Heritage Site in 2018.

## RHODES MEMORIAL CONTROVERSY

In 2015, an intruder defaced the Rhodes Memorial's bronze bust with graffiti denouncing its subject. This incident was sparked by the divisive #RhodesMustFall campaign, which argues that the removal of memorials to this poster boy of white supremacy and Victorian imperialism is a necessary step in the decolonization of African history. Detractors view it as historical revisionism; the controversy rages on.

state president's official Cape Town residence – the Rhodes Memorial overlooks the busy M3. The white granite, Doric-style temple on the slopes of Devil's Peak was designed by Sir Herbert Baker as a tribute to Cecil John Rhodes, and was unveiled in 1912. It contains a bust of Rhodes by J M Swan, who also sculpted the eight bronze lions that guard the stairs. Beneath the bust is an inscription from "The Burial", written by Rhodes' good friend Rudyard Kipling. The focus of the memorial, however, is the bronze equestrian statue, titled "Physical Energy", which was executed by George Frederic Watts.

The sweeping views from the monument across the southern suburbs and out to the distant Hottentots Holland mountains are superb. Mixed oak and pine woodlands cover the mountain slopes around the memorial, and there are hiking trails from the car park. The Rhodes Memorial Restaurant is a lovely spot for lunch or afternoon tea.

## Woodstock

**B7**

Concentrated around the two busy Main and Albert roads, Woodstock is one of the oldest of Cape Town's inner city suburbs. It features Victorian cottages and is undergoing an urban renewal with many new buildings and businesses. It is especially making itself known as the design quarter in town with decor, furniture and fabric shops as well as art galleries. The best time to visit is on a Saturday for the

Neighbourgoods Market at the Old Biscuit Mill. It is one of Cape Town residents' favourite weekend outings for the crafts shops, designer outlets, and food and drink stalls.

## Rhodes Memorial

**B7** Groote Schuur Estate Exit off M3 9am–5pm daily rhodes memorial.co.za

Directly opposite Groote Schuur homestead – the

The Rhodes Memorial, overlooking the city's lights

# A DRIVING TOUR
# THE CAPE PENINSULA

**Length** 160 km (100 miles) **Stopping-off points** Kommetjie, Simon's Town, Muizenberg **Difficulty** Easy, but Chapman's Peak Drive may be closed in bad weather

Tours of the Cape Peninsula should start on the Atlantic Seaboard and include Chapman's Peak Drive, a scenic route that took seven years to build. The drive, cut into the cliff face, has splendid lookout points with picnic sites. A highlight of the tour is the panorama at Cape Point, where the peninsula juts into the sea – the views encompass False Bay, the Hottentots Holland mountains and Cape Hangklip, 80 km (50 miles) away. The return journey passes the penguin colony at Boulders and also goes through charming Simon's Town.

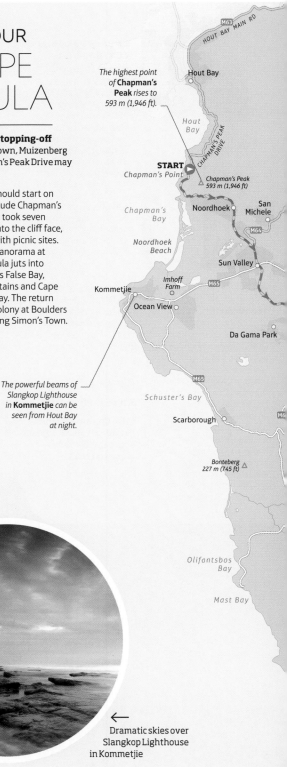

*The highest point of **Chapman's Peak** rises to 593 m (1,946 ft).*

**START**
*Chapman's Point*

HOUT BAY MAIN RD
M63

Hout Bay

*Hout Bay*

CHAPMAN'S PEAK DRIVE

Chapman's Peak
593 m (1,946 ft)

San Michele

Noordhoek

M64

*Chapman's Bay*

*Noordhoek Beach*

Sun Valley

*Imhoff Farm*

Kommetjie

M65

Ocean View

Da Gama Park

*The powerful beams of Slangkop Lighthouse in **Kommetjie** can be seen from Hout Bay at night.*

*Schuster's Bay*

M65

Scarborough

M6

*Bonteberg 227 m (745 ft)*

*Olifantsbos Bay*

*Mast Bay*

← Dramatic skies over Slangkop Lighthouse in Kommetjie

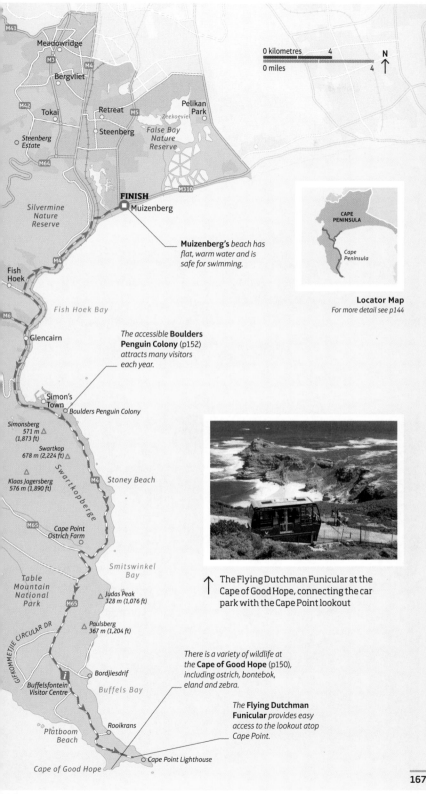

Meadowridge

Bergvliet

Tokai

Retreat

Steenberg

Pelikan Park

Steenberg Estate

*Zeekoevlei*

False Bay Nature Reserve

Silvermine Nature Reserve

**FINISH**
Muizenberg

**Muizenberg's** *beach has flat, warm water and is safe for swimming.*

Fish Hoek

*Fish Hoek Bay*

Glencairn

The accessible **Boulders Penguin Colony** (p152) *attracts many visitors each year.*

Simon's Town

Boulders Penguin Colony

Simonsberg 571 m (1,873 ft)

Swartkop 678 m (2,224 ft)

Klaas Jagersberg 576 m (1,890 ft)

*Swartkopberge*

*Stoney Beach*

Cape Point Ostrich Farm

*Smitswinkel Bay*

Table Mountain National Park

Judas Peak 328 m (1,076 ft)

Paulsberg 367 m (1,204 ft)

GIFKOMMETJIE CIRCULAR DR

Buffelsfontein Visitor Centre

Bordjiesdrif

*Buffels Bay*

Rooikrans

*Platboom Beach*

Cape Point Lighthouse

Cape of Good Hope

↑ The Flying Dutchman Funicular at the Cape of Good Hope, connecting the car park with the Cape Point lookout

There is a variety of wildlife at the **Cape of Good Hope** (p150), including ostrich, bontebok, eland and zebra.

The **Flying Dutchman Funicular** provides easy access to the lookout atop Cape Point.

0 kilometres 4
0 miles 4

N

**CAPE PENINSULA**

Cape Peninsula

**Locator Map**
For more detail see p144

# THE CAPE WINELANDS AND WEST COAST

The focal point of the mountainous Winelands immediately inland of Cape Town, Stellenbosch is named after Simon van der Stel, who established it on the Eersterivier (First River) in 1679, making it South Africa's second oldest town. Only 25 km (15 miles) to its east, the hamlet of Franschhoek ("French Corner") is named for the many Protestant Huguenot refugees who settled there in the 1680s. These French settlers contributed to the development of agriculture in the verdant valleys around Stellenbosch and Franschhoek – much of which depended heavily on the use of slave labour – and several of the country's best-known wine estates date to 1680–95. The University of Stellenbosch, established in 1864 and accorded full academic recognition in 1918, is the country's joint-oldest; alumni include four former South African presidents as well as anti-apartheid activists such as Beyers Naudé. Today, the region's history is reflected in its wealth of gracious Cape Dutch buildings and the fine wine produced by its centuries-old vineyards.

0 kilometres 20
0 miles 20

N

**Atlantic Ocean**

Donkins Bay Private Nature

Soopjeshoogte Private Nature Reserve

LAMBERT'S BAY **17**
R364

Leipoldtville

Elands Bay

R366

Redelinghuys

**St Helena Bay**

Dwarskers-bos

Aurora

Stompneusbaai

St Helena Bay

Velddrif

PATERNOSTER **11**

Vredenburg

R399

Sauer

Bergrivier

R27

Langebaanweg

Groot Bergrivie

SALDANHA
**13**

Hopefield

R45

Langebaan

R27

**WEST COAST NATIONAL PARK**

Churchhaven

**4**

Swartwater

R307

Yzerfontein

R315

DARLING **14**

R31

*Dassen Island*

R307

Grotto Bay

Atlantis

**Atlantic Ocean**

R27

Philadelphia

Melkbosstrand

N

**BLOUBERGSTRAND**

*Robben Island*

**10**

Milnerton

Cape Town

**CAPE PENINSUL**
*p142*

Hout Bay

Noordhoek

Scarborough    Simon's Town

# THE CAPE WINELANDS AND WEST COAST

## Must Sees

**1** Stellenbosch
**2** Stellenbosch Winelands
**3** Franschhoek
**4** West Coast National Park

## Experience More

**5** Paarl
**6** Robertson
**7** Worcester
**8** Montagu
**9** Tulbagh
**10** Bloubergstrand
**11** Paternoster
**12** Malmesbury
**13** Saldhana
**14** Darling
**15** Clanwilliam
**16** Citrusdal
**17** Lambert's Bay
**18** Bushmans Kloof Wilderness Reserve
**19** Cederberg

# ❶
# STELLENBOSCH

**⛰B7 ✈Cape Town 🚉🚌 ⓘ47 Church St; www.visitstellenbosch.org**

A centre of viticulture and learning, the historic university town of Stellenbosch is shaded by avenues of ancient oaks and its streets are lined with venerable buildings in the Cape Dutch architecture style.

The heart of the Winelands, Stellenbosch was founded in 1679 and is the cradle of Afrikaner culture. Its proud educational heritage began in 1863 with the establishment of the Dutch Reformed Theological Seminary. The Stellenbosch College, completed in 1886, was the forerunner of the university, which was established in 1918. Today, the university buildings are beautifully integrated with the surrounding historic monuments.

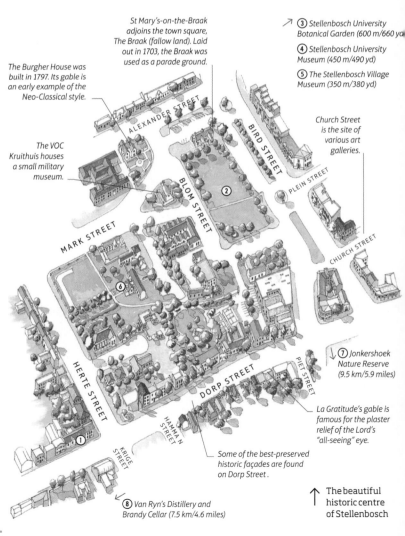

St Mary's-on-the-Braak adjoins the town square, The Braak (fallow land). Laid out in 1703, the Braak was used as a parade ground.

The Burgher House was built in 1797. Its gable is an early example of the Neo-Classical style.

The VOC Kruithuis houses a small military museum.

③ Stellenbosch University Botanical Garden (600 m/660 yd)

④ Stellenbosch University Museum (450 m/490 yd)

⑤ The Stellenbosch Village Museum (350 m/380 yd)

Church Street is the site of various art galleries.

⑦ Jonkershoek Nature Reserve (9.5 km/5.9 miles)

La Gratitude's gable is famous for the plaster relief of the Lord's "all-seeing" eye.

Some of the best-preserved historic façades are found on Dorp Street.

⑧ Van Ryn's Distillery and Brandy Cellar (7.5 km/4.6 miles)

↑ The beautiful historic centre of Stellenbosch

The quaint exterior of the Oom Samie se Winkel village store ↑

## ① Oom Samie se Winkel

 84 Dorp St ☎ 021 887 0797 ⏰ 9am–5pm Mon–Fri, 9am–4pm Sat, 9am–1pm Sun ⏳ 1 Jan, Good Fri, 25 Dec

This charming, restored Victorian shop, whose name means "Uncle Samie's Store", has been operating as a general store since 1904. Its original proprietor, bachelor Samie Volsteedt, lived in the house next door. The store, a Stellenbosch institution and a national monument, has an eclectic stock including bottled preserves, biltong and other South African delicacies, basketry, candles and curios, 19th-century butter churns, plates and kitchen utensils, and clothing

### Did You Know?

Stellenbosch is nicknamed "Eikestad", which means "City of Oaks".

and straw hats. Visitors may also browse in Samie's Victorian Wine Shop for a special vintage.

## ② Rhenish Complex

 Herte St

This lovely group of old buildings is representative of most of the architectural styles that have appeared in Stellenbosch over the centuries. Some parts of the Cape Dutch-style Rhenish Parsonage are much older than the date of 1815 that is marked on the building's gable. Leipoldt House, which was built around 1832, is an interesting combination of Cape Dutch and English Georgian architectural styles, while the Rhenish Church, on the south side of The Braak (the town's main square), was erected in 1823 by the Missionary Society of Stellenbosch as a training centre and school for enslaved and Coloured people. Also overlooking the Braak is St Mary's-on-the-Braak, an Anglican church that was completed in 1852.

# SHOP

### Karoo Classics

This centrally located family business specializes in handcrafted items made from mohair, ostrich leather, game skins and natural African fibres, most of which are sourced from small local contractors.

🏠 Church St
🌐 karooclassics.com

### Vineyard Connection

A must-visit for serious wine buyers, this emporium stocks 500 of the Cape's finest vintages, and offers global door-to-door shipping for overseas customers.

🏠 R44, between Stellenbosch and Paarl
🌐 vineyard connection.co.za

## Stellenbosch University Botanical Garden

🏠 Van Riebeeck St ⏰ 8am-4pm daily 🌐 sun.ac.za

Founded in the 1920s, these gardens have a fine collection of ferns, orchids and bonsai trees, as well as tropical and succulent plants housed in four glasshouses. There is a pleasant tearoom under the shade of a red-flowering gum tree *(Corymbia ficifolia)*, and university students can be seen revising on the lawns.

## Stellenbosch University Museum

🏠 52 Ryneveld St ⏰ 9am-4:30pm Mon-Sat 🚫 Good Fri, 25 Dec 🌐 sun.ac.za

The interesting exhibition at the Stellenbosch University Museum focuses on anthropology, cultural history and art. Of particular interest to many visitors are the prehistoric artifacts, reproductions of San rock art, and crafted utensils and ritual objects from South, West and Central Africa. There are also a number of paintings depicting the Cape in the 19th century.

→
Soaking up the scenery during a hike through the Jonkershoek Nature Reserve

## The Stellenbosch Village Museum

🏠 18 Ryneveld St ⏰ 9am-5pm Mon-Sat, 10am-1pm Sun (to 4pm Sun Sep-Mar) 🚫 Good Fri, Easter Sun, 25 Dec 🌐 stelmus.co.za

This complex features houses dating from Stellenbosch's early settlement years to the 1920s, although the later houses are not open to the public. Schreuder House was built in 1709 by Sebastian Schreuder. It is the oldest of the homes and shows the

💬 INSIDER TIP
**Self-Guided Walk**

The best way to explore Stellenbosch's historic buildings is by walking. A brochure for a self-guided walk is available from the tourist information centre on Church Street.

spartan, simple lifestyle of the early settlers. Bletterman House belonged to a wealthy 18th-century magistrate, while the elegant Grosvenor House dates back to 1782, with later additions representing the Classicism of the 1800s. The interiors of the Victorian-style Bergh House reflect the comfortable lifestyle of a wealthy burgher of the 1850s.

## Toy and Miniature Museum

🏠 Market St ⏰ 9am-4:30pm Mon-Fri, 9am-2pm Sat 🚫 Good Fri, 25 Dec 🌐 stelmus.co.za

Housed in the Rhenish Parsonage of 1815, this museum offers a world of

↑ An exhibition hall at the fascinating Stellenbosch University Museum

# EAT

### Die Wijnhuis
This bar serves 300-plus wines, along with craft beers and light meals and tapas.

**Cnr Church and Andringa sts**
**wijnhuis.co.za**

®®®

### Kleine Zalze
Oak-shaded gourmet restaurant using seasonal local ingredients.

**Kleine Zalze Estate, on the R44 to Strand**
**kleinezalze.co.za**

®®®

# STAY

### Oude Werf
Established in 1802, this hotel is steeped in character and has a fine-dining restaurant.

**30 Church St**
**oudewerf.co.za**

®®®

### Boschendal Farm
Secluded self-catering cottages set in the beautiful grounds of the Cape's second-oldest wine estate.

**Helshoogte Rd**
**boschendal.com**

®®®

### Stumble Inn
This central backpackers lodge has a pool and runs wine tours and hiking excursions.

**12 Market St**
**stumbleinn backpackers.co.za**

®®®

enchantment for both young and old. It displays an amazing collection of toys, such as dolls and toy motor cars, and also contains a number of finely detailed and exquisite 1:12 scale miniature rooms, each with delicate filigree work.

⑦

## Jonkershoek Nature Reserve

**Jonkershoek Rd** **8am-6pm daily** **Heavy rains**
**capenature.co.za**

The Jonkershoek Nature Reserve lies in a valley 10 km (6 miles) southeast of Stellenbosch. The valley is flanked by *fynbos*, which in spring and summer includes tiny pink and white ericas, blushing bride (*Serruria florida*) and the king protea. Elsewhere, the waterfalls and streams of the Eerste River provide abundant water for hikers, mountain bikers and horse riders. For the less energetic, there is a 12-km

(7-mile) scenic drive into the mountains. Baboons and dassies may be sighted, along with the elusive klipspringer if you are lucky.

⑧

## Van Ryn's Distillery and Brandy Cellar

**R310 from Stellenbosch, exit 33** **Hours vary, check website** **Public hols** **vanryn.co.za**

The rich history of Van Ryn's Distillery and Brandy Cellar in the heart of the Vlottenburg Valley just southwest of Stellenbosch dates back to 1845 when the Dutch immigrant Jan van Ryn arrived at the Cape. Today, well-known local brands Van Ryn and Viceroy are made here, and guided tours introduce the visitor to the intricate art of brandy production. A tasting is included in which brandy is paired with hand-made Belgian chocolate and Brazilian coffee.

**Housed in the Rhenish Parsonage of 1815, the Toy and Miniature Museum offers a world of enchantment for both young and old.**

**②**

# STELLENBOSCH WINELANDS

**🗺B7** **📍Stellenbosch** **ℹ️www.winelands.co.za; www.wineroute.co.za**

The Stellenbosch wine route was launched in April 1971 by the vintners of three prominent estates: Spier, Simonsig and Delheim. Today, the route comprises a great number of estates, and tastings and cellar tours are offered throughout the week at most of the vineyards.

①⊘🍴

## Tokara

**🏠Off R310** **🕘9am-9pm daily** **🌐tokara.co.za**

Located up on the Helshoogte Pass, the Tokara estate has sweeping views across False Bay to Table Mountain. As well as excellent wines, the estate produces brandy and olive oil. The restaurant is housed in a striking elevated glass-and-steel cube with wonderful mountain views and tapestries by William Kentridge. The delicatessen has a child-friendly, sunny deck for breakfast and light meals, and sells Tokara's own olive oil and kalamata olives, as well as handmade Belgian chocolates and South African cheeses.

The public buildings are also a showcase for the work of local artists.

②⊘🍴🏠

## Spier Wine Estate

**🏠N2, then R310** **🕘Tastings: 9am-5pm daily (to 7pm in summer)** **🌐spier.co.za**

Bounded by the Eerste River, the Spier Wine Estate made its first wine in 1712. Spier grows all the major South African red grape varietals – Merlot, Cabernet, Shiraz and Pinotage – and produces a good range of everyday reds and whites, along with some award-winning winemaker's specials aimed at connoisseurs. There is plenty to do at this

family-friendly estate besides wine tasting. Gourmet dining is on offer at Eight Restaurant, while at the Farm Kitchen deli you can assemble (or prebook) a picnic to enjoy on the lawns beside the lake. You

↑ Enjoying some of Spier's wines in the estate's airy tasting room

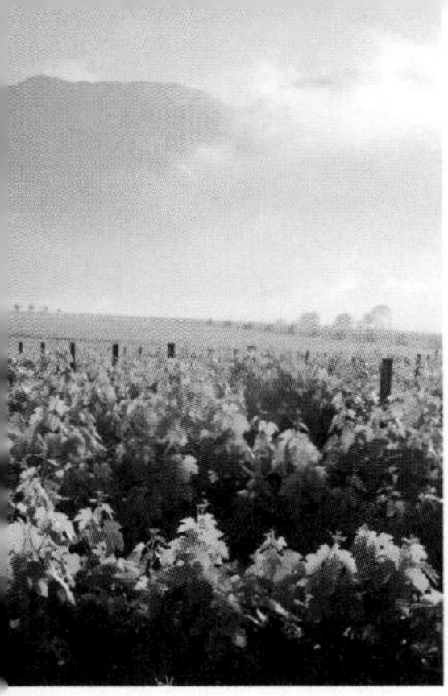

↑ The lush green vines of the picturesque Stellenbosch Winelands

can walk around the Protea Garden, visit Eagle Encounters (a bird of prey rehabilitation centre) and take a self-guided audio tour that tells the story of Sannie de Goede, a fictional woman enslaved on the estate in the 19th century. There is also a luxury hotel with a spa open to day visitors.

③

## Vergelegen

**Somerset West, Lourensford Rd from R44 8am-5pm daily Good Fri, 1 May, 25 Dec vergelegen.co.za**

The vines and the five old camphor trees in front of this estate's magnificent manor house were planted in 1700, when the property belonged to Cape Governor Willem Adriaan van der Stel. Today the manor is filled with period furniture and fine paintings, a tasting room, a shop, displays on the history of the estate, and two restaurants: Camphors at Vergelegen is the formal à la carte option and Stables at Vergelegen is a café/bistro open for breakfast, lunch and teas. From November to April, picnics complete with white tablecloths can be arranged under the shade of van der Stel's camphor trees.

④

## Boschendal

**On R45 Manor House: 9:30am-5pm daily; wine tastings: 10am-4:30pm daily boschendal.com**

Set in a pretty green valley, the Boschendal Estate ranks among the oldest and most enjoyable of Wineland destinations. It was founded in 1685, when Simon van der Stel granted a farm named "Bossendaal" to Jean le Long, a French Huguenot who planted the first vines there.

Reached via a beautiful tree-lined drive, the H-shaped manor house – a magnificent example of Cape Dutch architecture constructed in 1812 – is now a museum featuring vintage furniture. Boschendal also features a wine-tasting facility, a wine shop, and a classy restaurant serving farm-to-table food and irresistible French-style picnics on the lawn. Activities include informative guided tours of the organic fruit and vegetable gardens, hiking and running trails, and mountain bike and horseback excursions.

TOP 5

### BEST OF THE REST

**Saxenburg**

C1 saxenburg.co.za

The terroir at award-winning Saxenburg is ideally suited to Shiraz.

**Neethlingshof**

C1 neethlingshof.co.za

A famous avenue of pines leads to this iconic gabled homestead.

**Thelema**

C1 thelema.co.za

A family-run estate atop the Helshoogte Pass.

**Seven Sisters Vineyards**

C1 sevensisters.co.za

Owned by the seven sisters of the Brutus family.

**Delheim**

C1 delheim.com

Delheim's brick wine cellar is particularly atmospheric.

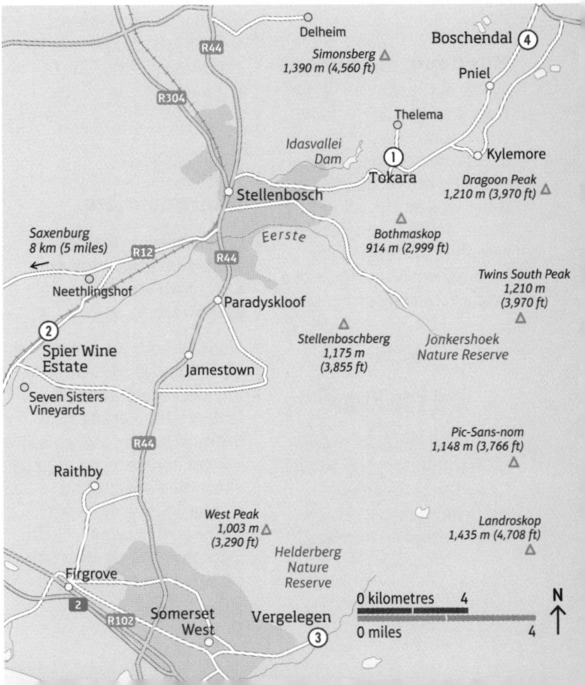

↑ The scenic surrounds of Franschhoek, home to numerous vineyards

**3**

# FRANSCHHOEK

B7 ✈ Cape Town 🛈 62 Huguenot St; www.franschhoek.org.za

This beautiful valley encircled by the Franschhoek and Groot Drakenstein mountains was settled by several French Huguenot families in 1694. Its main attraction, besides an exquisite setting, is its gourmet cuisine, accompanied by the area's excellent wines. Around 30 restaurants offer superb Malay, country and Provençale dishes.

## ① Huguenot Monument

Visible at the top end of the main street is the Huguenot Monument, unveiled in 1948 to commemorate the arrival of the French settlers. Here, a wide, semicircular colonnade frames three tall arches representing the Holy Trinity. Before them is the figure of a woman standing on a globe,

### Did You Know?

Franschhoek's French heritage is reflected in the town's name, which means "French Corner" in Dutch.

with her feet on France. On a tall spire that surmounts the central arch is the "Sun of Righteousness".

---

## ②  Haute Cabrière

🏠 Lambrechts Rd 🕘 9am–5pm Mon–Fri, 10am–4pm Sat, 11am–4pm Sun 🌐 cabriere.co.za

Franschhoek's wine route was established in 1980 with five founder cellars, and today features 20 estates. One of the most memorable to visit is Haute Cabrière. Here, after an interesting cellar tour, a sommelier cleanly shears the neck off a bottle of Pierre Jourdan sparkling wine with a sabre – an old technique

known as sabrage – before serving the wine. The estate's supremely elegant cellar restaurant is regularly named one of the top ten places to eat in South Africa.

↑ A barrel-lined cellar at the Haute Cabrière wine estate

## Huguenot Memorial Museum

📍 Lambrecht St 🕐 9am-4pm Mon-Fri, 10am-4pm Sat, 1:30-4:30pm Sun & public hols 🌐 museum.co.za

This museum celebrates the Cape's Huguenot heritage. Some 270 Huguenots fled here from France in 1685, when King Louis XIV revoked the 1598 Edict of Nantes permitting freedom of worship to Protestants.

Displays in this excellent museum document the daily life of the settlers, who brought with them skills as farmers and viticulturists. Of special note is a collection of old Bibles, including one dated 1636.

## Franschhoek Motor Museum

📍 L'Ormarins Wine Estate, on the R45 🕐 10am-5pm Mon-Fri, 10am-4pm Sat-Sun 🌐 fmm.co.za

Located in the prestigious L'Ormarins Estate, this museum is a magnet for car enthusiasts. It charts the evolution of the automobile with memorabilia and a collection of some 220 vehicles (including bicycles and motorcycles), more than 80 of which will be on show at any one time. Rare vehicles in the collection include an 1898 Beeston motor tricycle and a 2003 Ferrari Enzo.

# EAT

### Le Quartier Français
This plush boutique hotel has stylish rooms and suites, but it is best known for its dazzling and multiple award-winning restaurant.

📍 Cnr Berg and Wilhelmina sts 🌐 leeucollection.com/SA/le-quartier-francais

Ⓡ Ⓡ Ⓡ

### Otter's Bend Lodge
A unique lodge located on a farm on the Franschhoek River, an easy walk from the town centre.

📍 Dassenberg Rd 🌐 ottersbendlodge.co.za

Ⓡ Ⓡ Ⓡ

### Café des Arts
Simple food using fresh local ingredients served in a relaxed courtyard setting, with a good local wine selection.

📍 7 Reservoir St West 🌐 cafedesarts.co.za

Ⓡ Ⓡ Ⓡ

### The Werf Restaurant
A fine dining restaurant next to Boschendal's historic manor house, Werf offers excellent wine pairings.

📍 Helshoogte Rd 🌐 boschendal.com

Ⓡ Ⓡ Ⓡ

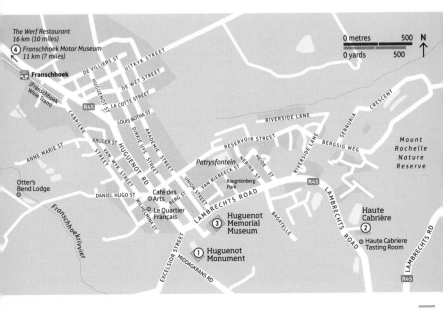

**4**

# WEST COAST NATIONAL PARK

⚠ A6  🚪 Gates on the R27 and Langebaan  🕐 National park: Sep-Mar: 7am-7pm daily, Apr-Aug: 7am-6pm daily; Postberg Nature Reserve: open only during flower season (usually Aug-Sep)  🌐 sanparks.org

**Extending around the sparkling salt waters of the Langebaan Lagoon, this pristine coastline is famous for its spring wildflowers. The park's many wetland bird species are a draw for bird enthusiasts, and its recreational zone is popular with watersports fans.**

The West Coast National Park encompasses Langebaan Lagoon, the islands Schaapen, Jutten, Marcus and Malgas, and the Postberg Nature Reserve, which is opened to the public each spring, when it is carpeted with colourful wildflowers such as daisies and gazanias. The park is one of South Africa's most important wetlands, harbouring some 250 species of waterbird including plovers, herons, ibis, and black oyster-catchers. Offshore islands support breeding colonies of ten different species. Terrestrial wildlife that can be found in the park includes antelope species such as elands, kudus, bontebok and springbok, as well as zebras. The park can be explored by car or on hiking trails; accommodation consists of chalets and houseboats on the lagoon.

> 💬 INSIDER TIP
> **Watersports at Langebaan**
>
> Langebaan Lagoon is ideal for watersports, particularly kite- and wind-surfing, kayaking, waterskiing and sailing. Watersports centres in the town rent out equipment and offer lessons.

↑ Strolling through the spring wildflowers in the West Coast National Park

↑ Lesser flamingoes, one of hundreds of bird species that can be found within the park

↑ Geelbek Homestead, home of the park's visitor centre and a restaurant specializing in Cape cooking

## TOP 5 LAGOON BIRDS

**Cape Cormorant**
Abundant on the coast, they feed on pelagic shoaling fish.

**Great White Pelican**
Langebaan houses one of a handful of white pelican breeding colonies in southern Africa.

**Hartlaub's Gull**
Endemic to the West Coast, this gull forages for food along the shore in the early morning.

**Lesser Flamingo**
Distinguished from greater flamingoes by their smaller size and black wings.

**Curlew Sandpiper**
Its curved bill enables it to probe for crustaceans.

# EXPERIENCE MORE

### ⑤

## Paarl

🅰B7 ✈Cape Town
🚌🚐 ℹ216 Main
Rd; www.paarl
online.com

In 1687, farms were allocated to early Dutch colonists in the pretty Berg River Valley, which is flanked to the north by Paarl Mountain. The name Paarl comes from the Dutch *peerlbergh* (pearl mountain), given to the outcrops by early Dutch explorer Abraham Gabbema when he spotted the three

smooth domes after a rain shower. Mica chips embedded in the granite glistened in the sun, giving it the appearance of a shiny pearl. The town of the same name was established in 1690.

Paarl is a major player in the industry of the Western Cape, but its many tree-lined streets and graceful gabled homes still lend it a certain country charm. The town's Main Street makes a good starting point from which to explore. A number of well-preserved 18th- and 19th-century Cape Dutch and

Georgian houses are found along both sides of Main Street, some of the later ones displaying marked Victorian architectural influences.

La Concorde, a stately Neo-Classical structure built in 1956, is the headquarters of the Kooperatiewe Wijnbouwers Vereeniging (KWV), the Cooperative Wine Farmers Association. The KWV, now privatized, was a controlling body that aimed to administer wine production, check quality and develop export markets.

←

The soaring column of the Afrikaans Language Monument

↑ Orderly rows of vineyards, which criss-cross the Paarl region

Further along Main Street, the **Paarl Museum** presents historical aspects of the town. Exhibits include a collection of stinkwood chairs and a Dutch linen press. An excellent porcelain collection features VOC, Imari, Kang Hsi, and Canton pieces, and the kitchen is crammed with authentic utensils and furniture. Temporary displays on a variety of related themes, such as the Khoe, are arranged regularly.

Picturesque wine farms spread out to either side of the imposing Paarl Mountain. The region's vineyards produce about one-fifth of South Africa's total wine crop, and many offer wine tasting and sales most days. Certain farms arrange cellar tours by appointment only. Just off Paarl's Main Road lies **Laborie Estate**, first granted to a Huguenot settler in 1688. In 1774 it was acquired by Hendrick Louw, who built the Cape Dutch homestead on it. Today, Laborie is best known for producing Méthode Cap Classique sparkling wines.

Opposite La Concorde is Jan Phillips Drive, an 11-km (7-mile) route to Paarl Mountain. The 500 million-year-old massif is the world's second-largest granite outcrop, after Uluru in Australia, and can be climbed with the aid of handholds.

The entrance to the Paarl Mountain Nature Reserve also lies on Jan Phillips Drive. From here, visitors can gain access to the **Afrikaans Language Monument** (Afrikaanse Taalmonument). Designed by the architect Jan van Wyk, it was constructed around 1975, and is a tribute to the official recognition of the Afrikaans language 100 years earlier. The monument's various elements acknowledge the linguistic influence and contribution of a different culture.

**Paarl Museum**

⊛ 🏠 303 Main Rd 📞 021 872 2651 🕔 9am–4pm Mon–Fri, 9am–1pm Sat, 9am–2pm public hols 🔒 Good Fri, 25 Dec

**Laborie Estate**

⊛ ⊛ 🍷 🏠 Taillefer St, off Main Rd 🕔 Tastings: 9am–4:30pm Mon–Sat; 10am–3pm Sun 🔒 1 Jan, 25 Dec  laborie wines.co.za

**Afrikaans Language Monument**

⊛ ⊛ 🏠 11 Pastorie Ave 🕔 8:30am–4:45pm Mon–Fri 🔒 Public hols ⓦ taalmuseum.co.za

**TOP 5 PAARL VINEYARDS**

**Rhebokskloof Estate**
🅰 B7 ⓦ rhebokskloof.co.za
Named after the rhebok antelope that once lived in its valleys.

**Fairview**
🅰 B7 ⓦ fairview.co.za
Delicious goat's milk cheeses from the estate's Saanen goats are sold here.

**Rupert & Rothschild Vignerons**
🅰 B7 ⓦ rupert-rothschild vignerons.com
Combines French and local wine-making on the historic Huguenot farm of Fredericksburg.

**Avondale**
🅰 B7 ⓦ avondalewine.co.za
A top-quality organic producer, whose wines are allowed to develop naturally as possible.

**Nederburg**
🅰 B7 ⓦ nederburg.com
Famous for its annual Wine Auction.

# Robertson

**⚑B7** **ℹ** Cnr Voortrekker & Reitz sts; www.robertson tourism.co.za

Established as a town in 1852, Robertson lies in the Breede River Valley, where sunny slopes create perfect conditions for vineyards and orchards. As well as wine and grapes, dried fruit is a major industry here. The Robertson Wine Route – a section of the renowned Route 62 (p210) – comprises more than 50 cellars, many of which are acclaimed for their choice Chardonnays.

Situated in a townhouse originally constructed in 1860, the **Robertson Museum** is furnished in period style and has some interesting displays relating to local history and culture.

### Robertson Museum

⌂ 50 Paul Kruger St
☎ 023 626 3681
🕑 9am–noon Mon–Sat

---

# Worcester

**⚑B7** **🚉** Worcester Station **ℹ** Mountain Mill Mall, Entrance 2; www. worcester tourism.com

This city, named after the Marquis of Worcester, brother of one-time Cape governor Lord Charles Somerset, lies

**INSIDER TIP**
**Boesmanskloof Hiking Trail**

This five-hour trail just south of Robertson follows a gap through the Riviersonderend mountains. The views are impressive, and the Oakes Falls, near Greyton, are ideal for swimming.

↑ A candlemaker using traditional methods at the fascinating Worcester Museum

some 110 km (68 miles) east of Cape Town. It is the biggest centre in the Breede River Valley and the largest producer of table grapes in South Africa. Its wineries produce a substantial amount of wine too, and Worcester is known for everyday affordable reds, whites and fortified wines. Twelve estates on the Worcester Wine and Olive Route are open for tastings and cellar tours, most in the Breede River Valley.

The attraction of a trip to Worcester is the drive through the Du Toitskloof Pass, which climbs to a height of 823 m (2,700 ft). Construction of the Huguenot Tunnel in 1988 shortened the pass by 11 km (7 miles), but the route still affords scenic views of Paarl and the Berg River Valley. At Church Square in Worcester, there is a Garden of Remembrance designed by Hugo Naude; the World War I Memorial; and a stone cairn erected at the time of the symbolic *Ossewa* (ox wagon) Trek of 1938, undertaken to commemorate the Great Trek of the 19th century (p63). Worcester's Dutch Reformed

Church was built in 1832. Its imposing Gothic-style steeple was added in 1927 after the original blew away in gales.

The open-air **Worcester Museum** is a re-creation of an early Cape farm, complete with a shepherd's hut, horse mill, labourer's cottage and harness room. Visitors can watch bread being baked outdoors, a traditional blacksmith at work and seasonal activities such as brandy distillation.

The **Karoo Desert National Botanical Garden**, a short drive north of Worcester, contains plants that thrive in a semi-desert environment. Jewel-bright mesembryanthemums are lovely in spring, while the unusual year-round species include the prehistoric welwitschias, and the *halfmens* (half-human) and quiver trees. One area features plants grouped by regional and climatic zones. The succulent plant collection, the largest in Africa, is ranked by the Organization for Succulent Plant Study as one of the most authentic of its kind in the world. There is also a trail with Braille text signs.

> **Established as a town in 1852, Robertson lies in the Breede River Valley, where sunny slopes create perfect conditions for vineyards and orchards.**

### Worcester Museum

🏛 Robertson Rd
🕐 9am–4pm Mon–Fri
🚫 Good Fri, 25 Dec, 1 Jan
🌐 worcestermuseum.org.za

### Karoo Desert National Botanical Garden

🦋🍷⚠🚻 🏛 Roux Rd
🕐 7am–6pm daily 🌐 sanbi.org

---

## ❽ Montagu

📍 B5 🛈 27 Bath St; www.
montagu-ashton.info

The charm of Montagu lies in its many houses dating back to the early 1850s. In Long Street alone there are 14 national monuments. But the area's best known feature is the thermal springs 2 km (1 mile) from town, with a temperature of 43° C/109° F.

The scenery of the northern edge of the Langeberg range has led to the establishment of trails for hikers, mountain bikers and 4WD enthusiasts. The route to Montagu from Robertson passes through a

---

### PINOTAGE WINE-MAKING

Pinotage is a unique South African cultivar developed in 1925 by Stellenbosch University professor Abraham Perold, from a cross of Pinot Noir and Cinsaut (then called Hermitage). The world's first commercially bottled Pinotage was released in 1961 under the Lanzerac label, and the fruity wine has since then achieved much international acclaim.

16-m- (52-ft-) long tunnel, above which stands the ruined Sidney Fort built by the British during the South African War.

---

## ❾ Tulbagh

📍 B6 🛈 4 Church St; www.
tulbaghtourism.co.za

In 1700, Governor Willem Adriaan van der Stel initiated a new settlement in the Breede River Valley, naming it Tulbagh after his predecessor. It is South Africa's fourth-oldest town.

Encircled by the Witzenberg and Winterhoek mountains, in 1969 the town was hit by an earthquake measuring 6.3 on the Richter scale. Eight people died and many historic buildings were badly damaged. The disaster resulted in a five-year restoration project undertaken along Church Street, which is lined with no less than 32 18th- and 19th-century Victorian and Cape Dutch homes. The oldest building, Oude Kerk (old church) Volksmuseum, dates back to 1743 and contains the original pulpit, pews and Bible. De Oude Herberg, Tulbagh's first boarding house (1885), is now a guesthouse and restaurant.

↑ Whitewashed buildings from the 18th and 19th centuries along Church Street in Tulbagh

# STAY

### Bushman's Kloof
A first-rate resort in a private reserve rich in endemic wildlife and rock art.

🏠 Agert Palhuis Paa, Clanwilliam
🌐 bushmanskloof.co.za

®®®

---

### Saldanha Bay Protea Hotel
This harbourfront hotel is well located for exploring West Coast National Park.

🏠 15B Main Rd, Saldanha 🌐 protea.marriott.com

®®®

---

### Paternoster Dunes Boutique Guest House
A friendly guesthouse with a superb ocean-front setting.

🏠 18 Sonkwas, Paternoster 🌐 paternosterdunes.co.za

®®®

---

**10**

## Bloubergstrand

🅰 B7

Literally "Blue Mountain Beach", Bloubergstrand owes its name to the peerless views it offers to majestic Table Mountain, 10 km (6 miles) to the southwest across Table Bay. Weather permitting, the iconic mountain's unmistakeable flat-topped profile is seen at its very best advantage from the beach, making Bloubergstrand one of the most photographed spots anywhere in the vicinity of Cape Town. Even without the draw of the mountain views, though, Bloubergstrand would be a superb beach. Wide and sandy for the most part, there are enough rocky protrusions to keep it visually interesting. As with South Africa's other Atlantic beaches, the beach can be rather exposed in windy weather and the water is somewhat icy, but it remains a firm favourite with walkers and watersports enthusiasts.

**11**

## Paternoster

🅰 A6  🛈 Seeduiker St; www.visitpaternoster.com

One of the West Coast's oldest villages, Paternoster is a cluster of traditional fishermen's cottages whose name reputedly refers to the Lord's Prayer, recited by shipwrecked Portuguese sailors in the 17th century. It is the gateway to the scenic **Cape Columbine Nature Reserve**, which protects a wild

---

> ### OPEN-AIR SEAFOOD FEASTS
> Along the West Coast, there are several open-air eating places known as *skerms* (Afrikaans for "shelters"). Reed roofs provide shade and mussel shells are used as utensils, but the major appeal is the fresh seafood on offer: smoked angelfish, snoek, mussel stews, *perlemoen* (abalone) and calamari.

 Dramatic views of Table Mountain, as seen from Bloubergstrand

estates and coops that offer tastings and sales around the Riebeek Valley, Malmesbury, Piketberg and Porterville.

### Swartland Wine and Olive Route

 Cnr Voortrekker & Church sts 8am–5pm Mon-Fri, 9am–2pm Sat swartlandwineandolives.co.za

### ⑬ Saldhana

A6 Van Riebeeck St; 022 715 1142

The largest town on the West Coast stands on the northern shore of Saldanha Bay, which is the country's deepest harbour. Named after one of the Portuguese captains who sailed to South Africa with Albuquerque's fleet in 1503, Saldanha is a down-to-earth spot whose economy is dominated by commercial fishing, a modern harbour built primarily to export iron ore, and an important naval base. It's also a great site for watersports. The Saldanha Nature Reserve, run through by four walking and cycling trails, is best visited in spring, when it hosts magnificent wildflower

coastline that bursts into spectacular bloom come August. Attractions include sea kayaking, a variety of birds and South Africa's only manually operated lighthouse.

### Cape Columbine Nature Reserve

 St Augustine Rd 022 752 2718 8am–4:30pm Mon-Fri, 8am–2pm Sat & Sun

### ⑫ Malmesbury

B6 3 Church St; www.malmesburytourism.co.za

Malmesbury, the heart of South Africa's wheatland, lies in the Swartland (black country), a term that has at times been attributed to the region's soil, and at other times to its renosterbush, a local shrub that turns a dark hue in winter. The wheatfields, with their velvety shoots rippling in the breeze are a lovely sight. Wine is also produced in the region. The **Swartland Wine and Olive Route** features 24

 **HIDDEN GEM**
**San Heritage**

Learn about San culture at !Khwa ttu *(www.khwattu.org)*, an award-winning heritage centre and nature reserve with a museum, shop, restaurant, accommodation, and walking and mountain-biking trails.

displays and offers good land-based whale-watching opportunities.

### ⑭ Darling

A6 Pastorie St; www.hello darling.org.za

Darling is surrounded by a farming region of wheatfields, vineyards, sheep and dairy cattle, but is best-known for its spring flower show.

The town also lays claim to satirist Pieter-Dirk Uys, who has gained fame for his portrayal of his female alter ego, Evita Bezuidenhout, fictitious ambassadress of Baphetikosweti. His bar, **Evita se Perron** (Evita's platform), is set on a defunct railway platform and attracts crowds to hear analyses of local politics.

### Evita se Perron

 8 Arcadia St evita.co.za

A sculpture outside the popular Evita se Perron comedy venue in Darling

## Clanwilliam

**⬛B6 🛈 Main Rd; www. clanwilliam.info**

Clanwilliam is the head-quarters of the *rooibos* (red bush) tea industry. The shoots of the wild shrub have for centuries been used by the Khoe-San people of the remote Wupperthal valley to make a caffeine-free tea that is low in tannin and also considered to have medicinal properties.

Clanwilliam Dam, encircled by the Cederberg Mountains, stretches for 18 km (11 miles) and is popular with water-skiers. Wooden holiday cabins line the banks, and a pleasant campsite has been established right at the water's edge.

## Citrusdal

**⬛B6 🛈 89 Muller St; www.citrusdal.info**

Frost-free winters and the Olifants River Irrigation Scheme have made Citrusdal South Africa's third-largest citrus district. The first orchard was planted with seedlings from Van Riebeeck's garden at the foot of Table Mountain (*p126*). One tree, after bearing fruit for some 250 years, is now a national monument. The Goede Hoop Citrus Co-operative has initiated scenic mountain bike trails

>  **INSIDER TIP**
> **Buchu Tea Tour**
>
> Buchu is a rare fynbos shrub with medicinal qualities. On this two-hour tour of Skimmel-berg organic farm (*www.skimmelberg. co.za*) you can see buchu growing in its natural habitat, before ending with a delicious tasting.

↑ The clamouring gannet colony at Lambert's Bay Bird Island Nature Reserve

around Citrusdal, such as the old Ceres and Piekenierskloof passes, and there are also several hiking trails situated close to town.

## Lambert's Bay

**⬛A6 🛈 Main Rd; www. lambertsbay.co.za**

This little fishing town, an hour's drive west of Clanwilliam on the R364, was named after Rear Admiral Sir Robert Lambert, a senior Royal Navy officer who monitored the marine survey of this section of coastline. For visitors, the main attraction is **Lambert's Bay Bird Island Nature Reserve**, about 100 m (328 ft) offshore. It is accessible via a breakwater-cum-harbour wall. The island is a breeding ground for thousands of African penguins, Cape cormorants and the striking Cape gannet with its yellow-painted face. There is a small museum, and a viewing tower allows visitors to remain unobtrusive while observing the birds' behaviour. The reserve is the world's only gannet breeding ground easily accessible to the public.

**Lambert's Bay Bird Island Nature Reserve**
 ⏰ 8am–6pm daily
🖥 capenature.co.za

## Bushmans Kloof Wilderness Reserve

**⬛B6 🛈 www.bushmans kloof.co.za**

Extending across an area of 7,500 ha (18,500 acres) over the northeastern foothills of the Cederberg, Bushman's Kloof is a multiple award-winning wilderness reserve centred on a sump-tuous five-star spa resort. Explorable on foot or by canoe, mountain bike or open 4WD, the ruggedly scenic reserve protects more than 750 *fynbos*, forest and Karoo plants as well as 150 bird species including the striking black harrier. Other wildlife includes the endemic bonte-bok, red hartebeest and Cape mountain zebra, along with leopard, bat-eared fox, Cape fox, African wild cat, caracal and aardwolf. More than 100 prehistoric rock art sites are exclusively accessible to overnight guests, the most spectacular being the beautifully pre-served Elephant Hunt Panel.

**⓳**

# Cederberg

**🅰 B6** **ℹ️ Cape Nature office, Algeria; www.capenature. co.za**

The Cederberg range is a surreal wilderness of sandstone peaks that have been eroded over the millennia into jagged formations. It is reached from the north via Pakhuis Pass and the Biedouw Valley, 50 km (31 miles) from Clanwilliam; from the south, it can be accessed via the N7 from Citrusdal.

The range is part of the Cederberg Wilderness Area, which was proclaimed in 1973 and covers 710 sq km (274 sq miles). Its main attraction is its recreational appeal – walks, hikes, camping and wonderful views (anyone wishing to hike or stay in the area will require a permit). The southern part, in particular, is popular for its dramatic rock formations, inlcuding the Maltese Cross and the Wolfberg Arch. The snow protea (*Protea cryophila*), endemic to the upper reaches of the range, occurs on the Sneeuberg which, at 2,028 m (6,654 ft), is the highest peak. The Clanwilliam cedar, after which the area was named, is an endemic species that is protected in the Cederberg Wilderness Area – some 8,000 trees are planted annually to ensure its survival.

At the southern end of the Cederberg is the **Kagga Kamma Private Nature Reserve**, where visitors can go on game drives, view San rock art and take part in activities such as bird-watching and stargazing. Accommodation is in thatched chalets, unique

## ROCK FORMATIONS OF THE CEDERBERG

During the Palaeozoic pre-Karoo period several hundred million years ago, the formations that later became the Cape Folded Mountains were under water. Of the elements comprising these Cape formations, Table Mountain sandstone was the most resilient. In the Karoo Period, tectonic forces produced the rumpled Cape mountains. Subsequent erosion wore away the soft rock, leaving the harder layer and resulting in the Cederberg's twisted landscape.

cave rooms and a campsite. Pre-booked day visitors are welcome.

**Kagga Kamma Private Nature Reserve**
🔷 🍷 🏠 🅰 Southern Cederberg 🕐 Daily
🌐 kaggakamma.co.za

↓ The spectacular Cederberg rock formations, often tackled by expert climbers (*inset*)

# NORTHERN CAPE AND FREE STATE

Prior to European settlement, the Northern Cape's harsh climate ensured it was one of the last places on earth to be inhabited by hunter-gatherers whose lifestyles differed little from those of our prehistoric forebears. Known collectively to outsiders by derogatory names such as Bushmen, these ancient San cultures fell victim to a succession of genocidal incursions that took place over the course of the 18th and 19th centuries. Ordered by the Dutch and British, the raids were carried out by Khoe pastoralists and "Basters" who had escaped from slavery, bearing imported firearms, farmers with drought-resistant merino sheep, and fortune seekers bound for the copper mines of Springbok/ Okiep.

The provincial capital Kimberley was established in 1871 to exploit the world's richest diamond vein, while the implementation of the ambitious Orange River Irrigation Scheme in the 1960s transformed Upington into a major centre of agriculture and wine production. Despite this, the Northern Cape remains very thinly populated, accounting for almost a third of the country's surface area but only 2 per cent of the population.

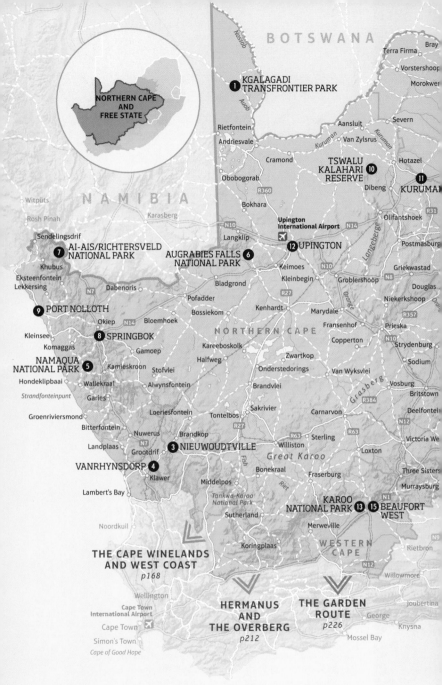

NORTHERN CAPE AND FREE STATE

BOTSWANA

Bray
Terra Firma
Vorstershoop
Morokwer

**1** KGALAGADI
TRANSFRONTIER PARK

Aansluit
Severn

Rietfontein
Andriesvale
Cramond
Van Zylsrus
Hotazel

Obobogorab
TSWALU
KALAHARI
RESERVE **10**

Bokhara
Dibeng
**11**
KURUMAN

Witpüts
Karasberg
Olifantshoek

Rosh Pinah
N10
Upington
International Airport
N14
Postmasburg

Sendelingsdrif
Langklip
**12** UPINGTON
Griekwastad

**7** AI-AIS/RICHTERSVELD
NATIONAL PARK
**6** AUGRABIES FALLS
NATIONAL PARK
Keimoes
Groblershoop
N8
Douglas

Khubus
R360
Kleinbegin
N10
Niekerkshoop
R357

Eksteenfontein
Lekkersing
Dabenoris
Bladgrond
Orange
Prieska

**9** PORT NOLLOTH
Pofadder
Kenhardt
Marydale
Copperton
N10
Strydenburg

Okiep
Bloemhoek
Bossiekom
NORTHERN CAPE
Fransenhof
Sodium

Kleinsee
**8** SPRINGBOK
Kareeboskolk
Van Wyksvlei
Vosburg

Komaggas
Gamoep
Halfweg
Zwartkop
Britstown

NAMAQUA
NATIONAL PARK **5**
Kamieskroon
Stofvlei
Onderstedorings
Grasberg
Deelfontei

Hondeklipbaai
Wallekraal
Alwynsfontein
Brandvlei
R384
N12

Strandfonteinpunt
Garies
Loeriesfontein
Sakrivier
Carnarvon
Victoria We

Groenriviersmond
Bitterfontein
Tontelbos
R27
Sterling
R63
Loxton
Three Sisters

Landplaas
Nuwerus
Brandkop
Williston
Great Karoo
Murraysburg

VANRHYNSDORP **4**
Grootdrif
**3** NIEUWOUDTVILLE
Bonekraal
Fraserburg

Klawer
Middelpos
Fish
Riet
KAROO
NATIONAL PARK **13** **15** BEAUFORT
WEST
N1

Lambert's Bay
Tankwa-Karoo
National Park
Sutherland
Merweville

Noordkuil
Koringplaas
WESTERN
CAPE
Rietbron

THE CAPE WINELANDS
AND WEST COAST
p168
N12
Willowmore

Wellington
HERMANUS
AND
THE OVERBERG
p212
THE GARDEN
ROUTE
p226
Joubertina

Cape Town
International Airport
George
Knysna

Cape Town
Simon's Town
Cape of Good Hope
Mossel Bay

Atlantic
Ocean

NAMIBIA

Nossob
Auob
Kuruman
Kurumen
Langeberge

0 kilometres    100
0 miles          100
N

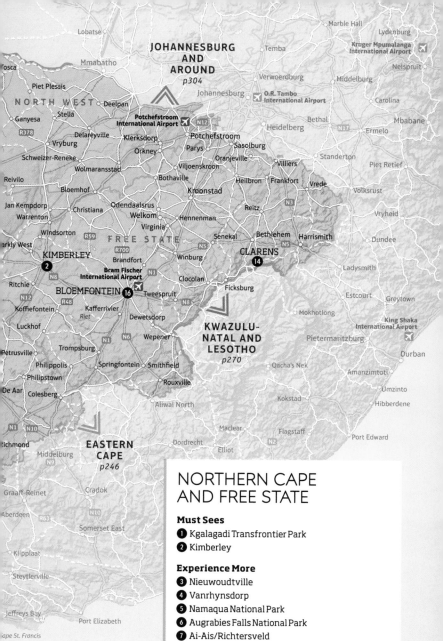

## NORTHERN CAPE AND FREE STATE

**Must Sees**
1. Kgalagadi Transfrontier Park
2. Kimberley

**Experience More**
3. Nieuwoudtville
4. Vanrhynsdorp
5. Namaqua National Park
6. Augrabies Falls National Park
7. Ai-Ais/Richtersveld National Park
8. Springbok
9. Port Nolloth
10. Tswalu Kalahari Reserve
11. Kuruman
12. Upington
13. Karoo National Park
14. Clarens
15. Beaufort West
16. Bloemfontein

**1**

# KGALAGADI TRANSFRONTIER PARK

**B3** ⌂ **R360, Upington** ⊕ **Hours vary, check website** 🅦 **sanparks.org**

An immense wilderness of grass-covered dunes traversed by two dry, ancient riverbeds, this national park is Africa's largest and extends for 34,390 sq km (13,278 sq miles), absorbing much of the distinctive red Kalahari desert. Jointly managed by South Africa and Botswana, the border within the park is unfenced and the wildlife is free to migrate.

From Upington the tarred R360 cuts a course across a landscape that seems devoid of human habitation until it reaches the southern entrance, largest rest camp and the park administrative headquarters at Twee Rivieren. Here there are chalets, a campsite, swimming pool and the park's only restaurant. Additionally, it has immigration facilities for those crossing between South Africa and Botswana or Namibia via the park. From Twee Rivieren, two gravel roads follow the dry courses of the Auob and Nossob rivers on their way to the other two main rest camps of Mata Mata and Nossob. There are also six wilderness camps in the dunes, accessible by 4WD only.

Although the Kgalagadi is located in a particularly arid region, wildlife is surprisingly plentiful, with an astonishing 19 species of carnivore present, including the black-maned Kalahari lion and honey badger. Several species of raptor – including tawny and bateleur eagles, plus the pale chanting goshawk – are also often sighted. A string of waterholes, pumped by solar or windmill power, sustain wildlife.

### Did You Know?

The Kalahari is classed as a desert because rain drains straight through the sand, leaving the surface bone dry.

1 Bateleur eagles spend around eight hours a day flying in search of food.

2 Lions in Kgalagadi have very large ranges, due to the low density of prey.

3 Leopards are among the many carnivores that freely roam the arid, sandy landscapes.

↑ Wave-like patterns in the park's unusual red sand, seen in the morning light

# LIFE IN THE DESERT

The Kalahari Desert forms part of a vast inland steppe that stretches from the Orange River (also known as the Gariep River) to the equator. It extends across portions of the Northern Cape and Namibia, and also covers much of Botswana. Rainfall in this region varies from 150 mm to 400 mm (6–16 inches) per year and is soon soaked up or simply evaporates. There is little surface water and the flora consists mainly of grass, shrubs and the hardy camelthorn acacias that line the dry beds of ancient rivers. Although the harsh landscape may appear to be lifeless, it supports an astonishing variety of wildlife.

## THE SAN

These nomads have inhabited southern Africa for over 20,000 years. However, their population has been severely diminished due to the impact of colonialism and apartheid, under which the San were designated as "Coloured" and forced to hide their heritage. A small community remains in the Northern Cape, living on land south of the Kgalagadi Transfrontier Park allocated to them in 1997. The modern age has severely affected their culture, limiting the San's hunting area and diminishing their food resources. Even in the remote reaches of Botswana, clans now live in settlements around waterholes – the nomadic lifestyle replaced by a sedentary existence. Before these camps were established, water and food were obtained from the bush: the San knew of 20 edible insects and 180 plants, roots and tubers, including fruits such as the Tsamma melon.

## Did You Know?

The Kalahari is the second-largest desert in Africa, after the Sahara.

↑ Seasonal river beds, such as that of the Auob, carry water only every few years

↑ A San family gather at their settlement in the desert

## DESERT ANIMALS

The wildlife of the Kalahari is superbly adapted to survive in this arid environment.

### Steppe Buzzard
Steppe buzzards are migrant visitors to the Kalahari, arriving in southern Africa during October and departing in March.

### Gemsbok
Gemsbok (oryx) feed on grass, leaves and roots, and can do without water for many days. The animal's temperature fluctuates in response to climatic changes.

### Kalahari Lion
Kalahari lions are unique to the Kgalagadi Transfrontier Park, and have learned to depend on smaller prey, such as bat-eared foxes, when antelopes migrate.

### Bat-Eared Fox
Bat-eared foxes' large ears allow them to detect underground prey, such as beetle larvae, in the barren areas.

### Brown Hyena
Restricted to the drier desert regions of southern Africa, the brown hyena can survive without fresh water for extended periods of time.

### Barking Gecko
Barking geckos herald sunset in the desert by emitting a series of sharp clicking sounds.

### Scarab Beetle
The *Sparrmannia flava* scarab beetle has a furry coat that enables it to remain active at night when temperatures drop.

### Puff Adder
The highly venomous puff adder leaves deep, straight tracks that can sometimes be seen on the Kalahari sand dunes.

### Namaqua Sandgrouse
Namaqua sandgrouse males fly distances of up to 60 km (37 miles) every three to five days to drink and soak their specially adapted chest feathers. The water retained in these feathers sustains the chicks.

1 Steppe buzzard.

2 Gemsbok.

3 Kalahari lion.

4 Bat-eared fox.

5 Namaqua sandgrouse.

**②**

# KIMBERLEY

⛰D4 ✈🏠🚌 📍121 Bultfontein Rd; www.kimberley.co.za

The first Diamond Rush in the Kimberley district took place in 1869 when diamonds were found in the walls of a house, and by 1873 the town had become home to 50,000 miners. Famed for its "Big Hole" – an enormous open diamond mine – Kimberly today has an attractive historic centre with an interesting collection of museums and galleries.

**①**

## The Big Hole: Kimberley Mine Museum

🏠 West Circular Rd
🕐 8am-5pm daily 🚫 25 Dec
🌐 thebighole.co.za

Kimberley Mine, or the Big Hole, as it is known, is the only one of four diamond mines in the Kimberley area that is still open. Within two years of the discovery of diamond-bearing kimberlite pipes in 1871, the mining claims were being worked by up to 30,000 miners at a time. With little more than picks and shovels to aid them, the miners dug deep into the earth, and by 1889,

the hole had reached an astounding depth of 150 m (488 ft). The deeper the miners delved, the more difficult it became to extract the diamond-bearing soil, and the chaotic arrangement of cables, precipitous paths and claims lying at varying heights encouraged the miners to form syndicates. These groupings were later acquired by Cecil John Rhodes.

Centred around the Big Hole, the Kimberley Mine Museum tells South Africa's diamond-mining history through several elements. The Old Mining Village consists of cobbled streets lined with buildings dating to the late 19th century, while the 90-m (295-ft) viewing platform

over the Big Hole allows visitors to look into the murky lake below. There is also a model of a mine shaft and the Real Diamond Display holds replicas of uncut stones.

---

**②**

## Duggan-Cronin Gallery

🏠 Egerton Rd 📞 053 839 2700 🕐 9am-4pm Mon-Fri

This gallery contains 8,000 photographs of anthropological interest taken over 20 years by Alfred Duggan-Cronin from 1897.

↑ A tram in Kimberley Mine Museum's Old Mining Village

↑ Kimberley's famous Big Hole, once an important diamond mine

**③**

## Wildebeest Kuil Rock Art Centre

🏠 R31, 16 km (10 miles) from central Kimberley
🕐 9am-6pm Mon-Fri, by appt only on Sat & Sun

One of South Africa's finest prehistoric rock engraving sites, Wildebeest Kuil Rock Art Centre is a dolerite hill set on San community land. There are more than 400 individual engravings here, some thought to be several thousand years old. Most engravings depict large animals such as elephant, rhino and eland. Guided tours by local community members provide fascinating insight into the shamanistic rituals with which this ancient art is associated.

**④**

## William Humphreys Art Gallery

🏠 1 Cullinan Crescent, Civic Centre 🕐 8am-3:30pm Mon-Fri, 10am-4:45pm Sat 🚫 Good Fri, 25 & 26 Dec, 1 Jan 🌐 whag.co.za

Situated in the grounds of the Oppenheimer Memorial Gardens, this gallery houses a superb collection of paintings and other artworks. It covers a broad spectrum of styles, ranging from 17th-century Dutch and Flemish Old Masters to works by contemporary South African artists.

**⑤**

## McGregor Museum

🏠 7-11 Atlas St, Belgravia
🕐 9am-5pm Mon-Sat, by appt only on Sun
🌐 museumsnc.co.za

Constructed in 1897, this former sanatorium, hotel and school now houses a museum of natural and cultural history, with ethnological and archaeological displays, as well as rock paintings.

### THE BIG HOLE IN FIGURES

Covering an area of 17 ha (43 acres), the Big Hole has a perimeter of 1.6 km (1 mile). It initially reached a depth of 800 m (2,600 ft), the first 240 m (780 ft) of which was laboriously dug by hand. An underground shaft increased the depth to 1,098 m (3,569 ft) and by 1914 some 22.6 million tonnes of rock had been excavated, yielding a total of 14.5 million carats of diamonds.

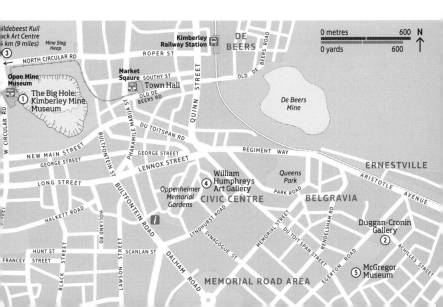

↑ Nieuwoudtsville's
sandstone Dutch
Reformed Church

# EXPERIENCE MORE

## ❸
### Nieuwoudtville

B5 *i*www.nieuwoudt
ville.com

Nieuwoudtville stands on
semi-desert plains known
as the Bokkeveld (Land of
Antelope), after the herds
of migratory wildlife it once
attracted. Its cluster of sandstone buildings include a Neo-
Gothic Dutch Reformed Church
dating from 1906–7. Nieuwoudtville comes into its own in
spring, when wildflower displays are dominated by the
world's largest diversity of
geophytes (plants with bulbs,
corms or tubers). The best
wildflower routes vary by week
and season, so seek local
advice, but the Nieuwoudtville

> **INSIDER TIP**
> **Flower Spotting**
>
> Consult Namaqualand
> Tourism (namaqualand.
> com) to find the best
> viewing areas. Flowers
> open only on sunny
> days, and look their best
> between 11am and 4pm;
> drive facing them, with
> the sun behind you.

Wildflower Reserve and
Hantam National Botanical
Garden are both reliable sites.

Just outside town, the
Nieuwoudtville Falls can be
spectacular after spring or
summer rains, but is usually dry
in winter. The world's second-
largest *kokerboom* (quiver
tree) forest lies about 25 km
(15 miles) to the northeast.

## ❹
### Vanrhynsdorp

A6 *i*www.namaqua
westcoast.com

The southern gateway to
Namaqualand, Vanrhynsdorp
was founded as a mission
called Trutro in 1751 and
renamed after the prominent
Van Rhyn family 130 years
later. The original 18th-century
Trutro House – later converted
to a Dutch Reformed Church –
can still be seen, while the Van
Rhyn Museum, housed in a
building from 1897, focuses
on local history. Vanrhynsdorp
lies in a succulent-dominated
semi-desert known, somewhat
ominously, as the Knersvlakte
(literally, "Gnashing Plains") in
reference to the crunching
sound made by wagon wheels

as they traversed its surface
of quartzite gravel. This dry
country ecosystem is known
both for dramatic spring
wildflower displays and for
the unique dwarf plants that
grow here. It was finally
accorded official protection in
2014 with the proclamation of
the vast Knersvlakte Nature
Reserve (not yet formally open
to the public, though parts are
accessible by public road).

## ❺
### Namaqua National Park

A5 🏛Springbok 🕐8am-
5pm daily 🌐sanparks.org

Established in 1999 and
extended to cover 1,410 sq km
(544 sq miles) in 2008, this
national park is centred on the
Skilpad Wildflower Reserve,
which erupts into a dazzling
extravaganza of spring flowers
from July through September.
The park's attractions are more
nuanced at other times of year,
but still appealing. Rocky plains
traversed by walking and
biking trails slope down to
the scenic coastline between
the Groen and Sproeg river
mouths. Wildlife includes
springbok and baboon, and
several dry country endemics
are found on the bird checklist
of 150 species.

# NAMAQUALAND

Extending over 48,000 sq km (18,500 sq miles) between the Olifants and Orange rivers, Namaqualand is a region of sharp seasonal contrasts. For most of the year, its cover of rocky semi-desert shows few signs of floral activity. But come spring, a scattering of rain transforms it into a blaze of colour – pink, yellow, purple, orange – as a bewildering diversity of daisies and flowering succulents come into blossom.

Springflower displays are the most flamboyant facet of the floral wealth that has led to the Succulent Karoo of Namaqualand being listed among the world's top 34 biodiversity hotspots. Of its estimated 3,000-4,000 plant species, half are endemic, while 17 per cent are on the IUCN Red Data List. Drought-resistant annuals include daisy-like *Ursinias* such as *botterblom* (butter flower) and *gousblom* (goose flower). Succulents are well-represented, most famously the carpet-like *vygies* (mesembryanthemums) and oddities such as the forbidding kokerboom, a tree aloe whose spiked crown protrudes skywards like fortifications.

### TOP 3 WILDFLOWER SITES

**Namaqua National Park**
The higher rainfall resulting from the park's proximity to the West Coast guarantees excellent displays of bright orange daisies and gazanias *(p200)*.

**Postberg Nature Reserve**
Located in the West Coast National Park *(p180)*, this popular flower-viewing spot is an easy day-trip from Cape Town.

**Goegap Nature Reserve**
Situated 15 km (9 miles) east of Springbok *(p203)*, the Goegap Nature Reserve's flat plains and granite koppies support hundreds of succulents.

↑ A kokerboom, or quiver tree, with characteristic spiky leaves

A colourful carpet of ↑ flowering daisies in Goegap Nature Reserve

## Augrabies Falls National Park

🅰 B4  🄰 Augrabies  🕘 7am-6pm daily  🆆 sanparks.org

This national park was founded in 1966 to protect the Augrabies Falls (known by the Khoe as *Aukoerebis*, or "place of Great Noise"), which rush through the largest granite gorge in the world. During periods of normal flow, the main waterfall plunges 56 m (182 ft) into the gorge. The lesser Bridal Veil Waterfall cascades 75 m (244 ft) into the river.

At the main complex near the entrance to the park stands a shop, restaurant and bar. Paths lead from here down to the falls. There are safety fences to prevent visitors from falling into the chasm,

but you should take care near the waterfall, as the rocks are very slippery.

Apart from the waterfall itself and the attractive rest camp, Augrabies has much to offer. The 39-km (24-mile) Klipspringer Trail explores the southern section of the park and affords superb views of the gorge and surrounding desert. Wildlife to look out for includes klipspringer and kudu.

---

## Ai-Ais/Richtersveld Transfrontier National Park

🅰 A4  🄰 Port Nolloth  🕘 May-Sep: 7am-6pm daily; Oct-Apr: 7am-7pm daily  🆆 sanparks.org

A favoured tramping ground for self-sufficient 4WD enthusiasts, the Richtersveld is a

Dramatic terrain in Augrabies Falls National Park, a popular hiking spot *(inset)*

true desert: searingly hot by day and surprisingly chilly at night, with some areas receiving an annual average rainfall of less than 5 mm (0.19 inches). Antelope such as gemsbok and springbok are present, together with several bird species endemic to the arid west, but for most visitors the primary attraction is the park's uncompromised wilderness feel. Also on display

↑ A herd of Hartmann's mountain zebra grazing in Goegap Nature Reserve near Springbok

**Hester Malan Wildflower Garden showcases a wealth of local succulents and is brightened by dazzling wildflower displays in spring.**

are some peculiar native plants, most strikingly the halfmens (half-human) tree, which resembles a hunch-backed person in silhouette.

Richtersveld amalgamated with Namibia's Ai–Ais Hot Springs Game Park in 2003, to form a vast 6,045-sq-km (2,334-sq-mile) transfrontier park bisected by the Orange River. The Richtersveld Community Conservancy, immediately south of the park and considered to be in more pristine condition, was inscribed as a UNESCO World Heritage Site in 2005.

---

**8**

## Springbok

🄰A5  www.springbok-information.co.za

Springbok, self-styled capital of Namaqualand, can lay fair claim to being the most remote town of comparable size in South Africa. Founded in 1850, it owes its existence to the combination of wealthy copper deposits and a water supply adequate to support mining operations. The nearby Goegap Nature Reserve, traversed by a short road loop, is home to 600 plant, 45 mammal and 95 bird species, including South Africa's only

---

💬 INSIDER TIP
**The Augrabies Rush**

Thrill-seekers should check out this four-hour rafting trip, which takes in several patches of rapids along a scenic stretch of the Orange River (www.kalahari-adventures.co.za).

---

population of Hartmann's mountain zebra (a species otherwise restricted to Namibia). Within the reserve, Hester Malan Wildflower Garden showcases a wealth of local succulents and is brightened by dazzling wildflower displays in spring.

Only 8 km (5 miles) north of Springbok, Okiep is South Africa's oldest working mining town, founded in around 1869 to exploit what were then the world's largest known copper deposits. Relicts of these days include a Cornish Beam Pump, built in 1882 to keep the mine dry, and a tall ventilation tower of similar vintage.

---

**9**

## Port Nolloth

🄰A5  www.portnolloth info.co.za

Head north from Springbok along the N7 as far as Steinkopf, turn left onto a quiet asphalt road that leads across the Annienous Pass, and you will emerge at the sleepy fishing village of Port Nolloth. First developed in 1855 to ship out copper ore carried there by horse-drawn cart from Springbok, the vil-lage's sheltered harbour was expanded in 1876 following the opening of a 154-km (96-mile) narrow-gauge railway from Okiep. It enjoyed a second lease of life in 1926 with the discovery of alluvial diamond deposits around the Orange River Mouth 85 km (53 miles) to the north.

Today, Port Nolloth has a charming, resort-that-time-forgot atmosphere, which is enhanced by sensational sun-sets over the Atlantic Ocean; a strong Portuguese influence (from Angola) in the seafood-dominated cuisine; and a surrounding of dune-lined beaches and lagoons notable for their marine birdlife. The Port Nolloth Museum, housed in a 19th-century building, explores the region's history.

A stylish game lodge within Tswalu Kalahari Reserve ↑

## ⑩ 🦒
## Tswalu Kalahari Reserve

🅰C3 📍115 km (71 miles) NW of Kuruman 🅦tswalu.com

An ambitious project without equal, Tswalu is South Africa's largest private reserve. It protects around 750 sq km (285 sq miles) of red Kalahari dunes and the picturesque Korannaberg mountains. The reserve came into existence through the tireless efforts of British businessman Stephen Boler. First, he bought and amalgamated 26 cattle farms. Work teams then removed some 800 km (500 miles) of fencing from the land, as well as 2,300 km (1,440 miles) of electric lines, 38 concrete dams and the farmsteads. Thousands of cattle were sold off and the reserve was fenced.

Boler invested R54 million to develop the reserve. A total of 4,700 animals, representing 22 species, have been reintroduced, including lion, cheetah, buffalo, three types of zebra, blue and black wildebeest, red hartebeest, giraffe, gemsbok, kudu, impala and wild dog. But the jewels in Tswalu's crown are, without doubt, the small number of desert black rhino (subspecies *Diceros bicornis bicornis*), relocated with the permission of the Namibian government. The reserve is now owned by the wealthy Oppenheimer family (of gold and diamond mining fame).

Tswalu's two luxury, all-inclusive lodges have their own airstrip, and most visitors arrive by charter plane.

## ⑪
## Kuruman

🅰C4 ℹ️www.visit kuruman.co.za

The gateway to the Northern Cape coming from Gauteng, the modest town of Kuruman owes its existence to the 20 million litres (5.3 million gallons) of clear, drinkable

---

# STAY

**Le Must Residence**
A Georgian-style house set on the banks of the Orange River. The gardens are immaculate and the decor stylish.

🏠12 Murray Ave, Upington 🅦lemus tupington.com

ⓇⓇⓇ

# EAT

**Café Zest**
This café specializes in European and meaty Karoo-style cooking.

🏠24 Schröder St
☎054 337 8546

ⓇⓇⓇ

water that flow from a natural spring known as Die Oog (The Eye). The spring empties into a lily-covered pool that supports a variety of aquatic life, including a rare cichlid species, and attracts plenty of birds.

Improbable though it might seem today, this was one of the first parts of the South African interior to be explored by Europeans. The Kuruman Mission, founded by Robert Moffat in 1821, later became the first African posting held by the missionary and future explorer David Livingstone. The stump of the tree beneath which Livingstone proposed to Robert's daughter Mary still stands, as does the church – then seven years old – where they were wed in 1845, and the old homestead where Robert Moffat and his family lived. The leafy mission grounds and their old stone buildings – which are open to visitors – exude a tranquil and historic ambience that is at odds with these otherwise harsh surrounds.

### 12
## Upington

**A**B4 **🚂🚌** **ℹ** 4 Schröder St; www.upington.co.za

Originally established in 1875 as a mission station, the bustling town of Upington lies in a vast plain dotted with low shrubs. Only where the road reaches the Orange River does the landscape change abruptly, as the river paints a wide green stripe across the barren territory. As the second-largest settlement in the Northern Cape after Kimberley, Upington serves a district of lucerne, cotton, fruit and wine farms, which line a fertile corridor along the river.

The original 1875 mission church built by the Reverend Christiaan Schröder now forms the centerpiece of the **Kalahari-Oranje Museum**, which houses various items dating from the town's early years. There's also a life-size statue of a donkey that honours the contribution

these doughty beasts made to the economic development of the Orange River Valley in the late 19th century.

Occupying an island in the Orange River, just outside town, Die Eiland is a municipal resort which has an avenue of more than 200 palm trees that were planted in 1935. The five wine cellars in this arid region all belong to the **Orange River Cellars**, which offers tastings alongside complementary snack platters. On the southern bank of the river, the South African Dried Fruit Co-op on Louisvale Road is capable of processing up to 250 tonnes of dried fruit daily.

### Kalahari-Oranje Museum
**A** 4 Schröder St **⊙** 9am–12:30pm & 2–5pm Mon–Fri; 9am–noon Sat **🌐** upington. co.za

### Orange River Cellars
**♿** **A** 158 Schröder St **⊙** Tastings: 10am–5pm Mon–Fri, 10am–2pm Sat **🌐** orangeriverwines.com

## Did You Know?

The Orange River contains hidden treasure in the form of diamond deposits along its shores.

← Aerial view of Die Eiland, a municipal resort in the Orange River

# STAY

**Castle in Clarens**
Built to resemble a
fairytale castle, this
boutique hotel is a
fantasy lover's delight.

📍Bokpoort Farm, R712,
Clarens 🌐castle
inclarens.co.za

Ⓡ Ⓡ Ⓡ

---

**Golden Gate Hotel**
This 70s-style hotel
underwent an Africa-
themed makeover in
2013, and offers lush
views over the park.

📍Golden Gate National
Park 🌐golden
gatehotel.co.za

Ⓡ Ⓡ Ⓡ

---

**Liedjiesbos B&B**
An innovative
guesthouse that
combines airy modern
architecture with
African and Eastern-
influenced decor.

📍13 Frans Kleynhans
Rd, Bloemfontein
🌐bloemfontein
accommodation.biz

Ⓡ Ⓡ Ⓡ

# Karoo National Park

📍C6 📍Beaufort West
🕐5am–10pm daily
🌐sanparks.org

The Karoo National Park was established on the outskirts of Beaufort West in 1979, to conserve a representative sample of the region's unique heritage. It has been enlarged over the years and now encompasses vast, flat plains as well as the rugged Nuweveld Mountains. Animals such as mountain reedbuck, grey rhebok, kudu, steenbok, jackal and aardwolf occur naturally, while reintroduced species include lion, springbok, hartebeest, gemsbok (oryx), black wildebeest, Cape mountain zebra and the endangered riverine rabbit. Some 196 bird species have been recorded, and the park is well known for sustaining more than 20 Verreaux's (black) eagle pairs.

A comfortable rest camp is situated at the base of the Nuweveld Mountains. Its spacious Cape Dutch chalets provide a convenient overnight stop that is easily accessible from the N1. The camp has good facilities, including a shop, swimming pool, restaurant and caravan park. Nearby, the historic Ou Skuur Farmhouse contains the park's information centre. A 4WD trail has been laid out in the rugged western region of the park, and night drives here provide the very best chances of seeing many of the region's shy nocturnal animals, such as the aardwolf.

In addition to its plentiful wildlife population, the park is also home to an extremely rich fossil history. The short Fossil and Bossie trails are accessible from the rest camp and allow visitors to explore the Karoo's fascinating 250-million-year-old geological history and its unique vegetation.

The 400-m (1,300-ft) Fossil Trail is especially popular; it is designed to accommodate wheelchairs and incorporates Braille boards and informative plaques. A bird hide and an easy hike of 3 km (2 miles) are also accessible from the rest camp.

↑ The 19th-century Town Hall and Dutch Reformed Church in Beaufort West

## 14
## Clarens

🅰 E4 **𝒊** www.clarens.co.za

Far less developed than its KwaZulu-Natal counterpart, the western Drakensberg – also known as Maloti – is nevertheless very scenic. Set within unglamorous Free State province, the region's closest approximation of a resort town is Clarens, which

stands in a lush valley below a striking sandstone cliff nicknamed Titanic Rock. Founded in 1911 and named after the Swiss town where President Paul Kruger spent his last years in voluntary exile, today Clarens supports a thriving art colony and is a great base for outdoor activities, from trout fishing and canoeing to hiking and mountain biking.

Clarens is also the springboard for **Golden Gate Highlands National Park**, which encompasses 340 sq km (131 sq miles) of grassland and sandstone formations in the Maloti foothills. Proclaimed in 1963, the park is named for its most distinctive feature, a magnificent pair of facing cliffs that take on a burnished hue towards sunset. Best explored on foot, this scenic park supports plenty of wildlife, notably black wildebeest, blesbok and eland, while birds in the area include the endangered bearded vulture, soaring Verreaux's eagle and endemic southern bald ibis.

Rock art enthusiasts might consider basing themselves at Ladybrand, a quaint highland

← Dramatic sandstone cliffs dominating the Golden Gate Highlands National Park

town set within striking distance of 300 different sites. The pick of the region is Tandjesberg, a national monument whose 530 individual painted images include polychrome elands, a group of female dancers, and an elephant whose trunk appears to morph into a human.

### Golden Gate Highlands National Park

 🕓 7am-5:30pm daily
🅦 sanparks.org

---

## 15
## Beaufort West

🅰 C6 **𝒊** www.beaufort west.com

The Karoo's largest town, Beaufort West was founded in 1818 and its historic Donkin Street is lined with national monuments including the Neo-Gothic Dutch Reformed Church and the adjacent Town Hall. The surrounding semi-arid plains have thrived as a centre of sheep farming since the hardy merino breed was introduced in the 1840s, and even today Karoo lamb is a staple on local menus.

In Victorian times, Beaufort West's dry climate made it a popular winter retreat for asthmatic Capetonians, but these days the town is of interest mainly as a convenient overnight stop between Johannesburg and Cape Town.

> 💬 INSIDER TIP
> **The Cherry on Top**
>
> Situated halfway between Clarens and Ladybrand, the agricultural town of Ficksburg is known as the cherry capital of South Africa. It hosts a popular and enjoyable festival *(free-state-info. co.za)* each year in mid-November, when the cherry season peaks.

## ⑯ Bloemfontein

**ⒶE4 🚗🚌✈️ ℹ️**Bloemfontein Tourist Centre, 60 Park Rd; www.mangaung.co.za

Situated in the heartland of South Africa, Bloemfontein, capital of the Free State and seat of the province's parliament, is also the country's judicial capital. Part of the municipality of Mangaung, it lies at the hub of five national road routes. An altitude of 1,400 m (4,593 ft) means that summers are moderate and winters mild to cool.

The city was named after a fountain where early travellers used to stop on their treks through the interior. The city's history – and that of many of its stately old sandstone buildings – is firmly connected with the Afrikaners'

**The city's history - and that of many of its stately old sandstone buildings - is firmly connected with the Afrikaners' struggle for independence.**

struggle for independence. In 1854, when Major Henry Warden, the region's official British representative, was recalled to the Cape, the Afrikaners established a republic, with Bloemfontein as its capital.

Although Major Warden's fort has long disappeared, a portion of Queen's Fort, dating back to 1848, can still be seen south of the city centre. President Brand Street is lined with many fine old sandstone buildings, such as the Appeal Court, built in 1929, opposite the Fourth Raadsaal, which now houses the Free State's

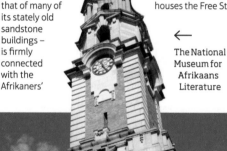

← The National Museum for Afrikaans Literature

provincial legislature. This brick-and-sandstone building was constructed around 1893, during the presidency of Frederick Reitz.

Not far from the Appeal Court are two interesting museums. The **National Museum** contains a good collection of dinosaur fossils, and a reconstruction of a 19th-century Bloemfontein street, while the **National Museum for Afrikaans Literature** is devoted to leading Afrikaans writers.

Three blocks south from the Literature Museum stands the **Old Presidency**, an attractive building completed in 1861. It was the home of the republic's Afrikaner presidents before the British invasion in 1900, and now houses a small museum with a pleasant café in the stables.

The oldest building in the city is the **First Raadsaal Museum**, a satellite of the National Museum. Built on Warden's instructions in 1849, it was first used as a school, but after 1854 it became the meeting place of the republic's *Volksraad* (people's council).

Also in the city centre is the **Tweetoringkerk** (twin-spired church), which was dedicated in 1881. Unique in the country, it was inspired by Europe's Gothic cathedrals. Inside, the decorative woodwork is especially noteworthy. South

### Did You Know?

Bloemfontein is more evocatively known in Sesotho as Mangaung, meaning "Place of Cheetahs".

The Fourth Raadsaal, located on Bloemfontein's central President Brand Street

of the city, the **National Women's Memorial and Anglo-Boer War Museum** commemorates the countless Boer and Black African women and children who died in British concentration camps during the South African War. Emily Hobhouse, a British woman who campaigned for better treatment of the prisoners, is buried at the foot of the monument.

North of the city centre, the **Franklin Nature Reserve** occupies Naval Hill, where the University of Michigan built an observatory in 1928. Over 7,000 star systems were discovered before it closed in 1972. Further north still, the **Oliewenhuis Art Museum** has a superb collection of South African art.

### National Museum
⊗ ⊚ ⊛ ⌂ 36 Aliwal St ⊙ 9am–3pm Mon–Fri, 10am–5pm Sat ⊠ Good Friday & 25 Dec
ⓦ nasmus.co.za

### National Museum for Afrikaans Literature
⌂ 40 Miriam Makeba St ⓒ 051 405 4711
⊙ 8am–4pm Mon–Fri

### Old Presidency
⊚ ⌂ President Brand St
ⓒ 051 448 0949
⊙ 10am–4pm Tue–Sat

### First Raadsaal Museum
⌂ 95 St George St ⊙ 9am–3pm Mon–Fri, 10am–3pm Sat & Sun ⊠ Good Fri, 25 Dec ⓦ nasmus.co.za

### Tweetoringkerk
⌂ Charles St ⓒ 051 430 4274

### National Women's Memorial and Anglo-Boer War Museum
⊗ ⌂ Monument Rd ⊙ 8am–4:30pm Mon–Fri, 10am–5pm Sat, 11am–5pm Sun ⊙ 1 Jan, Good Fri, 25 Dec
ⓦ wmbr.org.za

### Franklin Nature Reserve
⌂ 2–22 Delville Dr, Naval Hill
⊙ 7am–6pm daily

### Oliewenhuis Art Museum
⌂ Harry Smith St ⓒ 051 447 9609 ⊙ 9am–3pm Mon–Fri, 9am–3pm Sat
⊙ Public hols

# EAT

### De Oude Kraal Country Estate & Spa
A five-course set menu and excellent wine list provide gastronomic adventures at this high-ceilinged farmhouse with antique furniture.

⌂ N1, south of Bloemfontein
ⓦ deoudekraal.com

Ⓡ Ⓡ Ⓡ

### Margaritas
Steak, *sosaties* (kebabs) and fresh seafood are the specialities at this family-friendly Mediterranean-influenced restaurant.

⌂ 59 Milner Rd
⊠ Sun ⓦ margaritas restaurant.co.za

Ⓡ Ⓡ Ⓡ

← *Flowers* by Walter Altman, Oliewenhuis Art Museum

# A DRIVING TOUR
# ROUTE 62

**Length** 250 km (155 miles) **Stopping-off points**
Montagu, Barrydale, Ladismith, Calitzdorp **Difficulty** Easy

An increasingly popular route heading east from the
Cape Winelands, the R62 runs between Ashton in the
Breede River Valley and Oudtshoorn in the Klein
Karoo. En route, it traverses scenic passes flanked by
the dramatically stratified Cape Fold Mountains,
pretty rural towns distinguished by their time-warped
architecture and agricultural bounty, and some fine
off-the-beaten-track wine estates. In theory, you could
cover the route in one longish day, but a more relaxing
option is to take an overnight break to soak up the
scenic surrounds and legendary Karoo hospitality.

*Studded with 19th-century
architectural gems including
a local history museum in a
converted church,* **Ladismith**
*lies below the spectacular,
fortress-like protrusion of
Towerkop Peak.*

*Crossing the Langeberg Mountains
between Ashton and Montagu, the
spectacular* **Cogmanskloof Pass**
*is overlooked by a stone fort built
by the British in 1899.*

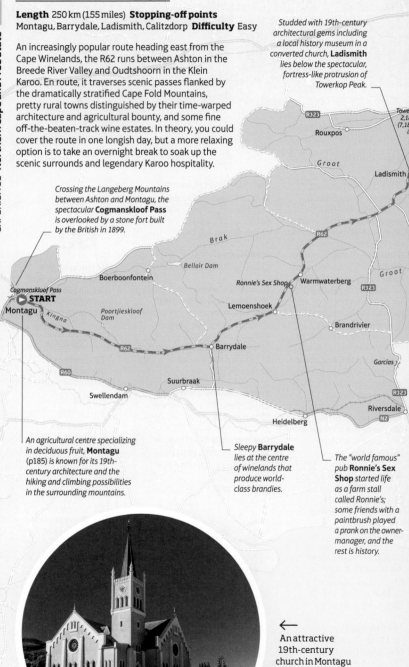

R323
Rouxpos

Towerko
2,189 r
(7,182 fi

Ladismith

Groot

Brak

Bellair Dam

R62

Boerboonfontein

Groot

*Cogmanskloof Pass*
▶ **START**
Montagu

*Kingna*

*Poortjieskloof
Dam*

Ronnie's Sex Shop ◇ Warmwaterberg

R323

Lemoenshoek

Brandrivier

R62

Barrydale

Garcias

R60

Suurbraak

R323

Swellendam

Riversdale

N2

Heidelberg

*An agricultural centre specializing
in deciduous fruit,* **Montagu**
*(p185) is known for its 19th-
century architecture and the
hiking and climbing possibilities
in the surrounding mountains.*

*Sleepy* **Barrydale**
*lies at the centre
of winelands that
produce world-
class brandies.*

*The "world famous"
pub* **Ronnie's Sex
Shop** *started life
as a farm stall
called Ronnie's;
some friends with a
paintbrush played
a prank on the owner-
manager, and the
rest is history.*

← An attractive
19th-century
church in Montagu

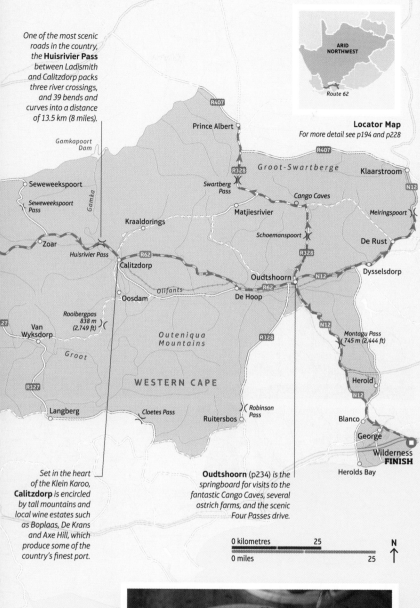

One of the most scenic roads in the country, the **Huisrivier Pass** between Ladismith and Calitzdorp packs three river crossings, and 39 bends and curves into a distance of 13.5 km (8 miles).

**ARID NORTHWEST**

Route 62

**Locator Map**
For more detail see p194 and p228

Gamkapoort Dam

Prince Albert

R407

R407

Groot-Swartberge

Klaarstroom

N12

Seweweekspoort

Seweweekspoort Pass

R328

Swartberg Pass

Cango Caves

Meiringspoort

Matjiesrivier

Gamka

Kraaldorings

Schoemanspoort

De Rust

R328

Zoar

Huisrivier Pass

R62

Calitzdorp

Oudtshoorn

N12

Dysselsdorp

Olifants

De Hoop

R62

Oosdam

Rooibergpas
838 m
(2,749 ft)

Outeniqua
Mountains

N12

Montagu Pass
745 m (2,444 ft)

27

Van Wyksdorp

R328

Groot

Herold

N12

R327

WESTERN CAPE

Langberg

Cloetes Pass

Robinson Pass

Blanco

Ruitersbos

George

Wilderness
**FINISH**

Herolds Bay

Set in the heart of the Klein Karoo, **Calitzdorp** is encircled by tall mountains and local wine estates such as Boplaas, De Krans and Axe Hill, which produce some of the country's finest port.

**Oudtshoorn** (p234) is the springboard for visits to the fantastic Cango Caves, several ostrich farms, and the scenic Four Passes drive.

0 kilometres — 25
0 miles — 25

N
↑

→
A plate of local Klein Karoo appetizers being served at a restaurant in Calitzdorp

# HERMANUS AND THE OVERBERG

Incorporating Africa's most southerly headland in the form of Cape Agulhas, the productive agricultural region known as the Overberg was inhabited by Khoe fish-trappers and pastoralists prior to 1488, when the Portuguese navigator Bartolomeu Dias became the first European to sail past its treacherous rocky extremity. Following the establishment of a settlement on the Cape in 1652, Dutch settlers entered into regular trade with the Khoe as far inland as Swellendam, which became South Africa's third magisterial district in 1743 and rebelled to form a short-lived breakaway republic in 1795. The region became more settled in the first half of the 19th century, when several other towns – including the port of Hermanus and the mission at Elim – were established. The loss of hundreds of vessels off the coast of Agulhas led to the erection of a lighthouse there in 1842. The Overberg today remains a predominantly rural area whose agriculture-based economy is boosted by a burgeoning wine industry and growing tourism.

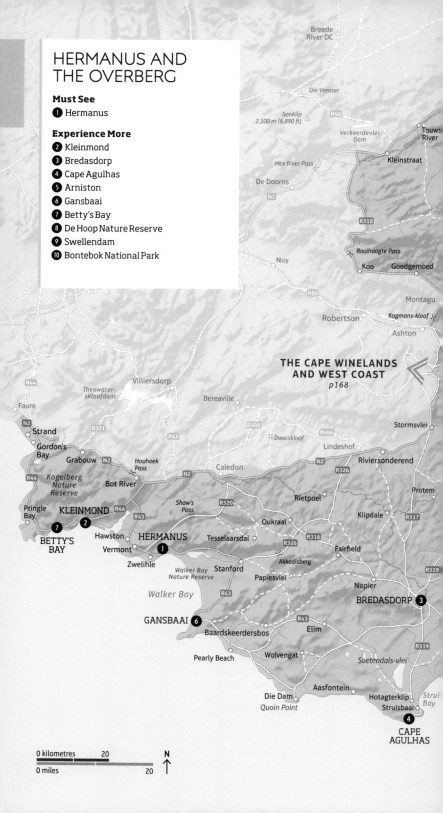

# HERMANUS AND THE OVERBERG

**Must See**

**1** Hermanus

**Experience More**

**2** Kleinmond
**3** Bredasdorp
**4** Cape Agulhas
**5** Arniston
**6** Gansbaai
**7** Betty's Bay
**8** De Hoop Nature Reserve
**9** Swellendam
**10** Bontebok National Park

Breede
River DC

*Die Venster*

*Sonklip
2,100 m (6,890 ft)*

R46

*Verkeerdevlei
Dam*

Touws
River

*Hex River Pass*

Kleinstraat

De Doorns

R318

N1

*Rooihoogte Pass*

Koo  Goedgemoed

Nuy

R60

Montagu

Robertson

*Kogmans-kloof*

Ashton

**THE CAPE WINELANDS
AND WEST COAST**
*p168*

Villiersdorp

*Theewater-
skloofdam*

Bereaville

R46

Faure

R321

R406

*Dwarskloof*

R406

Stormsvlei

N2

Strand

Gordon's
Bay

Grabouw

N2

*Houhoek
Pass*

Caledon

N2

Lindeshof

Riviersonderend

R326

Protem

*Kogelberg
Nature
Reserve*

Bot River

R320

Rietpoel

Klipdale

R317

R44

Pringle
Bay

KLEINMOND

R44

R43

*Shaw's
Pass*

Oukraal

R316

Fairfield

R319

**7**

**2**

Hawston

HERMANUS

Tesselaarsdal

R326

BETTY'S
BAY

Vermont

**1**

*Akkedisberg*

Napier

Zwelihle

Stanford

Papiesvlei

BREDASDORP **3**

*Walker Bay
Nature Reserve*

*Walker Bay*

R43

GANSBAAI **6**

Baardskeerdersbos

Elim

R43

R319

Pearly Beach

Wolvengat

*Soetendals-vlei*

Aasfontein

Hotagterklip

*Strui
Bay*

Die Dam

*Quoin Point*

Struisbaai

CAPE
AGULHAS

**4**

0 kilometres    20

0 miles    20

N
↑

**1**

# HERMANUS

**A** B7 **🚌** Bot River **ℹ** Old Station Building, Mitchell Street;
www.hermanustourism.info

First established as a farming community, this sunny, well-located town soon became a fashionable tourist destination. The grandeur of Hermanus is now a little faded, but it remains a popular holiday hub.

Today, Hermanus is famous for its superb whale-watching sites. Every year, southern right whales *(p218)* migrate from the sub-Antarctic to calve in the shelter of Walker Bay. They arrive in June and leave again by December, with the peak whale-watching season during September and October. The town's official whale crier blows his kelp horn as he walks along Main Street, bearing a signboard that shows the best daily sighting places.

Hermanus's focal point is the Old Harbour Open-Air Museum, which traces the history of the town's whaling days and contains a whale skull and old weapons. Fishermen's boats dating from 1850 to the mid-1900s lie restored and hull-up. There are also bokkom stands, racks on which fish are hung to dry in the sun, and reconstructed fishing shacks.

Hermanus has a beautiful coastline. Unspoiled beaches such as the 12-km (7-mile) stretch of Die Plaat are perfect for walks and horse riding. A clifftop route extends from New Harbour to Grotto Beach – the regularly placed benches allow walkers to rest and to enjoy the superb views. Swimming is generally safe, and there is a tidal pool below the Marine Hotel.

↑ Historic row houses, part of the Old Harbour Open-Air Museum

# EAT

**Bientang's Cave**
An award-winning seafood restaurant, dramatically carved into a cave that extends to the water's edge.

⌂ Marine Dr, Hermanus ⓦ bientangs cave.com

Ⓡ Ⓡ Ⓡ

---

**Origins at The Marine**
Head here for ocean-fresh seafood, listed on a menu that expertly blends local and international flavours.

⌂ Marine Dr, Hermanus ⓦ collection mcgrath.com

Ⓡ Ⓡ Ⓡ

The picturesque coastline of Hermanus, known for its excellent whale-watching *(inset)* ↑

Other activities nearby include the Rotay Way, a 10-km (6-mile) scenic drive, and the Hermanus Wine Route, which features four vineyards in the pretty Hemel en Arde Valley. Just east of Hermanus lies Stanford, a rustic crafts centre. The heart of this little village contains many historic homes built in the late 1800s and early 1900s, and has been proclaimed a national conservation area.

↑ The craggy cliff overlooking the sands of Grotto Beach

💬 INSIDER TIP
**Call of the Wild**

The World Wide Fund for Nature (WWF) has recognized Hermanus as one of the earth's best land-based whale-watching spots. The mammals can be seen as close as 10 m (33 ft) away, while the Old Harbour Museum's sonar link-up transmits whale calls to an audio room on shore.

# WHALE-WATCHING

Some 37 whale and dolphin species and around 100 different types of shark occur in southern African waters. A large proportion of the world's 4,000–6,000 southern right whales migrate here annually, leaving their subantarctic feeding grounds from June onwards to mate and calve in the warmer waters of the protected rocky bays and inlets that occur along the South African coastline.

## THE SOUTHERN RIGHT WHALE

Early whalers named this species "southern right" (*Eubalaena australis*) because it occurred south of the Equator and was the perfect species to hunt. Its blubber was rich in oil, the baleen plates (filter-feeders made of keratin) supplied whalebone for corsets, shoe horns and brushes, and when dead the whale floated, unlike other types of whale, which sank. A protected species, it can migrate up to 2,600 km (1,615 miles) annually.

↑ A characteristic V-shaped "blow", seen when the southern right whale exhales

**LOCATIONS FOR WHALE-SPOTTING**

**Hermanus**
The whale-watching capital of South Africa, Hermanus (p216) is renowned for its spectacular sightings.

**False Bay**
The Cape Peninsula (p142) has numerous whale-watching sites around False Bay, from both land and boat.

**Addo Elephant National Park**
In addition to the Big Five, this national park (p250) is also home to seasonal populations of southern right whale in its Marine Sector.

↑ A breaching humpback whale, with the extremely long flippers that are a striking feature of this species

## WHALE BEHAVIOUR

Certain types of behaviour are common among whales, such as breaching, where the whale lifts its upper body out of the water and falls back into the sea with a massive splash. Humpbacks in particular are well-known for their spectacular breaching, lifting themselves well above the ocean. Other antics you might see on a whale-watching trip include lobtailing, where the flukes (the two lobes of the tail) slap on the surface to produce a loud clap, and spyhopping, where the whale lifts its head vertically from the sea to observe what is happening on the surface.

## WHALE EXPLOITATION

In the years from 1785 to around 1805, some 12,000 southern right whales were killed off the southern African coast, but the northern right whale was even more ruthlessly hunted and is virtually extinct today. After the introduction of cannon-fired harpoons in the late 19th century, humpbacks became the first large whale to be exploited; around 25,000 were killed between 1908 and 1925. By 1935, when the League of Nations' Convention for the Regulation of Whaling came into effect, fewer than 200 southern right whales remained in southern African waters. Although numbers are increasing steadily – by around seven per cent every year – today's total population is only a fraction of what it once was.

↑ Enjoying a close-up sighting during a whale-watching trip

# EXPERIENCE MORE

**2**

## Kleinmond

B7 📍Protea Centre, Main Rd; www.kleinmond tourism.co.za

Surrounding Kleinmond, the stony hills with their thin green veneer of *fynbos* scrub once harboured small bands of Khoe and escapees from slavery. In the 1920s, Kleinmond, nestled at the foot of the Palmietberg, was a fishing settlement; today it is a holiday spot where rock angling for

---

🔍 HIDDEN GEM
**Salmonsdam Nature Reserve**

Wildlife fans shouldn't miss this pretty reserve to the east of Kleinmond; bontebok, grey rhebok, klipspringer, the Cape rockjumper and king proteas might all be spotted along a trio of walking trails.

---

*kabeljou* (kob) and fishing for yellowtail and tunny are popular pastimes. Kleinmond Lagoon, where the Palmiet River reaches the sea, offers safe swimming and canoeing. Visitors can enjoy beautiful views from a well-planned network of hiking trails in the **Kogelberg Nature Reserve**, and maybe even glimpse some of the shy gazelles such as klipspringers, as well as the grysbok and steenbok that inhabit the coastal *fynbos* and the mountain's lower slopes.

**Kogelberg Nature Reserve**

 Off R44, 8 km (5 miles) W of Kleinmond ⏱7:30am–4pm daily 🌐capenature.co.za

---

**3**

## Bredasdorp

B7 📍19 Long St; 087 721 5377

Bredasdorp lies in a region of undulating barley fields and sheep pasture. The town is a

---

## Did You Know?

Bredasdorp was named after its founder, Michiel van Breda, the first mayor of Cape Town.

---

centre for the wool industry, but serves mainly as an access route to Cape Agulhas and Arniston (via the R319 and R316 respectively).

The town's most interesting feature is the **Shipwreck Museum**, which pays tribute to the southern coast's tragic history. This treacherous length of coastline has been labelled the "graveyard of ships" as its rocky reefs, gale-force winds and powerful currents make it one of the most dangerous areas to sail through in the world. Since 1552, more than 130 ships have foundered here, an average of one wreck per kilometre of coast.

A deserted bay in Kleinmond, ↑ ringed by the dramatic Kogelberg Mountain Range

→ The intriguing Shipwreck Museum in Bredasdorp

The museum was officially opened in April 1975 and is housed in an old rectory and church hall, both of which have been declared national monuments. The rectory, built in 1845, contains artifacts from the many shipwrecks that occurred along this capricious stretch of coastline. The salvaged wood, as well as ships' decor, frequently appear in door and window frames and in the ceiling rafters.

The museum itself is full of shipwrecked figureheads, anchors, old bottles and coins. The beautiful marble-topped washstand in the bedroom was salvaged from the *Queen of the Thames*, which sank in 1871, while the medicine chest came from the *Clan MacGregor*, which was shipwrecked in 1902.

The church hall, dating back to 1864, is now called the Shipwreck Hall. Its rather gloomy interior is a suitable environment for the interesting and diverse relics displayed in glass cases, all of which were recovered from major local shipwrecks.

The best time to visit Bredasdorp's Heuningberg Nature Reserve is from mid-September to mid-October, when the countryside is bathed in colourful blooms. It is home to a number of South African endemic plants and of these, the Bredasdorp lily *(Cyrtanthus guthriea)* is found only on the Heuningberg Mountain.

### Shipwreck Museum
⊛ 🏠 Independent St
📞 028 424 1240 🕒 9am-4:45pm Mon-Wed & Fri, 9am-3pm Thu 🚫 Good Fri, 25 Dec, 1 Jan

# STAY

### Oudebosch Eco Cabins
An ideal retreat for nature lovers, the six glass-fronted wooden cabins in this scenic reserve all have two bedrooms, and a spacious well-equipped kitchen, lounge and dining room. Two of the cabins also come with wheelchair access.

🏠 Kogelberg Nature Reserve
🌐 capenature.co.za

ⓇⓇⓇ

### Bredasdorp Country Manor
Moulded in the image of its welcoming live-in owner, this small but sumptuous bed-and-breakfast has a tranquil French country feel, a lovely swimming pool, and a great location for exploring downtown Bredasdorp on foot and making driving excursions further afield.

🏠 9 Kloof St, Bredasdorp
🌐 bredasdorpcountry manor.co.za

ⓇⓇⓇ

## 4

### Cape Agulhas

**B7**

Cape Agulhas was named by the early Portuguese navigators who first rounded Africa in the 15th century. At the southernmost point of their journey, the sailors noticed that their compass needles were unaffected by magnetic deviation, pointing true north instead. They called this point the "Cape of Needles".

At this promontory, where the tip of the African continental shelf disappears quietly into the sea to form what is known as the Agulhas Bank, the Atlantic and Indian oceans merge.

It is one of the world's most treacherous stretches of coast: shallow, rock-strewn and subject to heavy swells and currents. This is the graveyard of more than 250 once-proud vessels, including the Japanese trawler *Meisho Maru 38*, whose rusting wreck can be seen 2 km (1 mile) west of the **Cape Agulhas Lighthouse**. Southern Africa's second-oldest working lighthouse, it was built in 1848 based on the design of the ancient Pharos Lighthouse of Alexandria. The lamp at the

→

The brightly striped tower of Cape Agulhas Lighthouse

top is visible for 30 nautical miles and affords superb views over the coastline in Agulhas National Park. After the Green Point lighthouse in Cape Town, it is the oldest working lighthouse in southern Africa. It fell into disuse, but was restored and reopened in 1988 – today, its lamp is visible for 30 nautical miles. There are 71 steps to the top of the tower, which affords superb views of the coast and seascape.

The area around the southernmost tip of Africa is now part of the Agulhas National Park.

**Cape Agulhas Lighthouse**
 Lighthouse St ☎028 435 7185 ⏰9am–5pm daily

## 5

### Arniston

**B7** ℹ www.overberg-info.co.za

Arniston's name originates from the British vessel *Arniston*, which was wrecked east of the settlement in May

1815. Of the 378 soldiers on board, only six survived. The little fishing settlement is located some 24 km (15 miles) southeast of Bredasdorp *(p220)*, and is characterized by its turquoise waters. The locals refer to Arniston as Waen-

↑ Spectacular colours inside the yawning Waenhuiskrans cave, located close to Arniston

huiskrans (wagonhouse cliff), after a large nearby cave that can accommodate several fully spanned ox wagons. The cave is accessible only at low tide, however, and visitors should be aware of freak waves washing over the slippery rocks.

Kassiesbaai is a cluster of rough-plastered and thatched fishermen's cottages. This little village lies to the north of Arniston, close to undulating white sand dunes. Further to the south lies Roman Beach, with its gently sloping seabed, rock pools and caves. Further from here is a windy, wild rocky point that attracts many hopeful anglers.

 HIDDEN GEM
**Elim Mission**

Established in 1824, this former Moravian mission, inland of Cape Agulhas, is noted for its charming whitewashed cottages, the craftsmanship of its thatchers, and the fine Sauvignon Blanc and Shiraz produced in surrounding winelands.

## ❻
## Gansbaai

 **B7** 🚌 **i Kapokblom St; www.gansbaaiinfo.com**

The twin towns of Gansbaai and Kleinbaai are separated by Danger Point, whose most famous victim was HMS *Birkenhead*; it sank offshore in 1852.

Outside Kleinbaai lies **African Penguin and Seabird Sanctuary**. Overseen by the Dyer Island Conservation Trust, this rehabilitation centre treats injured marine birds before re-releasing into the wild. The trust is funded by Fair Trade-certified commercial boat trips. Marine Big 5 trips offer a chance of spotting dolphins and whales en route to the seal colony on Geyser Island and marine bird colonies on Dyer Island. Depending on season, caged shark-diving takes place in the offshore shallows.

**African Penguin and Seabird Sanctuary**
🏠 Dyer Rd ⏰ 9am-4pm daily 🌐 dict.org.za

## ❼
## Betty's Bay

 **B7** **i Protea Centre, Main Rd, Kleinmond; www. kleinmondtourism.co.za**

This seaside village, named after Betty Youlden, daughter of a property developer who lived here in the 1900s, is a popular weekend retreat. Holiday cottages are scattered throughout the dunes, while the beach offers tremendous views across False Bay.

Of significance is the **Harold Porter National Botanical Garden**, which rises behind Betty's Bay. Porter, a local businessman, bought this tract of land in 1938 to preserve the rich *fynbos* vegetation. More than 1,600 species of ericas, proteas and watsonias attract sugarbirds and sunbirds. There is also a penguin reserve at Stoney Point (open daily).

**Harold Porter National Botanical Garden**
♿🔵😊🏠 Cnr Clarence Dr and Broadwith rds ⏰ 8am-4:30pm Mon-Fri, 8am-5pm Sat & Sun 🌐 sanbi.org

A path cutting through the terrain of De Hoop Nature Reserve, down to the ocean ↑

# EAT

### The Old Gaol

Local dishes rule at this rustic eatery. The speciality is *roosterkoek*, a delicious filled bread.

🏠 8A Voortrek St, Swellendam 🌐 oldgaol restaurant.co.za

Ⓡ Ⓡ Ⓡ

# STAY

### The Hideaway

This Victorian-era B&B offers an indoor pool, and great breakfasts.

🏠 10 Hermanus Steyn St, Swellendam 🌐 hideawaybb.co.za

Ⓡ Ⓡ Ⓡ

### De Kloof Luxury Estate

This five-star hotel sits in vast gardens. There's a koi pond, as well as a pool and cigar lounge.

🏠 8 Weltevrede St, Swellendam 🌐 dekloof.co.za

Ⓡ Ⓡ Ⓡ

8

## De Hoop Nature Reserve

🅐 C7 🚗 R319, 56 km (35 miles) W of Bredasdorp 🕐 7am–6pm daily (to 7pm Oct–Apr) 🌐 capenature. co.za

This reserve encompasses a 50-km (31-mile) stretch of coastline, weathered limestone cliffs and spectacular sand dunes, some of which tower as high as 90 m (295 ft). De Hoop's main attraction is a 14-km (9-mile) wetland that is home to 12 of South Africa's 16 waterfowl species.

Thousands of red-knobbed coot, yellow-billed duck and Cape shoveller, as well as Egyptian geese, can be seen here, although populations do fluctuate with the water level of the marshland. The bird-watching is best between the months of September and April, when migrant flocks of Palaearctic waders arrive. Of the 13 species that have been recorded, visitors may expect to see ringed plover, wood and curlew sandpiper, greenshank and little stint.

The rich variety of *fynbos* species includes the endemic Bredasdorp sugarbush (*Protea obtusifolia*), stinkleaf sugarbush (*Protea susannae*) and pin-cushion protea (*Leucospermum oliefolium*). Wildlife species to look out for include the rare Cape mountain zebra and bontebok, eland, grey rhebok, baboons and the yellow mongoose.

A mountain bike trail traverses the Potberg section of the reserve, which contains a breeding colony of the rare Cape vulture. Comfortable campsites and cottages are available and overnight visitors can experience the spectacular southern night sky almost free of light pollution. De Hoop is also the start of the popular 5-day Whale Trail hike along the coast, which must be booked well in advance.

9

## Swellendam

🅐 B7 🚆 22 Swellengrebel Street; www.visit swellendam.co.za

Nestling in the shadow of the Langeberg Mountains, Swellendam is one of South Africa's most picturesque small towns. It is the country's third-oldest town, after Cape Town and Stellenbosch, and was founded by the Dutch in 1742 and named after the governor and his wife.

The thatched-roofed and whitewashed **Drostdy** was built by the Dutch East India Company in 1747 as the seat of the *landdrost*, or magistrate.

It now serves as a museum of Dutch colonial life. The adjacent Old Gaol was originally a single-storey building, but it was subsequently enlarged to include an enclosed courtyard.

Near the museum is the *Ambagswerf* (trade yard), which features a smithy and wagon-maker's shop, a mill and bakery, a tannery and a coppersmith. Also on site is the Mayville Cottage. Built between 1853 and 1855, it represents a transition of architectural styles, using both Cape Dutch and Cape Georgian influences.

> Nestling in the shadow of the Langeberg Mountains, Swellendam is one of South Africa's most picturesque small towns.

Swellendam is renowned for its many fine old buildings. The Oefeningshuis was built in 1838 as a school for those freed from slavery. An interesting feature of the building is the clock designed for the illiterate: when the time painted on the sculpted clock face matches that on the real clock below, then it is time for worship. Also noteworthy are the Dutch Reformed Church, the wrought-iron balconies of the 19th-century Buirski & Co shop and the elegant Auld House.

### Drostdy

⊛ ⊛ ⊜  🏠 18 Swellengrebel St ⏲ 9am–4:45pm Mon–Fri, 10am–3pm Sat & Sun ✕ 1 Jan, Easter, 25 Dec 🌐 drostdy.com

---

🔟

### Bontebok National Park

🅰 B7 🚩 Swellendam ⏲ 7am–6pm daily (to 7pm Oct–Apr) 🌐 sanparks.org

The southern outskirts of Swellendam are home to South Africa's smallest national park, which extends

across 28 sq km (11 sq miles) of undulating terrain bounded by the Breede River at the base of the Langeberg Mountains. As its name suggests, the park was set aside as a reserve for the bontebok, and it now hosts around 200 of these endemic antelopes. Other native mammals include Cape mountain zebra, red hartebeest, grey rhebok and Cape grysbok. The park is also great for birders, with more than 200 species recorded. Look out for the Denham's bustard and Agulhas long-billed lark in areas of open cover, and Acacia Pied Barbet, southern boubou and swee waxbill in thickets along the river and around the park's campsite. As there is no dangerous wildlife in the park, the game-viewing roads are supplemented by three self-guided walking trails.

←

Interior of the Drostdy colonial museum in Swellendam

# THE GARDEN ROUTE

Archaeological deposits near Mossel Bay and Plettenberg Bay indicate that human habitation along the Garden Route goes back 150,000 years, but little is known about the history of these early societies. In 1488, a Portuguese naval expedition led by Bartolomeu Dias landed at Mossel Bay, becoming the first Europeans to set foot on South African soil before being chased away in a hail of stones. Nine years later, Vasco da Gama landed at the same site and bartered goods for cattle with the local Khoe, the first such transaction recorded in South Africa. Settlers started farming the area now known as the Garden Route in the 1750s and woodcutters arrived in the 1770s. By this time, the region's traditional Khoe inhabitants had either been killed by settlers or enslaved, with the only trace of their culture left in place names such as Outeniqua (the name of a Khoe clan) and Tsitsikamma. The mountains around George and Knysna were heavily exploited for timber in the 19th and early 20th centuries, and plantation forestry remains an important industry in the region. Today, however, the Garden Route – more, perhaps, than any other part of South Africa – has a strongly tourism-driven economy, though other key activities include agriculture and offshore gas extraction at Mossel Bay.

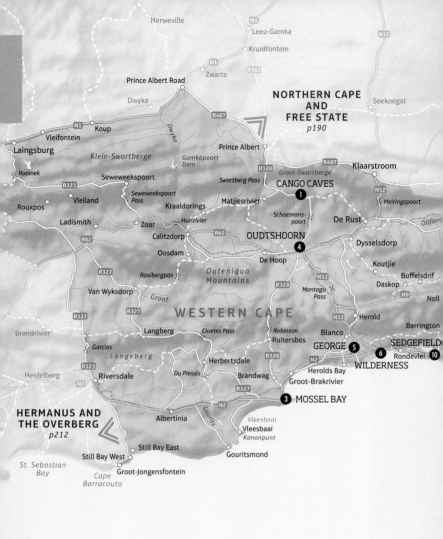

Merville

Leeu-Gamka

N1

N12

Kruidfontein

N1

Zwarts

R353

Prince Albert Road

**NORTHERN CAPE
AND
FREE STATE**
*p190*

Dwyka

Seekoegat

R407

Koup

Prince Albert

Vleifontein

N1

*Klein-Swartberge*

Laingsburg

*Gamkapoort
Dam*

R328

*Groot-Swartberge*

R407

Klaarstroom

*Rooinek*

*Swartberg Pass*

**CANGO CAVES**

N12

R323

Seweeksport

*Swartberg Pass*

➊

*Meiringspoort*

Vleiland

*Seweeksport
Pass*

Kraaldorings

Matjiesrivier

*Schoemans-
poort*

De Rust

Rouxpos

Ladismith

Zoar

*Huisrivier*

*Olifant*

R62

Calitzdorp

R62

**OUDTSHOORN**

Dysselsdorp

R327

Oosdam

De Hoop

➍

Koutjie

*Rooibergpas*

*Outeniqua
Mountains*

R328

Buffelsdrif

Van Wyksdorp

*Groot*

*Montagu
Pass*

N12

Daskop

N9

Noll

R327

**WESTERN CAPE**

N12

Herold

Brandrivier

R323

Langberg

*Cloetes Pass*

*Robinson*

Blanco

Barrington

*Garcias*

Ruitersbos

**GEORGE**

**SEDGEFIELD**

*Langeberg*

Herbertsdale

R328

N2

➎

➏

Rondevlei

➓

Heidelberg

Du Plessis

Brandwag

Herolds Bay

**WILDERNESS**

Riversdale

R327

Groot-Brakrivier

N2

N2

➌ **MOSSEL BAY**

Albertinia

*Gourits*

*Vleesbaai*

**HERMANUS AND
THE OVERBERG**
*p212*

Vleesbaai

*Kanonpunt*

*St. Sebastian
Bay*

Still Bay East

Gouritsmond

Still Bay West

*Cape
Barracouta*

Groot-Jongensfontein

*Indian Ocean*

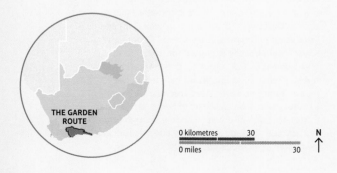

**THE GARDEN
ROUTE**

0 kilometres          30

0 miles          30

N
↑

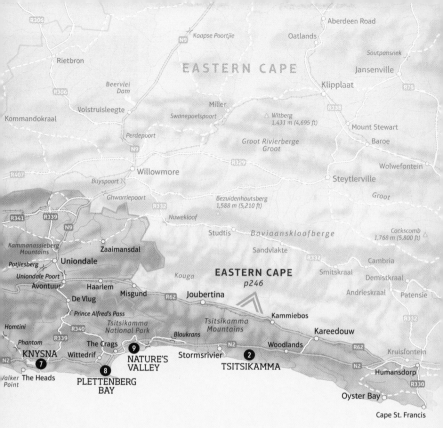

# THE GARDEN ROUTE

### Must Sees
**1** Cango Caves
**2** Tsitsikamma

### Experience More
**3** Mossel Bay
**4** Oudtshoorn
**5** George
**6** Wilderness
**7** Knysna
**8** Plettenberg Bay
**9** Nature's Valley
**10** Sedgefield

**1** 🏂 🎿 🍴 🛍️

# CANGO CAVES

🅰️ C6  🅰️ R328 from Oudtshoorn  📞 044 272 7410
🕐 9am–4pm daily

Located just north of Oudtshoorn, the Cango Caves are home to some of the biggest dripstone formations in the world. Over a quarter of a million visitors flock to explore this fascinating subterranean network each year.

Deep in the foothills of the Swartberg Mountains lies an underground network of chambers and passages where dissolved minerals have crystallized to form stalactite and stalagmite dripstone formations that resemble fluted columns and delicate, ruffled drapes.

The first European to explore the complex was Jacobus van Zyl, after his herdsman stumbled upon the cave opening in 1780, but rock paintings and stone implements discovered near the entrance indicate that the site was occupied as early as 80,000 years ago.

Of the three caves, only Cango 1 is open to the public. Access to Cango 2 and 3, rediscovered in 1972 and 1975 respectively, is prohibited in order to preserve the crystals. Some of the dramatic dripstone formations in Cango 1, which is 762 m (2,500 ft) in length, are the 9-m- (30-ft-) high Cleopatra's Needle – believed to be some 150,000 years old – a dainty Ballerina and a Frozen Waterfall. The largest chamber is Van Zyl's Hall, 107 m (350 ft) long and 16 m (52 ft) high.

An hour-long standard tour takes in the first six chambers, while the full tour is a 90-minute hike that includes 416 stairs and is best attempted only by the fit. The temperature inside is a constant 18° C (64° F), but humidity can reach an uncomfortable 99.9 per cent. Book ahead; the last tour begins at 4pm daily.

### FORMATION OF THE CANGO CAVES

The tunnels of Cango burrow through a 20-million-year-old limestone stratum at the base of the quartzite Swartberg. Situated in a wide fault, the limestone was gradually washed away by seepage water, which carried with it the particles of semi-soluble calcite that form the caves' many drip formations.

## Did You Know?

Cango contains the only piece of South African cave art to have been created in a totally dark area.

↑ Dramatic drip formations inside Cango 1, which is open to tour groups *(inset)*

**2**

# TSITSIKAMMA

🅰 D7  🕐 6:30am–7pm daily  Ⓦ sanparks.org

Tsitsikamma is a Khoe word meaning "place of abundant waters". The scenic reserve is known for its indigenous forests – which are heavily populated with giant yellowwood trees – and stunning coastline with an abundance of marine life.

Tsitsikamma is part of the larger Garden Route National Park and extends for 68 km (42 miles) from Nature's Valley to Oubosstrand. It stretches seawards for some 5.5 km (3 miles), offering licensed snorkellers and divers a unique "underwater trail". Within the park's boundaries lie two of South Africa's most popular hikes, the Tsitsikamma and Otter trails. Both take five days to complete; the former is a relatively easy inland route that winds through primeval forest in the Tsitsikamma mountains. The Otter Trail was the country's first official hike, and is a scenic coastal path along which whales, dolphins and otters may be spotted.

> 💬 INSIDER TIP
> **Walking Kit**
>
> Visitors should be fit and wear sturdy walking shoes. On longer hikes, all provisions and gear must be carried, as the overnight huts are equipped only with mattresses. Some trails involve swimming or wading, so waterproof backpacks are advisable.

**Did You Know?**

The park is home to the world's highest commercial bungee jump, the Bloukrans Bungy.

Turquoise waters and coastal scenery within the Tsitsikamma reserve ↑

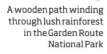

A hiker examining The Big Tree, an ancient yellowwood near the Tsitsikamma Trail ↑

→

A wooden path winding through lush rainforest in the Garden Route National Park

**LAND RESTITUTION**

The Mfengu people settled in the Tsitsikamma area in the 1830s after being left landless as a result of King Shaka's Mfecane wars *(p62)*. They were once again torn from their land in the 1970s, this time by the Apartheid government. In 1994, the Mfengu were the first group of Black South Africans to receive their land back under the Land Claims Restitution Act. The community has since benefitted from government investment.

# EXPERIENCE MORE

## ③ Mossel Bay

**A** C7 **i** Cnr Church and Market sts; www.visitmosselbay.co.za

One of the main attractions in the seaside town of Mossel Bay, situated 397 km (246 miles) east of Cape Town, is the interesting museum complex and the historic centre, both overlooking the harbour.

Seafaring history is the subject at the **Bartolomeu Dias Museum Complex**. Established in 1988, the complex celebrates the 500th anniversary of Dias's historic landfall; the Portuguese explorer dropped anchor off the South African coast in February 1488. The inlet he named after São Bras (St Blaize) is today called Mossel Bay. A full-sized replica of Dias's ship was built in Portugal in 1987 and set sail for Mossel Bay, arriving right on time on 3 February 1988. Here, the 130-ton vessel was lifted from the water and lowered into the specially altered museum. Alongisde this outstanding reconstruction, there are old maps, photographs and documents detailing the first explorations around the tip of Africa. The complex also includes the Protea Hotel Mossel Bay, which dates back to 1846 and is thought to be the oldest building in town.

Mossel Bay is probably best known for its controversial and costly Mossgas development, initiated by the discovery of natural offshore gas fields.

The real charm of the settlement lies in its natural beauty, fine beaches and walks. The 15-km (9-mile) St Blaize Hiking Trail winds along an unspoiled stretch of coastline, while Santos Beach, the only north-facing beach in South Africa, guarantees sunny afternoons and safe swimming.

Regular cruises take visitors out to Seal Island, while White Shark Africa offers shark cage dives or snorkelling and certification diving courses.

### Bartolomeu Dias Museum Complex

⊘ ⊙ **A** 1 Market St
⊙ 9am–2pm Mon–Fri
⊙ Good Fri, 25 Dec
**W** diasmuseum.co.za

**Did You Know?**

One ostrich egg is equivalent to approximately 24 chicken's eggs.

## ④ Oudtshoorn

**A** C7 **i** 80 Voortrekker St; www.oudtshoorn.com

The town of Oudtshoorn was established in 1847 at the foot of the Swartberg Mountains, to cater for the needs of the Little Karoo's growing farming population. It gained prosperity when the demand for ostrich feathers – to support Victorian, and later Edwardian fashion trends – created a sharp rise in the industry in 1870–80.

The Karoo's hot, dry climate proved suitable for big-scale ostrich farming; the loamy soils yielded extensive crops of lucerne,

A hops field outside George, a crop that flourishes in the farming valleys of the region ↑

which forms a major part of the birds' diet, and the ground was strewn with the small pebbles that are a vital aid to their somewhat unusual digestive processes (ostriches have neither teeth nor a crop in the oesophagus to store food, so they eat stones as a means of helping to grind and digest their food).

Oudtshoorn's importance as an ostrich-farming centre continued for more than 40 years, and the town became renowned for its sandstone mansions built by wealthy ostrich barons. However, World War I and changes in fashion resulted in the industry's decline, and many farmers went bankrupt. Ostrich farming eventually recovered in the 1940s with the establishment of the tanning industry, and Oudtshoorn remains known as the "ostrich capital of the world". Today, ostrich products include eggs, leather, meat and bonemeal. The town also produces crops of tobacco, wheat and grapes.

The lifesize replica of Bartolomeu Dias's ship, displayed in Mossel Bay

### 5
# George

C7 124 York St; www.visitgeorge.co.za

The wide streets of George were laid out in 1811 during the British occupation of the Cape. Named after King George III, the town is today the Garden Route's largest centre, primarily serving the farming community.

The Outeniqua Transport Museum provides an insight into the history of steam train travel in South Africa. Nearby, the appealing **Outeniqua Nature Reserve** is the starting point for 12 day walks in the indigenous forest of the Outeniqua Mountains. At least 125 tree species grow here, and more than 30 forest birds have been recorded. The Tierkop Trail is a circular overnight route that covers 30 km (19 miles), while the difficult Outeniqua Trail between here and Knysna covers 108 km (67 miles) in seven days.

#### Outeniqua Nature Reserve

Witfontein, on R28 NW of George 7:30am–4pm daily capenature.co.za

# STAY

**Fancourt Hotel**
Gracing a spectacular golfing estate below the Outeniqua Mountains, this elegant hotel features several pools and a tennis court.

Montague St, George
fancourt.com

®®®

**Queens Hotel**
This renovated, colonial-style hotel dates from 1880 and offers great service and a convenient location in the historic heart of town.

05 Baron van Rheede St, Oudtshoorn
queenshotel.co.za

®®®

**Rosenhof Country House**
Guests will delight in the period furnishings, pretty rose garden and scenic swimming pool at this sumptuous boutique hotel.

264 Baron van Rheede St, Oudtshoorn
rosenhof.co.za

®®®

Walkers strolling along the water's edge as the sun sets over a pristine Wilderness beach ↑

### 6

## Wilderness

🅰 C7  ℹ 198 George Rd; www.visitgeorge.co.za

Ten kilometres (6 miles) east of the city of George is South Africa's lake district. This chain of salt- and fresh-water lakes at the foot of forested mountain slopes forms part of the Wilderness sector of the Garden Route National Park. Protecting some 30 km (19 miles) of unspoiled coastline, the park features two long white beaches: Wilderness and Leentjiesklip. Despite the appealing backdrop, note that

> At Wilderness Heights lies the Map of Africa, a forested area run through by a stretch of the Keurbooms River shaped like the African continent.

swimming is not safe here due to the strong undercurrents. Of the five lakes in this region, the three westernmost ones – Island Lake, Langvlei and Rondevlei – are all linked and fed by the Touw River via a natural water channel called the Serpentine. Swartvlei is the largest and deepest lake, and it is connected to the sea by an estuary, although its mouth silts up for six months

of the year. Groenvlei, which is the only lake not located within the park, is not fed by any river and has no link to the sea. Instead, it receives its water through springs and rainfall; as a result, it is the least brackish.

Birdlife viewing in the park is excellent, with as many as 79 of the country's waterbird species having been recorded here. Five species of kingfisher can be spotted – pied, giant, half-collared, brown-hooded and malachite. The area is also popular for angling and watersports, and a scenic drive starting at Wilderness runs along Lakes Road, which skirts the lake chain and meets up with the N2 at Swartvlei.

There are many hiking trails in and around Wilderness. With the magnificent Outeniqua range stretched along the northern perimeter of the area, visitors can ramble through natural forests on routes that cover a range of durations and difficulty levels, including the Brown-Hooded Kingfisher Trail. Another popular activity

### THE ENDEMIC KNYSNA SEAHORSE

Listed as Endangered by the IUCN (International Union for Conservation of Nature), the Knysna seahorse possesses a chameleon-like capacity to change colour to reflect its mood and environment. Native to the Garden Route, it is known only from the Keurbooms River Estuary, Swartvlei Estuary and Knysna Lagoon, placing it at high risk of extinction.

is hiring a canoe from Eden Adventures and paddling up the Touw River into a forested gorge situated within Garden Route National Park and inhabited by monkeys and a wide variety of colourful forest birds.

For the most daring visitor, one-day paragliding courses or short tandem flights are available at Cloudbase Paragliding. At Wilderness Heights lies the Map of Africa, a forested area run through by a stretch of the Keurbooms River shaped like the African continent.

Off the N2, between Wilderness and Sedgefield, is **Timberlake Farm Village**, a collection of charming wooden cabins with a café, a country-style restaurant deli and a wine shop. Numerous activities are available, including a delightful fairy-themed garden, an adventure playground for children and a zipline cable ride in the trees.

**Timberlake Farm Village**
🍷 😊 👶 🚗 N2 between Wilderness and Sedgefield 🕐 8am–5pm daily 🌐 timberlakeorganic.co.za

# EAT

### Pomodoro
The terrace at this Italian joint is a local favourite, with the family-friendly menu offering something for everyone.

🚗 George Rd, Wilderness
🌐 pomodoro.co.za

Ⓡ Ⓡ Ⓡ

### Salinas Beach Restaurant
The wide balconies at Salinas offer fine views over Wilderness Beach and the Mediterranean-fusion menu focuses on fresh seafood.

🚗 458 Zundorf Ln
🌐 salinas.co.za

Ⓡ Ⓡ Ⓡ

# STAY

### The Old Trading Post
This charming guesthouse features a lush garden where plenty of birdlife can be observed.

🚗 Vleie Rd, Wilderness
🌐 oldtradingpost.co.za

Ⓡ Ⓡ Ⓡ

### The Fairy Knowe
This popular base for birdwatching and canoeing has an idyllic location on the Touw River facing Garden Route National Park.

🚗 Dumbleton Rd
🌐 fairyknowehotel.co.za

Ⓡ Ⓡ Ⓡ

Scenically located chalets along the banks of the Touw River

The popular Knysna Quays district, bristling with shops and restaurants ↑

## ⑦
## Knysna

 C7 ⊞ 🛈 40 Main Rd; www.visitknysna.co.za

A significant figure in Knysna's history was George Rex, who, according to local legend, was the son of Britain's King George III and his first wife Hannah Lightfoot, a Quaker. The claim, made as a result of Rex's opulent lifestyle, was never proved, but he played a key role in developing the harbour and was a prominent landowner in the area.

Today, Knysna is one of the Garden Route's most popular tourist destinations. The Knysna Quays is a modern complex developed around the old harbour, packed with restaurants, boutiques and souvenir shops. A marina has been built on Thesen Island, linked to the town by a causeway, which has a man-made beach and a pleasant park with bird hides.

One of Knysna's most attractive features is the 17-km (11-mile) Knysna Lagoon, which is protected from the sea by two sandstone cliffs, the Knysna Heads. George Rex Drive provides access to the Eastern Head, from where there are superb views. On the Western Head, accessible via a ferry, is the private Featherbed Nature Reserve. A four-hour excursion there includes the boat trip, a guided nature walk called the Bushbuck Trail, a short 4WD ride to the top of the Western Knysna Head and a buffet lunch.

South Africa's largest commercial oyster-farming centre is based at Knysna Lagoon. Pacific oysters can be sampled on tasting tours, or at one of the restaurants on Thesen Island. Another popular culinary activity is a gin-tasting session and a distillery tour at **Knysna Gin**, which was founded in 2018 and has won awards for its range of imaginatively flavoured gins..

---

### PINK LOERIE MARDI GRAS AND ARTS FESTIVAL

Established in 2001 to attract visitors during the quiet month of May, Knysna's LGBTQ+ carnival has a celebratory atmosphere and an inclusive ethos. Behind the fun façade, it aims to empower the local LGBTQ+ community and to raise awareness of the damage caused by bullying, violence and hate crime.

---

## 50,000

The average number of attendees at Knysna's annual oyster festival.

Only 200 m (656 ft) from Knysna's main road, the **Pledge Nature Reserve** is an urban reclamation project comprising a former brickfield. Created in 1991, the reserve has been restored to near pristine condition due to the planting of indigenous trees and the creation of dams to purify streams. Criss-crossed by a network of wheelchair-friendly footpaths offering lovely views to the lagoon and Knysna Heads, the reserve contains more than 250 plant species, while a checklist of 80 bird species includes forest specialists such as Knysna loerie and olive bush shrike.

East of Knysna, a turnoff to Noetzie ends at a clifftop parking area. From here visitors can descend a path to a secluded bay with a pristine beach and an estuary guarded by five castles, all of which are now private homes.

Surrounding Knysna is some of South Africa's most magnificent indigenous forest, which supports many impressively old Outeniqua ironwood, yellowwood and stinkwood trees. Plenty of wildlife also inhabits the forest, including the elusive Knysna elephant – this is the last free-ranging population in South Africa, with only half a dozen individuals surviving.

A scenic drive north of Knysna leads to the **Diepwalle Forest Station**, home to both the circular Elephant Walk and the King Edward Tree, a gigantic Outeniqua yellowwood that is approximately 650 years old.

East of Knysna, **Harkerville Forest** is traversed by a set of mountain bike trails that emerge from the trees to reveal some dramatic coastal scenery. The nearby Kranshoek Trail is surely a contender for South Africa's loveliest coastal day hike; only 9 km (6 miles) long, it passes through an exceptional variety of habitats, including rocky seashore and patches of Protea-studded coastal *fynbos*. On the north side of the N2, shortly after it exits Harkerville Forest, lies **Knysna Elephant Park**, a refuge and rehabilitation centre for unwanted elephants: orphans, individuals rescued from culls, former circus animals. The park is a particular hit with children, who delight in feeding or walking with these relaxed animals.

### Knysna Gin

⌂ 5 Uil St ⏰ 10am-6pm Mon-Thu, 10am-10pm Fri, 2pm-7pm Sat ⧉ knysna-gin.com

### Pledge Nature Reserve

⌂ Bond St ⏰ Summer: 7am-6pm daily; winter: 8am-5pm daily ⧉ pledgenature reserve.org

→
Some of the residents of Knysna Elephant Park, cavorting in the sunshine

# EAT

### Drydock Food Company

This lovely lagoon-side restaurant offers tasty dishes and is an ideal spot for sundowners.

⌂ Knysna Quays, Knysna
⧉ drydock.co.za

Ⓡ Ⓡ Ⓡ

# STAY

### St James of Knysna

A five-star country hotel set in a sprawling landscaped estate facing the Knysna Heads.

⌂ The Point, Knysna
⧉ stjames.co.za

Ⓡ Ⓡ Ⓡ

### Diepwalle Forest Station

⌂ R339 ☎ 044 382 9762 ⏰ 6am-6pm daily

### Harkerville Forest

⌂ N2 ☎ 044 532 7770 ⏰ 6am-6pm daily

### Knysna Elephant Park

⌂ N2 ⏰ 9am-3pm daily
⧉ knysnaelephant park.co.za

## 8

# Plettenberg Bay

🅰 C7 🚌 Shell Ultra City, Marine Way 🛈 Melville's Corner, Main St; www. pletttourism.co.za

Upmarket Plettenberg Bay, 30 km (19 miles) east of Knysna *(p238)*, is a holiday playground of the wealthy. A coast of rivers, lagoons and white beaches, "Plett", as it is called by the locals, earned the name Bahia Formosa ("beautiful bay") from early Portuguese sailors.

The town is perched on red sandstone cliffs that rise above the coastline. To its south, the **Robberg Nature Reserve** juts out into the sea, its cliffs rising to 148 m (486 ft) in places. The three trails range from a 30-minute stroll to a four-hour hike, all offering fantastic views of churning seas, pristine bays, and the seal colony for which the peninsula is named. The reserve also extends 2 km (1 mile) offshore, protecting a range of vulnerable fish. Dolphins and whales are often seen in spring.

Situated south of the N2, about 10 km (6 miles) east of Plettenberg Bay, **Jukani Wildlife Sanctuary** is a refuge for carnivores rescued from breeding facilities and other non-viable circumstances. Indigenous animals such as lion, leopard, cheetah, honey-badger and spotted hyena are all present, along with a few exotic creatures such as a white tiger and a jaguar. Expert-led guided tours take around 90 minutes.

Further east is the popular **Monkeyland**, the world's first multispecies free-roaming primate sanctuary. More than a dozen primate species here include baboons from South Africa, athletic squirrel monkeys from South

The dramatic coastal Robberg Nature Reserve, where dolphins can often be glimpsed *(inset)*

America and Madagascan lemurs, all rescued from domestic captivity.

**Birds of Eden**, situated next to Monkeyland, is the world's largest free-flight aviary. Its dome spans a gorge and is divided by a walkway and suspension bridge. It is home to more than 3,500 birds, from colourful, forest-loving macaws, toucans and turacos to majestic blue cranes (the national bird of South Africa) and 30 types of waterfowl.

**Robberg Nature Reserve**
🈯 🅰 Robberg Rd 🕐 7am–5pm daily (to 8pm Dec & Jan) 🌐 capenature.co.za

**Jukani Wildlife Sanctuary**
🈯🈲 🅰 The Crags 🕐 9am–4pm daily 🌐 jukani.co.za

### Monkeyland

 **The Crags**
⏰ 8am–5pm daily 🌐 monkey
land.co.za

### Birds of Eden

⚿ **The Crags** ⏰ 8am–5pm
daily 🌐 birdsofeden.co.za

---

**⑨**

# Nature's Valley

🅰 C7

Tucked away in a forested
gorge about 10 km (6 m) south
of the N2, Nature's Valley is
one of the prettiest but least-
visited villages on the Garden
Route. It runs down to a magnificent sandy beach separated
from the eastern border of the
Garden Route's Tsitsikamma
Sector by a wide lagoon whose
surface is usually as calm as
the forested surrounds. The
village lies at the centre of a
50-km (31-mile) network of
day trails that lead deep into
an ancient forest, which is
inhabited by a wealth of
colourful birds, along with
several types of antelope.
Non-hikers who want to
explore the scenic forest can
cruise slowly along a looping
pair of backroads that connect

↑ Holidaymakers enjoying safe swimming and
surfing at Sedgefield's picturesque beach

Nature's Valley to the N2.
Nearby, the Bloukrans River
Bridge marks the provincial
boundary between the
Western and Eastern capes,
and is also the platform used
for the world's third-highest
commercial bungee jump.

---

**⑩**

# Sedgefield

🅰 C7 📧 ℹ 30 Main Street;
**www.discover-sedgefield-
south-africa.com**

Located between Wilderness
and Knysna, Sedgefield is
an attractive small town set
around a network of lagoons
that lead to a pristine beachfront scattered with small
resort-type developments.

Sedgefield Beach offers
safe swimming (perfect for
families), and bass fishing
opportunities at Cola Beach,
Myoli Beach, Swartvlei Beach
or Gerike's Point. In addition
to the several lakes and
beaches, there are a variety
of pretty forests and lakeside
walking trails.

Bordering Sedgefield, the
**Goukamma Nature Reserve**
is home to flora such as *fynbos*
and milkwood and wildlife
that include Cape grysbok,
blue duiker and Cape clawless
otters. The circular Bush
Pig Trail within the reserve
runs along a ridge of dunes

offering fine views of
the ocean. There are also
kayaks available for rent.

**Goukamma Nature
Reserve**

🅰 8 km (5 miles) from
the N2 on Buffalo Bay Rd
⏰ 8am–6pm daily
🌐 capenature.co.za

---

# A LONG WALK
# ROBBERG
# NATURE RESERVE

**Distance** Gap Circuit: 2 km (1 mile); Witsand Circuit: 5.5 km (3 miles); Point Circuit: 9.2 km (6 miles) **Walking time** Gap Circuit: 30 minutes; Witsand Circuit: two hours; Point Circuit: four hours **Difficulty** Various **Nearest town** Plettenberg Bay

Protecting a peninsula that juts 4 km (2.5 miles) into the Indian Ocean, the tall cliffs of the stunning Robberg Nature Reserve offer fantastic views over a dramatic seascape of wave-battered rocks and pristine secluded bays. Wildlife here includes a large resident colony of Cape fur seals, and – less reliably – sharks, dolphins and whales. Three circular hiking trails are on offer: the relatively undemanding Gap Circuit, the Witsand (White Sand) Circuit and the more strenuous Point Circuit.

*The shortest of the reserve's circular trails turns back west at a striking rock formation known as **The Gap**.*

Park Entrance
**START**
**FINISH**
Nelson Bay Cave
*Nelson Bay*
*The Gap*
*Robberg Beach*
*Die Eiland (The Island)*

**Nelson Bay Cave** *contains evidence of Stone Age occupation dating back 120,000 years, when Robberg also supported now-extinct giant forms of horse and buffalo.*

*Portuguese survivors of the Sao Gonçalo shipwreck in 1630 camped at the south end of **Robberg Beach**.*

**Die Eiland** *(The Island) is a small, climbable hill separated from the rest of the peninsula by the lovely sandy beach that rises northwards to the Witsand dune.*

← Steps down to one of the reserve's pretty beaches

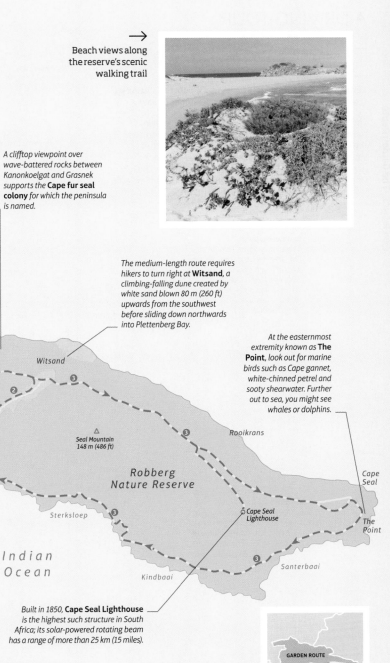

→ Beach views along the reserve's scenic walking trail

*A clifftop viewpoint over wave-battered rocks between Kanonkoelgat and Grasnek supports the* **Cape fur seal colony** *for which the peninsula is named.*

*The medium-length route requires hikers to turn right at* **Witsand**, *a climbing-falling dune created by white sand blown 80 m (260 ft) upwards from the southwest before sliding down northwards into Plettenberg Bay.*

*At the easternmost extremity known as* **The Point**, *look out for marine birds such as Cape gannet, white-chinned petrel and sooty shearwater. Further out to sea, you might see whales or dolphins.*

Witsand

❷ ❸

❸

❷

❷

❸

❸

△ Seal Mountain 148 m (486 ft)

Rooikrans

Cape Seal

Robberg Nature Reserve

…andbaai

❸

Sterksloep

○ Cape Seal Lighthouse

The Point

Indian Ocean

❸

❸

Kindbaai

Santerbaai

*Built in 1850,* **Cape Seal Lighthouse** *is the highest such structure in South Africa; its solar-powered rotating beam has a range of more than 25 km (15 miles).*

## HIKING TRAILS

❶ Gap Circuit
❷ Witsand Circuit
❸ Point Circuit

| 0 metres | 500 |
| 0 yards | 500 |

N ↑

**Locator Map**
*For more detail see p228*

GARDEN ROUTE

● Robberg Nature Reserve

# A DRIVING TOUR
# FOUR PASSES

**Length** 380 km (235 miles) **Stopping-off points** Calitzdorp, Oudtshoorn, Prince Albert **Difficulty** Some gravel roads

The Little Karoo is a region sharply defined by mountain ranges. Sandwiched between the Swartberg to the north and the Langeberg and Outeniqua mountains to the south, it is surrounded by spectacular peaks that severely tested the genius of South Africa's famous road engineer Thomas Bain. Of the four different passes constructed here, the most majestic is the one that winds its way through the Swartberg.

**Locator Map**
*For more detail see p228*

Four Passes
THE GARDEN ROUTE

**Seweweekspoort**
*("seven weeks pass") is a 15-km (9-mile) gravel route through sheer walls of rough-hewn rock, criss-crossing a river course. Local legend claims that its name refers to the time it used to take brandy smugglers to cross this route.*

*Swartberg Nature Reserve*

*Kariegasberg 2,053 m (6,736 ft)*

S w a r t b e r g   M o u n t a i n s

*Gamka*

*Waboomsberg*

Seweweekspoort

R323

Zoar

○ Ladismith   R62

R62

**START**
Calitzdorp

Buffelskloof ○

R62

*The streets of the village of **Calitzdorp** are lined with Victorian houses. Nearby is a natural hot-spring spa, while some of the best port wines in the country are produced at Boplaas, Die Krans Estate and the Calitzdorp Wine Cellar.*

*Gamka*

| 0 kilometres | 10 |
|---|---|
| 0 miles | 10 |

N ↑

←
Ostriches at a commercial farm near Oudtshoorn

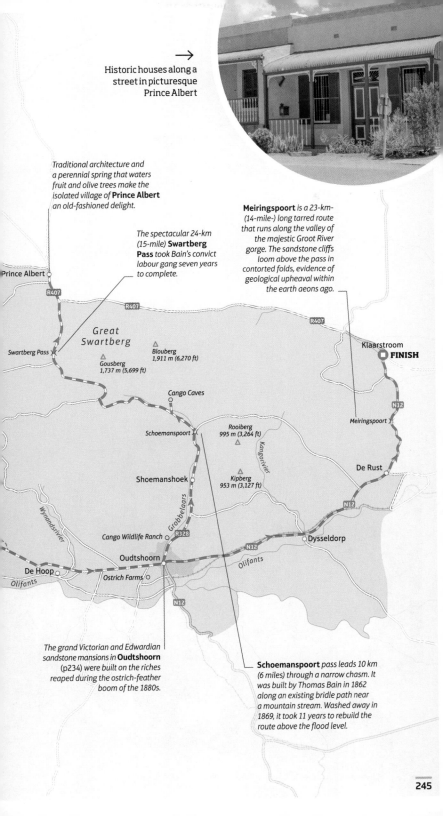

→
Historic houses along a
street in picturesque
Prince Albert

Traditional architecture and
a perennial spring that waters
fruit and olive trees make the
isolated village of **Prince Albert**
an old-fashioned delight.

**Meiringspoort** *is a 23-km-
(14-mile-) long tarred route
that runs along the valley of
the majestic Groot River
gorge. The sandstone cliffs
loom above the pass in
contorted folds, evidence of
geological upheaval within
the earth aeons ago.*

*The spectacular 24-km
(15-mile)* **Swartberg
Pass** *took Bain's convict
labour gang seven years
to complete.*

Prince Albert ○

R407

R407

R407

*Great
Swartberg*

△
*Blouberg
1,911 m (6,270 ft)*

Klaarstroom
● **FINISH**

Swartberg Pass ✕

△
*Gousberg
1,737 m (5,699 ft)*

N12

*Meiringspoort* ⟩

Cango Caves

*Rooiberg
995 m (3,264 ft)*
△

Schoemanspoort ⟩

*Kangorivier*

De Rust ○

Shoemanshoek ○

△
*Kipberg
953 m (3,127 ft)*

N12

*Grobbelaars*

Cango Wildlife Ranch ○
R328

N12

○ Dysseldorp

*Wynandsrivier*

Oudtshoorn ○

*Olifants*

De Hoop ○
*Olifants*

○ Ostrich Farms ○

N12

*The grand Victorian and Edwardian
sandstone mansions in* **Oudtshoorn**
*(p234) were built on the riches
reaped during the ostrich-feather
boom of the 1880s.*

**Schoemanspoort** *pass leads 10 km
(6 miles) through a narrow chasm. It
was built by Thomas Bain in 1862
along an existing bridle path near
a mountain stream. Washed away in
1869, it took 11 years to rebuild the
route above the flood level.*

# EASTERN CAPE

The Eastern Cape is home to the Xhosa, a pastoralist people who form part of the same Nguni linguistic subgroup as their Zulu neighbours, and are divided into two main political groupings, the amaGcaleka and amaRharhabe. The Xhosa were among the first of South Africa's Indigenous peoples to come into conflict with European settlers, and have a proud history of resistance to colonialism. In 1820, the British shipped 4,000 settlers to Port Elizabeth (now Gqeberha) to buffer the established Cape Colony against the Xhosa living east of the Great Fish River. Tensions came to a head in 1857, when, inspired by a visitation received by a teenage girl called Nongqawuse, the Xhosa elders ordered the sacrificial killing of 350,000 cattle and widespread burning of crops to encourage the ancestral spirits to smite the British intruders. The ensuing famine left 30,000 people dead and forced many Xhosa chieftaincies to submit to colonial rule. Under apartheid, Xhosa leaders such as Nelson Mandela, Walter Sisulu and Oliver Tambo played a major role in the struggle. The Eastern Cape was created in 1994 when the nominally independent Xhosa homelands of Transkei and Ciskei were reincorporated into South Africa and merged with the eastern part of the old Cape Province.

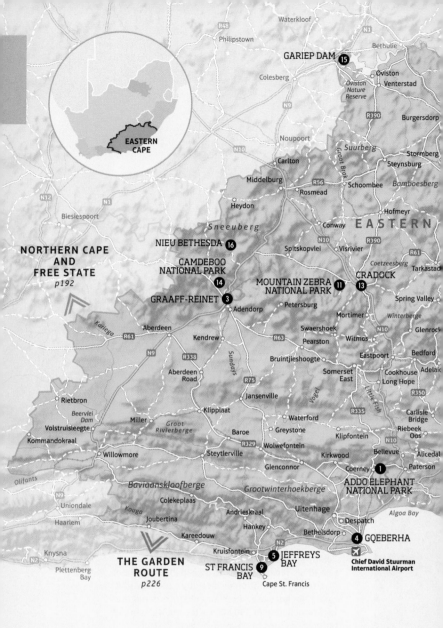

*Indian
Ocean*

# EASTERN CAPE

## Must Sees

1. Addo Elephant National Park
2. Wild Coast
3. Graaff-Reinet

## Experience More

4. Gqeberha
5. Jeffreys Bay
6. Port Alfred
7. East London
8. Great Fish River Nature Reserve
9. St Francis Bay
10. Makhanda
11. Mountain Zebra National Park
12. Hogsback
13. Cradock
14. Camdeboo National Park
15. Gariep Dam
16. Nieu Bethesda

**Did You Know?**

Elephants are one of the few animals that are able to recognize their own reflection.

1 ⌁ Ⓜ ☕ 🏛

# ADDO ELEPHANT NATIONAL PARK

**△D6** **⌂Addo** **⌅Gqeberha** **⌚7am–7pm daily** **🆆sanparks.org**

Rivalling Madikwe Game Reserve as South Africa's premier malaria-free game-viewing destination, Addo Elephant National Park is the third-largest national park in the country. It is unique among its peers for not only being inhabited by the Big Five, but also – in the marine section – providing a home to the southern right whale and great white shark.

The park and a cluster of associated private reserves lie a short drive inland and northeast of Gqeberha (formerly Port Elizabeth). Addo's focal point is the fenced main game area, which extends over some 200 sq km (77 sq miles) and supports around 600 very relaxed elephants. Crisscrossed by a good network of game-viewing roads and serviced by a rest camp, this sector is ideal for self-drive safaris; elephant sightings are a near certainty and there is plenty of other wildlife too. In addition to self-drive, it's also possible to book guided game drives at reception, including night drives. For a more upmarket, exclusive safari experience, nearby private game reserves such as Shamwari, Amakhala and Kwantu offer five-star bush accommodation and all-inclusive packages along similar lines to their counterparts in Sabi Sands *(p342)* and Madikwe *(p320)*.

↑ A bokmakierie, with characteristically vibrant green and yellow plumage

↑ Elephants roaming the plains of Addo Elephant National Park

## ①
### Addo Main Game Area

Offering independent travellers the most rewarding self-drive game-viewing experience anywhere in the Eastern or Western Cape, Addo's fenced main game area extends over 200 sq km (77 sq miles) of dense tangled thicket dominated by the spekboom (bacon tree), a 2–3 m (7–10 ft) succulent whose leaves reputedly taste like cured meat.

The park started life as a 68-sq-km (26-sq-mile) municipal reserve set aside in 1921 to protect Africa's most southerly elephant population. At that time it constituted 15 or so misanthropic survivors of a vermin eradication scheme, during which Major Philip Pretorius, under contract to Uitenhage Town Council, had hunted down 120 members of their kin. In 1931, the reserve was upgraded to national park status, and by 1954 it had been fenced off to prevent the elephants from raiding nearby farms. For many years after this, Addo resembled a large zoo where oranges were placed below the rest camp at night to lure out the shy beasts, while stout fences separated them from visitors.

It is all very different today. Around 600 elephants freely roam the core park, which is one of the best places anywhere in Africa to witness the interaction and behaviour of these wonderful creatures at close quarters. Leopard, buffalo, greater kudu, eland, bushbuck and red hartebeest also occur naturally, while the reintroduction of black rhino, lion and spotted hyena has elevated Addo to the status of a full-on Big Five reserve. Conspicuous smaller mammals include black-yellow mongoose, meerkat and ground squirrel, while the rich bird population of 170 species includes the endemic jackal buzzard, bokmakierie, southern tchagra, southern boubou, Cape weaver and Cape bulbul. One of the park's most fascinating creatures is often overlooked by visitors: the flightless dung beetle (p252). Signs warn motorists not to drive over these precious insects.

> **The park started life as a reserve set aside to protect Africa's most southerly elephant population.**

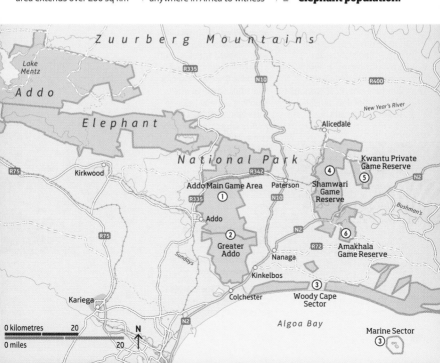

## THE FLIGHTLESS DUNG BEETLE

Endemic to Addo and its environs, the flightless dung beetle has evolved an arid-adapted, water-conserving breathing mechanism, which uses the empty space below the sheath that protects the wings of related beetles. The beetles are often seen on the roads, valiantly pushing one of the buffalo- or elephant-dung balls wherein they lay their eggs.

### Greater Addo

Like the Mountain Zebra and Bontebok national parks, Addo was created primarily to preserve one single species, and that remained the case until 1997, when a visionary proposal was put forward to allow the park to stretch from the peaks of the Zuurberg to the coastal dunes west of Port Alfred. Today, the Greater Addo Elephant National Park extends over a full 1,640 sq km (633 sq miles) and protects five of South Africa's seven terrestrial biomes, with habitats that range from montane forest and coastal *fynbos* to 100-m- (330-ft-) high dunes and the euphorbia-studded plains of the Karoo.

Elephants remain the main tourist draw, but there are also a couple of scenic day trails that can be undertaken across the mountainous Zuurberg, the most accessible of the appended terrestrial sectors of the park.

Zebra, one of the many herbivore species found in the Addo area

### Woody Cape and Marine Sectors

The 250-sq-km (97-sq-mile) Woody Cape sector of Addo protects the Alexandria forest, home to 170 tree species, as well as South Africa's largest active dune system. It is best explored on the two-day, 35-km (22-mile) Alexandria Hiking Trail, a circular route that passes through dense indigenous forest and climbs 150-m- (500-ft-) high sand dunes to form one of the finest coastal walks in South Africa. Plentiful small wildlife includes vervet monkey, bushpig, bushbuck, Cape grysbok and forest birds such as trumpeter hornbill, crowned eagle and Narina trogon. It is accessed via the attractive hamlet of Alexandria, which was founded in 1856 around a Dutch Reformed Church. Offshore, the marine sector offers fine seasonal whale-watching (June to January) and islands that host the world's largest breeding colony of Cape gannets (120,000 birds), as well as Cape fur seals, African penguins and other species.

### Shamwari Game Reserve

Only to lodge guests
shamwari.com

The Eastern Cape's largest private reserve, Shamwari protects 200 sq km (77 sq miles) of undulating bushveld in the catchment area of the Bushmans River. The recipient of several international awards, it was the brainchild of entrepreneur Adrian Gardiner, who originally bought the ranch in the hills near Paterson as a family retreat. It was gradually expanded, before becoming the first private reserve in the Eastern Cape to reintroduce large mammals. Today, Shamwari is home to all of the Big Five as well as zebra, giraffe, eland, greater kudu, impala, gemsbok, hartebeest, springbok and black wildebeest. It offers an exclusive, all-inclusive safari experience similar to the private reserves adjoining Kruger.

**100,000**
—
muscles can be found in an elephant's trunk, giving it great dexterity when picking things up.

## Kwantu Private Game Reserve

🚙 Game drives for day visitors: 9am and 2pm daily
🌐 kwantu.co.za

Extending across 60 sq km (23 sq miles) of biodiverse and scenic plains verged by the Bushman's River, this award-winning private reserve offers expertly guided morning, afternoon and evening game drives in search of the rein-troduced Big Five as well as naturally occurring wildlife such as greater kudu, blue duiker, aardwolf, caracal and porcupine. It is particularly rewarding for birdwatchers, with more than 250 species recorded. Other amenities

include a world-class spa, swimming pool, domestic animal farm, reptile centre, museum and sports facilities.

## Amakhala Game Reserve

🚙 Game drives for day visitors: 9:30am daily
🌐 amakhala.co.za

Among the finest of the 20-odd malaria-free private sanctuaries now scattered around the borders of Greater Addo, Amakhala Game Reserve extends across 85 sq km (33 sq miles) of former sheep and cattle ranchland that was given over to conservation in 1999. It comprises six contiguous and jointly managed farms, all of which are owned by descendants of 1820 Settlers, and several of its five-star lodges consist of old country houses. All of the Big Five have been reintroduced, and 16 antelope species can be seen, along with giraffe and zebra. Game drives are supplemented by boat trips on the Bushman's River.

# STAY

### Addo Rest Camp
Well-run facility with chalets, standing tents, campsites, shop, restaurant, swimming pool and a waterhole that attracts plenty of wildlife.

🏠 Inside the main park entrance gate
🌐 sanparks.org.

Ⓡ Ⓡ Ⓡ

### Long Lee Manor
The most characterful accommodation in Shamwari Game Reserve comprises the original 1910 manor house.

🏠 Shamwari Game Reserve
🌐 shamwari.com

Ⓡ Ⓡ Ⓡ

### Hillsnek Safari Camp
Set below a sandstone cliff, the most exclusive lodge in Amakhala comprises four large and stylishly furnished tents bordering the Bushman's River.

🏠 Amakhala Game Reserve
🌐 hillsnek safaris.com

Ⓡ Ⓡ Ⓡ

### Woodbury Tented Camp
Relatively affordable en-suite standing tents on stilted bases with private decks, in the big game country of Amakhala.

🏠 Amakhala Game Reserve
🌐 woodbury tentedcamp.co.za

Ⓡ Ⓡ Ⓡ

↑ A close encounter with Addo's elephants on a game drive

**Did You Know?**

The Xhosa word for Hole in the Wall, *esiKhaleni*, means "the place of sound".

**②**

# WILD COAST

**⚐ E6–F6  🛈 www.wildcoast.co.za**

The appropriately named Wild Coast is an outdoor paradise with rugged cliffs, sheltered bays and dense coastal forests. The region stretches around 280 km (175 miles) from East London to the Umtamvuna Nature Reserve next to Port Edward in KwaZulu-Natal. Much of the area is communally owned by the Xhosa, whose rural communities live off the land and adhere to age-old traditions. Spectacular beaches front a section of the Indian Ocean that is notorious for its shipwrecks.

**①**
## Coffee Bay

**🛈 Ocean View Hotel, Main Rd; www.oceanview.co.za**

Allegedly named after a ship carrying coffee which was wrecked at the site in 1863, Coffee Bay is popular for fishing, swimming and beach walks. There are a number of superbly sited hotels set above the sandy beaches. A prominent detached cliff, separated from the mainland by erosion, has been named Hole in the Wall; it is a conspicuous landmark located 6 km (4 miles) south along the coast. Many centuries

of swirling wave action have carved an arch through the centre of the cliff. More intriguingly, Xhosa legend tells that the hole was created by mystical sea people who used a large fish to batter through the rock.

↑ Small thatched huts speckling the lush, green hillside that overlooks Coffee Bay

← Sunset over the striking Hole in the Wall formation near Coffee Bay

### ③ Kei Mouth to Mbashe River

The Kei River marks the start of the Wild Coast. A total of 20 rivers enter this 80-km- (50-mile-) long stretch, along which is strung a succession of old-fashioned family hotels. North of Kei Mouth, Dwesa Nature Reserve extends along the coast from the Nqabara River. The reserve is home to rare tree dassies and samango monkeys, and the grassland, coastline and forest are all pristine. On the eastern banks of the Mbashe River is the adjacent Cwebe Nature Reserve; like Dwesa, it conserves dense forest, which is home to bushbuck and blue duiker, as well as coastal grasslands inhabited by eland, hartebeest, wildebeest and zebra. A hiking trail follows the entire Wild Coast, but the section that runs from Mbashe to Coffee Bay is the most spectacular.

### ② Morgan Bay and Kei Mouth

 www.morganbay.co.za; www.keimouth.co.za

These coastal villages lie on a stretch of coast renowned for its scenery. At Kei Mouth, a pont transports vehicles across the Great Kei River to the former Xhosa "homeland" known as Transkei. The village is only an hour's drive from East London, making it a popular weekend destination.

In Morgan Bay, the Ntshala Lagoon offers safe swimming, while walks along the cliffs afford superb views of the sea. Other activities on offer include fishing, canoeing and rock climbing.

Further south, at Double Mouth, a spur overlooking the ocean and estuary provides one of the finest views in the whole country.

💬 INSIDER TIP
**Exploring the Wild Coast**

The resorts, reserves and villages of the Wild Coast are accessible from the N2, and most of the roads are tarred – though some are not in great condition and potholes are a hazard. There is no public transport to speak of, but buses ply the N2 and some of the resorts arrange transfers.

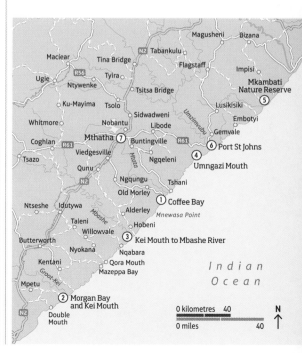

> **Horseshoe Falls in Mkambati Nature Reserve is striking – it is also unusual for being one of the few waterfalls in the world to cascade directly into the sea.**

 ④

### Umngazi Mouth

An idyllic estuary framed by forested hills, the Umngazi offers superb opportunities for snorkelling, canoeing and board-sailing. **Umngazi River Bungalows & Spa**, on the northern bank, is one of the leading resorts on the Wild Coast and is renowned for its first-class food and service. There is a lovely sandy beach and the rugged coastline extends south to the cliffs that are known locally in isiXhosa as Ndluzulu, after the crashing sound of the surf at their base.

**Umngazi River Bungalows & Spa**

▲ 25 km (16 miles) S of Port St Johns ▥ umngazi.co.za

 ⑤

### Mkambati Nature Reserve

🛈 www.visiteasterncape.co.za

Wedged between the Mzikaba and Mtentu rivers, Mkambati is the Wild Coast's largest nature reserve. Apart from conserving a 13-km- (8-mile-) long strip of grassland and unspoiled, rocky coastline, the reserve is known for its endemic plants such as the Mkambati palm, found only on the north banks of the rivers. Cape vultures breed in the Mzikaba Gorge, and the surrounding forest is home to an incredible variety of other bird species, including trumpeter hornbill and Rameron pigeon. Large

grazing herbivores such as eland, red hartebeest, blue wildebeest and blesbuck have been introduced into the open grasslands.

The Mkambati River flows through the reserve in a series of waterfalls, of which Horseshoe Falls is the most striking – it is also unusual for being one of the few waterfalls in the world to cascade directly into the sea. There is a variety of scenic walking trails to explore, while canoeing trips offer the opportunity to see the birdlife along the river up close. Accommodation in the reserve ranges from a stone lodge to cottages.

**15**
___
click sounds are contained in the Xhosa language.

↑ Crossing the Mthatha River mouth by boat during a cycle tour of the Wild Coast

## ⑥ Port St Johns

www.portstjohns.org.za

Named after a Portuguese shipwreck that actually occurred 100 km (60 miles) further northeast, Port St Johns, set on the south bank of the navigable Mzimvubu River, is a veritable metropolis by the standards of the Wild Coast. Once a thriving settler outpost, it later served as the main port of the defunct Republic of Transkei – an ostensibly self-governing Xhosa "homeland" accorded nominal independence from South Africa in 1976 and reintegrated into it in 1994. The town is now the region's main tourist hub, offering fabulous angling opportunities as well as housing a vibrant alternative art scene. The best time to visit is June and July, when the annual Sardine Run – comprising millions of tiny fish in shoals up to 10 km (6 miles) long – moves northwards from the Antarctic, attracting hordes of marine predators, from dolphins, sharks and sailfish to penguins and gannets.

## ⑦ Mthatha

Set on the banks of the eponymous river 50 km (30 miles) inland of the Wild Coast, Mthatha (formerly Umtata) was the capital of the former Transkei. A large but rather humdrum town, it boasts one genuine highlight in the form of the **Nelson Mandela Museum**, which follow its namesake's life story from his childhood in Qunu, 30 km (20 miles) out of town, to his return to the same village after his retirement from politics. The museum is housed in the Bhunga Building, which was constructed in 1903 as the regional headquarters and later served as the Parliament of the Transkei. The museum also offers tours of some of Mandela's favourite haunts in Qunu.

### Nelson Mandela Museum

◉◉◉ 🏠Nelson Mandela Drive & Owen St ⏰8am-4:30pm Mon-Fri, 9am-3pm Sat & Sun 🚫Good Friday & 1 May 🌐nelsonmandela museum.org.za

← The serene waters of the Umngazi Mouth, bathed in golden light

---

**MANDELA AND THE WILD COAST**

Nelson Mandela was born into a Thembu royal clan in 1918 in Mvezo, 55 km (35 miles) south of Mthatha. He attended primary school in nearby Qunu, and completed his schooling at Engcobo, 80 km (50 miles) to the northeast. Although his adult life was enacted on a larger stage, Mandela spent much of his retirement in Qunu and is now buried there. His maternal home in Qunu and the church where he was baptized are preserved as an annexe of Mthatha's Nelson Mandela Museum, and plans exist to make his grave a public memorial.

# ❸
# GRAAFF-REINET

🅐D6 ✈Gqeberha ⛔ ℹ17 Church St; www.graaffreinet.co.za

**The gardens and tree-lined avenues of Graaff-Reinet form a striking contrast to the bleak expanse of the surrounding Karoo. This pretty town has hundreds of historic buildings, many of which have been painstakingly restored.**

Founded in 1786, the town was named after Governor Cornelis Jacob van de Graaff and his wife, Hester Cornelia Reinet. Nine years later, the citizens of Graaff-Reinet expelled the landdrost (magistrate) and declared the first Boer Republic in South Africa. Within a matter of a few months, however, colonial control was re-established.

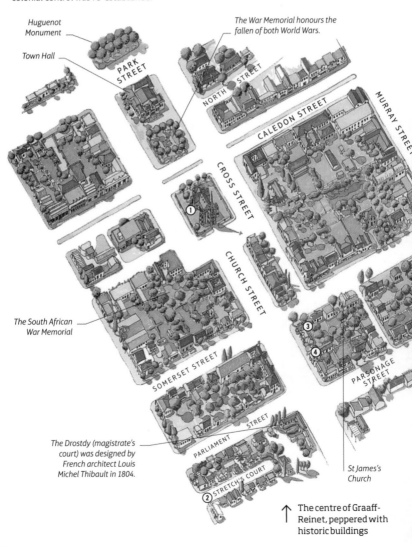

Huguenot Monument

Town Hall

PARK STREET

The War Memorial honours the fallen of both World Wars.

NORTH STREET

CALEDON STREET

MURRAY STREET

CROSS STREET

①

CHURCH STREET

The South African War Memorial

③

④

PARSONAGE STREET

SOMERSET STREET

The Drostdy (magistrate's court) was designed by French architect Louis Michel Thibault in 1804.

PARLIAMENT STREET

STRETCH'S COURT

②

St James's Church

↑ The centre of Graaff-Reinet, peppered with historic buildings

## ① Dutch Reformed Church

The beautiful Groot Kerk (great church) is considered to be one of the finest examples of Neo-Gothic architecture in the country. Completed in 1887, it was modelled on Britain's Salisbury Cathedral and was constructed using two different types of local stone.

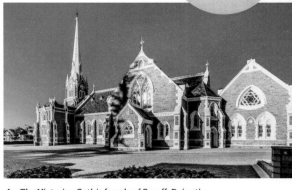

↑ The Victorian Gothic façade of Graaff-Reinet's handsome Dutch Reformed Church

## ② Stretch's Court

In 1855 Captain Charles Stretch bought land near the Drostdy to build cottages for labourers and those emancipated from slavery. Carefully restored in 1977, these pretty buildings with colourful shutters and doors are now an annexe of the Drostdy Hotel.

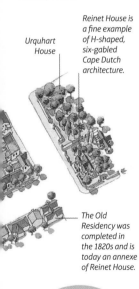

*Urquhart House*

*Reinet House is a fine example of H-shaped, six-gabled Cape Dutch architecture.*

*The Old Residency was completed in the 1820s and is today an annexe of Reinet House.*

**220**

national monuments can be found in Graaff-Reinet - more than any other town or city in the country.

## ③  Old Library Museum

🏠 Church St ⏰ 9am-5pm Mon-Fri 🚫 Public hols 🌐 graaffreinetmuseums.co.za

Established in 1847, this building served as the town's library until 1981. Today it is one of four buildings – along with Reinet House, Urquhart House and the Old Residency – that make up the Graaff-Reinet Museum. On display here are Karoo fossils, old photographs, furniture and reproductions of rock art.

## ④  Hester Rupert Art Museum

🏠 Church St ⏰ 9am-12:30pm, 2-5pm Mon-Fri, 9am-noon Sat & Sun 🚫 Good Fri & 25 Dec 🌐 rupertartmuseum.co.za

Built and consecrated as a Dutch Reformed Mission Church in 1821, this elegant building was narrowly saved from demolition in the 1960s. It was subsequently converted into an art museum, and now displays a small collection of works by contemporary South African artists, among them Irma Stern (*p40*) and Cecil Skotnes.

# EAT

**Pioneers Restaurant**
Housed in a national monument and serving traditional dishes like Karoo lamb, bobotie and venison steaks.

🏠 3 Parsonage St 📞 084 433 0612 🚫 Mon

Ⓡ Ⓡ Ⓡ

**Coldstream Restaurant**
Serves a varied mix of international seafood, steaks and vegetarian cuisine.

🏠 3 Church St 📞 087 285 4587 🚫 Sun

Ⓡ Ⓡ Ⓡ

# STAY

**Buiten Verwagten Guest House**
Set in an 1840 mansion, this characterful hotel - with spa - is easily the town's most appealing.

🏠 58 Bourke St 🌐 buitenverwagten.co.za

Ⓡ Ⓡ Ⓡ

→ Turquoise waves breaking against the rocky coastline of Gqeberha

# EXPERIENCE MORE

**4**

## Gqeberha

**D7** 🚗🚌🚆 **ℹ️** Donkin Lighthouse building, Donkin Reserve; www.nmbt.co.za

Facing east towards the wide sweep of Algoa Bay, the land on which Gqeberha sits was inhabited by the Xhosa people prior to the arrival of European setters in the 18th century. Competition for resources led to wars between the two groups, and it was against this backdrop that a township was established here by the British. Known originally as Port Elizabeth, it became the landing point for the 1820 Settlers, 4,000 British economic refugees shipped here to bolster the colony's English-speaking population. Ironically, this former bastion of British-settler culture today forms the centrepiece of a municipality named after the most celebrated of Xhosa leaders – Nelson Mandela Bay. In 2021, the township was renamed Gqeberha, the Xhosa name for the Baakens River that flows through the city.

Often referred to as the Friendly City, Gqeberha is lined with beaches and historic buildings. Donkin Reserve is a central park that includes the Donkin Lighthouse. Built in 1861, it now houses a tourism office. The lighthouse is also the country's tallest flagpole and a memorial to the horses killed during the South African War (1899–1902). The adjacent Port Elizabeth Opera House, the oldest in the southern hemisphere, was built in 1862 on a site once used for public hangings; its two stages still host many plays and shows.

Most safely explored with a local guide, lovely St George's Park is home to South Africa's oldest cricket ground and a collection of exotic plants,

### EARLY SETTLER ARCHITECTURE

Gqeberha is studded with buildings associated with the 1820 Settlers. No 7 Castle Hill, a settler's cottage from 1827, is now a museum, while the quaint double-storey 19th-century houses along Donkin Street are a national monument. Overlooking them all is the Campanile, a 52-m-(170-ft-) tall tower built in 1923 to commemorate the settlers' arrival, which has a lofty viewing platform reached via a spiral staircase.

← The Horse Memorial that stands outside the city's Donkin Reserve

> **The adjacent Port Elizabeth Opera House, the oldest in the southern hemisphere, was built in 1862 on a site once used for public hangings; its two stages still host many plays and shows.**

housed in the 19th-century Pearson Conservatory. Further south, the Boardwalk is a slick seafront complex that hosts numerous restaurants and bars, as well as entertainment venues such as an open-air theatre and a 24-hour casino. Near the harbour is **Fort Frederick**, named after the Duke of York and built in 1799 to prevent an invasion by French supporters of the rebel republic of Graaff-Reinet. The arrival of the 1820 Settlers was overseen by the fort's commander, Captain Francis Evatt, whose grave can be seen here.

Just along the coast is Humewood Beach, a recreation hub that provides quick access to all the sea-side attractions. A covered promenade hosts a weekend flea market. There is a freshwater and tidal pool complex in addition to the main beaches, and sailing and scuba diving are very popular.

The beach is also home to **Bayworld**, an unusual combination of museum, aquarium and snake park. The museum includes a gallery of salvaged items and an exhibition featuring original artifacts of

the Khoe, the area's earliest known inhabitants. On view at the snake park are the likes of puff adder and green mamba, while the aquarium's observation windows allow visitors to view penguins swimming underwater.

Further south, at the entrance to Algoa Bay, the **Cape Recife Conservancy** can be explored along a hiking trail that traverses rocky shores and dune vegetation, and passes the 1850 Cape Recife Lighthouse. Nearby, the South African Foundation for the Conservation of Coastal Birds centre rescues marine birds, especially penguins. Visitors can watch the penguins being fed at 2:30pm daily.

### Fort Frederick
🄰 Belmont Terrace
🄲 Sunrise–sunset daily

### Bayworld
🄰 Beach Rd 🄲 9am–4:30pm daily 🅦 bayworld.co.za

### Cape Recife Conservancy
🄰 13 km (8 miles) S of Gqeberha 🄲 Sunrise–sunset daily 🅦 caperecife.co.za

↑ Gqeberha's palm-lined Boardwalk, which is dotted with restaurants and entertainment venues

# EAT

### Royal Delhi
This family-run Indian restaurant is a good-value favourite. The deboned lamb curry is delicious, and there's an excellent vegetarian selection too.

🄰 10 Burgess St, Gqeberha 🄲 Sun 🅦 royaldelhi.co.za

---

### Natti's Thai Kitchen
An informal eatery that's been serving up authentic Thai dishes since 1997 – try the searingly hot "angry duck".

🄰 5 Park Lane, Gqeberha 🄲 041 373 2763 🄲 Mon & Sun

# STAY

### The Boardwalk
This five-star hotel is attached to the entertainment complex, offering easy access to both the beach and boutiques.

🄰 Beach Rd, Summer Strand, Gqeberha 🅦 suninternational.com/boardwalk

---

### Brighton Lodge
A small guesthouse with luxury suites, a swimming pool and a good range of other amenities.

🄰 21 Brighton Dr, Summer Strand, Gqeberha 🅦 brightonlodge.co.za

## ⑤

# Jeffreys Bay

**🗺 D7** **🛈 Da Gama St; www.jeffreysbay tourism.org**

This once sleepy seaside town, reputedly named after the whaler Captain Jeffreys and referred to as "J-Bay" by locals, is now the centre of South Africa's surfer scene. It is often ranked among the world's top 10 surfing spots, with a tubing right-hand break that offers a ride of over 1 km (0.5 miles) in the right conditions. The town is busiest in early July, when the World Surf League (WSL) holds its only African championship tour event there.

Jeffreys Bay's blue flag beach is perfect for swimming and sunbathing, while the **Jeffreys Bay Shell Museum** is the finest collection of its kind in the country. Established in 1945 by Charlotte Kritzinger, a local resident who first began collecting shells in her own home, the museum now showcases more than 600 different types of shell from all around the world.

**Jeffreys Bay Shell Museum**
**🏠 Da Gama St** **📞 082 852 4056** **🕐 10am–3pm Mon–Fri, 9am–2pm Sat**

### COELACANTH

In 1938, a boat fishing off the Chalumna River mouth netted an unusual fish. The captain sent it to the East London Museum, whose curator, Marjorie Courtenay-Latimer, contacted Professor JLB Smith, ichthyologist at Rhodes University. The fish - distinguished by its six primitive, limb-like fins - belonged to a species believed to have become extinct with the dinosaurs. The reward offered for another coelacanth, as the fish was named, was claimed only in 1952.

## ⑥

# Port Alfred

**🗺 E7** **🛈 Causeway Rd; www.sunshinecoast tourism.co.za**

Port Alfred, an upmarket seaside resort in the Eastern Cape, is well known for its superb beaches. Those west of the river mouth are more developed; those to the east are unspoiled and excellent for long walks. Kelly's Beach offers safe bathing, while the entire stretch of coast is perfect for surfing and is also popular with rock and surf fishermen.

Nearby, the **Kowie Nature Reserve** has an 8-km (5-mile) hiking trail with various exit points for those wanting shorter walks. It passes through a thickly forested canyon, with picnic sites next to the river.

**Kowie Nature Reserve**
**♿ 🏠 R67, 5 km (3 miles) N of Port Alfred** **🕐 7am–7pm daily**

## 7

### East London

**A** E6 ✕▢▦ **i** www. eastlondon.org.za

East London was founded as a military camp on the banks of the Buffalo River in 1847, and its strategic position as a river port was soon recognized. Originally known as Port Rex, East London was accorded city status in 1914, and today is the second-largest city in the Eastern Cape. It is an industrial centre, dominated by a Mercedes-Benz plant that manufactures vehicles for both domestic use and export.

East London is known for its swimming beaches washed by the warm waters of the Indian Ocean. The **East London Museum** has a collection of ethnographic and natural history exhibits, including the only surviving dodo egg, and the first live coelacanth specimen *(see box)*. In front of the City Hall is a statue of Steve Biko, the iconic Black Consciousness Movement leader who was detained without trial and beaten to death by security police in 1977. It was unveiled 20 years later by Nelson Mandela.

**East London Museum**

⊗ **A** 319 Oxford St **O** 9am-4:30pm Mon-Fri, 9am-1pm Sat **W** elmuseum.za.org

---

## 8

### Great Fish River Nature Reserve

**A** E6 **A** 34 km (21 miles) N of Makhanda **O** Sunrise-sunset daily **W** visiteastern cape.co.za

After the Fifth Frontier War of 1819, the land between the Great Fish and Keiskamma

←

A local surfer taking advantage of the legendary waves in Jeffreys Bay

---

→

Seal Point Lighthouse, which guards St Francis Bay

rivers was declared neutral territory, and British settlers were brought in to act as a buffer against the Xhosa incursions. Today this area forms the Great Fish River Nature Reserve, where the semiarid bushveld vegetation sustains large populations of plains game, including blue wildebeest, waterbuck and giraffe, as well as buffalo, black rhino and hippo. There are tracks suitable for cars along the two rivers, and the area is also suitable for hiking.

---

## 9

### St Francis Bay

**A** D7 **i** Municipal Offices, Assissi Dr; www.stfrancis tourism.co.za

This picturesque seaside town is known for its superb surfing, though it lacks the trendy scene associated with neighbouring Jeffreys Bay. It is also very popular with hikers and nature lovers thanks to the five nature reserves and abundant walking trails in the area. The pick among these is the **Cape St Francis Nature Reserve**, which protects a rocky headland and unspoiled coastline immediately south of town. Bottlenose dolphins and, from August to December, southern right whales, are often spotted offshore, while Cape grysbok, yellow mongoose and African penguin inhabit dry land.

Since 1878, the Cape has been guarded by the Seal Point Lighthouse, which houses a small museum and offers fantastic views of the bay.

**Cape St Francis Nature Reserve**

**A** Cape St Francis **W** stfrancistourism.co.za

---

---

↑ Makhanda's attractive, pastel-coloured buildings and *(inset)* one of its historic churches

## NATIONAL ARTS FESTIVAL

Founded in 1974 when the 1820 Settlers Monument officially opened, Makhanda's annual National Arts Festival *(nationalarts festival.co.za)* is now the largest event of its type in Africa. Held annually in June/July, the festival runs for 11 days and comprises a curated main pro-gramme of 600 acts – including opera, stand-up comedy, cabaret and live music – as well as a Fringe programme that is open to all. Bed space is at a premium during the festival, so book your tickets and accommodation early.

## ⑩ Makhanda

🅰 E6   ✈ Gqeberha   🚌 Bathurst St   ℹ 63 High St; www.grahamstown.co.za

After the Fourth Frontier War of 1812, Colonel John Graham established a military post on an abandoned farm near the southeast coast. In an attempt to stabilize the region, the Cape government enticed 4,500 British families to the farmlands. Many of these "1820 Settlers" preferred an urban life, and Grahamstown became a thriving centre of trade and artisanship.

In 2018, Grahamstown was renamed in honour of Makhanda ka Nxele, a prophet and military advisor who was instrumental in uniting the Xhosa against British coloniza-tion. In 1819, Makhanda was captured by the British for instigating an attack on the Grahamstown garrison. He was imprisoned on Robben Island. In 1820, he drowned while trying to escape, but such was his status among the Xhosa that a full 50 years passed before all hope of his return was abandoned.

Today Makhanda is known for its 50 plus churches, uni-versity and schools. Some 60 buildings have been declared national monuments, and a host of well-restored Georgian and Victorian residences line the streets.

Owned by Rhodes University, the **Albany Museum Complex** incorporates seven separate venues. Two of them, the History and Natural Sciences museums, display fossils, settler artifacts and Xhosa dress. Another, the Old Provost, was built in 1838 as a military prison. Drostdy Gateway, which frames the university entrance, is all that remains of the 1842 magis-trate's offices. Fort Selwyn was built in 1836 as an artillery barracks.

Also part of the Albany Complex, but located on a different site, the **Observatory Museum** is the historic home and workshop of a 19th-century jeweller. A Victorian camera obscura in the turret projects images of the town onto a wall.

The beautiful old campus of **Rhodes University** houses the world-famous **South**

> **Many of these "1820 Settlers" preferred an urban life, and Grahamstown became a thriving centre of trade and artisanship.**

**African Institute for Aquatic Biodiversity**, where the most interesting displays are two rare embalmed coelacanth fishes (p262). There is also a collection of other marine and freshwater fish. Visitors interested in traditional African music should call in to the university's **International Library of African Music**. Multientry tickets are available.

Adjoining the university, the **Makana Botanical Gardens** was laid out in 1853 and is a national monument. Indigenous plants including aloes, cycads and proteas attract more than 100 species of birds.

The town's most prominent landmark is the **Cathedral of St Michael and St George**, which stands out with its towering 51-m (166-ft) spire. The original St George's Church, built in 1824, is the oldest Anglican Church in South Africa, and the organ is one of the country's finest.

Close to the cathedral, the **National English Literary Museum** began as a personal collection of Indigenous manuscripts. Declared a cultural institution in 1980, it now preserves various documents and correspondence relating to some of South Africa's most prominent writers. Entrance is free, but donations are welcomed.

Reminiscent of an old fort, the ship-shaped **1820 Settlers Monument** on Gunfire Hill was built in 1974 to commemorate the British families who arrived in the area in 1820. The nearby Monument Theatre

complex is the main venue for the annual 11-day National Arts Festival. Many paintings decorate the impressive foyer.

**Albany Museum Complex**
🏛 Various venues
🌐 am.org.za

**Observatory Museum**
⊘ 🏛 Bathurst Street
🕐 9am-5pm Mon-Fri
🌐 am.org.za/observatory

**Rhodes University**
⊘ 🏛 Artillery Road
🌐 ru.ac.za

**South African Institute for Aquatic Biodiversity**
🏛 Somerset St 🕐 8am-4pm Mon-Fri 🚫 Good Fri, 25 Dec
🌐 saiab.ac.za

**International Library of African Music**
🏛 Off Prince Alfred Street
📅 By appt 🌐 ilam. africamediaonline.com

**Makana Botanical Gardens**
🏛 Lucas Ave
🕐 8am-4:30pm daily
🌐 ru.ac.za/groundsand gardens/botanicalgardens

**Cathedral of St Michael and St George**
🏛 High St 🕐 9am-3pm Mon-Fri, 9am-noon Sat 🌐 grahams towncathedral.org

**National English Literary Museum**
🏛 25a Worcester St ☎ 046 622-7042 🕐 9am-4:30pm Mon-Fri 🚫 Good Fri, 25 Dec

**1820 Settlers Monument**
⊙ 🏛 Gunfire Hill ☎ 046 603 1100 🕐 8am-4:30pm Mon-Fri

# STAY

### The Cock House
This 200-year-old guesthouse has a cosy ambience. There's an elegant restaurant on-site, with a lovingly curated wine list.

🏛 10 Market St, Makhanda
🌐 cockhouse.co.za

Ⓡ Ⓡ Ⓡ

### Makana Resort
Simple chalets and cottages, each with their own barbecue area. The accommodation is set within large central grounds that have a swimming pool and restaurant.

🏛 Grey St, Makhanda
🌐 makana resort.co.za

Ⓡ Ⓡ Ⓡ

### The Rat & Parrot
This landmark student haunt offers regular live entertainment and a varied menu of comfort foods. Try the signature biltong, avocado and sour cream beef rump.

🏛 59 New St, Makhanda
🌐 046 622 5002

Ⓡ Ⓡ Ⓡ

→

Statue of a Victorian family, set in the grounds of the 1820 Settlers Monument

# STAY

### Away with the Fairies

This hugely popular backpackers' retreat has a quirky Lord of the Rings theme and amazing forest views. There's a campsite, plus a good mix of dorms and cottages.

 Ambleside Close, Hogsback
 awaywiththefairies. co.za

Ⓡ ⓡ ⓡ

---

### Die Tuishuise

Choose from among this cluster of characterful 19th-century cottages, which have been immaculately restored for overnight visitors.

 Market St, Cradock
 tuishuise.co.za

Ⓡ ⓡ ⓡ

---

### Mountain Zebra National Park Rest Camp

This beautifully sited rest camp is located deep in the heart of the park, and comes complete with a swimming pool.

 Mountain Zebra National Park
 sanparks.org

Ⓡ ⓡ ⓡ

---

### The Ibis Lounge

A comfortable guesthouse with colour-themed rooms and an excellent on-site restaurant serving traditional South African fare.

 Martin St, Nieu Bethesda
 theibislounge.co.za

Ⓡ ⓡ ⓡ

↑ Zebras drinking from a lake in the tranquil Mountain Zebra National Park

⑪ ⊘ 🍴 🏠

## Mountain Zebra National Park

🅐 D6 🅐 26 km (16 miles) W of Cradock 🕑 Apr-Sep: 7am-6pm daily; Oct-Mar: 7am-7pm daily 🌐 sanparks.org

This national park west of Cradock was originally conceived as a sanctuary to rescue the Cape mountain zebra from imminent extinction. When the park was proclaimed in 1937, there were six zebras; by 1949 only two remained. Conservation efforts were successful, however, and the park now protects about 1,000 zebras.

The plains and mountains of this Karoo landscape also support a wide variety of other mammals, including black wildebeest, kudu, eland, red hartebeest, springbok, buffalo, black rhino and caracal. More than 200 species of bird have been recorded, including many raptors and the endangered blue crane.

The park's rest camp, which overlooks a valley, consists of chalets, a campsite, a restaurant, shop and information centre. A short walk past the chalets leads to the swimming pool, which is set at the base of a granite ridge. Further into the park are a guesthouse and two mountain cottages.

For convenience, the park can be split into two sections. From the camp, a circular drive of 28 km (18 miles) explores the wooded Wilgeboom Valley, noted for its rugged granite land forms. The road passes Doornhoek Cottage where the screen adaptation of Olive Schreiner's *The Story of an African Farm* was filmed, and leads to a shady picnic site. The northern loop, which starts just before Wilgeboom, climbs steeply to the Rooiplaat Plateau and offers views across the Karoo, where most of the park's wildlife congregates. Early morning and late afternoon are the best times to visit the area.

Recently reintroduced to the national park, lions are now quite often seen on game drives, and cheetahs can be tracked on foot on a guided activity that leaves the rest camp every morning.

### Did You Know?

Zebras are black with white stripes, rather than vice versa. Each individual's stripes are unique.

→
The imposing façade of Cradock's Dutch Reformed Church

## ⑫ Hogsback

**Ⓐ E6** **ℹ Main Rd; www. hogsback.com**

The quiet village of Hogsback lies at an altitude of 1,200 m (4,000 ft) in the beautiful forested surroundings of the Amatola Mountains. Its name derives from one mountain peak that resembles the back of a hog when viewed from a particular angle.

The earliest known written reference to "Hogsback" was found in the journal of the painter Thomas Baines, who passed the "Hogs Back" while on his travels deeper inside South Africa in 1848. The Amatola Forest is often claimed as J R R Tolkien's inspiration for *The Lord of the Rings*, in particular for his fictional forest of Mirkwood. Tolkien was born in South Africa in 1892, although his family relocated to England when he was a young boy.

The village is made up of a string of cottages, tea gardens, guesthouses and craft shops. It is well-known for its lovely English-style gardens of flowering plants such as rhododendrons and azaleas and its orchards full of soft fruits such as blackcurrants, blackberries and gooseberries. There are delicious jams for sale in Hogsback's shops. Local hikes ranging from 30 minutes to two hours lead up to some pretty waterfalls in the forests.

---

## ⑬ Cradock

**Ⓐ D6** **🚉 Church St** **🚌**
**ℹ JA Calata St www. visitcradock.co.za**

In 1812, towards the end of the Fourth Frontier War, Sir John Cradock established two military outposts to secure the eastern border. One was at Grahamstown (now Makhanda), the other at Cradock. Merino sheep flourished in this region, and Cradock soon developed into a sheep-farming centre.

The Dutch Reformed Church, was inspired by London's St Martin-in-the-Fields. Completed in 1867, it dominates the town's central square. Behind the town hall, the Great Fish River Museum preserves the history of the early pioneers. In Market Street, Die Tuishuise is the result of an innovative project to restore a series

---

### OLIVE EMILIE SCHREINER

*The Story of an African Farm* is widely regarded as the first South African novel of note. Olive Schreiner wrote it while working as a governess on farms in the Cradock district. The book was released in 1883 under the male pseudonym Ralph Iron. Schreiner, a campaigner for women's equality and an advocate of the rights of Indigenous Africans, wrote extensively on politics. She was buried just south of Cradock upon her death in 1920.

of 30 mid-19th-century Karoo cottages and to create comfortable accommodation for visitors to the town. Each cottage is furnished charmingly in the style of the period, with meals taken in the adjoining Victoria Manor hotel.

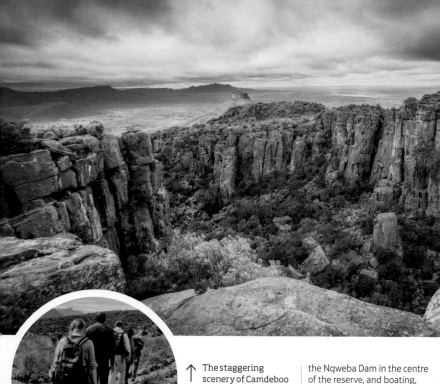

↑ The staggering scenery of Camdeboo National Park, popular with hikers *(inset)*

## 14

### Camdeboo National Park

🗺️ D6  🚗 8 km (5 miles) NW of Graaff-Reinet  🕐 Apr-Sep: 6am-6pm daily; Oct-Mar: 6am-7pm daily  🌐 sanparks.org

In a bid to conserve Karoo landforms and wildlife, 145 sq km (56 sq miles) of land around Graaff-Reinet *(p258)* was set aside. West of the town is the Valley of Desolation, where columns of weathered dolerite tower 120 m (390 ft) over the valley floor. A 14-km (9-mile) road leads to a view site and a short walk, while the circular day hike is reached from the Berg-en-dal gate on the western edge of town.

The eastern region of the nature reserve includes the Driekoppe peaks, which rise 600 m (1,950 ft) above the plains. This section sustains more than 250 species of bird. The populations of Cape mountain zebra, buffalo, red hartebeest, springbok, kudu and blesbok are expanding, and many may be seen. There are game-viewing roads and picnic sites situated around

---

📷 PICTURE PERFECT
**Valley of Desolation**

This other-worldly landscape of looming dolerite columns, located in Camdeboo National Park, is at its most beautiful and photogenic in the late afternoon - although it's certainly worth staying on for sunset.

---

the Nqweba Dam in the centre of the reserve, and boating, canoeing, fishing and windsurfing are permitted.

---

### 15

### Gariep Dam

🗺️ D5  ℹ️ www.gariep dam.com

In 1779 Colonel Robert Gordon reached the banks of a watercourse that was known to the Khoena as Gariep, renaming it the Orange River, in honour of the Dutch Prince of Orange. In 1928, Dr A D Lewis advanced the idea of building a tunnel linking the Orange River to the Eastern Cape, but work did not begin until 1966. In September 1970 the last gap in the wall was closed.

The Orange River (also known as the Gariep River) is South Africa's longest river, and the Gariep reservoir forms the country's largest body of water. The dam wall rises 90 m (297 ft) and has a crest length of 948 m (3,110 ft). When full, it covers an area of 374 sq km (144 sq miles).

A corridor of bushveld surrounds the Gariep Dam, and is home to a few spring-bok, black wildebeest and blesbok. **Gariep, A Forever Resort** is situated at the dam wall, and offers comfortable chalets, a campsite and a range of activities such as fishing and boating. There are also tours of the dam wall. Day visitors must call ahead.

**Gariep, A Forever Resort**
⊛ ⓨ 🅰 Gariep Dam
ⓦ forevergariep.co.za

### Nieu Bethesda
🅰 D6  🅸 Martin St; www. nieu-bethesda.com

The turn-off to this village lies on the N9, 27 km (17 miles) north of Graaff-Reinet. From there, a good-quality dirt road traverses the Voor Sneeuberg ("in front of snow mountain") and leads to Nieu Bethesda.

At 2,502 m (8,131 ft), the Kompasberg (Compass Peak) is the highest point in the Sneeuberg range. It was named

in 1778 when Cape Governor Baron van Plettenberg visited the mountain and noted that the surrounding countryside could be surveyed from all angles from its summit.

Nieu Bethesda was founded by Reverend Charles Murray, minister of Graaff-Reinet's Dutch Reformed Church. The fertile valley in the arid terrain reminded him of the Pool of Bethesda (*John 5:2*), and so he named the town after it.

In 1875 he acquired a farm in the valley and by 1905 the church (now in Parsonage Street) was completed. It cost £5,600 to build, but at the time of its consecration two-thirds of the amount was still outstanding. To raise funds, arable church land was divided into plots and sold at a public auction. The debt was finally settled in 1929.

Today, Martin Street, the quaint main road, is lined with pear trees and quince hedges. Pienaar Street crosses over the Gat River and passes an old water mill that was built in 1860. The first water wheel was made of wood, but it was later replaced with the existing steel wheel.

The peaceful village has attracted much artistic talent, including one of South Africa's leading playwrights, Athol Fugard. This legacy is on display at **The Owl House**, one of South Africa's top 50 heritage sites. Its garden is packed with an intriguing assembly of concrete statues: owls, people, sphinxes and religious symbols, created over more than 30 years by Helen Martins and her assistant, Koos Malgas. The walls, doors and ceilings of the house are decorated with finely ground

coloured glass. Mirrors reflect the light from candles and lamps. Martin's unusual work has been classified as "Outsider Art" (art that falls outside the artistic mainstream as a result of isolation or insanity) and "Naive" (an expression of innocence and fantasy).

**The Owl House**
⊛ 🅰 Martin St
🕒 9am–5pm Thu–Mon
ⓦ theowlhouse.co.za

→
Unusual sculptures found at the Owl House in Nieu Bethesda

# KWAZULU-NATAL AND LESOTHO

Prior to the 19th century, what is now KwaZulu-Natal supported a scattering of small fiefdoms of Nguni-speaking pastoralists. That changed over the course of 1816–27, after an illegitimate prince called Shaka usurped the throne of the Zulu fiefdom to instigate an era of violent social turmoil and intertribal bloodshed remembered throughout Southern Africa as the Mfecane *(p62)*. Using innovative military tactics, Shaka had seized all of present-day KwaZulu-Natal by 1828, when he was assassinated by his half-brother and successor Dingane. Under Dingane, the Zulu Kingdom faced up to two new threats in the form of the British port of Durban, founded in 1824, and the arrival of the Boer Voortrekkers from the southwest. In December 1838, 3,000 spear-wielding Zulus were mowed down by Boer guns at the Battle of Blood River, a defeat that shook the kingdom to its core. An uneasy Anglo-Zulu truce followed, but it collapsed in 1879 when the Zulu army famously defeated the British army at Islandwana. Superior European firepower held sway thereafter, and by 1880 Zululand was effectively part of the British Empire. KwaZulu-Natal came into being in 1994, when the nominally independent homeland of KwaZulu was integrated into the province of Natal.

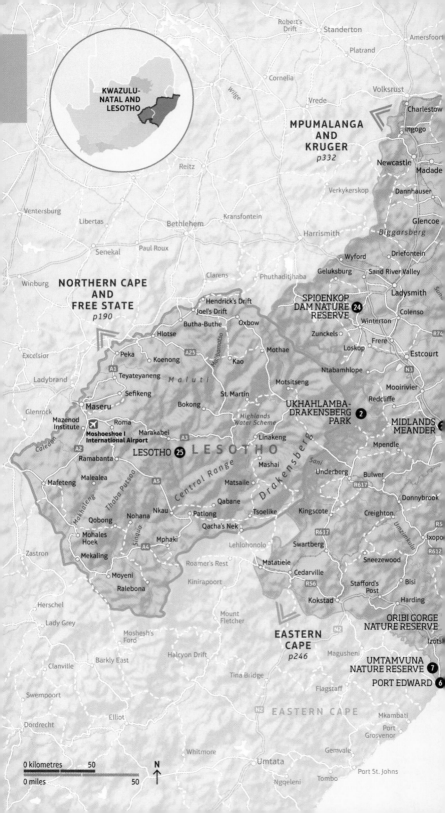

ESWATINI
*p354*

**20** TEMBE ELEPHANT PARK

**18** ITHALA GAME RESERVE

**4** ISIMANGALISO WETLAND PARK

**19** PHINDA PRIVATE GAME RESERVE

**3** HLUHLUWE-IMFOLOZI GAME RESERVE

KWAZULU/NATAL

**15** SHAKALAND

**16** ESHOWE

**17** UMLALAZI NATURE RESERVE

**23** HOWICK

**22** PIETERMARITZBURG

**14** BALLITO
✈ King Shaka International Airport

**13** UMHLANGA

**1** DURBAN

**12** AMANZIMTOTI

**11** SCOTTBURGH

**8** PORT SHEPSTONE

**10** UVONGO

**9** MARGATE

*Indian
Ocean*

## KWAZULU-NATAL AND LESOTHO

### Must Sees

**1** Durban
**2** uKhahlamba-Drakensberg Park
**3** Hluhluwe-Imfolozi Game Reserve
**4** iSimangaliso Wetland Park

### Experience More

**5** Oribi Gorge Nature Reserve
**6** Port Edward
**7** Umtamvuna Nature Reserve
**8** Port Shepstone
**9** Margate
**10** Uvongo
**11** Scottburgh
**12** Amanzimtoti
**13** Umhlanga
**14** Ballito
**15** Shakaland
**16** Eshowe
**17** Umlalazi Nature Reserve
**18** Ithala Game Reserve
**19** Phinda Private Game Reserve
**20** Tembe Elephant Park
**21** Midlands Meander
**22** Pietermartizburg
**23** Howick
**24** Spioenkop Dam Nature Reserve
**25** Lesotho

↑ The Durban skyline, with the distinctive arch of the Moses Mabhida Stadium

**❶**

# DURBAN

🅰F5 ✈🚗🚌 🏠Ithala Trade Centre, 29 Canal Quay Rd; www.zulu.org.za

Vasco Da Gama's Port Natal was renamed Durban in honour of Cape Governor Benjamin D'Urban, after Zulu chief Shaka gave the land to the British in 1824. Today, it is South Africa's principal harbour and the holiday capital of KwaZulu-Natal. Most attractions are on the Golden Mile, and central Durban also offers historic buildings, museums, theatres and exciting markets.

 INSIDER TIP
**Exploring Durban**

Most of the attractions located along the beach front are within easy walking distance of the hotels. By far the most useful of Durban's bus services is the People Mover *(muvo.co.za)*, which has three different loops around the city and passes by every 15 minutes (5am–10pm).

## ①
### The Golden Mile

**🚏OR Tambo Parade**

The land side of this 6-km-(4-mile-) long holiday precinct is lined with hotels, while the seaward edge consists of typical seaside attractions such as amusement parks, ice-cream parlours, piers, sandy beaches and a promenade.

At the southern end, the leading Golden Mile attraction is **uShaka Marine World**, a massive beachfront complex that offers numerous entertainments. The Sea World aquarium has a unique phantom ship that visitors can walk through to see ragged-tooth sharks and game fish;

Wet 'n' Wild has swimming pools, waterslides and rides; Dangerous Creatures is a snake and reptile park; and the Village Walk is an attractive open-air mall.

↑ The beachfront promenade that runs along the Golden Mile

At the northern end of the Golden Mile, behind Battery Beach, is the **Moses Mabhida Stadium**. Built for the 2010 FIFA World Cup, it is named after an anti-apartheid activist. As well as hosting football matches and concerts, the stadium has the SkyCar, a funicular railway car that climbs the curve to the top of the arc, and activities including the Adventure Walk up and down the 550 steps and the Big Rush Swing, a bungee-like 220-m (720 ft) swing beneath it.

**uShaka Marine World**
♿🐟👶🏖🍴 🏠1 King Shaka Ave, Point 🕐9am–5pm daily 🌐ushakamarine world.co.za

## Moses Mabhida Stadium

 44 Isaiah Ntshangase Rd ⏰9am-5pm daily 🌐mmstadium.com

---

## Juma Mosque

📍Cnr Denis Hurley & Dr Yusuf Dadoo sts 📞031 306 0026 ⏰9am-4pm Mon-Sat

The impressive Juma Mosque, with its glittering golden domes, lies across the road from Victoria Street Market. Completed in 1927, it is the largest mosque in the southern hemisphere and can accommodate 7,000 worshippers. Visitors are allowed inside, except at prayer times. A strict dress code is enforced, and shoes must be removed before entering.

## Durban Botanic Gardens

📍John Zikhale Rd ⏰7:30am-5:45pm daily 🌐durbanbotanicgardens.org.za

Located near the Greyville Racecourse, these attractive gardens were established in 1849 as an experimental station for tropical crops. The spectacular cycad and palm collection is one of the largest of its kind in the world and includes several rare species. Other attractions include a sensory garden, a Victorian sunken garden, an orchid house and an ornamental lake. From May to August, a series of Sunday afternoon concerts is held here.

# EAT

**Circus Circus Beach Café**
Serves a global menu of freshly prepared dishes.

📍1 Snell Parade 🌐circuscircus.co.za

Ⓡ Ⓡ Ⓡ

**Roma Revolving Restaurant**
Offers 360-degree views from the 32nd floor.

📍John Ross House, Margret Mncadi Ave 🌐roma.co.za 🗓Sun

Ⓡ Ⓡ Ⓡ

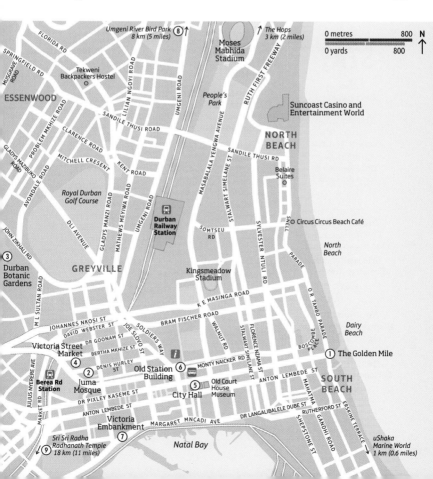

## ④ Victoria Street Market

 Cnr Bertha Mkhize & Denis Hurley sts ⏰ 8am-5pm Mon-Fri, 8am-4pm Sat, 9am-3pm Sun 🌐 victoria streetmarket.co.za

Situated at the end of the N3 flyover, the covered Victoria Street Market is striking – each of its 11 domes was modelled on a notable building in India. In this crowded bazaar, visitors can sample many different tastes and aromas as they browse through more than 200 stalls, which offer spices and incense, fabrics, leather goods, brassware, ceramics and delicious street food.

---

# STAY

### Tekweni Backpackers Hostel
A budget lodge set in a 19th-century mansion.

 169 9th Ave 🌐 tekweniback packers.co.za

Ⓡ Ⓡ Ⓡ

---

### Belaire Suites
Comfortable self-catering apartments.

 15 Snell Parade 🌐 belairesuites.co.za

Ⓡ Ⓡ Ⓡ

---

### Southern Sun Elangeni & Maharani
Large and luxurious beachfront high-rise.

 63 Snell Parade 🌐 tsogosunhotels.com

Ⓡ Ⓡ Ⓡ

---

## ⑤  City Hall

 Anton Lembede St ⏰ 8:30am-4pm Mon-Sat, 11am-4pm Sun 🔒 Good Fri, 25 Dec 🌐 durban.gov.za

Completed in 1910, Durban's City Hall was modelled after that of Belfast, in Northern Ireland. On its ground floor is the free Natural Science Museum, with exhibits that vary from a display of South African wildlife to an Egyptian mummy. Most fascinating are the oversized insects that are featured in the KwaNunu section. Upstairs, the pioneering Durban Art Gallery showcases a leading collection of Black South African art.

Next door, the **Old Court House Museum** contains relics of early colonial life in what was then Natal, while the mock-Tudor Playhouse Theatre opposite offers top-class entertainment by the Playhouse Company. The neighbouring streets are lined with cafés and restaurants.

### Old Court House Museum
 77 Samora Machel St ⏰ 8:30am-4pm Mon-Fri, 8:30am-12:30pm Sat 🔒 Public hols 🌐 durban historymuseums.org.za

---

## ⑥ Old Station Building

 160 Monty Naicker Rd

Durban's former railway station was completed in 1894. The building's most curious feature is its roof, which is designed to carry the weight of 5 m (16 ft) of snow. The London firm of architects accidentally switched the plans with those for Toronto station in Canada, whose roof caved in during the first heavy snow.

The Tourist Junction has maps and brochures; the staff can advise on all the local sights. There are also booking offices for accommodation at the national parks (the only other offices are in Cape Town and Pretoria), and for Durban Tourism's walking tours.

South African artworks on display in Durban Art Gallery, City Hall

### Durban Maritime Museum

Samora Machel St
8:30am–4pm Mon–Sat, 11am–4pm Sun Good Fri & 25 Dec durbanhistory museums.org.za

 ⑧
### Umgeni River Bird Park

490 Riverside Rd, 8 km (5 miles) N of Durban off the M4 9am–3pm daily 25 Dec umgeniriver birdpark.co.za

Bordered on three sides by steep cliffs, and overlooking the north bank of the Umgeni River, 2 km (1 mile) from its mouth, the Umgeni River Bird Park enjoys a superb location. Four waterfalls cascade down the cliffs into ponds fringed by palms and lush vegetation. The four large walk-through aviaries allow visitors a face-to-face encounter with some of the 700 birds. Among the 180 resident species are rare exotic parrots, toucans, cranes, macaws and hornbills.

Educational bird shows are held every day (except Mondays) at 11am and 2pm.

 ⑨
### Sri Sri Radha Radhanath Temple

Bhaktivedanta Swami Circle, Chatsworth
9:30am–6pm Mon–Sat, 9:30am–5pm Sun iskcon durban.net

This large, ornate temple of the International Society for Krishna Consciousness was designed by the Austrian architect Hannes Raudner. It is encircled by a moat and a garden laid out in the shape of a lotus flower.

The daily guided tours take in the awe-inspiring marble temple room and the inner sanctuary, and there is also a good vegetarian restaurant and takeaway on the ground floor called Govinda's.

⑦
### Victoria Embankment

Margaret Mncadi Avenue

Lined with skyscrapers, the Victoria Embankment – also known as Margaret Mncadi Avenue – was built in 1897 as an upmarket residential area. At the eastern end is the cast-iron Da Gama Clock, erected in 1847 to commemorate the 400th anniversary of Vasco Da Gama's discovery of a sea route to India.

Photographs and other memorabilia of Durban's seafaring past is displayed in the **Durban Maritime Museum**, where the tugboats *Ulundi* and *J R More* and the minesweeper SAS *Durban* are on display. The Durban Club, built in 1904, on the opposite side of the road, is one of the few original buildings remaining on the embankment, while further to the west, the Royal Natal Yacht Club was founded in 1858 and is the oldest yacht club in Africa. Its restaurant is open to the public.

### THE HINDU POPULATION OF KWAZULU-NATAL

When the first sugar was produced from sugar cane in 1851, the Natal Colony required cheap labour to work in the plantations. Between 1860 and 1911, 152,000 indentured labourers were shipped to Durban from India. Despite enduring terrible conditions, many workers opted to remain in South Africa once their period of indenture ended, becoming active as retailers and farmers, and later in other industries. Of the current population of 900,000 (the largest Indian community outside Asia), an estimated 50 per cent are Hindu.

**2** 🏷️ 🗺️

# UKHAHLAMBA-DRAKENSBERG PARK

🅐F5 🏠100 km (60 miles) W of Pietermaritzburg 🌐kznwildlife.com

**This breathtaking park is a nature lover's nirvana. Comprising South Africa's greatest mountain wilderness, it is also a vast outdoor art gallery, housing thousands of ancient rock paintings.**

Extending over 2,350 sq km (907 sq miles), the uKhahlamba-Drakensberg Park, a UNESCO World Heritage Site, protects a dramatic and rugged escarpment that provides an awesome backdrop to the pastoral midlands of KwaZulu-Natal. A hiker's paradise, this scenic range of secluded valleys, green highland meadows

→

Prehistoric rock paintings by the San tribes that once inhabited the area

The spectacular peaks of the Drakensberg range, a magnet for hikers *(inset)* and nature lovers ↑

and dense mist-shrouded forests incorporates all of South Africa's tallest peaks. Wildlife ranges from the massive eland antelope and vociferous Chacma baboon to majestically soaring raptors such as the jackal buzzard and bearded vulture. Elsewhere, the rock overhangs of the Drakensberg shelter some of the world's most prolific and best-preserved prehistoric rock art.

### THE DRAKENSBERG RANGE

The Drakensberg, "dragon mountains", follow the border of Lesotho for 250 km (155 miles) - an escarpment that separates the high interior plateau from the subtropical coast of KwaZulu-Natal. The range is divided into the rocky High Berg and the pastoral Little Berg, both of which are superb areas for hiking.

### Exploring uKhahlamba-Drakensberg

The provincial conservation authority Ezemvelo KZN Wildlife has subdivided uKhahlamba-Drakensberg into individually administered wilderness and conservation areas. Several government rest camps and private hotels have been set up in the foothills as a base for exploring the middle and upper slopes on foot. Shorter hikes range from hour-long rambles to ancient rock art sites (many of which can be visited only on guided tours, to protect them from vandalism), to a demanding full-day hike to Cathedral Peak. Within the park, unequipped caves and camp sites cater to more intrepid mountaineers.

## TOP 3 DRAKENSBERG HIKES

**Gorge Trail, Royal Natal Park**
This reasonably flat trail (8 km/5 miles; three hours in either direction) follows a pretty gorge to the Amphitheatre base and Thukela Falls, with natural swimming pools en route.

**Rainbow Gorge, Didima**
This route (5 km/3 miles; two hours in either direction) runs along a riverbank through pockets of riparian forest, to a narrow gorge adorned with waterfalls and swimming pools.

**Battle Cave, Injisuthi**
Tours of this guided trail (10-km/6-mile round trip; five hours) near Champagne Valley depart daily at 8:30am, leading to a spectacular rock art site comprising 700-plus paintings.

① ⊛

## Kamberg Nature Reserve

🖈 Estcourt  🕑 Apr-Sep: 6am-6pm daily; Oct-Mar: 5am-7pm daily

Nestling in the park's foothills, Kamberg is known for its trout-fishing. There are several small dams near the trout hatchery, and fishing gear can be hired from the reserve reception.

Walking trails in the area last from one hour to a full day. Game Pass Shelter cave has some superb San rock paintings and can be visited with a guide – the return walk takes about three hours.

② ⊛ 🏠

## Royal Natal National Park

🖈 Bergville  🕑 24 hrs daily

The Royal Natal National Park comprises some of the most spectacular scenery in all of

> **The Royal Natal National Park comprises some of the most spectacular scenery in all of Africa.**

Africa. One of its main features is an awe-inspiring natural Amphitheatre – a crescent-shaped basalt wall 6 km (4 miles) wide and 1,500 m (4,875 ft) high. Here, the Tugela River plunges 948 m (3,080 ft) into the valley below, making this the second-highest waterfall in the world. Chalets at the award-winning Thendele Resort, above the Tugela River, provide unrivalled views of the Amphitheatre and countryside below.

In the valleys, the Mahai campsite provides easy access to an extensive network of hiking trails that can be used to explore the 88-sq-km (34-sq-mile) reserve.

↑ Exploring Royal Natal National Park on horseback

## Giant's Castle Game Reserve

**Estcourt** **Apr–Sep: 6am–10pm daily; Oct–Mar: 5am–10pm daily**

In 1903 a sanctuary was established here to protect some of the last surviving eland in South Africa. They now number around 2,000 – one of the largest populations in the country. The area is also home to several breeding pairs of the endangered bearded vulture (lammergeyer), which can be viewed from a camouflaged hide.

The main camp overlooks the Bushman's River, with Giant's Castle dominating the skyline. A short walk away are the Main Caves, where 500 San rock paintings can be seen.

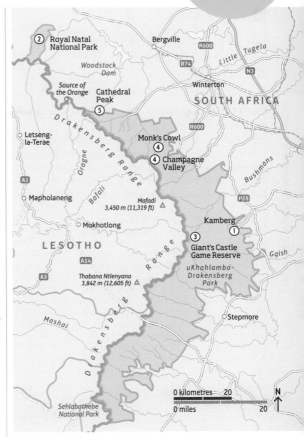

## Champagne Valley and Monk's Cowl

**Winterton** **Monk's Cowl: 6am–6pm daily**

Champagne Castle, at 3,377 m (10,975 ft), is South Africa's second-highest peak. It juts out from the escarpment and dominates the delightful Champagne Valley, so-named for the cluster of luxury hotels and timeshare resorts that line the 31-km (19-mile) road from Winterton to Monk's Cowl. Monk's Cowl is the peak between Champagne Castle and Cathkin, where there is a campsite and hiking trails.

---

> **INSIDER TIP**
> **Hiking Advice**
>
> The Drakensberg is extremely remote, so even for a day hike be sure to pack water, food, sun protection, a mobile phone and first aid kit, and bear in mind that the weather can be highly changeable.

## Cathedral Peak

**Winterton** **Apr–Sep: 6am–6pm daily; Oct–Mar: 5am–7pm daily**

Some of the Drakensberg's finest scenery is to be found in this region. The road from Winterton winds for 42 km (26 miles) through Zulu villages that are scattered across the folds of the Mlambonja Valley, with the Drakensberg as a spectacular backdrop.

The strenuous hike to the top of Cathedral Peak (3,004 m/9,855 ft) in the Drakensberg is exciting and will reward you with fantastic views. There are also guided drives to the top of Mike's Pass, and the Rock Art Centre at Ezemvelo KZN Wildlife's Didima Resort explains the complicated meaning of many of the San paintings.

↑ The majestic view of Cathedral Peak across the Mlambonja Valley

③

# HLUHLUWE-IMFOLOZI GAME RESERVE

🅰 G4  🅰 237 km (147 miles) N of Durban  🕒 Mar-Oct: 6am-6pm daily; Nov-Feb: 5am-7pm daily  Ⓦ kznwildlife.com

One of Africa's leading wildlife sanctuaries, this unspoiled wilderness of rolling hills, subtropical forest, acacia woodland and palm-fringed rivers is world-renowned for its rhino conservation programme. The varied vegetation also supports an astonishing array of other animals, including large herds of nyala, impala, kudu, zebra and buffalo, as well as elephant, rhino, giraffe, lion, leopard, hyena and cheetah.

In 1895 two wildlife reserves, Hluhluwe and Imfolozi, were established to protect the last rhinos in South Africa. A corridor of land was added between the two in the 1950s. The park was consolidated in 1989, and now sprawls across 964 sq km (372 sq miles).

In 1958 a single male lion suddenly appeared, possibly from the Kruger National Park some 350 km (220 miles) to the north. Two lionesses were relocated from Kruger some time later, and their offspring have re-established prides throughout the park. The reserve's hilly terrain provides great vantage points for viewing.

> 💬 INSIDER TIP
> ### A Room with a View
>
> The reserve's Hilltop Camp (hilltop camp.co.za), set at an altitude of 450 m (1,460 ft), offers panoramic views and can accommodate up to 210 guests in its rustic, self-catering chalets. Facilities at the central complex include a restaurant, bar, shop, petrol station and a swimming pool, perfect for cooling off beneath the blazing African sun.

**20,000**
southern white rhinos
are estimated to
exist in the wild
worldwide.

↑ A young African elephant spraying mud on his body as protection from the sun

## Exploring the Park

Nyalazi Gate, the park's main entrance, is reached from the N2 at Mtubatuba. It is a perfect starting point for exploring the park's 220-km (138-mile) road network. Heading south, the route traverses open woodland before fording the Black Imfolozi River. Then it ascends to the magnificently located Mpila Camp.

> **In 1958 a single male lion suddenly appeared, possibly from the Kruger National Park some 350 km (220 miles) to the north.**

A trio of exclusive reed-and-thatch rest camps on the banks of the Black Imfolozi, Sontuli, Gqoyeni and Nselweni rivers allow visitors to savour the most secluded corners of this wilderness. Seasoned game rangers conduct game-viewing walks.

From Nyalazi Gate north, the route follows a tarred road that curves across rolling hills teeming with wildlife. The journey to Hluhluwe climbs a range of hills, 400 m (1,300 ft) above the Hluhluwe River. These hills trap moisture-laden clouds, resulting in an average rainfall of 985 mm (38 inches) per year. In the dense woodland and forests live red duiker, bush-buck, nyala and samango monkeys. Buffalo, zebra, white rhino and elephant can be seen roaming the northeastern grasslands near Memorial Gate. Parts of the reserve's forest are also excellent for bird-watching.

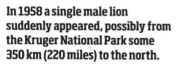

← A white rhino roaming the Hluhluwe-Imfolozi Game Reserve, which is also home to a large zerba population *(inset)*

### RHINO CONSERVATION

In 1916, Hluhluwe-Imfolozi's southern white rhino population was at a low of 15–30. Amazingly, this group were progenitors not only to the 1,600 indi-viduals now roaming the reserve, but also – thanks to a 1960s trans-location programme – to every white rhino population worldwide. Indeed, despite ongoing poaching, the southern white rhino is now listed as Not Threatened by the IUCN.

↑ Hippos wallowing in the waters of iSimangaliso Wetland Park

# ISIMANGALISO WETLAND PARK

**⚠ G4 🏠 Accessed from the N2 or R22 ⏰ Apr–Oct: 6am–6pm daily; Nov–Mar: 5am–7pm daily 🌐 isimangaliso.com**

A UNESCO World Heritage Site, this 3,320-sq-km (1,282-sq-mile) park is the country's most biodiverse protected area. Comprising more than half a dozen reserves and sanctuaries, iSimangaliso – a Zulu phrase meaning "something wondrous"– has habitats such as coral reefs, mountains, grassland and coastal forests.

### St Lucia

Carved into a jungle-like peninsula, this is perhaps the only South African urban centre patrolled nocturnally by hippopotamus, warthog, red duiker and bushbaby. Walking trails from the village offer excellent birding, while launch trips on the estuary provide good hippo and crocodile sightings. The village is flanked by a gorgeous sandy beach, while the Crocodile Farm to its north is one of the best in the country.

### Cape Vidal and the Eastern Shores

Set below forested dunes on a beach 32 km (20 miles) north of St Lucia, Cape Vidal offers seasonal land-based whale- and dolphin-viewing and is also a vital nesting site for loggerhead and leatherback turtles. The Eastern Shores sector has some of the world's tallest forest dunes, while a game-viewing loop to Lake Bhangazi offers a chance of sighting buffalo, rhino, elephant and cheetah.

### uMkhuze Game Reserve

Created in 1912, this 400-sq-km (154-sq-mile) inland spur of iSimangaliso offers excellent game viewing, with large numbers of rhino, elephant, giraffe and antelope. The park is also known for its birdlife, with more than 420 species recorded. Nsumo Pan is an excellent spot for water birds, while sand forests harbour "iSimangaliso specials" such as yellow-spotted nicator, Neergard's sunbird and African broadbill. Geared mainly to self-drivers, uMkhuze offers activities such as the guided Fig Forest Walk near Nsumo Pan and a cultural village providing insights into Zulu lifestyle and crafts.

INSIDER TIP
**Exploring the Park**

The park is well suited to self-drive exploration, ideally starting in St Lucia for a few nights then striking out to the more northerly sites. Even without your own vehicle St Lucia makes a great base for organized day excursions.

## Sodwana Bay

Located on an unspoiled stretch of coast, Sodwana Bay is South Africa's premier scuba destination. The closest and most popular spot is Two Mile Reef, which offers dives from 9 m (30 ft) to below 30 m (100 ft) in depth. Quarter Mile Reef is famed for the ragged-toothed sharks that gather there in January and February, while the deeper Five Mile Reef comprises a stunning variety of branching, table and plate corals. Further out, Seven Mile Reef is considered one of the world's most beautiful dive sites. For non-divers, there are several good snorkelling spots, while a wealth of birds and small mammals are likely to be seen along a 5-km (3-mile) trail starting at the reserve headquarters.

## Kosi Bay Nature Reserve

iSimangaliso's most northerly component, this reserve protects eight lakes and a labyrinth of streams and channels abutting the Mozambican border. A large rocky reef within the estuary offers some of the region's best snorkelling conditions, while canoe trips along the Sidhadla River into Lake Amanzamnyama often yield sightings of samango monkey, crocodile and hippo.

## Lake Sibaya

With a relatively modest area of 65 sq km (25 sq miles), Lake Sibaya is the country's largest natural freshwater body. Aquatic wildlife includes an endemic fish, the Sibaya goby, as well as around 150 hippos and plenty of crocodiles. The lake also hosts more than 20,000 water birds, including several rarities regularly observed in the area.

# STAY

### St Lucia Wetlands Guesthouse

Good value B&B set in a verdant garden.

🏠 20 Kingfisher St, St Lucia village
🌐 stluciawetlands.com

Ⓡ Ⓡ Ⓡ

---

### Kosi Forest Lodge

This lovely bush camp overlooks Lake Shengeza.

🏠 Kosi Bay
🌐 kosiforestlodge.co.za

Ⓡ Ⓡ Ⓡ

---

### Makatana Bay Lodge

Exclusive lakeside lodge that offers boat trips and game drives.

🏠 Western Shores
🌐 makakatana.com

Ⓡ Ⓡ Ⓡ

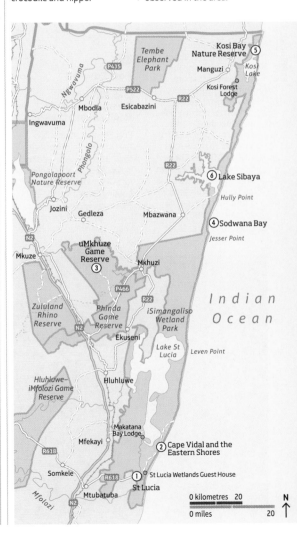

# EXPERIENCE MORE

**5**

## Oribi Gorge Nature Reserve

**F5** **21 km (13 miles) inland of Port Shepstone** **24 hrs daily** **kznwildlife.com**

In a region where population densities are high and sugar cane plantations and coastal resorts have replaced most of the natural vegetation, this impressive ravine carved by the Umzimkulwana River is a delight for nature lovers.

There is a scenic circular drive, as well as walking trails with many beautiful picnic spots along the river and at viewpoints overlooking the waterfalls in the gorge.

Small, forest-dwelling animals such as bushbuck, duiker and samango monkey occur in the dense forest while the cliffs provide nesting sites for birds of prey.

### SARDINE RUN

Lying approximately 120 km (75 miles) south of Durban, the Hibiscus coastline is home to the famous "Sardine Run". Each June or July, over several weeks, millions of the tiny fish head north from their Eastern Cape spawning grounds to the waters of Port Edward. They are dogged by predators such as dolphins, sharks and seals, while seabirds rain down from above to take their fill.

**6**

## Port Edward

**F5** **Margate** **Panorama Parade, Margate; 039 312 2322**

Port Edward, situated on the Umtamvuna River, is the southernmost beachside resort in KwaZulu-Natal. It is popular for swimming, fishing and boating. Established in 1925, the resort was named in honour of the Prince of Wales, later King Edward VIII.

> **Did You Know?**
>
> Port Edward is home to the wreck of the *Sao João*, a treasure-laden Portuguese ship that sank in 1552.

A casino resort, the Wild Coast Sun, was built here in 1981 to lure visitors from Durban and the South Coast. Today, it overlooks an unspoiled coastline covered in dense forest and grassland, and offers one of the country's top golf courses.

The Mzamba Village Market opposite the resort's main entrance sells a varied range of local crafts.

**7**

## Umtamvuna Nature Reserve

**F5** **Rennies Beach, Port Edward** **6:30am-5:30pm daily** **kznwildlife.com**

Protecting a 30-km (19-mile) stretch of the Umtamvuna River as it flows through a

←

Visitors crossing the suspension bridge that cuts through Oribi Gorge

← The rocky coastline of Margate, a popular holiday destination

deep forested gorge on the Eastern Cape border, this scenic reserve can be explored through a network of steep but well-marked walking trails, ranging in duration from three to eight hours. Large mammals such as bushbuck, chacma baboon, samango monkey and even leopard are present but mostly seldom seen. The mountainous scenery, dense subtropical forest, wealth of native plants and tranquil atmosphere, however, more than compensate. Birdlife in the area includes African fin-foot, Knysna loerie, gorgeous bush-shrike and Gurney's sugarbird. Sadly, the reserve's much-touted breeding colony of endangered Cape vulture has abandoned its cliffside roost for reasons that are unclear.

 **Port Shepstone**

🏞 F5  ℹ️ www.visitkzn southcoast.co.za

Named after the prominent colonial administrator Sir Theophilus Shepstone, the largest town on the KwaZulu-Natal South Coast was founded in 1867 to exploit the plentiful white granite deposits at the mouth of the Umzimkulu River. It has a pivotal location at the junction of the N2 and the coastal R61, but tourism

development is focused 3 km (2 miles) further south at the fast-growing resort town of Shelly Beach. Offering great swimming conditions, this popular beach – actually a sandy strand, but named for the many shells that wash ashore here – has several tidal pools and lagoons for snorkelling and diving.

 **Margate**

🏞 F5  🏖 Beachfront
ℹ️ Panorama Parade; www. visitkznsouthcoast.co.za

Self-proclaimed tourist capital of the South Coast, Margate comprises a broad expanse of golden sand hemmed in by well-tended, palm-shaded lawns and overlooked by a row of multi-storey hotels and holiday apartments.

Seaside activities include paddling pools, a freshwater swimming pool, water slides, mini-golf and there are plenty of amenities such as restaurants, ice-cream parlours and tackle shops. Designated surfing and boogie-boarding areas are on Main Beach and at Lucien Point. For a change of pace, try the two-hour walking trail through the diverse habitats of the Uvongo River Nature Reserve, home to a rich variety of birdlife.

# STAY

### The Estuary Hotel & Spa
Set in a handsome manor house, this mid-sized hotel is a short walk from the beach.

🏠 Main Rd, Port Edward
🌐 estuaryhotel.co.za

Ⓡ Ⓡ Ⓡ

### Emerald Cove
Head here to stay in an attractive thatched chalet, with good amenities and a sea-front location.

🏠 1286 Marine Rd, Shelly Beach
🌐 emeraldcove.co.za

Ⓡ Ⓡ Ⓡ

### The Oyster Box
An elegant 1930s icon. Located right on the beach, this Art Deco hotel boasts an infinity pool and a renowned high tea service.

🏠 2 Lighthouse Rd, Umhlanga Rocks
🌐 oysterboxhotel.com

Ⓡ Ⓡ Ⓡ

# EAT

### Enzo Pizzeria

A family-run trattoria serving pasta and pizzas.

 **129 Marine Terrace, Scottburgh**
**W** enzopizzeria.co.za

Ⓡ Ⓡ Ⓡ

---

### The Chef's Table

This stylish fusion restaurant serves a regularly changing menu that features fresh local ingredients.

 **Protea Mall, Chartwell Dr, Umhlanga Rocks**
**W** thechefstable.co.za

Ⓡ Ⓡ Ⓡ

---

### Mozambik

Head here for tasty Portuguese dishes.

 **4 Boulevard Centre, Ballito W** mozambik.co.za

Ⓡ Ⓡ Ⓡ

---

## Uvongo

**F5** **𝒊** www.visit kznsouthcoast.co.za

Just before it empties into the sea, the iVungu River plunges down a 23-m (75-ft) waterfall into a lagoon. High cliffs, overgrown with wild bananas, protect the lagoon with its sandy beach separating the river from the ocean. It is a popular swimming spot, and pedal boats can be hired to explore the upper reaches of the river.

There are also walking trails in the River Valley Nature Reserve, which falls on both sides of the river. A two-hour circular walk winds through beautiful coastal forest full of a wide variety of indigenous plants and plentiful birdlife.

---

## Scottburgh

**F5** 🚌 **𝒊** Scott St; www. visitkznsouthcoast.co.za

An almost continuous carpet of sugar cane plantations lines this stretch of the South Coast, and the town of Scottburgh was once used as a harbour for exporting the crop. Today, the compact little town has a distinct holiday atmosphere, and is a popular beach resort. It occupies the prominent headland overlooking the mouth of the Mpambanyoni River, and most of the hotels and holiday apartments offer superb sea views.

In the 19th century, a spring used to cascade from the bank above the river, but today a large water slide occupies the site. A restaurant, shops, a miniature railway and tidal pool are added attractions. Further south, a caravan park adjoins the beach and there is also a popular golf course, with a prime site overlooking the Indian Ocean surf.

> **An almost continuous carpet of sugar cane plantations lines this stretch of the South Coast, and the town of Scottburgh was once used as a harbour for exporting the crop.**

A photographer setting up his equipment at sunrise, on the rock-strewn sands of a beach in Umhlanga ↑

## Amanzimtoti

**⚑F5** 🚘**Durban** 🚌 **ℹ95 Beach Rd; www.sapphire coasttourism.co.za**

It is claimed that Amanzimtoti derives its name from a remark made by Shaka Zulu. In the 1820s, returning home from a campaign further down the South Coast, Shaka drank from a refreshing stream and is said to have exclaimed, "amanzi umtoti" (the water is sweet). Today, Amanzimtoti is a lively coastal resort. Its warm-water beaches are lined with hotels, holiday apartments, take-away outlets, restaurants and vibrant beachwear shops.

The area's most popular beach extends for 3 km (2 miles) north of the Manzimtoti River and offers safe bathing, picnic sites and a fine salt-water pool.

The N2 passes within 400 m (400 yrds) of the coast, providing easy access to the town's other attractions. These include a small bird sanctuary, a nature reserve and two fine golf courses.

### SHARKS ON THE INDIAN OCEAN COAST

The warm waters off KwaZulu-Natal are favoured by 12–14 types of shark, including the great white, Zambezi (or bull), ragged-tooth (or sand tiger) and hammerhead. The harmless whale shark also visits this coast in summer. Major beaches in the area are protected by shark nets beyond the surf. These are maintained by the KZN Sharks Board, which finds about 1,200 sharks in the nets each year.

## Umhlanga

**⚑F5** 🚌 **ℹChartwell Drive; www.umhlanga rockstourism.co.za**

Now a suburb of Durban, modern development lines the ridge above Umhlanga and includes shopping malls and business parks. But the town retains its atmosphere as the premier holiday resort on the North Coast and has excellent beaches, timeshare resorts, hotels and restaurants. The promenade, which extends for 3 km (2 miles), provides stunning views of the golden sands that have made Umhlanga famous. A local landmark is the red-and-white Umhlanga Lighthouse, located in front of the Oyster Box hotel.

Further north, at the mouth of the Ohlanga River, forested dunes form part of a nature reserve. A boardwalk crosses the river and the forest teems with blue duiker, birds and acrobatic monkeys.

---

## Ballito

**⚑G5** 🚌 **ℹBallito Drive; 032 437 5021**

Ballito and the neighbouring Salt Rock extend for 6 km (4 miles) along a coast known for its beaches, rocky headlands and sheltered tidal pools. Lining the main coastal road are many good restaurants. Accommodation ranges from luxury holiday apartments and timeshare resorts to family hotels and attractive caravan parks.

↑ Zulu dancers performing a traditional display in the village of Shakaland (inset)

Mhlatuze Valley, is the site of Shaka's famed military stronghold, KwaBulawayo. Construction of this historic facility began in 1823, but today almost nothing remains of the citadel that once held so much of southern Africa in its grasp.

**15** 🏞️ 🍴 🛍️

## Shakaland

**▲ G4** 🏠 Eshowe, R68 **☎** 035 460 0912 🕐 6am–9pm daily

For the 1984 TV series *Shaka Zulu*, several authentic 19th-century Zulu *kraals* were constructed. They were destroyed when filming finished, but that of Shaka's father was spared and opened to the public as Shakaland.

The unique Zulu village is open for day visits, and also offers overnight accommodation at the Shakaland Hotel. A video explaining the origin of the Zulu people is shown, and guests enjoy Zulu fare, followed by a traditional dancing display.

On a tour of the 40-hut village, visitors are introduced to a variety of traditional skills such as hut-building, spear-making, beer-brewing, artistic beadwork and pottery.

Framed by thorn trees and aloes, Goedertrou Dam in the valley below is an attractive body of water. The sunset river boat cruises are an added attraction. In the hills east of Shakaland, and commanding a superb view over the wide

**16**

## Eshowe

**▲ G4** ℹ️ www.eshowe.com

Perched at an altitude of 520 m (1700 ft), Eshowe is an attractive small town whose

---

### TRADITIONAL MUTHI HEALING

A key aspect of Zulu culture is *muthi* (traditional medicine). Historically, it was practised by a male *inyanga* (herbalist), who concentrated on medicinal cures, and a female *isangoma* (diviner), who possessed psychic powers and the ability to communicate with the ancestral spirits, but today this division is less strict. *Muthi* is an assortment of medicine and remedies made from indigenous plant life. Animal products such as fat, claws, teeth and skin are also often used. Faith in traditional healing methods is still widespread and, in order to meet the demand for the plants, special "*muthi* gardens" have been established in a number of nature reserves.

misty midland climate feels especially invigorating after the sticky coast. The oldest town in Zululand, Eshowe has a significant place in the region's history. It was the birthplace of King Cetshwayo c 1825, and served as a British military and administrative outpost in the aftermath of the 1879 Anglo-Zulu War.

Bordering the town centre, the 3-sq-km (1-sq-mile) Dlinza Forest Reserve protects a stand of mist-belt forest inhabited by the diminutive blue duiker and 90 bird species, notably crowned eagle, trumpeter hornbill, and the globally threatened spotted ground-thrush. An aerial boardwalk through the forest terminates at a 20-m- (66-ft-) high tower, which offers views to the Indian Ocean. Fort Nongqai, built by the British in a forest clearing in 1883, now houses the **Vukani Museum**'s peerless collection of Zulu ethno-graphic artifacts, as well as an outdoor dome showcasing some of the 85 butterfly species occurring in Dlinza.

### Vukani Museum

 7 Nonggai Rd 035 474 2281 7:30am-4pm Mon-Fri, 10am-4pm Sat, Sun & public hols

 **17**

## Umlalazi Nature Reserve

G4 Entrance in Mtunzini village 5am-10pm daily kznwildlife.com

This underrated reserve packs a huge amount of biodiversity into its 10 sq km (4 sq miles). A short circular walking trail leads through South Africa's most accessible mangrove swamp, home to mudskippers, hermit crabs and the gorgeous mangrove kingfisher.

A second walk leads through the dune forest to a wide, sandy beach and reveals glimpses of fish eagles and kingfishers. Shy forest animals such as vervet monkeys, red duiker and bushbuck can often be spotted.

The reserve is entered through the pretty hillside village of Mtunzini, whose name means "in the shade". Its streets are lined with coral trees and in winter their red flowers add splashes of colour to the townscape. Mtunzini is well-known for its grove of raffia palms; the nearest other known group of these scarce plants is on the Mozambique border, 260 km (163 miles) north. The palms have been

# STAY

**George Hotel**
Established in 1906 and located adjacent to Dlinza Forest Reserve, this characterful hotel has an on-site craft brewery and offers a selection of local tours.

36 Main St, Eshowe thegeorge.co.za

Ⓡ Ⓡ Ⓡ

**Umlalazi Camp**
This attractive and isolated beachfront camp comprises a dozen rustic log cabins aimed at self-caterers.

Umlalazi Nature Reserve kznwildlife.com

Ⓡ Ⓡ Ⓡ

designated a National Moniment, and can be seen with the swamp forest from a raised boardwalk. The rare palm-nut vulture, a fruit-eating raptor, may also be spotted here.

Visitors wandering the boardwalk in Dlinza Forest Nature Reserve, just outside Eshowe ↑

# ZULU CULTURE

The Zulu people's reputation for being a fierce warrior nation, fuelled by written accounts of the 1879 Anglo-Zulu War, has been enhanced by dramatic films such as *Zulu* and the internationally acclaimed television series *Shaka Zulu*. Many sites associated with Zulu history can be visited in the Ulundi, Eshowe and Melmoth districts of KwaZulu-Natal. It is true that the Zulu fought determinedly to defend their land, but their culture also encompasses arts and crafts including beadwork, pottery, basketry and dancing.

### THE ZULU KRAAL

Historically, the *umuzi* (Zulu kraal) was a circular settlement that enclosed several *uhlongwa*, beehive-shaped huts made with grass or rushes. Similar-style huts were used as grain stores, which were built on long stilts to protect them from birds and rodents. These structures were grouped around an enclosure in which the cattle – an important symbol of wealth in Zulu society – were corralled at night. Although the principle of the kraal continues, traditional architectural styles are seldom seen nowadays. Cement, bricks, concrete blocks and corrugated iron sheeting are the modern choices.

### TRADITIONAL WEAPONS

Befitting the Zulus' fearsome reputation, weaponry is an integral part of Zulu culture – even today, men often carry wooden staffs and clubs. At political meetings and rallies, tempers tend to flare, and as a result the carrying of traditional weapons has been outlawed by the government.

↑ A woman preparing *utshwala* (beer), brewed from fermented maize and sorghum

↑ A group of dancers in traditional attire performing a dance known as the Ingoma

## TRADITIONAL DANCING

In Zulu society, social gatherings almost always involve dancing. Most Zulu dances require a high level of fitness – and a lack of inhibition. While ceremonial dances can involve large crowds of gyrating, clapping and stamping performers, small groups of performers need only the encouragement of an accompanying drum and singing, whistling or wailing onlookers. Lore and clan traditions may be related through the dance; alternatively, the movements may serve as a means of social commentary. The distinctive sound of a capella choral singing that accompanies the performances has become one of South Africa's best-known cultural exports.

## ZULU CRAFTS

The Zulu people are renowned for their weaving. Most baskets display the traditional triangle or diamond shape, a symbol representing the male and female elements. Glass beads introduced by the early 19th-century traders created a new custom, and today, beadwork forms an important part of Zulu culture. Every pattern and colour has symbolic significance, as shown in the *incwadi*, or love letters, that are made by young women and given to eligible men.

*A hide screen affords additional privacy for the hut's inhabitants.*

*Huts have built-in ventilation, to keep them warm in winter and cool in summer.*

↑ A typical Zulu kraal, composed of beehive-shaped grass huts

↑ Giraffes roaming the gold-hued landscape of Ithala Game Reserve

**18**

## Ithala Game Reserve

**G4** ☐ **Vryheid R69 via Louwsburg** ☐ **Mar-Oct: 6am–6pm daily; Nov-Feb: 5am–7pm daily** ☐ **kznwildlife.com**

From the unhurried village of Louwsburg on the R69, a tarred road descends an escarpment to the wilderness of Ithala, a 296-sq-km (114-sq-mile) tract of grassland with dramatic mountain scenery and densely wooded valleys.

The reserve was established in 1972 from previous farm-land and since then it has been stocked with large species of game and has reverted back to its natural state. The Pongolo River flows along the northern boundary for some 37 km (23 miles). Seven tributaries have carved the deep valleys that dissect this park and enhance its scenic splendour. The Ngoje escarpment rises dramatically to 1,446 m (4,700 ft), providing a striking backdrop.

A tarred road also leads from the entrance to the prestigious Ntshondwe Camp. Its 67 chalets have been carefully nestled between boulders and wild fig trees. The central complex contains a reception area, restaurant, store and coffee shop, and offers panoramic views over the entire reserve. In front of the building an extensive wooden platform overlooks a reed-fringed waterhole, and is perfect for bird-watching. As no fences surround the camp, animals such as warthog often wander between the chalets. A path leads to a swimming pool tucked into a clearing at the base of the mountain.

Lavish Ntshondwe Lodge is a three-bedroomed hilltop cabin. The far-reaching vista from its deck and sunken swimming pool is arguably Ithala's finest.

Game-viewing at Ithala is excellent. Visitors should see white rhino, hartebeest, kudu, giraffe, eland, impala, wilde-beest, warthog and zebra, as well as the only population in KwaZulu-Natal of the rare tsessebe antelope. Elephant, buffalo, leopard and black rhino are also present, but are more difficult to locate.

Ngubhu Loop is the best drive in the park. Another route winds down the thickly

### Did You Know?

The amount of methane gas produced daily by an elephant could power a car for 30 km (20 miles).

→ The cosy lounge of the Homestead lodge in Phinda Game Reserve

wooded Dakaneni Valley to the Pongolo River. Although game is not as plentiful here as on the higher grasslands, the scenery is spectacular.

---

**19**

## Phinda Private Game Reserve

**G4** **23 km (14 miles) NE of Hluhluwe off the R22** **Access for guests only** **andbeyond.com**

Extending over 170 sq km (65 sq miles) of bushveld, wetland, savannah and sand forest, the privately owned Phinda is sandwiched between the iSimangaliso Wetland Park and uMkhuze Game Reserve. It was established by &Beyond in 1991, a company that aims to create sustainable conservation through responsible luxury tourism. Similar wildlife to that seen at uMkhuze can be spotted, such as nyala, kudu, wildebeest, giraffe, zebra, elephant, lion, white rhino and cheetah. Activities on offer include sunset cruises on the Mzinene River and outdoor dining, as well as game-viewing drives, bush walks and fishing or diving expeditions. There are six lodges, each with its own unique atmosphere and bush or wetland views. The reserve can arrange air and road transfers.

**20**

## Tembe Elephant Park

**G3** **65 km (40 miles) north of Mbazwana on the R22** **Apr-Sep: 6am-6pm daily; Oct-Mar: 5am-7pm daily** **tembe.net.za**

This large wilderness reserve bordering Mozambique was established in 1983 to conserve the elephants that migrate between the two countries. Today it protects healthy numbers of the Big Five, but elephants and buffaloes will be more easily seen than lions, leopards and black rhinos. It also has South Africa's largest population of suni antelopes and 430 species of birds. Two hides overlook areas where elephants come to drink. Ten groups of day visitors are permitted (in 4WD vehicles only).

West of Tembe, the **Ndumo Game Reserve** is famous for its rich riverine life, especially waterbirds. The Nyamithi and Banzi pans also sustain populations of hippo, crocodile and white and black rhino.

### Ndumo Game Reserve

 **Apr-Sep: 6am-6pm daily; Oct-Mar: 5am-7pm daily** **kznwildlife.com**

# STAY

### Tembe Tented Camp
The only available accommodation in Tembe, the camp works in collaboration with the local community. Rates include meals and daily guided game drives in search of the Big Five.

**Tembe Elephant Park** **tembe.co.za**

ⓇⓇⓇ

---

### &Beyond Phinda Mountain Lodge
Of the four magnificent lodges set in KwaZulu-Natal's most exclusive Big Five destination, Mountain Lodge is the largest and - though not exactly cheap -the most affordable.

**Phinda Private Game Reserve** **andbeyond.com**

ⓇⓇⓇ

**21**

## Midlands Meander

⬛F5 ⬛Between Mooi River and Hilton ⬛www.midlandsmeander.co.za

The undulating hills of the KwaZulu-Natal Midlands, with their green patches of forest and their dairy farms, have long been a retreat favoured by artists and craftspeople. In 1985, six studios established an arts and crafts route as a means of boosting tourism: the Midlands Meander. The trail quickly gained popularity and now consists of around 400 members and studios.

There are five routes that meander between the small towns of Hilton, Nottingham

↑ Interior of the Msunduzi Museum, one of Pietermaritzburg's many cultural buildings

Road, Howick and Mooi River. Locally crafted goods available to purchase along the route include herbs, cheese, wine, pottery, woven cloth, stained glass and antiques.

The symbol of the Midlands Meander seen on road signs marking the routes is the endangered Karkloof blue butterfly, indigenous to this region of KwaZulu-Natal.

Accommodation along the way includes idyllic country hotels, tranquil guest farms, picturesque lodges and cosy bed and breakfast establishments. There are also many quaint country pubs.

buildings and monuments are located around the city centre and in the western suburbs. In Church Street, a statue of Ghandi recalls the occasion in 1893 when the future Mahatma – then a 23-year old lawyer – was forced off a first-class train carriage here because he wasn't white.

Visitors can ramble through the surrounding forests and botanic gardens, and visit several nature reserves and

---

# SHOP

Mix craft shopping and foodie fun at these Midlands Meander stops.

**Karkloof Farmers Market**
Fresh produce market with a plant nursery and children's activities.

⬛Howick ⬛7-11am Sat ⬛karklooffarmers market.co.za

**The Junction**
A shopping village in green surrounds, offering healthy food and a candle dipping shop.

⬛Nottingham Rd ⬛033 266 6116

**Piggly Wiggly Country Village**
Picnickers will enjoy the superb deli; kids head straight for the miniature steam train (weekends only).

⬛Lions River ⬛pigglywiggly.co.za

---

**22**

## Pietermaritzburg

⬛F5 ⬛Durban ⬛Pietermaritzburg ⬛⬛ ⬛Publicity House, 177 Chief Albert Luthuli Rd; www.pmb tourism.co.za

Since its humble establishment by Afrikaner farmers in 1836, Pietermaritzburg (part of the Msunduzi municipality) has developed into the commercial, industrial and administrative centre of the KwaZulu-Natal Midlands. An intriguing blend of Victorian, Indian, African and modern architecture and culture combine to produce a distinctly South African city. Many historical and cultural

recreation resorts located within the city or a few minutes' drive away.

---

## Howick

**A** F5 **i** www.howick tourism.co.za

Established in 1850, the agreeable town of Howick overlooks an eponymous waterfall known to the local Zulu as KwaNogqaza ("Tall One"). The bordering Midmar Dam Nature Reserve is popular as a venue for water sports enthusiasts and fishermen.

North of Howick, the **Nelson Mandela Capture Site** marks the spot where its namesake was arrested by security police, on 5 August 1962, with a striking sculpture of Mandela's face. A visitor centre and exhibition opened in 2019.

Further afield, Karkloof Nature Reserve protects a mist-belt forest inhabited by samango monkey, an endemic dwarf chameleon species and a wealth of birds. It can be explored via a scenic walking trail or along zip-lines on the Karkloof Canopy Tour.

### Nelson Mandela Capture Site
🕒 9am–5pm daily
🌐 thecapturesite.co.za

---

 24 

## Spioenkop Dam Nature Reserve

**A** F4 🚗 35 km (22 miles) SW of Ladysmith 🕒 Apr–Sep: 6am–6pm daily; Oct–Mar: 5am–7pm daily
🌐 kznwildlife.com

This picturesque dam nestles at the foot of the 1,466-m- (4,810-ft-) high Spioenkop, which in 1900 was the scene of a decisive battle between the British and Boer forces in the South African War. The battlefield site is accessible from the road, and countless graves and memorials are scattered across the peak's summit as a grim reminder of one of Britain's worst defeats during that conflict.

Today, Spioenkop is popular with outdoor enthusiasts. The dam offers fishing and boating, while zebra, giraffe, wildebeest, red hartebeest and oribi can be seen in the surrounding nature reserve, along with a variety of bird species. There is also a pleasant campsite, and picnic sites are situated along the southern shoreline. Two short trails encourage visitors to view game on foot.

Water tumbling over steep cliffs in Howick, which are often tackled by rock climbers *(inset)* ↓

# LESOTHO

**A**E5 **✈**Moshoeshoe International **ℹ**Cnr Parliament & Linare roads, Maseru; www.visitlesotho.travel

Surrounded by South Africa, this mountain kingdom, or "Kingdom in the Sky" as it is sometimes called, achieved independence from Britain on 4 October 1966. Its rugged highlands, formed by the Maluti, Drakensberg and Thaba-Putsoa mountains, are a popular destination for visitors who enjoy outdoor activities. Lesotho also features fertile river valleys and a strong cultural heritage that is very much kept alive by the Basotho people.

## ① Maseru

Lesotho's capital Maseru started life as a police camp established on the bank of the Mohokare (formerly Caledon) River when Basutoland became a British protectorate in the wake of the Free State-Basotho War of 1869. The market town that grew up around this British outpost soon took over from King Moshoeshoe's stronghold at Thaba Bosiu, 25 km (16 miles) to the east, as the country's largest settlement, and it remains so today. Maseru's main attraction is Makoanyane Square, site of a monument to the Basotho who died in the two World Wars.

## ② Teyateyaneng

Founded in 1886 by one of King Moshoeshoe's sons, this substantial highland town – whose tongue-twisting name is often abbreviated to T.Y. – is widely hailed as the "crafts capital" of Lesotho. The colourful woven jerseys, carpets and wall hangings made here are a local speciality, and there are several showrooms at which they can be purchased.

## ③ Ts'ehlanyane National Park and Bokong Nature Reserve

Connected by a 39-km (24-mile) hiking and pony-trekking trail, this is Lesotho's largest national park and nature reserve. It protects high-altitude wilderness areas that support a wide variety of forest, moorland and grassland habitats, including stands of the endemic bamboo (known locally as Ts'ehlanyane) for which the former is named, and a unique type of montane *fynbos*. Wildlife species that can be spotted here include bearded vulture and grey rhebok. The road to Bokong crosses the Mafika-Lislu Pass, the highest road in southern Africa at 3,090 m (10,140 ft).

Marquard • — Caledons — Butha-Buthe • Oxbow • — Bergville
FREE STATE
Excelsior •
Ts'ehlanyane National Park and Bokong Nature Reserve ③
Peka • — Mafika-Lislu Pass — Letsenga-Terae **A1**
Teyateyaneng ② — Lejone • — Mapholaneng • Mafadi 3,450 m △ (11,319 ft)
Maseru ① — Sefikeng • — Seshote
Mazenod • ④ Thaba Bosiu — ⑥ Katse Dam — Thabana Ntlenyana 3,842 m △ (12,605 ft)
Roma • **A3**
Kolo • — Marakabei • Thaba Tseka **A3** ⑤ Sani Pass
Ramabanta • — Semonkong ⑦ — Sehonghong
Mafeteng • — Malealea • — *Maletsunyane Falls*
Thabana Morena • — Mokopung • Tsoekike — ⑧ Sehlabathebe National Park
Mohale's Hoek • — Mphaki • Qacha's Nek — KWAZULU-NATAL
Matlakeng • **A4**
Quthing • — Matatiele
EASTERN CAPE

0 kilometres 50
0 miles 50
N ↑

↑ A traditional hut village in rural Lesotho, comprised of thatched-roof dwellings

 ④

## Thaba Bosiu

This sandstone plateau (the name of which is seSotho for "Mountain of Night") is where King Moshoeshoe I and his followers took refuge from the rampant Zulu army during the Mfecane in the 1820s *(p62)*. Widely regarded as the founder of the modern Basotho nation, Moshoeshoe later chose this natural fortress as his capital.

Thaba Bosiu was tested most severely during 1865-6, when the site was bombarded by a 6,000-strong Boer army from the nearby Free State Republic led by General Louw Wepener. Moshoeshoe and his subjects survived the siege, but were so weakened by it that they eventually signed a treaty surrendering vast tracts of land to the aggressors. In 1869, under threat of another attack from the Boers, Basutoland was named as a British protectorate at the request of Moshoeshoe.

Thaba Bosiu is still regarded as a sacred site by Basotho traditionalists, who believe it grows in height during the night to make it more difficult for attackers to conquer. The summit can be reached from the visitor's centre at its base, following a short but steep pass. It houses the restored remains of a stone house built for Moshoeshoe by a Scottish soldier called David Webber in 1837, as well as the royal cemetery where the king was buried in 1870. Also visible from here is the distinctive rock pinnacle known as Qiloane, or the Basotho Hat.

### ROCK PAINTINGS AND DINOSAUR TRACKS

Due to its remoteness, Lesotho has remained relatively uncommercialized. The mountains, where stout Basotho ponies are often the only form of transport, contain some of the finest examples of rock art in southern Africa. Thaba Bosiu near Maseru and the Sekubu Caves at Butha-Buthe are just two of the more than 400 worthwhile sites. Fossilized dinosaur tracks can also be found in the region.

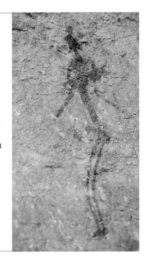

The dramatic switchbacks of the route through the mountainous Sani Pass ↑

## ⑤
## Sani Pass

The only motorable track to breach the craggy escarpment that forms the border between KwaZulu-Natal and Lesotho, the 4WD-only Sani Pass climbs 1,300 m (4,300 ft) uphill via a remote Lesotho border post (passport required), to **Sani Mountain Lodge**. The lodge stands in spectacular isolation at a windswept altitude of 2,874 m (9,400 ft), and is home to Africa's highest pub. The Alpine scenery of Sani Pass is almost other-worldly: a treeless plateau of tussocked grass, mossy boulders and clumped heather inhabited by high-altitude endemics such as Drakensberg rockjumper and mountain pipit. Though somewhat off the beaten track, Sani Pass is the only part of Lesotho to receive a regular stream of tourists.

**Sani Mountain Lodge**
🏠 Sani Top 🌐 sani mountain.co.za

---

## ⑥
## Katse Dam

This is Africa's second-largest double-curvature arch dam – and the second-tallest dam of any kind. The Katse stands 185 m (607 ft) tall, just below the Malibamat'so River's confluence with the Bokong.

---

> 💬 **INSIDER TIP**
> **Sani Pass Tours**
>
> Those reluctant to make this challenging drive themselves can join a commercial 4WD or quad bike day tour, or take the shuttle provided by Sani Mountain Lodge, departing from the town of Himeville.

The dam forms part of the Lesotho Highlands Water Project, an ambitious scheme to divert water from Lesotho to the densely populated but drought-prone province of Gauteng while also genera-ting hydroelectric power for domestic use.

---

## ⑦
## Semonkong

This sleepy village is a well-established springboard for multi-day pony-trekking excursions in the highlands of Lesotho. Semonkong (Place of Smoke) is named for the rainy season spray kicked up by the spectacular waterfall formed by the Maletsunyane River as it plunges 192 m (633 ft) over a sheer basaltic ledge into the river to the south. The Maletsunyane Falls are also the site of the world's longest commercially

> The Alpine scenery of Sani Pass is almost other-worldly: a treeless plateau of tussocked grass, mossy boulders and clumped heather inhabited by high-altitude endemics such as Drakensberg rockjumper and mountain pipit.

has an average altitude of 2,400 m (7,870 ft). The park covers an area of 70 sq km (27 sq miles) and is accessible only on foot, with a high clearance 4WD, or – most alluringly – on horseback with a well-established local organization called **Khotso Horse Trails**. Due to its remote location, Sehlabathebe sees few visitors but it is serviced by a self-catering lodge and a few wild camp-sites. Those who do visit here come for the isolated wilderness atmosphere, stunning montane landscapes of rolling grassland, glassy tarns, natural rock arches and contorted sandstone forma-tions. There are also a few abandoned stone Basotho dwellings and an astonishing total of 60 prehistoric rock art sites to take in.

The chilly streams that run through Sehlabathebe offer exceptional trout fishing and support an endemic fish species known as the Maluti redfin. The park's population of birds is similarly impressive; a checklist of 117 bird species that may be sighted includes the endangered Cape vulture and Alpine specials such as lammergeyer (bearded vulture), Drakensberg siskin and Drakensberg rockjumper. Mammals are more thinly distributed across the land-scape but hikers should keep their eyes peeled – if lucky, they might well encounter eland, grey rhebok, oribi and chacma baboon.

**Khotso Horse Trails**
Ⓦ khotso.co.za

---

### Did You Know?

Lesotho's lowest point above sea level is 1,500 m (4,920 ft) – a higher low point than any other country.

---

operated, single-drop abseil (204 m/669 ft). The abseiling, along with a host of other activities such as pony-trekking and hiking, is operated by **Semonkong Lodge**, which also has a restaurant and offers a range of accommo-dation in traditional stone-and-thatch buildings.

**Semonkong Lodge**
Ⓐ Riverside Rd
Ⓦ semonkonglodge.com

---

 ⑧
## Sehlabathebe National Park

Protecting Lesotho's sector of the Maloti-Drakensberg UNESCO World Heritage Site, Sehlabathebe (literally "Shield of the Plateau") was gazetted in 1960 to protect a remote tract of undulating montane grassland that forms an important watershed and

↑ Admiring the Maletsunyane Falls, one of the highest single-drop waterfalls in the southern hemisphere

# A DRIVING TOUR
# BATTLEFIELDS

**Length** 380 km (236 miles). **Stopping-off points**
Ladysmith, Dundee **Difficulty** Easy

The peaceful, rolling grasslands and tree-covered hills of northwestern KwaZulu-Natal retain few reminders of the bloody battles that were waged in this corner of South Africa during the 19th century. In the 1820s, Zulu king Shaka's campaign to seize control of the scattered tribes plunged the entire region into turmoil. Over the following 80 years many wars were fought, pitting Zulu against Ndwandwe, Afrikaner against Zulu and British against Afrikaner and Zulu. A detailed guide to the battlefields lists more than 50 sites of interest and is available from the local publicity associations and the Talana Museum, where expert guides can also be hired.

*The **Talana Museum** commemorates the first battle of the South African War (29 October 1899), when 4,500 British soldiers arrived in Dundee to defend the town and its mines.*

*The Boer and British forces clashed at **Elandslaagte** on 21 October 1899, during a severe storm. The British were forced to retreat to nearby Ladysmith.*

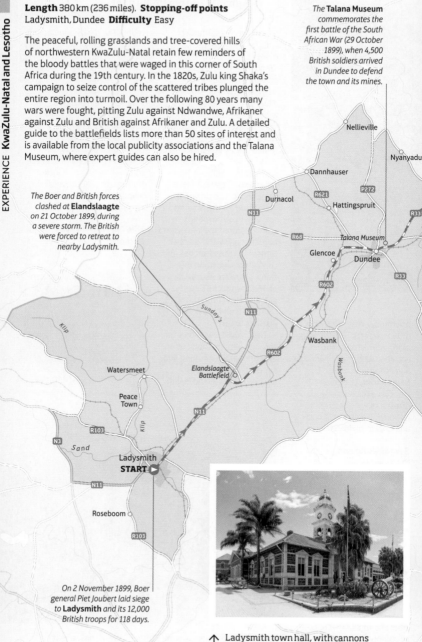

Nellieville

Nyanyadu

Dannhauser

Durnacol

R621

Hattingspruit

P272

R33

N11

R68

Talana Museum

Glencoe · Dundee

R602

R33

Sunday's

N11

R602

Wasbank

Wasbank

Watersmeet

Elandslaagte Battlefield

N11

Peace Town

Klip

R103

N3

Sand

Ladysmith
**START**

N11

Roseboom

R103

*On 2 November 1899, Boer general Piet Joubert laid siege to **Ladysmith** and its 12,000 British troops for 118 days.*

↑ Ladysmith town hall, with cannons from the Anglo-Boer War in front

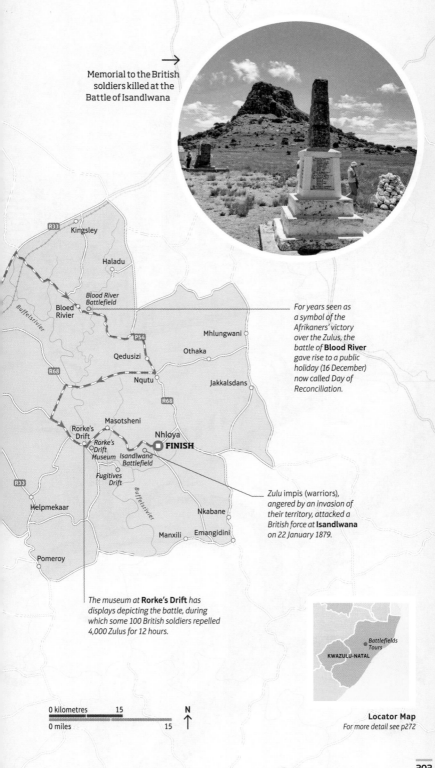

← Memorial to the British soldiers killed at the Battle of Isandlwana

For years seen as a symbol of the Afrikaners' victory over the Zulus, the battle of **Blood River** gave rise to a public holiday (16 December) now called Day of Reconciliation.

Zulu impis (warriors), angered by an invasion of their territory, attacked a British force at **Isandlwana** on 22 January 1879.

The museum at **Rorke's Drift** has displays depicting the battle, during which some 100 British soldiers repelled 4,000 Zulus for 12 hours.

0 kilometres     15

0 miles     15

N
↑

**Locator Map**
*For more detail see p272*

# JOHANNESBURG AND AROUND

Fossils unearthed in Gauteng's Cradle of Humankind site indicate that hominin habitation goes back at least three million years. Much of the region's early history is unknown, but around the 11th century AD Sotho and Tswana pastoralists arrived from the north to establish large stone settlements. These were evacuated in the mid 19th century in the aftermath of the Mfecane (*p62*), around the same time that Pretoria was founded as the capital of the 19th-century South African Republic; the city has been the national capital since 1910. Further south, Johannesburg owes its existence to the discovery of the world's richest gold deposits in 1886; by the turn of the 20th century, it was southern Africa's largest and wealthiest city. Residential segregation along racial lines was formalized under apartheid with the creation of "townships" such as Soweto (Blacks), Eldorado Park (Coloureds) and Lenasia (Indians). Gauteng, a seSotho name meaning "Place of Gold", is now the country's most progressive and urbanized province. Astonishingly, though it covers less than 1.5 per cent of South Africa's surface area, a full 20 per cent of the national population is crammed into Gauteng's cities, and the region generates 10 per cent of the entire African GDP.

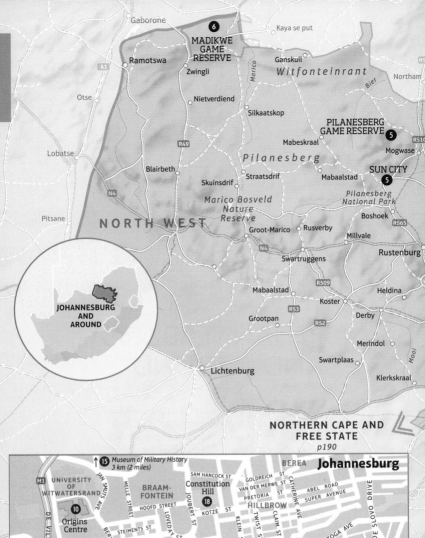

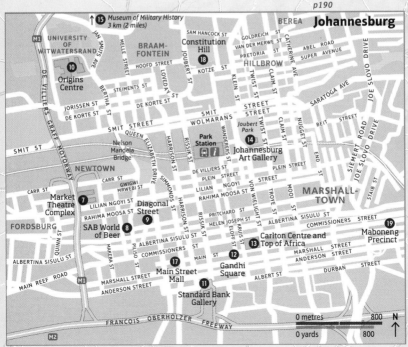

Johannesburg

LIMPOPO, MPUMALANGA AND KRUGER
*p332*

0 kilometres 30
0 miles 30

N

Holme Park

Warmbad

Settlers

Siyabuswa

Hereford

Groblersdal

*Borakalalo Nature Reserve*

Moretele

Radium

Pienaarsrivier

Rust de Winter

Assen

Atlanta

Klipvoor Dam

Babelegi

Witnek

*Vaalkop Dam*

Beestekraal

DINOKENG GAME RESERVE

Winterveld

**21**

Temba

Kwamhlanga

*Wilge*

Rashoop

Hammanskraal

Mabopane

N1

ANN VAN DYCK CHEETAH CENTRE

Ga-Rankuwa

Vaalplaas

Marikana

Brits

**23**

N4

Cullinan

Rayton

**26**

PRETORIA **27**

Bronkhorstspruit

Witbank

**24**

HARTBEES-POORT DAM

Verwoerdburg

Balmoral

MAGALIESBERG RANGE

**25** LESEDI CULTURAL VILLAGE

N4

Ogies

Coalville

R509

**4** CRADLE OF HUMANKIND

Bapsfontein

Kendal

MPUMALANGA

WALTER SISULU BOTANICAL GARDEN **22**

N14

SANDTON AND ROSEBANK

O.R. Tambo International Airport

Delmas

**16**

**20**

Johannesburg *see inset map below*

Kriel

FLORENCE BLOOM BIRD SANCTUARY

**2** GOLD REEF CITY

N14

**1**

Springs

Devon

Westonaria

SOWETO **3**

APARTHEID MUSEUM

N17

Nigel

N17

Bank

Walkerville

Kinross

Carletonville

Grasmere

N1

N3

Trichardt

Daleside

GAUTENG

Meyerton

Heidelberg

Balfour

Charl Cilliers

Fochville

Evaton

R59

N12

Vanderbijlpark

Vereeniging

N3

Viljoensdrif

Greylingstad

Parys

## JOHANNESBURG AND AROUND

### Must Sees

**1** Apartheid Museum
**2** Gold Reef City
**3** Soweto
**4** Cradle of Humankind
**5** Pilanesberg Game Reserve and Sun City
**6** Madikwe Game Reserve

### Experience More

**7** Market Theatre Complex
**8** SAB World of Beer
**9** Diagonal Street
**10** Origins Centre
**11** Standard Bank Gallery
**12** Gandhi Square
**13** Carlton Centre and Top of Africa
**14** Johannesburg Art Gallery
**15** Museum of Military History
**16** Florence Bloom Bird Sanctuary
**17** Main Street Mall
**18** Constitution Hill
**19** Maboneng Precinct
**20** Sandton and Rosebank
**21** Dinokeng Game Reserve
**22** Walter Sisulu Botanical Garden
**23** Ann Van Dyck Cheetah Centre
**24** Magaliesberg Range
**25** Lesedi Cultural Village
**26** Hartebeespoort Dam
**27** Pretoria

1 🤼 Ⓜ 🖥

# APARTHEID MUSEUM

🅰 E3  🅐 Northern Parkway and Gold Reef Rd, Ormonde, Johannesburg
🕐 9am–5pm daily  🅓 Good Fri, 25 Dec, 1 Jan  🅦 apartheidmuseum.org

**Documenting the triumph of the human spirit over adversity, the displays at this haunting museum recall the National Party's 1948 apartheid policy, which turned 20 million non-whites into legally defined second-class citizens.**

The darkest days of South Africa's turbulent past are chillingly evoked at this fascinating museum. To set the mood, visitors enter through separate "white" and "non-white" gates, which are randomly allocated on the entrance ticket. Particularly powerful exhibits include a room with 131 nooses representing the number of political prisoners executed during apartheid, BBC footage taken in 1961 of Nelson Mandela when he was in hiding, and a series of evocative photographs taken by Ernest Cole before he was sent into exile during the late 1960s.

Allow at least two hours to visit the museum. Note that it is not suitable for children under 11 because of the harrowing nature of much of the material on display.

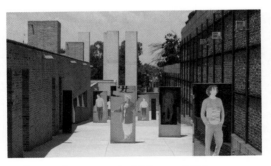

↑ "Journeys", a permanent exhibit representing South Africa's early migrant population

### ERNEST COLE

Born near Pretoria in 1940, Ernest Cole began his photographic career in 1958 at the magazine *Drum* and spent the next decade documenting life under apartheid. A book of his work, entitled *House of Bondage*, was published internationally in 1967 but banned in South Africa. He passed the rest of his life in exile in Stockholm and New York, and died of cancer in 1990. The discovery in 2006 of 60,000 missing negatives taken by Cole led to greater posthumous recognition of his pioneering work and the publication of another book - *Ernest Cole: Photographer*.

*Timeline*

*1948*

△ The National Party is elected on the promise of severely restricting Black rights. Their policy of apartheid begins.

*1960*
▽ Sixty-nine people are killed by police in the Sharpeville Massacre, following a riot over the use of passbooks for Black citizens.

*1974*
△ South Africa is expelled from the United Nations. The country was not allowed to return until after apartheid ended.

*1990*

▽ Nelson Mandela is freed from prison after 27 years. He became president in 1994, after South Africa's first democractic election.

An exhibition hall within the museum, ↑ displaying photographs that document the experience of life under apartheid

**2** 🛠️ 🅜 🖥️ 🛍️

# GOLD REEF CITY

🅰️ **E3** 🏠 **Northern Parkway, Ormonde, Johannesburg**
🕘 **9:30am-5pm Thu-Sun** 🔒 **25 Dec** 🌐 **goldreefcity.co.za**

**The past comes to life at this family-friendly amusement park, located 8 km (5 miles) south of Johannesburg. Themed around the city's gold-rush era, it offers fascinating historical exhibits alongside a plethora of thrilling rides.**

Reconstructing the Johannesburg of the early 1890s, Gold Reef City aims to recapture that transient time during which the town evolved from a mining camp to a modern city. An interactive tour includes a visit to the underground mine that the park is built around, a demonstration of gold panning, and a display of the heavy-footed Isicathulo "gumboot" dance (probably conceived by migrant miners as an alternative to traditional drumming, which was restricted by the authorities). Theme park rides include the Anaconda roller-coaster, and the complex also houses curio shops, eateries and a casino.

## Did You Know?

Johannesburg is also known as "Egoli", a Zulu name that means "place of gold".

## GOLD MINING IN SOUTH AFRICA

Vast natural resources make South Africa one of the richest countries on the continent. Ancient sediments in this geological treasure chest yield silver, platinum, chromite, uranium, diamonds – and gold. Over the years, small-scale miners have left behind evidence of their labour at numerous sites around the country. Today, South Africa is the world's sixth-largest gold producer, and the South Deep Mine in Mpumalanga, 45 km (28 miles) southwest of Johannesburg, is the second-biggest mine in the world.

←

The 19th-century-style Gold Reef City Theme Park Hotel

1 The lobby of the casino is centred around a giant clock.

2 The exhilarating Anaconda ride is one of several roller-coasters in the park.

3 The mine that the park is built around was closed in 1971.

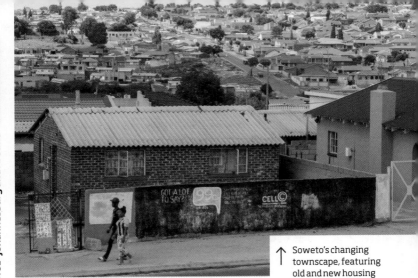

↑ Soweto's changing
townscape, featuring
old and new housing

**3**

# SOWETO

**⚐E3** **✈OR Tambo** **ℹN Walter Sisulu Square (cnr Klipspruit Valley & Union Rd); www.gauteng.net**

Soweto is the oldest, largest and best-known of the so-called "townships" in Gauteng. Several key events of the anti-apartheid struggle took place here, and revered figures including Nelson Mandela and Archbishop Desmond Tutu were among its former residents.

**①**

### Hector Pieterson Memorial and Museum

**⚐8287 Khumalo St, Orlando West** **☎011 536 0611/2** **⊙10am-5pm Mon-Sat, 10am-4pm Sun** **⊠Good Fri, Dec 25, 1 Jan**

On 16 July 1976, 13-year-old Hector Pieterson became the first victim of police action in the Soweto Uprising, a landmark wave of anti-apartheid clashes triggered by student protests against the proposed introduction of Afrikaans in local schools. More than 20,000 people took part in the protests, and a subsequent commission attributed 451 student deaths and 2,389 injuries to the police. The poignant Hector Pieterson Memorial, erected in the early 1990s two blocks from where its namesake was shot by police, is dominated by Sam Nzima's iconic photograph of the dying Pieterson being carried by another student, accompanied by his elder sister Antoinette. Next to the memorial, the Hector Pieterson Museum houses exhibits that illuminate and contextualize the Soweto Uprising – an event whose broader significance can be gauged by the fact that 16 June, the anniversary of the first protest, is now commemorated as Youth Day and is a public holiday.

**②**

### Mandela House Family Museum

**⚐Vilakazi St** **⊙9am-4:45pm daily** **⊠Good Fri, Easter Sun, 25 & 26 Dec, 1 Jan** **🌐mandelahouse.com**

This small museum preserves 8115 Orlando West, the modest house where Nelson Mandela lived from 1948 until he was imprisoned in 1963. The building was restored in 2009 and now functions as a museum dedicated to the history and legacy of the Mandela family.

---

### GUIDED SOWETO TOURS

The best and safest way to explore the suburb is on a day tour, which are typically guided by residents or former residents. Reliable specialist operators offering minibus tours are Soweto Day Tours *(sowetodaytours. com)* and MoAfrika Tours *(sowetotour.co.za)*. A more active option is the guided bicycle tours led by Cycle in Soweto *(cycleinsoweto.com)*.

## ③
### Regina Mundi Church

📍 149 Mkhize St ⏰ 9am-4pm Mon-Sat, 11am-3pm Sun 🌐 reginamundi soweto.com

Built in 1964, Regina Mundi is South Africa's largest Catholic church: its unusual A-frame structure can hold up to 5,000 people. The church served as a clandestine rendezvous for activists during the apartheid era, when overt political meetings were outlawed. It also provided refuge to demonstrators fleeing the police in the 1976 Soweto Uprising. Scars of gunfire associated with that event can still be seen on the walls.

## ④
### Soweto Towers

📍 Sheffield & Chris Hani rds, Orlando East ⏰ Noon-sun-set Thu, 10am-sunset Fri-Sun 🌐 sowetotowers.co.za

One of Soweto's most distinctive landmarks, the 100-m- (330-ft-) tall twin towers were constructed as cooling towers for the coal-fired Orlando Power Station, which was decommissioned in 1998. They received a facelift in 2002, when they became the canvas for a colourful mural featuring local icons such as the Soweto String Quartet and Nelson Mandela.

The disused towers now also double as a vertical adventure facility offering activities such as bungee jumping, abseiling and zip-lining.

## ⑤
### Walter Sisulu Square

📍 Cnr Klipspruit Valley & Union rds ⏰ 9am-5pm Mon-Fri (to 2pm Sat & Sun) 🌐 waltersisulusquare.co.za

Describing itself as "South Africa's first township enter-tainment explosion centre", Walter Sisulu Square is a modern shopping mall named after the deeply respected late ANC Deputy President who served 26 years in prison alongside Nelson Mandela. Its centrepiece is an open-air museum that celebrates the Freedom Charter – the docu-ment that forms the very cornerstone of the present-day South African constitution – drawn up on the site (then an empty field) in June 1955.

←

The Soweto Towers, brightly decorated with depictions of local scenes

🔍 HIDDEN GEM
**Credo Mutwa Cultural Village**

Set in the Oppenheimer Gardens, the Credo Mutwa Cultural Village is an outdoor museum-cum-sculpture garden, inspired by African culture and mythology.

## ⑥
### FNB Stadium

📍 Soccer City Avenue, Nasrec ⏰ For tours at 9am, 10:30am, noon, 1:30pm, 3pm Thu 🌐 stadium management.co.za

One of the world's ten largest stadiums, the 87,000-seat calabash-shaped arena known as "Soccer City" has hosted several legendary football matches, as well as a number of important national events, including the official memorial service to Nelson Mandela in December 2013. It also doubles as a music venue. The stadium is best visited when an inter-national or major domestic football fixture is underway, but tours of the grounds are also conducted on Thursdays.

④ 🖼 Ⓜ 🍽

# CRADLE OF HUMANKIND

🅰 E3 🅿 50 km (30 miles) NW of Johannesburg 🕐 9am–4pm daily
Ⓦ maropeng.co.za

Inscribed by UNESCO in 1999, the Cradle of Humankind World Heritage Site incorporates 13 paleontological sites that together offer an unparalleled insight into the evolution of humankind.

The Cradle of Humankind comprises an ancient Karstic landscape whose 2.5-billion-year-old dolomite bedrock started life as an ocean floor covered in blue-green algae. The dolomite is rich in soluble and erosive calcium carbonate, which seeps into the fault lines and gradually transforms them into gaping limestone caverns and sinkholes in which living creatures are frequently trapped and fossilized. Still under ongoing excavation, the caves have yielded numerous hominin fossils, representing a uniquely complete record of the last 3.2 million years of human evolution.

> 💬 INSIDER TIP
> **Combined Entry**
>
> Make the most of your excursion to the Maropeng Visitors Centre by purchasing a combined ticket that includes entrance to the Sterkfontein Caves.

↑ The award-winning Maropeng Visitors Centre, shaped like a giant tumulus (burial mound)

## Exploring the Site

The main focus for visitors is the innovative and child-friendly Maropeng Visitors Centre. Two-hour self-guided tours start with an exciting boat ride through a subterranean waterway, which emerges into a main hall with a series of well-thought-out displays documenting various aspects of human evolution. The only paleontological site open to the public is the Sterkfontein Caves, where "Mrs Ples" – a 2.3-million-year-old Australopithecus Africanus skull – was discovered in 1936, providing fossil confirmation of Darwin's theory that humankind evolved in Africa.

### HOMO NALEDI

During 2013–15, a palaeontological team unearthed more than 1,500 hominin fossils belonging to around 15 individuals from Dinaledi Chamber in the Cradle of Humankind's Rising Star Cave. These fossils were assigned to the previously unknown species *Homo naledi*, which combined typical *Homo* features with traits of other genera. The fossils are no more than 350,000 years old, suggesting that *H naledi* was not ancestral to *Homo sapiens* but lived alongside it.

### Did You Know?

The Cradle of Humankind's caves have yielded around 40 per cent of all known hominin fossils.

↑ Sterkfontein Caves, where the partial remains of more than 500 individuals *(inset)* have been discovered

5 ⟨✦⟩ ⟨✦⟩

# PILANESBERG GAME RESERVE AND SUN CITY

△E2-3 ⬡Accessed from R565 or R510 ⬡Mar-Apr: 6am-6:30pm daily; May-Sep: 6am-6pm daily; Nov-Feb: 5:30am-7pm daily ⬡pilanesbergnationalpark.org

Pilanesberg Game Reserve and neighbouring Sun City form the proverbial odd couple. Both are popular weekend retreats from congested Gauteng, but where the tranquil Pilanesberg dazzles with its Big Five game viewing, Sun City is an altogether more glitzy destination.

↑ An appealing elephant statue set within a square in Sun City

Pilanesberg and Sun City were established in what was then the homeland of the republic of Bophuthatswana, shortly after it accepted nominal independence from apartheid South Africa in 1977. The brainchild of hotelier Sol Kerzner, Sun City started life as a resort complex offering a bouquet of activities – gambling, pornographic movies, risqué stage shows – that were banned in South Africa but legal in Bophuthatswana.

Developed simultaneously to Sun City, Pilanesberg Game Reserve was forged from a 550-sq-km (193-sq-mile) tract of overgrazed, low-yield farmland. This was an ambitious

The wide landscape of
Pilanesberg Game Reserve, which
can be toured by jeep *(inset)* ↑

process that culminated in the relocation and release of thousands of individual animals across 19 different mammal species.

During apartheid, Pilanesberg rather languished in the background while Sun City flourished as a domestic tourism venue. Today, Pilanesberg is perhaps the bigger draw; the reserve offers the closest bona fide game-viewing to Johannesburg, home as it is to all of the Big Five and an astonishing 350 bird species. It also ranks as one of the most rewarding malaria-free self-drive safari destinations anywhere in Africa.

### HOT-AIR BALLOONING IN THE PILANESBERG

Balloon trips over Pilanesberg Game Reserve are a popular safari option. Drifting in total silence over the herds of wildlife that peacefully graze within the rim of the extinct volcano is a remarkable experience. The trips are operated by Air Trackers *(hotairballoonsafarisa.co.za)*, and can be booked either through the Pilanesberg accommodation or at the Welcome Centre in Sun City. Rates include a one-hour balloon ride and a game drive before breakfast at one of the lodges.

↑ African elephants walking through the reserve's grass as the sun begins to set

# PILANESBERG GAME RESERVE

The circular layout of this park can be traced to prehistoric times, when this area was the crater of a volcano. Three rings of little hills – mounds of cooled lava – enclose the reserve and the whole area is raised above the plain.

The decision to establish a reserve here was economic: to benefit the local people, and to complement the nearby resort of Sun City. Re-stocking the overgrazed farmland turned into one of the most ambitious game relocation ventures ever attempted in South Africa. Appropriately referred to

↑ A leopard in the dark, one of the park's most secretive mammals

as Operation Genesis, it involved the release of over 6,000 mammals into the new reserve. To ensure the success of this challenging venture, alien plants were removed and replaced with indigenous ones, telephone lines were diverted, farming structures demolished and the ravages of erosion repaired.

A safari to Pilanesberg will likely provide encounters with lions, elephants, white rhinos, buffaloes, giraffes, zebras and hippos, plus a wide variety of antelope. More than 200 km (125 miles) of good gravel roads traverse the park, and there are a number of walk-in viewing hides. For visitors staying overnight, guided night drives provide an opportunity to look for leopards, brown hyenas and other nocturnal species.

An impressive tally of 365 bird species has also been recorded in Pilanesberg. Cape vultures nest on the steep cliffs of the mountains and a number of feeding stations have been created to encourage the survival of this endangered bird.

# SUN CITY

Set in a fairly bleak part of the North West Province, Sun City was developed in the 1970s. The resort's casino was a key part of its initial success, since gambling was banned in South Africa at that time. It soon became apparent that the complex could not cope with the influx of visitors, and a further two hotels were added in 1980 and 1984. Then in 1992, the Palace of the Lost City opened, and today it is still Sun City's five-star flagship hotel. In the same year, the Valley of the Waves was constructed below the hotel and a second golf course added to the complex. The Valley of the Waves is one of Sun City's top attractions – a huge waterpark featuring a "roaring lagoon" with a wave machine, a mock volcano and a number of thrilling water-slides, including the 70-m (230-ft) Temple of Courage.

Although changes in gambling law introduced in 1996 mean that casinos have since sprung up around the country, Sun City continues to attract visitors with its many

↑ The honey-coloured walls of the Palace of the Lost City, Sun City's foremost hotel

other entertainment options, which include elaborate stage shows and music concerts, a man-made lake for parasailing, water-skiing and jet-skiing, stables and a ten-pin bowling alley. The complex also houses restaurants and boutiques, a cinema, a spa and swimming pools. At the entrance to the resort is Kwena Gardens, home to more than 7,000 Nile crocodiles that can be seen from elevated walkways.

The groomed greens and wide fairways of one of Sun City's two golf courses ↑

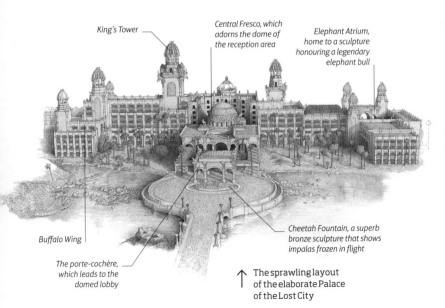

King's Tower

Central Fresco, which adorns the dome of the reception area

Elephant Atrium, home to a sculpture honouring a legendary elephant bull

Buffalo Wing

The porte-cochère, which leads to the domed lobby

Cheetah Fountain, a superb bronze sculpture that shows impalas frozen in flight

↑ The sprawling layout of the elaborate Palace of the Lost City

# MADIKWE GAME RESERVE

**🅰 E2  🅰 339 km (211 miles) NW of Pretoria  🅾 Access for lodge guests only  🅦 northwestparks.org.za**

**South Africa's premier malaria-free safari destination, the 750-sq-km (290-sq-mile) Madikwe Game Reserve abuts the Botswana border and is a leading model of community-based wildlife conservation.**

The Madikwe Game Reserve was established in 1991, following a government study which indicated that what was then an unproductive tract of former ranchland could be utilized more profitably for conservation, with greater benefits to local communities. Over the subsequent decade, around 8,000 head of game were introduced, including an elephant herd from drought-stricken southeast Zimbabwe. Today, giraffe, plains zebra, greater kudu, springbok, red hartebeest and tsessebe are conspicuous among the reserve's 65 mammal species. Of the Big Five, lion, elephant and white rhino are seen by most visitors, while buffalo and leopard are uncommon. Madikwe is possibly South Africa's most reliable reserve for sightings of the endangered African wild dog. More than 350 species of birds have been recorded.

Madikwe caters primarily for the middle and upper end of the safari market, studded as it is with around 15 exclusive bush camps offering all-inclusive guided safari packages.

① The park is home to predators such as cheetah, the world's fastest land mammal.

② The Southern Yellow Hornbill is among Madikwe's 350 species of birds, which also include pied babbler and crimson-breasted shrike.

③ The reserve is particularly reliable for glimpses of African wild dog, one of the world's most endangered mammals.

# STAY

**Buffalo Ridge Safari Lodge**
This spectacularly sited lodge treats guests to views of a watering hole.

🏠 Off the R48 🌐 buffalo ridgesafari.com

Ⓡ Ⓡ Ⓡ

**Sanctuary Makanyane Safari Lodge**
A bush lodge fringing the Marico River.

🏠 Off Derdepoort Rd 🌐 sanctuary retreats.com

Ⓡ Ⓡ Ⓡ

## Did You Know?

Giraffes have the same number of vertebrae in their necks as humans: seven.

←

Wildlife gathering at a park watering hole, and *(inset)* freely roaming the landscape

# EXPERIENCE MORE

**7**

## Market Theatre Complex

⚑E3 🏠 Lilian Ngoyi St, Newtown, Johannesburg
🌐 markettheatre.co.za

Originally an Indian fruit market, the Market Theatre Complex is the centre of the Newtown Cultural Precinct. A great effort has been made to make this a safe place to visit, and the complex now houses entertainment venues, restaurants and shops.

Opposite the Market Theatre, the Africana Museum (1935) was relaunched in 1994 as **Museum Africa**. The theme is Johannesburg and its people at various stages of sociopolitical transformation.

West of the theatre is the **Oriental Plaza** bazaar, where more than 300 shops and stalls sell everything from carpets to clothing. Many traders are descendants of the Indians who came here in the 19th century *(p297)*.

### Museum Africa

🏛 🏠 121 Lilian Ngoyi St, Newtown 📞 11 833 5624
🕐 9am–5pm Tue–Sun

### Oriental Plaza

🍴🏛 🏠 38 Lilian Ngoyi St, Fordsburg 🕐 9am–5pm Mon–Fri, 9am–3pm Sat
🌐 orientalplaza.co.za

**8** 🎨🎭🍴🏛

### SAB World of Beer

⚑E3 🏠 Entrance on Becker St, Newtown, Johannesburg
🕐 10am–6pm Tue–Sat, 10am–5pm Sun & Mon
🌐 worldofbeer.co.za

South African Breweries (SAB), established in 1895, is the largest brewer of beer by volume in the world. This modern museum offers an entertaining display of the company's long history. Other exhibits focus on the development of brewing in ancient Mesopotamia and illustrate how beer-brewing came to Africa and Europe, with excellent reconstructions of a "gold rush" pub and a traditional Soweto shebeen.

---

**9**

### Diagonal Street

⚑E3 🏠 Between Helen Joseph and Rahima Moosa sts, Johannesburg

This characterful street was first established in the mid-1880s by Indian and Chinese settlers who set up businesses to serve the original mining town. Today, the row of Victorian and Edwardian shops still sell fabrics, hardware and kitchen utensils.

At the end of the street is a delightful statue of anti-apartheid activists Walter and Albertina Sisulu. The figures sit opposite each other holding hands, and the inscription

> **CITY SAFETY**
>
> Soaring crime rates in central Johannesburg during the 1990s prompted a business and hotel exodus to more suburban locations. Regular visitors will tell you that much of the crime has since shuffled off to suburbia too, but still it would be reckless for a first-time visitor to explore the city centre independently; opt for a guided tour instead.

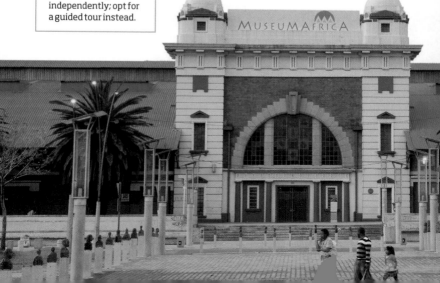

MUSEUMAFRICA

↑ *One Being* by Deborah Glencross, on display at Johannesburg's Origins Centre

reads: "Walter and Albertina Sisulu married in 1944. Through their enduring love and dedication they became parents to the nation."

At No 14, **Kwa-Zulu Muti** is a working herbalist shop, a traditional side of Africa still very much a part of daily life for many South Africans. Not all the potions and remedies are herbal; its stock includes animal skins, horns and claws, as well as dried bats, frogs and insects. Visitors can seek advice from a *sangoma*, a traditional African healer.

### Kwa-Zulu Muti
🏠 14 Diagonal St  🕐 7:30am-5pm Mon-Fri, 8am-1pm Sat

## ⑩ Origins Centre

🅰️ E3  📍 Yale Rd, Braam-fontein, Johannesburg  🕐 10am-5pm daily  🌐 wits.ac.za/origins

Part of the University of the Witwatersrand, this centre traces the origins of man from the Stone Age, and houses the country's most important Khoe and San rock art.

## ⑪ Standard Bank Gallery

🅰️ E3  📍 Cnr Simmonds and Fredericks sts, Johannesburg  📞 011 631 4467  🕐 8am-4:30pm Mon-Fri, 9am-1pm Sat

The unusual setting of a working bank conceals a sophisticated gallery that provides a showcase for talented local and inter-national artists. The building also hosts regular concerts.

←

The red exterior of Museum Africa, part of the Market Theatre Complex

**12**

## Gandhi Square

**△E3** ⬤ Johannesburg

The former Government Square, dating from 1893, was completely refurbished as a large piazza-style public space in 2002. It was also given a new name, after Mahatma Gandhi, who came to Johannesburg in 1903 and worked as a lawyer and civil rights activist. Gandhi's profession often brought him to the Transvaal Law Courts (now demolished), which were located in the square.

In 2003, a larger-than-life-sized statue of Gandhi by

← 
A statue of a young Gandhi, standing in Gandhi Square

sculptor Tinka Christopher was unveiled here. Trendy shops, restaurants and cafés line the southern side of the square.

---

**13**

## Carlton Centre and Top of Africa

**△E3** ⬤ 150 Commissioner Street, Johannesburg
📞 011 308 1331 🕐 9am-6pm Mon-Fri, 9am-5pm Sat, 9am-2pm Sun

A key downtown landmark, the 223-m- (730-ft-) high Carlton Centre was Africa's tallest construction prior to April 2019, when it was overtaken by the Leonardo building in suburban Sandton. For a small fee visitors can take the lift up to the Top of Africa observation deck on the 50th floor, which offers panoramic views of the city. On clear days, the Voortrekker Monument near Pretoria can be seen. The building was completed in 1973 and today there is a mall on the lower levels.

↑ Johannesburg, as seen from the Top of Africa in the Carlton Centre

**14**

## Johannesburg Art Gallery

**△E3** ⬤ King George St, Johannesburg 🕐 10am-5pm Tue-Sun 🚫 Good Fri, 25 Dec 🌐 friendsofjag.org

Situated in Joubert Park since it opened in 1915, this gallery has over 9,000 works in its collection. These include traditional, historical and modern South African art, as well as several works from European schools, including 17th-century Dutch and Flemish paintings and Pre-Raphaelite artwork. There are also interesting collections of ceramics, furniture and textiles.

### Did You Know?

Johannesburg is planted with 10 million trees, making it one of the world's largest man-made forests.

**15**

## Museum of Military History

🅰E3 📍20 Erlswold Way, Johannesburg ⏰8am-2pm Mon-Fri 🚫Good Fri, 25 Dec 🌐ditsong.org.za

Opened in 1947 to honour South Africa's role in the two World Wars, this outstanding museum also covers the Anglo-Zulu War, the Anglo-Boer War and the South African resistance movements. It displays more than 44,000 items, including the nation's official war art and war photography collections. It is also home to some of the world's rarest military aircraft.

**16**

## Florence Bloom Bird Sanctuary

🅰E3 📍Craighall Rd, Johannesburg ⏰Sunrise-sunset daily 🌐delta enviro.org.za/florence-bloom-bird-sanctuary

More than 250 bird species have been recorded in Florence Bloom, which is Johannesburg's oldest bird sanctuary. Various aquatic birds can be seen from carefully positioned hides, and a wide range of raptors includes black sparrowhawk. Bird-watching is most rewarding in summer, when resident species go into breeding colours and are supplemented by migrants such as steppe buzzard and European bee-eater.

**17**

## Main Street Mall

🅰E3 📍Johannesburg

In the heart of the central business district, this traffic-free section of Main Street is lined with office blocks that are home to many corporate and mining

companies. Dubbed the Mining District Walk, an outdoor museum includes relics from the gold-rush days as well as modern sculptures and water features. On weekdays Main Street is filled with office workers enjoying the street cafés, and with a high security presence it is a safe area to explore.

**18**

## Constitution Hill

🅰E3 📍11 Kotze St, Johannesburg ⏰9am-5pm daily 🚫Good Fri, 25 Dec 🌐constitutionhill.org.za

This remarkable development is a living museum documenting South Africa's turbulent past and its transition to democracy. The site incorporates the Old Fort Prison Complex, a notorious jail for more than a century where many, including Nelson Mandela, were imprisoned. South Africa's Constitutional Court, initiated in 1994 after the country's first democratic elections, occupies the eastern wing.

**19**

## Maboneng Precinct

🅰E3 📍286 Fox St & beyond, Johannesburg 🌐mabonengprecinct.com

This inner-city neighbourhood has been privately developed and is now a trendy place to live, work, eat and play. From restaurants and boutiques to art galleries and event spaces, there's lots to see and do. Highlights include William Kentridge's studio in Arts on Main and live music performances at The AntHill Club and Xavier, as well as a varied programme of activities such as yoga classes and night walks. You can even sip champagne while you paint or try a penthouse dinner experience.

# EAT

### Kitamu

This stylish pan-African restaurant offers a range of fusion and traditional dishes from all corners of the continent.

📍Melrose Arch, Johannesburg 🌐kitamu.co.za

Ⓡ Ⓡ Ⓡ

### Restaurante Parreirinha

Established in 1975, this family-run Portuguese restaurant is renowned for its Mozambican-style chicken, grilled prawns, and a relaxed beer garden.

📍6th St, La Rochelle, Johannesburg 🌐restaurante parreirinha.co.za

Ⓡ Ⓡ Ⓡ

### The Butcher Shop & Grill

This family-run restaurant is a one-stop-shop for excellent steak. It also has an adjoining butcher and deli.

📍Nelson Mandela Sq, Sandton 🌐thebutcher shop.co.za

Ⓡ Ⓡ Ⓡ

### Little Addis

A friendly owner-managed restaurant, Little Adis specializes in traditional Ethiopian dishes, which are well suited to vegans as well as fans of spicy food.

📍44 Stanley Ave, Milpark 🌐little-addis-cafe.business.site

Ⓡ Ⓡ Ⓡ

↑ Statue of Nelson Mandela in his eponymous square, next to Sandton City

## ⑳ Sandton and Rosebank

### Ⓐ E3

North of Johannesburg, the metropolitan sprawl blends into expensively laid-out residential areas with high walls, spacious gardens, swimming pools and tennis courts.

Affluent Sandton is a paradise for fashionable shoppers, with **Sandton City** reputedly the most sophisticated retail centre in the southern hemisphere. It is especially noted for its speciality shops, trendy boutiques, jewellers and dealers in

---

# SHOP

### Africa Rise

Founded by the award-winning designer Palesa Mokubung, this shop sells African fashion and accessories.

 Shop U73, Sandton City, Sandton
ⓦ africariseonline.co.za

---

African art, curios and leatherwork. The centre also has plenty of entertainment on offer, with cinemas and dozens of excellent bistros and restaurants. A number of five-star hotels adjoin the Sandton City complex and Nelson Mandela Square, where an Italianate fountain is the focal point in a little piazza lined with coffee shops and restaurants.

The residential suburb of Rivonia, north of Sandton, is home to **Liliesleaf Farm**, once a rural farmhouse and now an award-winning museum dedicated to the apartheid era. It was on this farm that, on 11 July 1963, the South African security forces carried out a raid that ended with the arrest of most of the leaders of the African National Congress. The ANC representatives, including Walter Sisulu and Govan Mbeki, were imprisoned after the Rivonia Trials later that year. Although Nelson Mandela had been arrested six months earlier, he was also part of the Rivonia Trials, which marked the

> The residential suburb of Rivonia, north of Sandton, is home to Liliesleaf Farm, once a rural farmhouse and now an award-winning museum dedicated to the apartheid era.

beginning of his 27-year incarceration. Liliesleaf opened to the public in June 2008, and since then thousands of local and international visitors have flocked to this important heritage site. South of Sandton is Rosebank, where the **Rosebank Mall** offers a buzzing mix of chain stores, upmarket boutiques, restaurants and entertainment, including a ten-pin bowling alley and a number of cinemas.

### Sandton City

🅟 🄳 🄿 Ⓐ Cnr Sandton Dr & Rivonia Rd Ⓒ 9am-8pm Mon-Sat, 9am-6pm Sun & public hols ⓦ sandtoncity.com

### Liliesleaf Farm

🄰 🄿 🅟 Ⓐ 7 George Ave, Rivonia Ⓒ 9am-4pm daily Ⓚ Good Fri, 25 Dec & 1 Jan ⓦ liliesleaf.co.za

### Rosebank Mall

🅟 🄳 🄿 Ⓐ Bath Ave, Rosebank Ⓒ 9am-6pm Mon-Thu, 9am-7pm Fri, 9am-5pm Sat & Sun ⓦ rosebankmall.co.za

## THE SPIRIT OF SOPHIATOWN

Sophiatown – located 10 km (6 miles) from Johannesburg's city centre – was a crowded shanty town, yet it was also the cradle of urban Black culture. Known as the "Harlem" or "Chicago" of South Africa, the multicultural and multiracial township was legendary for its vibrant music scene – particularly jazz – and a bohemian atmosphere that defied the apartheid ideal.

A number of townships were established around Johannesburg in the mid 20th century, but Sophiatown's vibe stood out from the others. Despite it being an area of poverty and crime, much of the creative Black African talent of Johannesburg lived in Sophiatown, including artists, journalists from *Drum* (the first "Black" magazine in South Africa) and numerous musicians. The streets and energetic dance halls were filled with the sounds of the penny whistle, saxophone, harmonica, piano, trumpet and clarinet, while at shebeens (illegal bars), such as the notorious Casbah Gang Den, workers and teachers, both Black and white, would meet to socialize and debate politics.

In the 1950s, the government ordered the forcible removal of Black residents of the suburb to the characterless Meadowlands (now Soweto) settlement. It took four years to remove all of the 60,000 inhabitants, and by 1959 Sophiatown had been demolished and replaced with the white suburb of Triomf (Triumph). The old name Sophiatown was reinstated for the suburb in 1997.

### Did You Know?

Sophiatown was named after the wife of Herman Tobiansky, who established the suburb in 1900.

↑ Locals at one of Sophiatown's lively shebeens (illegal drinking spots)

↑ A troupe of musicians giving an impromptu street performance

## 21

### Dinokeng Game Reserve Hammanskraal

**A** E3 **A** 40 km (25 miles) N of Pretoria **O** 6am–6pm daily **W** dinokengreserve. co.za

The only Big Five reserve set within the crowded confines of Gauteng province, Dinokeng – a seTswana name meaning "Place of Rivers" – opened in 2011 as a partnership between the public sector and more than 170 private landowners. It is divided into a self-drive section and a handful of semi-private concessions, with the latter offering guided game drives in open 4WDs. Wildlife at this reserve includes black-backed jackals and brown hyenas as well as lions, leopards, cheetah, white and black rhinos, elephants, buffaloes, giraffes and zebras.

## 22

### Walter Sisulu Botanical Garden

**A** E3 **A** Malcom Rd, Roodepoort **O** 9am–6pm daily **W** sanbi.org

Opened in 1983 and now entrenched as Gauteng's favourite back-to-nature venue, this 300-ha (740-acre) botanical garden is home to 600 varieties of indigenous plant, including aloes and proteas; more than 220 bird species, within which is a breeding pair of the spectacular Verreaux's eagle; and a variety of small to medium sized mammals.

Scenically, the garden is dominated by the Witpoortjie Falls and a small, forest-lined dam overlooked by a bird hide. There is a well-marked network of walking trails, and a variety of themed guided tours is available.

## 23

### Ann Van Dyck Cheetah Centre

**A** E3 **A** R513, Brits **O** Tours by appt **W** dewildt.co.za

Established in 1971 on what was then a chicken farm, the former De Wildt Cheetah and Wildlife Centre is a captive breeding programme where more than 800 cheetah cubs have been born. It was also the first place to breed a king cheetah – a blotchy-coated variant that was once thought to be a rare subspecies but is now known to be caused by a genetic mutation. Now renamed in tribute to its founder Ann Van Dyck, the centre also runs breeding programmes for other rare species, including African wild dog, brown hyena and the critically endangered riverine rabbit (one of the world's rarest mammals, with a wild population estimated at 500 adults). Other resident animals include honey badger, caracal and a playful family of meerkats. Guided tours run daily, but must be booked in advance.

### Did You Know?

The colouration of the king cheetah, white lion and black leopard are all attributable to recessive genes.

## 24

### Magaliesberg Range

**A** E3

The Magaliesberg is a chain of low hills that runs from west Pretoria towards Rustenburg, and forms a natural boundary between the hot lowveld of

the north and the relatively temperate highveld around Johannesburg. The name derives from Mogale's Berg – Mogale being the name of an important local chief who lived there in the 19th century (and berg simply meaning mountain). The mountains are serviced by many hotels and campsites, which mainly cater to domestic tourism rather than to foreigners. The area is also very popular with Gauteng's hiking fraternity.

For those with limited time or energy, the **Harties Cableway**, which climbs from close to Hartebeespoort Dam to the mountaintop, is an excellent short excursion offering stunning views in all directions. Costlier but even more thrilling are the morning ballooning excursions that are also available in the area.

### Harties Cableway

◈ ⬛ Plot 3, Melodie ◷ 9am-4:30pm Wed-Fri & Sun, 9am-6pm Sat & public holidays ⬛ harties cableway.co.za

---

 25 ◈ ⓂⓈ Ⓨ

## Lesedi Cultural Village

🄰 E4 ⬛ R512, Lanseria ⬛ aha.co.za/lesedi

Gauteng's equivalent of Shakaland (p290), Lesedi is a large open-air museum where a quintet of replica African villages represents five different South African ethnic groups: the Zulu, Xhosa, Pedi, Basotho and Ndebele. Though inevitably a little contrived, a three-hour tour of the villages is both fun and informative, offering first-time visitors some insight into traditional rural life in Africa. The tour culminates in a lively performance of singing, drumming and dancing.

←

The Witpoortjie Falls, tumbling through Walter Sisulu Botanical Garden

---

↑ Women making beadwork items in Lesedi Cultural Village

---

Taking the African theme one step further, the restaurant serves a pan-continental buffet that includes various game meats, and comprises three separate rooms: one dedicated to East Africa (Maasai-themed), another to South Africa (where murals represent the country's nine main Indigenous ethnic groups) and the third North Africa (where you will sit on floor cushions at low tables).

---

  26 Ⓨ ⬛

## Hartebeespoort Dam

🄰 E4 ⬛ Hartebeespoort ⬛ hartbeespoort online. co.za

Scenically located at the base of the Magaliesberg range, this 150-m- (492-ft-) long, 60-m- (197-ft-) high dam was built in the 1920s for irrigation. The associated 17-sq-km (7-sq-mile) reservoir has become a prime weekend destination for watersports enthusiasts. For families in particular, this site makes for an enjoyable day out, hosting as it does the **Hartbeespoort Dam Snake & Animal Park**, the base for the Harties Cableway and plenty of casual eateries.

### Hartbeespoort Dam Snake & Animal Park

◈ ⬛ Scott St ◷ 8am-sunset daily ⬛ hartbeespoort snakeanimalparkco.za

---

# EAT

### Restaurant Laurentina

Mozambican-style Portuguese cuisine is the speciality here - try the *espetada* kebabs.

⬛ Shop 10, Chameleon Village ⬛ laurentinas. co.za

ⓇⓇⓇ

---

### Silver Orange Bistro

A contemporary South African fusion restaurant, located on a working citrus farm. Over-18s only.

⬛ Altyd Mooi Farm, Hartbeespoort ◷ Mon ⬛ silverorange bistro.co.za

ⓇⓇⓇ

# STAY

### Lesedi Cultural Village

Head here to stay in thatched rondavels with bright ethnic decor.

⬛ R512, Lanseria ⬛ aha.co.za/lesedi

ⓇⓇⓇ

Melrose House,
a 19th-century
home *(inset)* with
much of its interior
still preserved

## ㉗
# Pretoria

**🅰E4  🅰Gauteng Province
✈Johannesburg 🚋🚌
ℹChurch Square; www.
tshwane.gov.za**

As the administrative capital
of South Africa and one of the
country's foremost academic
centres, Pretoria is home to
numerous monuments and
grandiose official buildings,
some of which date back to
the 1800s. This stateliness
is softened, however, by the
city's many parks and gardens,
whose jacaranda trees add
splashes of lilac to the
streets each spring.

In 2005 the name of the
larger municipality centred
on Pretoria was changed
to Tshwane, the Setswana
name of the Apies River.
However, the city itself has
retained the name Pretoria
(which comes from the
somewhat divisive figure
of a 19th-century Boer
leader, Andries Pretorius).

Historic buildings,
gracious parks, theatres
and restaurants can be found
throughout this elegant,
compact city, which centres
on the attractive, pedestri-
anized **Church Square**.

Among the buildings on
the square are the Raadsaal
(1890), one-time parliament
of the former Boer Republic,
and the Palace of Justice
(1899), used as a military
hospital until 1902 by the
British. Anton van Wouw's
statue of Paul Kruger was
cast in Italy in 1899, the
year the Transvaal Republic
went to war against the
British Empire.

Providing a stark contrast
to the square is the angular
concrete of the nearby **South
African State Theatre**. This
Japanese-style complex has
five theatres where ballets,
dramas, operas, musicals
and classical concerts are
performed regularly.

Other notable buildings
in the centre include the
imposing Neo-Classical

City Hall, built in 1931. In
front of it stand two statues
depicting Marthinus Pretorius,
founder of the city, and his
father, Andries. A statue of
the mythical chief Tshwane
is nearby. **Melrose House**,
meanwhile, was designed
in the 1880s by British
architect William Vale for
transport contractor George
Heys. The house, which
features nearly all forms
of precast embellishment
available, was inspired by
Cape Dutch architecture,
English country houses
and Indian pavilions. During
the South African War,
Melrose House was the
residence of Lord Kitchener,
British commander-in-chief,
and it was here that the

> **Historic buildings, gracious parks, theatres
> and restaurants can be found throughout
> this elegant, compact city, which centres on
> the attractive, pedestrianized Church Square.**

Treaty of Vereeniging was signed on 31 May 1902, ending the war. Today, it hosts a museum, which still contains many of the house's original contents

Nearby stands the **National Museum of Natural History**, which contains a remarkable collection of stuffed animals, as well as archaeological and geological exhibitions.

East of the zoo are the **Union Buildings**. Designed by the renowned architect Sir Herbert Baker, they were built to house the administrative offices of the Union of South Africa in 1910. Baker himself chose the imposing hill site from where the two large office wings overlook landscaped gardens and an impressive amphitheatre. Although it is not open to the public for reasons of security, the impressive Renaissance style building may be admired from the peaceful gardens.

Around the outskirts of the city, the **Voortrekker Monument** and museum is visible on the approach from the N1. The site commemorates the Afrikaner pioneers who trekked from the Cape in the 1830s to escape British domination. Construction began in 1938, the centenary of the Battle

↑ The massive Voortrekker Monument, set on Monument Hill

of Blood River (*p302*), and it became a focus of Afrikaner unity (*p44*). The structure features a cenotaph in the Hall of Heroes which is lit by a beam of sunlight at noon on 16 December, the date of the Battle of Blood River.

East of Pretoria on the R104 lies **Sammy Marks Museum**, once the elegant residence of industrial pioneer Sammy Marks (1843–1920), the founder of the South African Breweries. The house has been beautifully furnished in a Victorian style.

**Church Square**
🏠 Cnr WF Nkomo and Paul Kruger sts

**South African State Theatre**
🚇 🏠 320 Pretorius St
🌐 statetheatre.co.za

**City Hall**
🏠 Paul Kruger St

**Melrose House**
♿🚻 🏠 275 Jeff Masemola St
📞 012 322 2805 🕐 10am–5pm Tue-Sun 🚫 Public hols

**National Museum of Natural History**
♿ 🏠 432 Paul Kruger St
🕐 8am-4pm daily
🚫 Good Fri, 25 Dec
🌐 ditsong.org.za

**Union Buildings**
🏠 Government Ave, Meintjies Kop 🕐 Daily (grounds only)

**Voortrekker Monument**
♿🚻 🏠 Eeufees Rd, Groenkloof 🕐 8am-4pm daily 🚫 25 Dec 🌐 vtm.org.za

**Sammy Marks Museum**
♿♿🚻 🏠 Old Bronkhorstspruit Rd, Donkerhoek
🕐 9am-2pm Mon-Fri (tours every two hours)
🚫 Good Fri, 25 Dec
🌐 ditsong.org.za

**NDEBELE ARTS**

The hills around Pretoria are the historical home of the Ndebele people, who are noted for their colourful dress and their skill at art and crafts. An outstanding example is the beaded *nguba*, a "marriage blanket" that the bride-to-be makes under the supervision of the older women in her tribe. Traditionally, the women work the land and are the main artists, while the men fashion metal ornaments that are worn by women.

# LIMPOPO, MPUMALANGA AND KRUGER

Northeasterly Mpumalanga and Limpopo are the most ethnically diverse of South Africa's non-urban provinces, supporting a mix of Swazi, Zulu, Tsonga, Ndebele, North Sotho, Venda and various smaller tribes. The northeast was the last part of South Africa to be settled by Europeans, and little is known about its prehistory, despite the presence in Limpopo of several mysterious ruined medieval cities. In the late 19th century, Mpumalanga assumed importance as part of a trade route between Pretoria and Maputo (Mozambique). The province's oldest towns include Ohrigstad and Lydenberg, a pair of Voortrekker settlements established in the 1840s, and Pilgrim's Rest and Barberton, respectively founded in 1873 and 1883 on the back of local gold rushes. The Sabi Game Reserve, gazetted by former president of the Transvaal Paul Kruger in 1898, was later expanded to become the enormous 19,485-sq-km (7,525-sq-mile) Kruger National Park. Prior to 1994, Mpumalanga, Limpopo and Gauteng all formed part of the Transvaal; the first two are relatively poorly developed, with limited employment opportunities and almost exclusively agricultural economies, but Mpumalanga boasts a significant tourist industry.

LIMPOPO,
MPUMALANGA
AND KRUGER

BOTSWANA

❼
WATERBERG

# LIMPOPO, MPUMALANGA AND KRUGER

**Must Sees**

❶ Kruger National Park
❷ Pilgrim's Rest

**Experience More**

❸ Lydenburg
❹ Mbombela
❺ Dullstroom
❻ Blyde River Canyon
❼ Waterberg
❽ Polokwane
❾ Tzaneen
❿ Mapungubwe National Park

JOHANNESBURG
AND AROUND
p304

NORTHERN CAPE
AND
FREE STATE
p190

**Did You Know?**

The total area of Kruger National Park is equivalent in size to the country of Slovenia.

1 🔧 🏍 🍴 🛍

# KRUGER NATIONAL PARK

🅰 G2  📍 400 km (250 miles) E of Johannesburg  🚌 Nelspruit, Hoedspruit, Kruger Mpumalanga, Phalaborwa, Skukuza  🕐 Sep-Mar: 5:30am-6:30pm daily; Apr-Aug: 6am-6pm daily  🌐 sanparks.org

South Africa's largest national park, Kruger ranks among the most rewarding wildlife sanctuaries anywhere in the world. It is readily accessible to tourists, thanks to an excellent network of rest camps, picnic sites, and surfaced and unsurfaced roads.

Kruger's vast wilderness covers an area of 19,633 sq km (7,580 sq miles), extending for 352 km (220 miles) from the Limpopo River in the north to Crocodile River in the south. It comprises 16 distinct vegetation zones, ranging from open grassland to dense forest, and supports an astonishing species count, including 148 mammals, 505 birds and 118 reptiles.

←

Elephants and hippos enjoying the refreshing waters of the Sabie River

The park's vast habitat, home to hundreds of animal species, including *(inset)* lions ↑

## Exploring the Park

Tourism in Kruger is focused on the park's southern half, which offers superior game-viewing compared with the wilder, drier north. It also has better tourist amenities and is more accessible. Southern Kruger is divided into two sectors by the Sabie River, both of which are ideal for a self-drive safari, with a good road network and well-equipped, affordable rest camps. There are also privately managed lodges that offer a guided safari experience. Few organized safaris head up to northern Kruger, but a good network of surfaced roads means it is easily explored as an extension of a self-drive safari to the south, and its off-the-beaten track feel is a real draw for more experienced safari-goers.

## Private Reserves

Along the western boundary of the national park, and bordered by the Sabie and Olifants rivers, a mosaic of private reserves provides a vital buffer between the densely populated areas of Lebowa and Gazankulu and Kruger. Wildlife is able to travel freely between these zones, thanks to the removal of Kruger's boundary fence in 1994.

The reserves' luxury lodges offer exclusive "bush experiences" to small groups of guests. Emphasis is placed on personal attention, with experienced rangers guiding visitors on day and night drives and interesting bush walks.

## ① Crocodile River

Flowing eastwards along the park border, the Crocodile River forms a natural barrier between the untamed wilderness of Kruger and the lush farmland to its south. It is overlooked by Crocodile Bridge, the park's most easterly rest camp, set in an area renowned for its dense population of white rhino.

A short drive east of the camp, stands a hippo pool and a fascinating prehistoric rock painting site. The Mpanamana Concession, reserved for the private Shishangani Lodge, is good for spotting white rhino, lion and elephant.

↑ One of the 6,000–8,000 white rhinos that are estimated to live in the park

---

# STAY

Kruger's lodges offer a luxurious experience.

**Shishangani Lodge, Camp Shawu & Camp Shinga**
Ⓦ bonhotels.com/ shishangeni

Ⓡ Ⓡ Ⓡ

---

**Lukimbi Safari Lodge**
Ⓦ lukimbi.com

Ⓡ Ⓡ Ⓡ

---

**Hamilton's 1880 Tented Camp**
Ⓦ hamiltons tentedcamp.co.za

Ⓡ Ⓡ Ⓡ

---

**Singita Lebombo & Sweni**
Ⓦ singita.co.za

Ⓡ Ⓡ Ⓡ

---

**The Outpost**
Ⓦ rareearth.co.za

Ⓡ Ⓡ Ⓡ

---

## ② Berg-en-Dal

Situated 13 km (8 miles) northwest of Malalane Gate, this modern rest camp is well-positioned for a first night in the bush after travelling from Gauteng. The accommodation is perhaps the most comfortable of any public rest camp, and the hilly setting, overlooking a tree-lined dam, is lovely.

---

## ③ Pretoriuskop

Accessed via Numbi Gate, Pretoriuskop, the park's oldest rest camp, offers a diverse range of accommodation for different budgets. Game-viewing here is erratic, but the Voortrekker Road is a good place to look for the shy black rhino, stately eland and sable antelope.

---

## ④ Skukuza Camp

Overlooking the Sabie River 13 km (8 miles) east of Paul Kruger Gate, Skukuza is the park's second-oldest rest camp, and by far the largest, with a total capacity of 1,000-plus visitors. The camp doubles as the park's research and administrative headquarters, and its excellent range of facilities include an airport, car-hire service, bank, ATM, petrol station, post office, museum, restaurant and shop. Naysayers complain Skukuza is too large and impersonal, but these flaws are more than compensated for by its location at the junction of three superb game-viewing roads: the H3 to Malalane, H4–1 to Lower Sabie and H1–2/3 to Satara. Also in Skukuza's favour are the sprawling green grounds teeming with birds and small mammals, and the river below that attracts thirsty wildlife.

---

## ⑤ Lower Sabie

Favoured by many old Kruger hands, Lower Sabie, like Skukuza, stands at the intersection of three excellent game-viewing roads. The camp, however, is far smaller and more intimate. The chalets survey an expanse of the Sabie River regularly visited by elephant and buffalo, while nearby Sunset Dam is exceptional for hippo, storks, kingfishers and other aquatic birds. The roads south towards Crocodile Bridge are reliable for rhino.

> **Sunset Dam is exceptional for hippos, storks, kingfishers and other aquatic birds.**

### ⑥
#### The H4-1 and Nkuhlu Picnic Site

The surfaced H4-1 between Skukuza and Lower Sabie is probably the park's most reliably rewarding game-viewing road, but it also carries a high volume of tourist traffic. Following the south bank of the Sabie River for 43 km (27 miles), you might spot lion, elephant, rhino, buffalo, giraffe and greater kudu, and it's the best place in Kruger to look for leopards. Be sure to stop at Nkuhlu Picnic Site on the Sabie River, where you can see crocodiles, monkeys, African fish-eagles and half-collared kingfishers. To make it a round trip between Skukuza to Lower Sabie, return via the dirt Salitje Road.

### ⑦
#### The H10 from Lower Sabie to Tshokwane

This quiet road offers access to several superb vantage points overlooking reservoirs. Mlondozi Dam has picnic facilities and a shady terrace, while Nkumbe Lookout offers unparalleled views over the plains below. Orpen Dam often attracts greater kudu, elephant and giraffe. The H10 connects with the main H1-2 to Satara at Tshokwane Picnic Site, which is a pleasant place to stop for breakfast or lunch.

A malachite kingfisher, one of many bird species found in Kruger

## ⑧ Satara Camp and the Central Plains

North of Tshokwane, the countryside transforms into an open savannah of grassland and scattered trees. Situated in the thick of these central plains, Satara, Kruger's second-largest rest camp, is rather characterless but well positioned for game drives. Although no major rivers flow here, large herds of zebra, wildebeest and other grazers forage on the open grassland and its scattering of artificial waterholes attract plenty of

### HIDDEN GEM
**Balule Camp**

Kruger's most rustic rest camp, Balule – only 12 km (7 miles) from Olifants – is a no-frills, low-budget throwback. It comprises six small huts and a basic campsite, set in a wonderful riverside location with a compelling bush character.

predators. The open terrain is particularly suited to cheetah, which are often seen crossing the roads around Satara, and it also makes it relatively easy to see lion kills. About 50 km (31 miles) west of Satara, near Orpen Gate, the self-catering Tamboti Tented Camp offers a fabulous budget bush experience in standing tents carved into the riparian forest along the seasonal Timbavati River. At the other end of the price range are the ultra exclusive Singita Lebombo and Sweni lodges (p338).

## ⑨ Olifants Camp

The most northerly rest camp on the main tourist circuit, situated 55 km (34 miles) past Satara, Olifants has a stunning location on a tall cliff overlooking the broad flood plain of the river after which it is named. It offers arguably the best in-house game-viewing of any public rest camp, thanks to the large numbers of elephant that come to drink at the river below. The roads

↑ The restaurant terrace at Letaba Rest Camp, with expansive views

around Olifants are often crossed by large, thousand-strong herds of buffalo, and the area is also a stronghold for the handsome greater kudu and the smaller, cliff-loving klipspringer.

## ⑩ Letaba Camp

Enjoying a commanding position overlooking the seasonal Letaba river,

30 km (19 miles) north of Olifants, this rest camp has chalets overlooking the river, where tame bushbucks stroll past and fig trees attract colourful birds. Game drives along the river often yield elephant sightings, while the mopani-swathed plains running west towards Phalaborwa are the main stronghold of the rare sable antelope. Set within the camp, Letaba Elephant Hall, a museum dedicated to the evolution and ecology of elephants, displays the tusks of six of the "Magnificent Seven", a generation of huge tuskers in the 1970s.

### AVIAN WONDERS

Dedicated twitchers can easily notch up 100 species in a day in Kruger, especially during the southern summer. Even casual visitors should prepare to be wowed by the park's colourful array of rollers, bee-eaters, kingfishers and hornbills, as well as the outsized ostrich and Kori bustard, and raptors such as African fish-eagle and lappet-faced vulture.

## Mopani and Shingwedzi Camps

Mopani, 50 km (30 miles) north of Letaba, is a modern hillside rest camp overlooking an artificial reservoir that attracts thirsty wildlife out of the surrounding dry woodland. Elephants are plentiful, and the area supports several localized

antelope species, but game viewing tends to be erratic. It's far better to drive 63 km (38 miles) north to Shingwedzi, whose location alongside the Shingwedzi River makes it a contender for Kruger's best-kept game-viewing secret. The dirt road south to Kanniedood Dam runs through the territory of some of Kruger's biggest elephants. It is also good for buffalo and greater kudu, and the birdlife is spectacular.

## Punda Maria Camp

Set at the base of Dimbo Hill 72 km (43 miles) northwest of Shingwedzi, Punda Maria is an intimate rest camp with a remote wilderness feel and whitewashed thatched huts whose exteriors are little changed since their construction in 1933. The surrounding bush is a good place to look for the rare Lichtenstein's hartebeest and African wild dog. Punda Maria is the

← 

A family of elephants crossing the road during a game drive

closest public rest camp to Pafuri and the base for guided tours to the 16th-century stone ruins at the Thulamela Heritage Site.

## Pafuri and Makuleke

The shady woodland that verges the Luvuvhu River 60 km (37 miles) north of Punda Maria offers some of the best bird-watching in Kruger. The exquisite Narina trogon is the star of the public Pafuri Picnic Site on the south bank, and while wildlife viewing is erratic, the nyala antelope is abundant. North of the Luvuvhu, a triangle of land bounded by the Limpopo rivers was appended to Kruger in 1969 when its Makuleke inhabitants were forcibly ejected by the apartheid regime. Traditional ownership was restored in the 1990s and the triangle now forms Makuleke Contractual Park, which is managed as part of Kruger but hosts two exclusive private lodges – Pafuri Luxury Tented Camp and The Outpost – leased from the community. Both operate like the private reserves.

# PRIVATE RESERVES

### Sabi Sand Game Reserve

🏠 Access for lodge guests only 🅦 sabisand.co.za

This famous reserve is made up of a block of contiguous reserves north of the Sabie River, which include the Lion Sands, Londolozi, Mala Mala, Singita and Ulusaba private game reserves, and shares a 50-km (31-mile) boundary with Kruger National Park. There are no fewer than 30 all-inclusive luxury lodges and camps in Sabi Sand and entry is only open to overnight visitors. Thanks to the Sand and Sabie rivers, the area has a rich water supply, which results in a lush environment that animals enjoy all year round. Sightings of the Big Five are virtually guaranteed, and hyena, cheetah and wild dog may also be seen.

---

⑮

### Manyeleti Game Reserve

🏠 Access for lodge guests only 🅦 manyeleti.co.za

This reserve adjoins the Orpen area of Kruger National Park,

> Sabie Sand has a rich water supply, which results in a lush environment that animals enjoy all year round. Sightings of the Big Five are virtually guaranteed.

**Did You Know?**

Over a quarter of Kruger's total biomass comprises the park's estimated 17,000–20,000 elephants.

known for its varied wildlife. Visitors can stay in the two comfortable, mid-range tented Honeyguide Camps, or the luxurious Tintswalo Safari Lodge and Manor House.

---

⑯

### Timbavati Private Nature Reserve

🏠 Access for lodge guests only 🅦 timbavati.co.za

This 550-sq-km (210-sq-mile) reserve, adjoining Kruger's central region, extends from Orpen to the region just south of the Olifants River; it lies entirely in Limpopo province. There are a dozen lodges, each with access to a different part of the reserve, and they all offer drives and guided walks. Of these, Umlani Bushcamp is situated in the north, while the luxurious Ngala and Tanda Tula lodges lie in the central region.

↑ An adult leopard elegantly stalking through the grass

## STAY

Safari in style at these sumptuous lodges in the private reserves.

**MalaMala Rattray's Camp**
🏠 MalaMala Game Reserve
🌐 malamala.com

Ⓡ Ⓡ Ⓡ

**Earth Lodge**
🏠 Sabi Sabi Private Reserve 🌐 sabisabi.com

Ⓡ Ⓡ Ⓡ

**Singita Boulders Lodge**
🏠 Singita Sabi Sands Reserve 🌐 singita.com

Ⓡ Ⓡ Ⓡ

**Misava Safari Camp**
🏠 Klaserie Private Nature Reserve
🌐 klaseriedrift.co.za

Ⓡ Ⓡ Ⓡ

**Kings Camp**
🏠 Timbavati Private Nature Reserve
🌐 kingscamp.com

Ⓡ Ⓡ Ⓡ

## Klaserie Private Nature Reserve

🚪 Access for lodge guests only 🌐 klaseriereserve.co.za

Klaserie encompasses several different private reserves, which extend over a total area of 620 sq km (235 sq miles), bordering Kruger National Park and the Olifants River. The Klaserie River meanders across the semiarid bushveld

↑ A group of lionesses bask in the sunshine, keeping a careful eye out for potential prey

and is the reserve's central focus as many animals and birds gather on its banks to drink. There are nine accommodation options, ranging from tented camps to high-end lodges. Many of these are not in the top end of the luxury category and offer a more rustic experience.

---

**THE GREAT LIMPOPO TRANSFRONTIER PARK**

This impressive cross-border initiative links the Kruger National Park in South Africa, Limpopo National Park in Mozambique, and Gonarezhou National Park, Manjinji Pan Sanctuary and Malipati Safari Area in Zimbabwe, into one huge conservation area covering 37,700 sq km (14,556 sq miles) – roughly equivalent in size to the Netherlands. By taking down the fences along the country borders, which also divided conservation areas, the habitat available to the wildlife has been greatly increased, and the natural migratory routes of the animals have been extended. The floodplains and tributaries of five major river systems supply water to this vast area.

**2**

# PILGRIM'S REST

**F2** *Main St, Uptown; www.pilgrims-rest.co.za*

This village, in a picturesque valley of the Eastern Escarpment, was founded by gold prospectors in 1873. Its unique "tin and timber" buildings were originally intended to be temporary, but today – restored to their modest glory – they are a living part of history.

The entire village is a National Heritage Site. Historical displays and exhibits on gold-panning techniques can be found at the Pilgrim's Rest Information Centre and Museum, and several small museums are housed in old miners' cottages within walking distance.

At the Diggings Site Museum, visitors can try panning for alluvial gold, while the Pilgrim's & Sabie News Museum displays hand-printing equipment from the 1900s, when news of the expanding goldfields was distributed to interested stockbrokers, prospectors and the Boer government. The Victorian House Museum offers an insight into the simple life of the prospectors, as does the Dredzen Shop & House, a typical 1930s–50s general store with the owner's house at the back.

Stately Alanglade, a mine manager's residence built in 1916, is a large Edwardian mansion located in a wooded glen away from the village. It is now restored and furnished as a period museum, complete with a rose garden.

## Environs

Timber and tourism are the economic mainstays of the dramatic escarpment formed by the eastern Drakensberg Mountains. From the village, the R533 winds across Bonnet Pass to Graskop, a convenient centre for exploring the escarpment, and only 70 km (43 miles) from Skukuza, the main camp in Kruger National Park *(p336)*.

The R534, or Panorama Route, starts 3 km (2 miles) north of Graskop and passes cliff-top sites and lovely waterfalls *(p352)*. The escarpment drops almost 1,000 m (3,281 ft) to the Lowveld – among the most beautiful parts of South Africa – where the scenery offers spectacular vistas extending 100 km (60 miles) east to Mozambique.

> **The Lowveld - among the most beautiful parts of South Africa - offers spectacular vistas extending east to Mozambique.**

↑ Beautiful scenery along the Panorama Route, just outside Pilgrim's Rest

↑ The town's distinctive "timber and tin" architecture, and *(inset)* the Dredzen Shop & House

# EAT

**Vine Restaurant**
Serves simple but tasty fare.

🏠 Main St, Pilgrim's Rest
🌐 thevinerest.co.za

Ⓡ Ⓡ Ⓡ

# STAY

**Crystal Springs Mountain Lodge**
Self-catering cottages in a small game reserve.

🏠 Robber's Pass, 10 km (6 miles) E of Pilgrim's Rest
🌐 crystalsprings.co.za

Ⓡ Ⓡ Ⓡ

---

**Royal Hotel**
Offers rooms with period furniture.

🏠 Main St, Pilgrim's Rest
🌐 royalhotelpilgrims.co.za

Ⓡ Ⓡ Ⓡ

# EXPERIENCE MORE

**3**

## Lydenburg

**F3** **58 km (36 miles)**
**N of Dullstroom**

Lydenburg (literally "Town of Suffering") was founded in 1849 by the survivors of a malaria epidemic at Ohrigstad, a lower-lying Voortrekker settlement only 50 km (31 miles) to the north. Long before the Voortrekkers' arrival, however, the area was part of an Iron Age settlement. Artifacts found here include the Lydenburg Heads, replicas of which are housed in the **Lydenburg Museum**. These large terracotta masks are believed to have been used in ceremonial rituals circa AD 700.

Some 53 km (33 miles) east of Lydenburg, Sabie is reached via Long Tom Pass, an old wagon road whose rocks still bear the marks of metal-rimmed wheel ruts. Sabie is surrounded by plantations of exotic trees, established in the 19th century to provide timber for use in the local gold mines, and its **Forestry Industry Museum** is dedicated to wood and its many uses.

### Lydenburg Museum

 **Long Tom Pass Rd** **013 235 2213** **8am–4pm Mon–Fri, 8am–5pm Sat & Sun**

### Forestry Industry Museum

**Ford St, Sabie** **8am–4:30pm Mon–Fri, 8am–noon Sat** **safcol.co.za**

---

**4**

## Mbombela

**G3** **KLCBT House, cnr N4 and R40; www.krugerlowveld.com**

The provincial capital of Mpumalanga, rapidly growing Mbombela (a siSwati word meaning "Crowded Place") is an agricultural centre for oranges, mangoes, bananas, avocados and macadamia nuts. Formerly called Nelspruit, it has experienced a high level of industrialization since the 1990s, and has also grown in significance as a trade funnel on the main road and rail route between Gauteng and the Mozambican capital, Maputo.

The beautifully landscaped **Lowveld National Botanical Garden**, on the confluence of the Nels and Crocodile rivers, protects prehistoric cycads and other plants associated

 **HIDDEN GEM**
### Screaming Monster

Keen runners should check out the annual Race of the Screaming Monster – a half-marathon that enters the Sudwala Caves. There are shorter variations, so all ages can take part.

A group of visitors admiring the dramatic Sudwala Caves, found just east of Mbombela

with the subtropical lowveld. Hippo and vervet monkey are present, along with 250 bird species. **Chimp Eden**, 15 km (9 miles) along the R40, is the setting of South Africa's only chimpanzee sanctuary. Operated by the Jane Goodall Institute, it houses 30 chimps rescued from elsewhere in Africa in large enclosures overlooked by viewing platforms.

Alongside the N4, about 30 km (19 miles) east from Mbombela, guided tours into the impressive **Sudwala Caves** lead through cool subterranean passages past beautiful limestone formations to a natural dolomite chamber that can seat 500.

To the south of Nelspruit, **Barberton Museum** was established in 1883 to service a short-lived gold rush that led to it becoming the first stock exchange in the former Transvaal Republic. It sits below the Makhonjwa Mountains, whose 3.5-billion-year-old rocks comprise the planet's oldest exposed strata. It has an excellent history and geological museum, and several architectural relicts of its Victorian heyday survive. Another highlight is the black-and-white photo display of the town's development.

#### Lowveld National Botanical Garden
🏠 Madiba Drive 🕐 Apr-Aug: 9am-5pm daily; Sep-Mar: 9am-6pm daily 🌐 sanbi.org

#### Chimp Eden
🐾 😄 🏠 Turn Off 47, R40 🕐 Only for pre-booked guided tours noon Mon-Fri 🌐 chimpeden.com

> East of Lydenburg, Sabie is reached via the scenic Long Tom Pass, an old wagon road whose rocks still bear the marks of metal-rimmed wheel ruts.

↑ Dam water and lush greenery outside the town of Dullstroom

#### Sudwala Caves
🐾 🏠 R539 🕐 8:30am-4:30pm daily 🌐 sudwala caves.co.za

#### Barberton Museum
🏠 Crown St 📞 013 712 4208 🕐 8am-4pm Mon-Fri, 9am-4pm Sat & Sun

---

### ⑤
## Dullstroom
🏠 F3 ℹ️ www.dullstroom. co.za

The town of Dullstroom, set at a chilly altitude of 2,076 m (6,811 ft), houses the country's highest railway station, and experiences winter temperatures that drop to -13° C (9° F). It is a top destination for fly-fishing, an activity focused on the **Dullstroom Dams and Nature Reserve**, on the town's eastern outskirts, as well as various privately owned reservoirs. The **Mavungana Flyfishing Centre** has some excellent trout-stocked waters.

#### Dullstroom Dams and Nature Reserve
🐾 🕐 Sunrise-sunset daily 🌐 dullstroomonthedam.co.za

#### Mavungana Flyfishing Centre
🕐 Daily 🌐 flyfishing.co.za

# EAT

Breezy Dullstroom is a great place to break for lunch when driving between Gauteng and Kruger. Fresh trout is the local speciality.

**Mrs Simpson's Restaurant**
🏠 94 Teding van Berkhout St 🌐 mrssimpsons.co.za

Ⓡ Ⓡ Ⓡ

**Coachman Restaurant**
🏠 89 Naledi Dr 🌐 royalcoachman dullstroom.co.za

Ⓡ Ⓡ Ⓡ

**Duck & Trout**
🏠 Naledi Dr 📞 067 290 3822

Ⓡ Ⓡ Ⓡ

**Harrie's Pancakes**
🏠 Cnr Cunning & Hugenoten St 🌐 harriespancakes. co.za

Ⓡ Ⓡ Ⓡ

## 6
## Blyde River Canyon

 G2

The fast-flowing Blyde River has, over the centuries, carved its way through 700 m (2,300 ft) of shale and quartzite to create a scenic jumble of cliffs, islands, plateaus and bush-covered slopes that form a 20-km (12-mile) canyon. At the heart of this canyon lies the Blydepoort Dam.

Blyde means "river of joy", and the river was named when Voortrekker Hendrik Potgieter and his party returned safely from an expedition to Delagoa Bay (Mozambique) in 1844. The abundant flora in the canyon ranges from lichens and mosses to montane forest, orchids and other flowering plants.

Protecting the area is the Blyde River Canyon Nature Reserve. A 300-km (186-mile) circular drive from Graskop via Bosbokrand, Klaserie, Swadini and Bourke's Luck affords panoramic vistas of the escarpment rising above the plains, the Blydepoort Dam and the breathtaking view deep into the canyon itself. There are several overnight trails and short walks, and accommodation is available at **Swadini, A Forever Resort**. Set deep in the canyon on the shores of Blydepoort, this resort offers accommodation, a restaurant and a base for boating trips on the dam. The visitors centre and low-level view site have information on the dam and the Kadishi Falls, the world's largest active tufa (calcium carbonate) formation. There is also a Blyde Canyon sister resort.

The area has many stunning natural attractions, including the Three Rondavels. Resembling the traditional cylindrical huts of the Xhosa or Zulu, these three hills were shaped by the erosion of soft rock beneath a harder rock "cap" that eroded more slowly. The capping of Black Reef quartzite supports a growth of evergreen bush. The Three Rondavels is one of three sites that can be seen from the road that overlooks the canyon – the other two are World's End and Lowveld View.

Elsewhere, grit and stones carried by the swirling waters at the confluence of the Blyde ("joyful") and Treur ("sad") rivers have carved the extraordinary **Bourke's Luck Potholes**. The name "Bourke's Luck" comes from Tom Bourke, a prospector who worked a claim here in the vain hope that he would find gold. The visitor centre includes an exhibition outlining the geological history of the area.

The Panorama Route – an 18-km (11-mile) stretch of the R534 that loops along the top of the cliff – is a scenic marvel. God's Window and Wonderview may sound like fanciful names, but they are more than justified by the breathtaking scenery. Also visible on the route is the Pinnacle, an impressive column of rock that appears to rise sheer from a base of evergreen foliage. An optical illusion seems to place it almost within reach. Exposed layers of sandstone show the rock's sedimentary origins. It becomes clear that, even at this lofty height, the top of the escarpment was once covered by a primordial sea.

### Did You Know?

Blyde River Canyon is one of the biggest canyons in the world, and is also one of the greenest.

 The sun setting over the spectacular cliffs and winding waters of the Blyde River Canyon

### Swadini, A Forever Resort
⑲ 🅰 On R531 🆆 forever swadini.co.za

### Bourke's Luck Potholes
♻😊 🅰 On R531 🕐 7am–5pm daily 🆆 godswindow.info/bourkes-luck-potholes

---

**7**

## Waterberg

🅰 F2 ℹ www.waterberg-information.co.za

The Waterberg massif is a 14,500-sq-km (5,598-sq-mile) UNESCO biosphere reserve, one of Africa's two savannah biospheres. It rises to around 1,830 m (6,004 ft) some 200 km (120 miles) north of Gauteng. An attractive but rather unfocused region, it supports a mosaic of farms and private nature reserves, as well as the provincial Mokolo Dam, a popular site for water sports. A focal point is the 670-sq-km (259-sq-mile) **Marakele National Park**, which protects 90 mammal species including elephant, lion, leopard, black rhino, white rhino, giraffe and a variety of antelope. The proximity to Gauteng and the absence of malaria make it a popular choice with families.

A worthwhile stop en route between Gauteng and Waterberg is the **Nylsvley Nature Reserve**, which protects the Nyl Floodplain, one of South Africa's most important waterbird sites. More than 375 bird species – almost a third of which are water birds – have been recorded in this small reserve, including the rare slaty egret and rufous-bellied heron. Walking trails also offer a chance to get close to non-dangerous large mammals; the reserve supports about 1,000 of these larger animals, such as giraffe, wildebeest and warthog.

### Marakele National Park
😊 🅰 Thabazimbi 🕐 7:30am–5:30pm daily 🆆 sanparks.org

### Nylsvley Nature Reserve
🅰 Mookgophong 🕐 May–Aug: 6:30am–5:30pm daily; Sep–Apr: 6am–6pm daily 🆆 nylsvley.co.za

---

# EAT

### Canimambo Restaurante
This family-run venue serves tasty Mozambican-style dishes such as bean stew, piripiri chicken and grilled prawns.

🅰 Cnr Louis Trichardt & Hoof sts, Graskop 🆆 canimambo-restaurant-graskop.business.site

Ⓡ Ⓡ Ⓡ

---

### Kuka Café
All-day breakfasts, pizzas, craft beers and tasty cocktails can be enjoyed at this bright Afro-chic café.

🅰 Perry's Bridge Trading Post, Hazyview 🆆 kukasoup.co.za

Ⓡ Ⓡ Ⓡ

---

### Pioneer's Butcher & Grill
A modern steakhouse; meat is king, but their fish and vegetarian offerings are also strong.

🅰 Rendezvous Tourism Centre, Hazyview 🆆 pioneersgrill.co.za

Ⓡ Ⓡ Ⓡ

---

### The Greek Kouzina
Genuine Greek cuisine, with an impressively lengthy meze selection.

🅰 Sonpark Centre, 7 Faurie St, Mbombela 📞 013 741 5371

Ⓡ Ⓡ Ⓡ

← A small safari party in Marakele National Park, Waterberg

# STAY

### Marataba Safari Lodge

Luxury canvas-and-stone suites, plus an infinity pool overlooking the plains.

 Marakele National Park  marataba.co.za

ⓇⓇⓇ

---

### Leokwe Rest Camp

The largest camp in Mapungubwe, with comfortable self-catering chalets.

 Mapunggubwe National Park  sanparks.org

ⓇⓇⓇ

---

### Fusion Boutique Hotel

Limpopo's funkiest five-star accommodation.

 5 Schoeman St, Polokwane  fusion boutiquehotel.co.za

ⓇⓇⓇ

---

**8**

# Polokwane

🄰F2 🛈 Southern Gateway, N1; www.polokwane.gov.za

Polokwane, a Sepedi name meaning "Place of Safety", is the capital of Limpopo, South Africa's most northerly province. Established by the Voortrekker leader Andries Potgieter in 1886, it was named Pietersburg (after Commandant-General Piet Joubert of the Transvaal Republic) until 2005. The **Hugh Exton Photographic Museum**, set in a 19th-century Dutch Reformed Church, offers insights into the town's early history (particularly the Anglo-Boer War, when a British concentration camp housed 4,000 prisoners) through the thousands of images captured by its namesake between 1892 and 1945.

A network of game-viewing roads and walking trails through the **Polokwane Game Reserve** on the southern outskirts of town provides an opportunity for close encounters with white rhino, giraffe and several other reintroduced large mammals. Bordering the reserve, the **Bakone Malapa Open-Air Museum** offers guided tours through a faithful reconstruction of a traditional Pedi (North Sotho) homestead as it would have been in the 18th century. There are also demonstrations of local handcrafts.

### Hugh Exton Photographic Museum

🄰Church St 📞015 290 2186 🕒9am–3:30pm Mon–Fri

### Polokwane Game Reserve

🄰Silicon Rd 📞015 290 2331 🕒May–Sep: 7am–4:30pm daily

### Bakone Malapa Open-Air Museum

 🄰R37 📞083 245 2664 🕒8am–3:30pm Mon–Fri, by appt only Sat & Sun

---

**9**

# Tzaneen

🄰F2 🛈 www.greater tzaneen.gov.za/?q=tourism

Tzaneen is a pleasant town set within an agricultural area that is associated with tea, tomato, mango and avocado production. It stands next to the pretty Tzaneen Dam and is surrounded by lush tropical forests.

The **Tzaneen Museum** houses an interesting collection of ethnographic artifacts from all around Africa, including items associated with the Modjadji Rain Queen – a revered local monarch whose matrilineal line reputedly dates back to the 16th century.

Some 30 km (19 miles) north of Tzaneen, tiny Modjadjiskloof – also referred to by its Afrikaans name Duiwelskloof ("Devil's Gorge") – has two main claims to fame. The misty forests of **Modjadji Nature Reserve** support one of two extant populations of the eponymous cycad, a peculiar prehistoric palm-like tree that grows up to 12 m (39 ft) tall.

### Tzaneen Museum

🏠 44 Agatha St 📞 083 280 4966 🕐 9am-4pm Mon-Fri, 9am-noon Sat

### Modjadji Nature Reserve

🏠 Off the Mohlakamosoma Rd 📞 015 293 8300 🕐 7am-4:30pm daily

---

# Mapungubwe National Park

🅰 F1 🏠 Soutpansberg 🕐 Apr-Aug: 6:30am-6pm daily; Sep-Mar: 6am-6:30pm daily 🌐 sanparks.org

Once the capital of an important trade empire, Mapungubwe Hill was abandoned in the 13th century, when its inhabitants migrated north to establish the stone city of Great Zimbabwe.

Today, daily guided tours of the hilltop citadel reveal Mapungubwe's rise and fall as the first Indigenous kingdom in southern Africa. Flourishing between AD 900 and 1300, it was the first site in the region to have separate areas for the nobility and commoners, indicating the existence of wealth and a class-based society. Before being abandoned due to climate change (which made farming much harder), the powerful state traded gold and ivory with China, India, Egypt and Arabia, and was the largest kingdom on the sub-continent.

Inscribed as a UNESCO World Heritage Site in 2003, Mapungubwe is the centre-piece of South Africa's most northerly national park, inhabited by elephant, greater kudu and small populations of lion, leopard and cheetah.

The park's Interpretation Centre provides an excellent overview of its history, and displays artifacts including a gold-plated rhino sculpture.

Mapungubwe National Park, which is home to a number of bush elephants *(inset)*

# A DRIVING TOUR
# WATERFALLS

**Length** 100 km (60 miles) **Stopping-off points** Sabie, Graskop **Difficulty** Easy

High-lying ground, generous rainfall and heavy run-off have created spectacular waterfalls in this old gold-mining area along the eastern Drakensberg escarpment. There are, in fact, more waterfalls here than anywhere else in southern Africa. Several of them can be seen on an easy round trip between the towns of Sabie and Graskop. Most are well signposted and easy to reach by car. Enchanting as they are, waterfalls can be slippery and dangerous, and visitors are urged to heed the warning notices.

↑ The lush, green surrounds of the delightful Horseshoe Falls

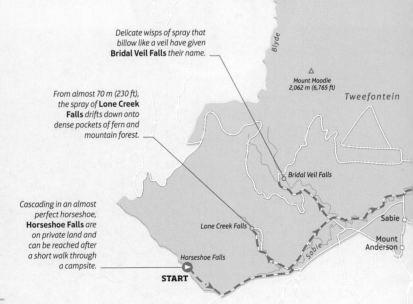

Delicate wisps of spray that billow like a veil have given **Bridal Veil Falls** their name.

From almost 70 m (230 ft), the spray of **Lone Creek Falls** drifts down onto dense pockets of fern and mountain forest.

Cascading in an almost perfect horseshoe, **Horseshoe Falls** are on private land and can be reached after a short walk through a campsite.

Blyde

Pilgrim's Rest

Jubilee
1,788 m (5,866 ft)

R533

Blyde

Blyde

Mount Moodie
2,062 m (6,765 ft)

Tweefontein

Bridal Veil Falls

Sabie

Mount Anderson

Lone Creek Falls

Sabie

Horseshoe Falls

**START**

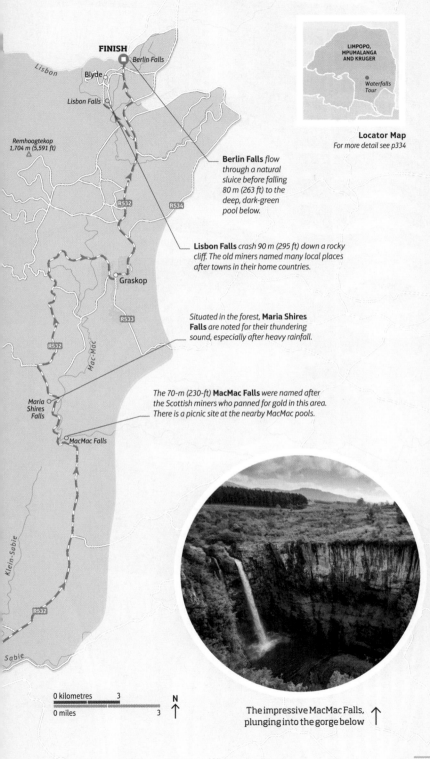

**FINISH**
*Berlin Falls*

**Blyde**

*Lisbon Falls*

*Remhoogtekop*
*1,704 m (5,591 ft)*

**Graskop**

*Mac-Mac*

**Maria Shires Falls**

**MacMac Falls**

*Klein-Sabie*

*Sabie*

R532
R534
R533

**Locator Map**
*For more detail see p334*

LIMPOPO, MPUMALANGA AND KRUGER

Waterfalls Tour

**Berlin Falls** *flow through a natural sluice before falling 80 m (263 ft) to the deep, dark-green pool below.*

**Lisbon Falls** *crash 90 m (295 ft) down a rocky cliff. The old miners named many local places after towns in their home countries.*

*Situated in the forest, **Maria Shires Falls** are noted for their thundering sound, especially after heavy rainfall.*

*The 70-m (230-ft) **MacMac Falls** were named after the Scottish miners who panned for gold in this area. There is a picnic site at the nearby MacMac pools.*

0 kilometres 3
0 miles 3

N ↑

The impressive MacMac Falls, plunging into the gorge below ↑

# ESWATINI

Africa's only absolute monarchy, Eswatini is
bordered by South Africa and Mozambique.
The country is home to the Swazi Kingdom, which
was consolidated in its present-day form under
Ngwane III, who ruled for roughly 35 years prior
to his death in 1780. Eswatini became a British
protectorate in 1906, but retains a cohesive identity
rare in more multi-ethnic societies. The kingdom's
dominant 20th-century personage was Sobhuza II,
who ascended the throne as a baby in 1899,
and reigned for almost 83 years. Following
independence in 1968, Sobhuza II scrapped the
Westminster-style political system bequeathed
by the British in favour of a traditional Swazi
constitution that placed absolute power in the
monarchy and outlawed meaningful opposition.
Calls for reform under Sobhuza's successor Mswati III
resulted in a 2008 constitution that allows for
a parliament comprising 55 elected members and
10 nominated by the king, who also selects the
cabinet and prime minister. The status of political
parties remains ambiguous, however, and to all
intents and purposes their participation in politics
is illegal. In 2018, Mswati III changed the kingdom's
name from Swaziland to the more correct Eswatini.

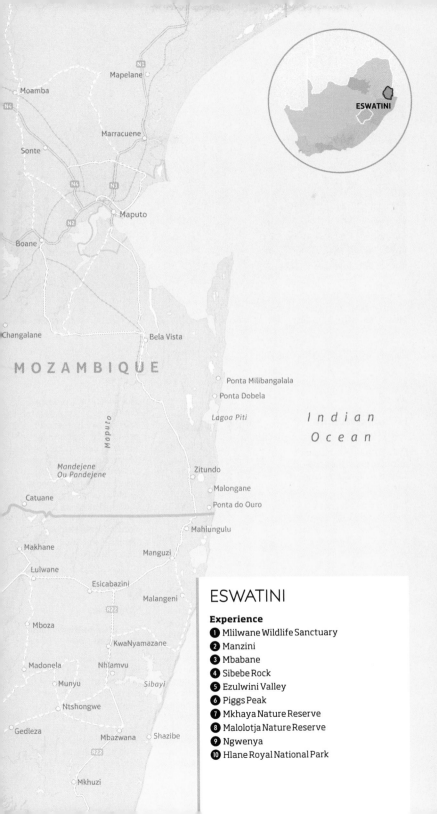

# ESWATINI

### Experience

1. Mlilwane Wildlife Sanctuary
2. Manzini
3. Mbabane
4. Sibebe Rock
5. Ezulwini Valley
6. Piggs Peak
7. Mkhaya Nature Reserve
8. Malolotja Nature Reserve
9. Ngwenya
10. Hlane Royal National Park

→

Atmospheric early morning mist hanging above a lake in Mlilwane Wildlife Sanctuary

# EXPERIENCE

### ①

## Mlilwane Wildlife Sanctuary

**🅰G3** 🅰 Between Mbabane and Manzini 🅾 Sunrise-sunset daily 🆆 biggame parks.org

The kingdom's oldest protected area, Mlilwane came into existence in 1961 when Ted and Liz Reilly, doyens of conservation in Eswatini, decided to convert their farm into a wildlife sanctuary (and an abundance of non-indigenous trees still betrays this past life). Guided and self-guided game drives are on offer, but the absence of dangerous game makes Mlilwane particularly well suited to more active exploration, whether it be mountain biking, horseback safaris or meandering along a 20-km (12-mile) network of self-guided trails. The siSwati name Mlilwane means "Little Fire" and refers to a hill where fires are frequently started by lightning strikes.

### Did You Know?

Eswatini's monarchs are polygamous. The current king, Mswati III, has 15 wives, and his father had 70.

### ②

## Manzini

**🅰G3** 𝒊 www.thekingdom ofeswatini.com

The most industrialized town in Eswatini, Manzini was also the largest prior to being outstripped by Mbabane around the turn of the millennium. Although it largely matches Mbabane in the blandness stakes, Manzini does possess a more down-to-earth character, and it tends to be somewhat warmer thanks to its lower elevation. Its central market, **Manzini Main Market**, is also excellent. The lower floor is

dedicated to fresh produce, while upper floor stalls sell the basketwork and other crafts for which the kingdom is famed (usually at better prices than the more touristy stalls in the Ezulwini Valley). The market is busiest on Thursday, when it hosts a macabre cluster of traditional medicine stalls.

**Manzini Main Market**
🅰 Mancishane St
🅾 6am-6pm Mon-Sat

### ③

## Mbabane

**🅰G3** 𝒊 www.thekingdom ofeswatini.com

In 1887, the pioneer Michael Wells established a rudimentary hotel and shop where the main trade route between Maputo (Mozambique) and the Transvaal Republic forded the Mbabane River. Set at an agreeable elevation of 1,250 m (4,100 ft), this simple trading post rapidly attracted further

European settlement, and in 1902 it was chosen as capital of the Swaziland Protectorate. Now a rather bland urban sprawl with a population of 100,000, Mbabane remains the capital of Eswatini, and is a useful base for exploring.

4

## Sibebe Rock

**G3 10 km (6 miles) N of Mbabane**

Southern Africa's oddly underpublicized counterpart to Uluru, Sibebe is the world's second-largest exposed rock monolith, rising a full 350 m (1,148 ft) from its 165-sq-km (64-sq-mile) base in the Mbuluzi River Valley.

Where its larger Australian rival is composed of sandstone, Sibebe is a 3-billion-year-old granite batholith whose sparsely vegetated lunar dome is merely the tip of a formation that extends for a full 15 km (9 miles) below the earth's surface. A truly startling apparition, its main face can be ascended on foot, a giddying three-hour climb that is not for the faint of heart (and could be genuinely dangerous after rain). Guided ascents are billed as the world's steepest commercial walk.

5

## Ezulwini Valley

**G3 www.thekingdomofeswatini.com**

The Ezulwini Valley thrived as a tourist centre in the apartheid era, when gambling was banned in South Africa, and it hosted a row of casinos to lure punters across the border. Three decades on, the valley remains the kingdom's most important tourist hub, though these days it attracts a more cosmopolitan clientele with a wholesome range of cultural, natural and outdoor attractions.

Foremost among these is the Mantenga Nature Reserve, where a reconstructed Swazi village offers fascinating tours and lively traditional musical performances. Mantenga's riverine scrub is set below Execution Rock, a foreboding granite outcrop from where convicted murderers used to be thrown to their death.

At the southern end of the valley, Lobamba, traditional seat of the Swazi monarchy, is home to the National Museum of Eswatini, whose displays include an absorbing collection of historical photographs. A more commercial attraction is the Swazi Candle Factory, which produces colourful, oddly shaped Swazi candles.

↑ The immense Sibebe Rock, towering over the countryside surrounding Mbabane

# EAT

**eDladleni Swazi Restaurant**

Tasty traditional Swazi fare in a log building with a tree-lined deck.

**Off the MR3, Ezulwini Valley edladleni.100webspace.net**

®®®

**Ramblas Restaurant**

A friendly eatery specializing in steak and seafood, with a broad wine list.

**Mantsholo Rd, Mbabane Sun ramblasmbabane.com**

®®®

# STAY

**Mlilwane Rest Camp**

Good value set-up with a range of accommodation options, including traditional beehive huts.

**Mlilwane Wildlife Sanctuary biggameparks.org**

®®®

**Royal Swazi Spa Valley**

A swish resort renowned for its golf course and casino.

**Ezulwini Valley suninternational.com/royal-swazi-spa**

®®®

**Mkhaya Stone Camp**

A tranquil camp of stone chalets. Rates include activities and meals.

**Mkhaya Game Reserve biggameparks.org**

®®®

## ⑥ Piggs Peak

**⚐ G3 🛈 www.thekingdom ofeswatini.com**

Founded by the prospector William Pigg, who discovered gold there in 1884, Piggs Peak is now best known as a centre of forestry and for the nearby Piggs Peak Casino. Close to the casino, the private **Phophonyane Nature Reserve** is named for an attractive waterfall that crashes 80 m (260 ft) over a bed of ancient sedimentary rocks. According to legend, it was formed, by the tears of a Swazi maiden abandoned by her suitor. Several small mammal species might be observed from the network of foot trails over the wooded slopes, but the reserve is primarily of interest for its escarpment forest avifauna.

### Phophonyane Nature Reserve

**⊛ ⚐ 10 km (6 miles) N of Piggs Peak 🌐 phophonyane lodge.squarespace.com**

Taking in the spectacular mountain views of Malolotja Nature Reserve ↓

**INSIDER TIP**
### White-water Rafting

Running through a starkly beautiful valley and navigable all year round, the challenging Grade I–IV rapids on the Great Usutu River can be tackled in unguided two-berth rafts.

## ⑦  Mkhaya Game Reserve

**⚐ G3 ⚑ 57 km (35 miles) E of Manzini ⧉ Pre-booked tours only 🌐 biggameparks.org**

Named after the *mkhaya* (knobthorn) acacia tree, this small lowveld reserve was originally set aside in 1979 to protect the kingdom's last herd of pure Nguni cattle, an indigenous breed resistant to several diseases that afflict its exotic counterparts. Today the reserve functions primarily as a refuge for endangered species such as elephant, roan antelope and sable antelope. It offers all-inclusive packages running out of a luxuriously rustic riverside lodge – but is slightly more wallet-friendly than most private reserves. The partitioning of the

reserve into fenced enclosures jars slightly, but there is no finer place in southern Africa for close-up encounters with both types of rhino, and the birding here is also superb.

## ⑧  Malolotja Nature Reserve

**⚐ G3 ⚑ 30 km (19 miles) N of Mbabane 🌐 sntc.org.sz/ reserves/mal.html**

Nestled up against the South African border, Malolotja is Eswatini's last true wilderness, with just 20 km (12 miles) of roads traversing its 180-sq-km (69-sq-mile) area. It is also the kingdom's premier hiking destination, transected by numerous day trails as well as a tough seven-day route.

The reserve protects a landscape of layered mountains and grassland plateaux studded with delicate wildflowers, blossoming proteas and the rare Barberton and Kaapsehoop cycads. Wildlife includes regional endemics such as black wildebeest and blesbok, and even a few resilient (and elusive) leopards. From May to January, a colony of 50 southern bald ibis frequents the cliffs above the Malolotja Falls, while breeding blue swallows swoop over the grassland in summer. Blue crane and Gurney's sugarbird are present year-round.

↑ A 4WD tour through Hlane Royal National Park

For adrenaline junkies, the privately run Malolotja Canopy Tour provides 11 elevated forest platforms connected by ten zip-line slides, and a suspension bridge across the Majolomba River.

 **9**

## Ngwenya

**🅰G3** **ℹ️ www.thekingdomofeswatini.com**

Situated close to the busy Oshoek border post, this village is the site of the **Ngwenya Glass Factory**, which uses recycled glass as the source of its wonderful handmade, mouth-blown products.

Close by are the world's oldest known mine workings, on the slopes of Ngwenya Mountain. Dated to before 40,000 BC, Ngwenya Mine was a source of specularite, a type of iron that glitters when crushed. The mine predates the craft of iron smelting by several millennia; the Stone Age humans who worked it presumably used the specularite for decorative purposes.

**Ngwenya Glass Factory**
🕐 8am–4pm daily 🚫 1 Jan, 25–26 Dec 🌐 ngwenyaglass.co.sz

## Hlane Royal National Park

**🅰G3** **📍 70 km (43 miles) NE of Manzini** 🕐 6am–6pm daily 🌐 biggameparks.org

The name Hlane translates as "wilderness", which slightly overstates the case, but this is Eswatini's largest and most diverse wildlife sanctuary.

Designated as a royal hunting ground since colonial times, the park is still owned by King Mswati III. Naturally occurring large mammals such as zebra and spotted hyena were joined more recently by reintroduced lion, cheetah, elephant and white rhino. Partitioned into several large enclosures as a measure against poaching, Hlane can feel uncomfortably artificial when explored by vehicle, and the lion enclosure can be visited on guided tours only. But the guided game walks are worthwhile, and often involve close encounters with white rhino and elephant.

> **REED DANCE CEREMONY**
>
> Adapted from an older chastity rite during the reign of Sobhuza II, the Umhlanga (Reed Dance) is Eswatini's largest annual festival. It attracts around 40,000 traditionally attired, virgin girls and young women, who must march to a river and cut down a reed to present as a tribute to the Queen Mother at her royal village of Ludzidzini.

# NEED TO KNOW

A game drive through the savannah

# BEFORE
# YOU GO

Things change, so plan ahead to make the most of your trip. Be prepared for all eventualities by considering the following points before you travel.

## AT A GLANCE

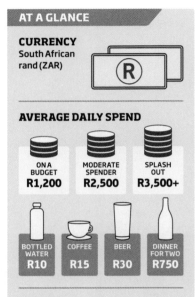

**CURRENCY**
South African rand (ZAR)

**AVERAGE DAILY SPEND**

| ON A BUDGET | MODERATE SPENDER | SPLASH OUT |
|---|---|---|
| **R1,200** | **R2,500** | **R3,500+** |

| BOTTLED WATER | COFFEE | BEER | DINNER FOR TWO |
|---|---|---|---|
| **R10** | **R15** | **R30** | **R750** |

## CLIMATE

 The longest days are in December and the shortest in June.

 Temperatures vary greatly between regions, from highs of 50°C (122°F) in summer to lows of -16°C (3°F) on winter nights.

 The east is generally wetter than the west.

## ELECTRICITY SUPPLY

Power sockets are type F and L, fitting two- and three-pronged plugs. Standard voltage is 220–230v.

## Passports and Visas

For entry requirements, including visas, consult your nearest South African embassy or check with South Africa's **Department of Home Affairs**. Citizens of the UK, US, Canada, Australia, New Zealand and most EU countries can stay in South Africa visa-free for up to 90 days on production of a passport at the point of entry. Those who do require a visa must buy one in advance at a South African embassy; check with the Department of Home Affairs for details. Visas to enter Eswatini are issued free of charge at the border. Visa requirements for Lesotho depend on your nationality; check the country's **E-Visa** website for details.
**Department of Home Affairs**
w dha.gov.za/index.php/applying-for-sa-visa
**E-Visa**
w evisalesotho.com/

## Government Advice

Now more than ever, it is important to consult both your and the South African government's advice before travelling. The **UK Foreign and Commonwealth Office**, the **US State Department**, the **Australian Department of Foreign Affairs and Trade** and the South Africa Department of Home Affairs *(above)* offer the latest information on security, health and other local regulations.
**Australian Department of Foreign Affairs and Trade**
w smarttraveller.gov.au
**UK Foreign and Commonwealth Office**
w gov.uk/foreign-travel-advice
**US State Department**
w travel.state.gov

## Customs Information

You can find information on the laws relating to goods and currency taken in or out of South Africa on the South African Tourist Board website.
**South African Tourist Board**
w southafrica.net

## Insurance

We recommend taking out a comprehensive insurance policy covering theft, loss of belongings, medical care, cancellations and delays; read the small print carefully. South Africa does not have reciprocal health care agreements with other countries, so medical cover is essential.

## Vaccinations

For information regarding COVID-19 vaccination requirements, consult government advice. If you arrive from a country where yellow fever is endemic, you will need a vaccination certificate. Malaria is still prevalent in parts of Mpumalanga, Limpopo and KwaZulu-Natal, so you might want to take prophylactics if visiting these regions.

## Accommodation

Accommodation ranges from backpacker dorms to luxury resorts and can be easily booked online. **SANParks** and **KwaZulu-Natal Wildlife** manage accommodation in national parks and reserves.

**KwaZulu-Natal Wildlife**
🅦 kznwildlife.com
**SANParks**
🅦 sanparks.org

## Money

ATMs are widespread and they generally offer the best rate of exchange. Banks and bureaux de change are also plentiful. Most businesses accept major credit cards, but keep your card in sight when making a payment to reduce the risk of it being "cloned". Informal traders do not usually accept credit cards, and it is advisable to carry some cash in rural areas just in case.

In restauraurants it is customary to tip waiting staff 10–15 per cent of the total bill; in hotels, porters will expect R5–10 per bag and housekeeping will expect R20 per night.

## Travellers with Specific Requirements

The rights of people with disabilities are enshrined in South Africa's constitution, and legislation requires that they are accommodated wherever possible in public buildings. All modern shopping malls, museums and tourist attractions have ramps, lifts and reserved parking. Local airlines provide assistance for disabled passengers, and newer urban transport systems, such as Cape Town's **MyCiTi** bus *(p368)* and Johannesburg's **Gautrain** *(p368)*, accommodate wheelchairs. Most national parks have specially adapted chalets for visitors with impaired vision, hearing, or mobility. **Disabled Travel** is a useful guide to facilities and accommodation for travellers with limited mobility.
**Disabled Travel**
🅦 disabledtravel.co.za

## Language

South Africa has 12 official languages: Afrikaans, English, IsiNdebele, IsiXhosa, IsiZulu, North Sotho, SeTswana, SiSwati, South African Sign Language, South Sotho, TshiVenda and XiTsonga. English is very widely spoken.

## Opening Hours

> **COVID-19** Increased rates of infection may result in temporary opening hours and/or closures. Always check ahead before visiting museums, attractions and hospitality venues.

Business hours are usually 8:30am–5pm Monday–Friday. Parks and reserves generally open from sunrise to sunset.

### PUBLIC HOLIDAYS

| | |
|---|---|
| 1 Jan | New Year's Day |
| 21 Mar | Human Rights' Day |
| Mar/Apr | Good Friday, Family Day (Easter Monday) |
| 27 Apr | Freedom Day |
| 1 May | Worker's Day |
| 16 Jun | Youth Day |
| 9 Aug | National Women's Day |
| 24 Sep | Heritage Day |
| 16 Dec | Day of Reconciliation |
| 25 Dec | Christmas Day |
| 26 Dec | Goodwill Day |

# GETTING AROUND

Whether you're exploring the cities, undertaking a long-haul road trip or embarking on a safari, discover how best to travel like a pro.

## TRANSPORT COSTS

### JOHANNESBURG TO CAPE TOWN

**R900+**

Single flight

**R700+**

Single train ticket

**R400**

Single bus journey

### TOP TIP
Domestic flight costs are highly variable so browse several airline websites and try to be flexible about times.

## SPEED LIMIT

**HIGHWAY**

**120** km/h (75mph)

**OTHER OPEN ROADS**

**100** km/h (60mph)

**URBAN ROADS**

**60** km/h (35mph)

**NATIONAL PARKS**

**30-40** km/h (20–25mph)

## Arriving by Air

The three main international airports are OR Tambo International Airport in Gauteng (for Johannesburg, Pretoria and Sandton), Cape Town International Airport in Cape Town and King Shaka International Airport in Durban. OR Tambo is the largest air travel hub in sub-equatorial Africa, and most major airlines fly there, but an increasing number also operate direct international flights to Cape Town and Durban. Cost-conscious travellers who want to fly directly to Cape Town or elsewhere will have more choice if they fly to OR Tambo, complete immigration formalities there, then take a domestic flight to their final destination.

Visitors travelling from OR Tambo to Pretoria and Johannesburg can access those cities by the Gautrain, provided their accommodation is close to one of its limited networks of stations. In Cape Town, there are MyCiTi buses to the city every 30 minutes, while in Durban, the King Shaka Airport Shuttle bus goes to Umhlanga, the city centre and beachfront every 30–45 minutes. Metered taxis can be found outside the main terminal buildings of all three airports, and most hotels and guesthouses can arrange transfers on request.

## Long-Distance Travel

### Domestic Flights
The most efficient way of covering long-haul trips within South Africa is by air. Various local private airlines operate several flights daily between Johannesburg, Durban, Cape Town, Gqeberha (formerly Port Elizabeth), Bloemfontein, East London, Nelspruit, George and Upington. Fares are wildly variable and dictated by demand, but usually the best prices are with low-cost, no-frills **Kulula**, **Safair** and **Mango Air**.

**Kulula**
w kulula.com
**Mango Air**
w flymango.com
**Safair**
w flysafair.co.za

## GETTING TO AND FROM THE AIRPORT

| Airport | Distance to city | Taxi fare | Journey time |
|---|---|---|---|
| Johannesburg (OR Tambo) | 28 km (17 miles) | R500 | 30–60 mins |
| Sandton (OR Tambo) | 35 km (20 miles) | R600 | 45–90 mins |
| Pretoria (OR Tambo) | 50 km (30 miles) | R750 | 45–90 mins |
| Cape Town (Cape Town) | 20 km (12 miles) | R250 | 15–30 mins |
| Stellenbosch (Cape Town) | 35 km (20 miles) | R500 | 30–45 mins |
| Wilderness (George) | 23 km (14 miles) | R250 | 15–30 mins |
| Knysna (George) | 70 km (45 miles) | R750 | 60–90 mins |
| Gqeberha (Chief Dawid Stuurman) | 5 km (3 miles) | R100 | 10 mins |
| Durban (King Shaka) | 32 km (20 miles) | R400 | 30–45 mins |
| Mbombela (Kruger Mpumalanga) | 30 km (19 miles) | R400 | 30–45 mins |

## Intercity Trains

The luxurious train safaris offered by the **Blue Train** and **Rovos Rail** are enormously popular (*p56*), especially with foreign visitors. Both offer a choice of routes, with all inclusive rates that include meals and most beverages.

Otherwise, train travel in South Africa is adequately comfortable and very economical, but not as fast as bus travel. **Shosholoza Meyl** operates trains from Johannesburg to Cape Town via Kimberley (four per week/27 hours), Gqeberha via Bloemfontein (three per week/21 hours), East London via Bloemfontein (three per week/21 hours), Durban (three per week/14 hours) and Komatipoort via Mbombela (Friday only/12 hours). There are two types of class: sitter and sleeper; the former is a standard seat and the latter comprises compartments with two or four bunks, a wash basin and a table. Simple meals are available from a restaurant coach. Booking in advance is necessary during school holidays.

**Blue Train**
w bluetrain.co.za
**Rovos Rail**
w rovos.com
**Shosholoza Meyl**
w shosholozameyl.co.za

## Coaches

Safe, comfortable and affordable coach services cover most major routes in South Africa, including the trio of through roads between Johannesburg and Cape Town via Kimberly, Bloemfontein and Upington; the coastal N2 between Cape Town and Durban via the Garden Route and Gqeberha; and the N3 between Johannesburg and Durban. The coaches are modern and air-conditioned, with onboard toilets and reclining seats, and they stop regularly for refreshments. The main operator is **InterCape**, which has route maps on its website and offers user-friendly online booking.

**InterCape**
w intercape.co.za

## BazBus

Aimed mainly at backpackers but open to all, the **BazBus** is a popular hop-on, hop-off service that runs between Johannesburg and Cape Town via the northern Drakensberg, Durban, Gqeberha and the Garden Route. A major advantage of this service is that it drops and picks up passengers by arrangement at selected backpacker hostels, saving a lot of hassle and the cost of taxi fares.

**BazBus**
w bazbus.com

## Minibuses

Known locally as taxis, minibuses are the main form of intercity transport in South Africa, and are very cheap. However, they generally have a poor safety record, tend to be overcrowded and leave from insalubrious neighbourhoods, so they are not recommended to foreign visitors.

# Local Transport

## City Buses

All South African cities have a system of public buses, which are inexpensive and easy to use. They can accommodate wheelchairs and prams and are monitored by security cameras. In Cape Town, bus services are run by **MyCiTi**, which also operates a service to and from the airport. In Durban, the **People Mover** runs up and down the beachfront and in a loop around the city centre, while in Johannesburg, **Metrobus** and **Rea Vaya** cover all the metropolitan areas. Minibus taxis follow the same routes as regular buses, and often several more, but are driven erratically and are not recommended.

**Metrobus**
W mbus.co.za

**MyCiTi**
W myciti.org.za

**People Mover**
W muvo.co.za

**Rea Vaya**
W reavaya.org.za

## Suburban Trains

Suburban train services run in most South African cities but are used mainly by commuters and can be overcrowded. Theft may also be an issue. Exceptions are the rapid-rail **Gautrain** linking Johannesburg, Pretoria, Sandton and OR Tambo International Airport, and the hop-on, hop-off **Southern Line Tourism Route** from central Cape Town to Simon's Town via the Southern Suburbs and False Bay.

**Gautrain**
W gautrain.co.za

**Southern Line Tourism Route**
W metrorail.co.za

# Taxis

Taxis are available in all major towns. They cannot usually be hailed in the street, but there are taxi ranks outside all airports, bus and railway stations and shopping malls, and at the major sightseeing attractions. Additionally, any hotel or restaurant can call a cab for you. All taxis are metered, and by law they must display a sticker on the side of the vehicle showing the price per kilometre. Uber and Bolt are also represented in larger cities and are generally much cheaper than other cab services.

# Driving

Renting a car provides the greatest travel flexibility and is the only way to visit South Africa's more remote areas. Overall, the country's road network is very good. In rural areas, only main arteries may be tarred, but dirt roads are usually levelled and in good condition. Along the major routes there are many service stations, and the main attractions are well signposted.

## Car Rental

Drivers need to be over 23 years of age and to have a photocard driving licence printed in English (or with an accompanying translation if the licence is in another language). Your licence must be carried in the vehicle at all times. A credit or debit card is essential to hire a car; check the small print for insurance cover. International companies include **Avis**, **Budget**, **Europcar** and **Hertz**, and equally good local companies include **First Car Rental** and **Tempest Car Hire**.

Many travel agents and car rental firms organize fly-drive packages. This is usually cheaper (and involves fewer formalities) than renting a car on arrival. **Around About Cars** is a national agency that is able to look for competitive rates across all the companies and has its own fleet of cars in Cape Town.

**Around About Cars**
W aroundaboutcars.com

**Avis**
W avis.co.za

**Budget**
W budget.co.za

**Europcar**
W europcar.co.za

**First Car Rental**
W firstcarrental.co.za

**Hertz**
W hertz.co.za

**Tempest Car Hire**
W tempestcarhire.co.za

## Rules of the Road

South Africa drives on the left side of the road. Except where granted right of way by a sign or by an official on duty, yield to traffic approaching from your right.

Stay alert for pedestrians and straying livestock when driving through rural villages, and be aware that speed traps are often strategically located to catch drivers on the outskirts of town, just as the speed limit drops from the rural to urban one. Seat belts are compulsory in the front and in the back. In the event of an accident, notify the police immediately and do not move the vehicles until they arrive.

South Africa has strict zero-tolerance drink driving laws. Anyone caught driving with a blood alcohol level above 0 is liable for a hefty fine, or up to six years' imprisonment.

## Fuel

Motor vehicles run on 97 Octane petrol, unleaded petrol or diesel fuel, and the unit of liquid measurement is the litre (0.22 UK gallons or 0.264 US gallons). Service station attendants see to refuelling and other checks such as tyre pressure, oil and water, and cleaning the front and rear windows; tips are not expected, but R5–10 is appreciated for good service. Due to the vast distances between towns, especially in the arid interior, it is advisable to refuel in good time, and to plan regular rest stops.

### Parking
Most South African towns and cities have street parking, with numbered bays painted on the tarmac or at the kerb; check for signs posted on a nearby pole. A fee may be paid to a parking marshal with a handheld meter. There are also numerous multi-storey car parks and almost all visitor attractions and shopping malls have parking areas. In unofficial parking areas such as side streets, informal parking attendants expect a tip for guarding your car when you leave it (p370).

## Cycling

Bikes can be rented in South Africa from numerous outlets in holiday regions such as Cape Town and along the coast. Tour operators can organize a variety of cycling tours – both off-road and on smooth tar – with popular options including the Garden Route and the Karoo.

## Walking

It is safe to walk in the centre of cities such as Cape Town, Johannesburg and Durban, and there are numerous walking tours available. Take advice from trusted locals about where not to go after dark.

Good-quality hiking trails can be found across the country. Popular routes such as the Otter Trail and Tsitsikamma Trail (p232) need to be booked more than a year in advance.

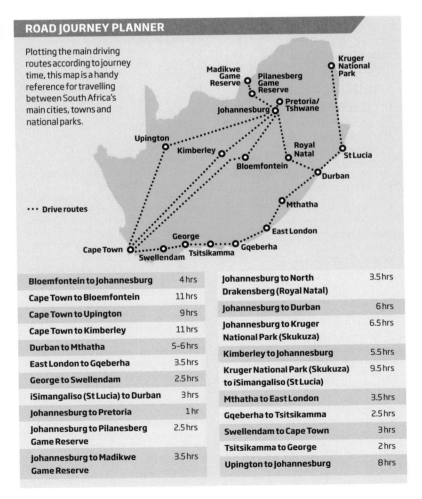

## ROAD JOURNEY PLANNER

Plotting the main driving routes according to journey time, this map is a handy reference for travelling between South Africa's main cities, towns and national parks.

••• Drive routes

| | | | | |
|---|---|---|---|---|
| Bloemfontein to Johannesburg | 4 hrs | Johannesburg to North Drakensberg (Royal Natal) | 3.5 hrs |
| Cape Town to Bloemfontein | 11 hrs | Johannesburg to Durban | 6 hrs |
| Cape Town to Upington | 9 hrs | Johannesburg to Kruger National Park (Skukuza) | 6.5 hrs |
| Cape Town to Kimberley | 11 hrs | | |
| Durban to Mthatha | 5–6 hrs | Kimberley to Johannesburg | 5.5 hrs |
| East London to Gqeberha | 3.5 hrs | Kruger National Park (Skukuza) to iSimangaliso (St Lucia) | 9.5 hrs |
| George to Swellendam | 2.5 hrs | | |
| iSimangaliso (St Lucia) to Durban | 3 hrs | Mthatha to East London | 3.5 hrs |
| Johannesburg to Pretoria | 1 hr | Gqeberha to Tsitsikamma | 2.5 hrs |
| Johannesburg to Pilanesberg Game Reserve | 2.5 hrs | Swellendam to Cape Town | 3 hrs |
| | | Tsitsikamma to George | 2 hrs |
| Johannesburg to Madikwe Game Reserve | 3.5 hrs | Upington to Johannesburg | 8 hrs |

# PRACTICAL
# INFORMATION

A little local know-how goes a long way in South Africa. Here you will find all the essential advice and information you will need during your stay.

## AT A GLANCE

### EMERGENCY NUMBERS

EMERGENCY
RESPONSE

**112**

AMBULANCE

**10177**

AA ROADSIDE
ASSISTANCE

**080 001
0101**

POLICE

**10111**

### TIME ZONE
South Africa Time Zone (UTC/GMT +2). There is no daylight saving.

### TAP WATER
Tap water is safe to drink in South Africa unless specifically stated otherwise.

### WEBSITES AND APPS

**South African Tourist Board**
For useful information on visiting South Africa see www.southafrica.net.

**SANParks**
For detailed information about South Africa's 20 national parks, and to make bookings for accommodation within them, visit sanparks.org.

**IOL**
A good free news service with an associated app is iol.co.za.

## Personal Security

Although South Africa has a reputation when it comes to crime, it's fairly rare for visitors to encounter anything other than the usual petty crime associated with large cities. Security is good in most places that tourists are likely to visit and the risk of serious crime is low, but there is a small chance that you may encounter bag-snatching or pickpocketing. Take sensible precautions when walking around – don't publicly flash expensive items such as jewellery and mobile phones, and avoid going out alone, especially after dark; if you do, stick to busy and well-lit tourist areas. Women should never walk alone anywhere after dark. If you are mugged, do not challenge the thief – simply hand over your phone or your money. Follow local advice about which areas to avoid, and be vigilant about the people around you. Report any incident immediately; you will need to obtain a case reference number from a police station in order to make an insurance claim.

On crowded public transport, be vigilant and guard possessions closely. When travelling by car, keep handbags and other valuables out of sight, keep the doors locked and the windows only slightly open. Use covered or supervised parking where possible, and as you leave the car make sure nothing of value is visible inside before you lock it. In the event of a breakdown in a remote area, stay in your locked vehicle if you can, and call for assistance from a mobile phone.

Apartheid legislation was repealed in 1991 and a new constitution that afforded equal rights to all racial groups has been in effect since 1996, although the legacy of segregation can still be felt in some areas. The rights of gay people are also enshrined in South Africa's constitution and gay marriage has been legal since 2006. But while Cape Town is the LGBT+ capital of Africa, and other cities have a host of gay venues, smaller towns and rural areas retain more conservative attitudes. If you do feel unsafe, the **Safe Space Alliance** pinpoints your nearest place of refuge.
**Safe Space Alliance**
🔲 safespacealliance.com

## Health

State and provincial hospitals offer adequate facilities, but tend to be under-funded and under-staffed, so members of medical insurance schemes are usually admitted to a private hospital. For all visitors, payment of medical expenses is the patient's responsibility. It is therefore important to arrange comprehensive medical insurance before travelling.

South Africa generally has no unusual or serious health risks, but there is a low seasonal risk of malaria in the Kruger National Park and immediate environs, and in the extreme north of KwaZulu-Natal. The main risk period is usually the rainy summer months of October to April. If you are travelling to these areas at that time, consult your doctor or travel clinic about taking antimalarial drugs.

Travellers are highly unlikely to be bitten or stung by a venomous creature, but should watch where they place their hands and feet on safari or on a hiking trail. Few snakes in South Africa are deadly, most are not poisonous at all, and those that are usually strike only when attacked or threatened. Most species of scorpion are harmless or only slightly venomous.

## Smoking, Alcohol and Drugs

Smoking is illegal and socially unacceptable in buses, trains, taxis, restaurants and most public buildings.

Alcohol is served in practically all hotels and licensed restaurants, as well as in bars. The consumption of alcohol on beaches is illegal, and drink driving legislation is strictly enforced (p368).

The personal consumption of cannabis by adults in private was decriminalized by the Constitutional Court in 2018, but laws prohibiting buying and selling it, or consuming it in public, remain in place. Travellers caught using illegal drugs may be arrested and face a heavy fine or jail time.

## ID

It is not a legal requirement to carry ID on one's person. Drivers must be in possession of their driving license whenever they are behind the wheel.

## Local Customs

South Africa is a relatively Westernized and cosmopolitan country, and visitors are unlikely to find themselves in any situations where they are culturally out of their depth. The dress code is casual, except for a few top restaurants and formal events. On the beach, it is illegal for women to swim or sunbathe topless.

Visitors should observe appropriate religious customs when visiting mosques, churches, temples and other places of worship.

## Mobile Phones and Wi-Fi

If you are set up for international roaming, you can use your GSM phone in South Africa. It is worth buying a local SIM card with airtime and a data bundle to allow you to make local calls, send texts and use the internet cheaply. This can be organized in the prominently signposted outlets of the main independent providers, **Vodacom**, **MTN** or **Cell C**, found in all airports and malls. Wi-Fi is available in virtually all hotels, as well as in many cafés, restaurants and shopping centres.

**Cell C**
W cellc.co.za
**MTN**
W wegotu.mtn.co.za
**Vodacom**
W vodacom.co.za

## Post

International post to and from South Africa is slow and unreliable – airmail to Europe takes at least two weeks and to North America even longer. Valuable items and time-sensitive packages are better entrusted to a courier service such as DHL.

## Taxes and Refunds

A 15 per cent VAT is levied on all purchases and services other than a select list of essential grocery items such as bread and milk. It is permitted for visitors to reclaim VAT on any goods bought to export home. This can be done at the VAT reclaim desk at any international airport or border post, provided you can produce the original receipts.

# Safaris

Arranging a safari is a fairly straightforward procedure. The biggest hurdles at the planning stage will be choosing between a self-drive adventure or an organized safari and deciding which reserves to visit – with the diversity of South Africa's national parks and wildlife reserves, visitors are spoilt for choice. If you're opting for the DIY approach, it's easy to book everything online – the South African National Parks (SANParks) website *(p365)* is extremely user-friendly. If your itinerary includes visits to more than one reserve, it may be worth investing in a SANParks Wild Card, which provides unrestricted access to most of South Africa's conservation areas for a year.

For the less adventurous, there are plenty of reputable tour operators in South Africa and elsewhere to offer specialist guidance and to set transport and accommodation arrangements in place. It is best to choose a company that is recognized by the **Southern Africa Tourism Services Association** (SATSA).

The best season for game viewing is winter (July to September), when the dry weather forces animals to gather around rivers and waterholes. The disadvantages are that animals are not in optimal condition and the winter landscape is stark. Summer (November to January) brings high rainfall, and the landscape becomes green and lush. This is the best time of year for viewing flora, though the wildlife will be more widespread and difficult to spot. The wide availability of water also leads to a higher threat of malaria in risk areas *(p370)*.

**Southern Africa Tourism Services Association**
🅦 satsa.com

## Self-drive

National parks and provincial game reserves such as Kruger, Kgalagadi, Addo Elephant, Hluhluwe-Imfolozi and Pilanesberg are generally far better suited to a self-drive safari than their counterparts elsewhere in Africa. Internal roads are generally either surfaced or well-maintained murram (gravel), so can be navigated in an ordinary saloon car. There are also well-equipped rest camps with amenities such as restaurants, grocery shops and self-catering facilities, though this should be checked for the specific reserve before you visit, as should the availability of fuel for larger or more remote places. Most conservation areas impose a speed limit of 40 km/h (25 mph) or less, but the ideal speed for game spotting is more like 25 km/h (15 mph), so bank on covering around 20 km (12 miles) per hour, allowing for stops to view and photograph wildlife. Driving at night is forbidden in most reserves. Allow animals the right of way, be cautious around elephants (especially single bulls or mothers with young), and under no circumstances get out of your car except at designated spots such as picnic sites.

## Guided Safaris

Guided safaris in an open-sided 4WD form part of the all-inclusive package offered by most upmarket private reserves or concessions such as Sabi Sands. They are also now offered at several rest camps in Kruger and other reserves around the country, and can be arranged via SANParks. Generally you will see more wildlife on a guided safari than self-driving, and spot-lighted night drives in particular offer the opportunity to encounter species you are unlikely to see by yourself.

# INDEX

# S

# T

# ACKNOWLEDGMENTS

DK would like to thank the following for their contribution to the previous editions: Philip Briggs, Michael Brett, Brian-Johnson-Barker, Mariëlle Renssen

The publisher would like to thank the following for their kind permission to reproduce their photographs:

Key: a-above; b-below/bottom; c-centre; f-far; l-left; r-right; t-top

**123RF.com:** Agami Photo Agency 101tc; benjaminboeckle 242bl; Patrice Correia 98crb; Ecophoto 98br; euregiocontent 28cr; Christopher Fell 95crb; mathieu gallet 80crb; humpata 199br; Ben McRae 99tr; Dave Montreuil 112tc; Jatesada Natayo 81tl; Anna Om 18cb, 212-3; PhotoSky 154tc; otto du plessis 151tr; Stuart Porter 95clb; Grobler Du Preez 95tl; Dmitrii Sakharov 156cra; Nico Smit 199crb; Donovan van Staden 88-9; utopia88 85br; Bradley van der Westhuizen 127ca.

**4Corners:** Justin Foulkes 26-7ca.

**akg-images:** Africa Media Online 327cr, / Graeme Williams 64-5t, 65bc.

**Alamy Stock Photo:** 19th era 62crb; AA World Travel Library 265bc; Africa Media Online / Anthony Van Tonder 257tl, 297cr, / Ilonde van Hoolwerff 154-5b; Afripics.com 94clb,104clb, 152br; age fotostock / Eric Baccega 104cb; Allstar Picture Library 129bl, 263tr; Diriye Amey 256-7b, 260t; Anka Agency International / Anka Petrovic 344-5b; Arco Images GmbH 26cla; Miles Astray 48-9b; Avalon / Photoshot License / Anthony Bannister 100tc; Brendan Bell 204t; Bleyer / Friedrichsmeier Archive 128; blickwinkel 218cl, / McPHOTO / PUM 107crb, / McPHOTO / Was 28bl; Chris Bloom 288-9b; Bluegreen Pictures / Onne van der Wal 160bl; Paul Boreham 338tr; Ger Bosma 100clb; botanikfoto / Steffen Hauser 126bl; Alex Bramwell 299br; Eden Breitz 217bl; Thomas Brissiaud 152bl; David Buzzard 8clb; David Cantrille 72-3t; Cavan Images / Alexandra Simone 189cl; Martin Chapman 111tr; Chronicle 267cr; Dennis Cox 311br; Rob Crandall 324bl; David Noton Photography 150-1b; Chris Davies 197br; dbimages / Jeremy Graham 131bl; Danita Delimont 292cr; Diadem Images / Jonathan Larsen 13t; Werner Dieterich 54-5b; David Dixon 44bl; Ulrich Doering 158tr, 241tr; Antony Souter / sculpture by Jean Doyle 158bc; dpa picture alliance 167crb; Education & Exploration 1 329tr; Education & Exploration 3 124t; Greg Balfour Evans 24t, 50tl, 151cra, 157b, 234b, 310-1, 311; F1online digitale Bildagentur GmbH / Jürgen Ritterbach 30-1t; Five-Birds Photography 296-7b; Gallo Images / Fiona McIntosh 239br, / Neil Overy 331bc, / Heinrich van den Berg 360b; GFC Collection / animals 30-1ca; Phil Gould 308cl; Greatstock / Brand SA 290t, / SATourism 52-3b, 184tr, 202clb, 268cla, 317cr; Jeff Greenberg 139br; Bjorn Grotting 260bl; Martin Harvey 220-1b; hemis.fr / Franck Guiziou 361t; / Ludovic Maisant 276-7t;/ René Mattes 22crb, 290cla, / Bertrand Rieger 322-3b; Heritage Image Partnership Ltd 41br; Hoberman Collection 17bl, 168-9; Cindy Hopkins 152crb; Lloyd Horgan 72tl; Friedrich von Hörsten 61tl, 244bl; hpbfotos 22bl, 127tr, 259tr; Ian Butler Photography 113tl; Iconpix 303tr; imageBROKER / Nigel Dennis 82clb, / Thomas Dressler 197cr, / jspix 82cb, / Günter Lenz 38-9t, / Christian Vorhofer 345tr; Imageplotter 173t; INTERFOTO / Travel 254-5t; ITPhoto 178t, 281br; jbdodane 254br; JL Photography 218-9b; John Warburton-Lee Photography / Will Gray 349bl; Vivien Kent 350-1b; KGPA Ltd / The Keasbury-Gordon Photograph Archive 63tr; David Kleyn 264cla; LatitudeStock 178br; frans lemmens 188tr, 211bl, 284t, 320-1b; Chris Van Lennep 286-7t; Martin Lindsay 201cl; lkpro 358t; Anina Lonte 202-3b; Look / Franz Marc Frei 70-1ca; Look / Michael Boyny 32tr; M.Sobreira 39cla, 41tr; Gregory Maassen 240clb; Benny Marty 320cl; mauritius images GmbH / ClickAlps 206-7b; Paul Mayall 319cra; Buddy Mays 301br; Angus McComiskey 252bl; Sean McSweeney 262b; Gillian Moore 141br; Juan Carlos Muñoz 181bl; Nadezda Murmakova 146clb; Eric Nathan 22t, 27cla, 125bl, 160-1t; Nature Picture Library 17t, 142-3; North Wind Picture Archives 219cr; Novarc Images / Annett Schmitz 240-1b; Gunter Nuyts 318bl; Christian Offenberg 298-9t; Fernando Quevedo de Oliveira 21bl, 354-5; Blaize Pascall 134-5t; The Picture Art Collection 62bc; Photogilio 50-1b; Grobler du Preez 31cla,187bc, 230cra; Edwin Remsberg 359bl; Robert Estall photo agency / Carol Beckwith & Angela Fisher 361br; robertharding / James Hager 103tr, 111crb, 266tr; / Andrew McConnell 120-1b, RooM the Agency / cormacmccreesh 92-3; RosalreneBetancourt 13 323tl; Suretha Rous 101clb; Dirk Rueter 151ca; Margaret S 325bl; Roger Sedres 163t; Nico Smit 104tl; Chakkrapan Na Songkhla 326b; Antony Souter 121cra, 185c; Tony Sparkes 27tr; Emanuele Stano 12clb; Friedrich Stark 137t, 313bl; Martin Strmiska 52-3t, 289tr; Survivalphotos 105tr; The Africa Image Library 342br; Steve Taylor ARPS 224-5t; Tierfotoagentur / W. Schaefer 31tr; Peter Titmuss 42br; 182-3t, 186clb, 264t; Ann and Steve Toon 269br; Morgan Trimble 104tc, 164-5b, 233tl, 237b, 282-3t; Trinity Mirror / Mirrorpix 308br; Genevieve Vallee 18tl, 192-3, 340tr; Ariadne Van Zandbergen 33tl, 51cl, 130t, 162b, 185b, 207tl, 208bl, 221tr, 225bl, 236-7t, 279cr, 291b, 277crb, 336bl, 344bl; Rudi Venter 330t, 330cra; wanderluster 59bl, 146bc; Monica Wells 37br, 121cla, 132-3t, 138cl;

Liam West 56-7t; Westend61 GmbH 19bl, 246-7, / Fotofeeling 195tr, 317bl; WildDrago 43cla; WILDLIFE GmbH 70-1t, 199tr, 296tr; World History Archive 308clb, 308bc; Hongqi Zhang 230bc, 235t.

**AWL Images:** Christian Kober 336-7t; Ian Trower 20cb, 46-7b, 304-5.

**Bridgeman Images:** Private Collection / Look and Learn 61tr, 63bl; Private Collection / Luisa Ricciarini 60t; Private Collection / The Stapleton Collection 62-3t; South African Library, Cape Town, South Africa 62tl.

**Depositphotos Inc:** EcoPic 83crb; kanuman 2-3; kovaricekpavel 82ca; mzphoto 80cla; zambezi 196cr.

**Dreamstime.com:** Riaan Albrecht 73tr; Steve Allen 111tl; Andrew Allport 110cb; Altaoosthuizen 104tr; Diriye Amey 261bl, 280b; Artushfoto 97tr, 316bl, 319tr; Avslt71 83tr; Avstraliavasin 48tl; Vanessa Bentley 328b; Peter Betts 101cb, 113clb; Cathywithers 30cla, 101tl, 113cb; Neal Cooper 106cra, 107tl, 112tr; Patrice Correia 72cla, 83cla, 83ca, 87br, 90-1, 99crb, 99br, 100tr, 105crb, 106clb, 107clb, 110clb, 339bl, 340-1b, 351c; Denys Denysevych 41cl, 153, 293cr; Deyan Denchev 19t, 226-27; Dirkr 96cr; Domossa 47cl; Sarah Dreyer 45bl; Ecophoto 8cl, 36tl, 37tr, 75t, 81crb, 82crb, 83cra, 85cr, 87cr, 94cla, 97crb, 98cr, 99cr, 100crb, 101tr,105cb, 108crb, 109crb, 109br, 110tc, 111tc, 113crb, 199cra; Simon Eeman 10ca, 80clb; Chris Fourie 80cra; Claire Fulton 75cra; Kevin Gillot 112cb; Oxana Gindo 75br; Golasza 106cla; Caglar Gungor 110crb; Halbrindley 85t; David Havel 102b; Rachel Hopper 104crb; Hpbfotos 70tl; Ivkuzmin 83clb; Jidewet 103cr; Vladislav Jirousek 100tl; Helen Jobson 315tl; Johncarnemolla 109tr; Chris Kruger 106crb; Sergio Lacueva 222b; Linncurrie 112crb; Temistocle Lucarelli 196b; Rodney Jackson / sculpted by Kobus Hattingh and Jacob Maponyane 13br; Marciparavia 283cr; MarionSmithPhotos 108tr; Arno Meintjes 109cr; Julia Middleton 146cra; Mikelane45 110tr; Hamish Mitchell 108cr; Gunter Nuyts 51br; Photogallet 97cra; Photographerlondon 57br; Picture.jacker 78-9; Jennifer Pillinger 353crb; Fabian Plock 81clb; Marek Poplawski 129cra; Stu Porter 74b, 75crb, 87tr, 97br, 113tr; Grobler Du Preez 53crb, 135b, 136b, 182bl, 200t, 209t, 331tr, 245tr; Ondřej Prosický 83cb 111cb; Rido 11br; Rixie 72-3ca; Gabriel Rojo 98tr; Rudix 47tr; Annette Rüppel 243tr; Siegfried Schnepf 8cla, 49br; sculpies 186-7t; Alexander Shalamov 103br; David Steele 30tl, 112clb; Alexey Stiop 26-7t, 57cla; Thomasgehmacher 70cla; Tobie1953 195tl; Sergey Uryadnikov 86b; Michael Valos 219tl; Wrangel 100cb, 107tr.

**FLPA:** Minden Pictures / Suzi Eszterhas 105clb, / Jelger Herder 105tc; Richard Du Toit 95tr.

**Getty Images:** 500px / Roman Betk 132bl; AFP 64crb, / Rodger Bosch 65cra, / Gianluigi Guercia 308-9, / Marco Longari 65tr, / Jean-Pierre Muller 55crb, / Anna Zieminski 123bl; Sergio Amiti 16, 116-7; Anadolu Agency / Ihsaan Haffejee 40-1b; Doug Armand 308crb; Daniel Berehulak 65clb; Bloomberg 324t; Luís Henrique Boucault 126cra; Peter Van Der Byl 223t; claudialothering 66-7; Corbis Historical / Barry Lewis 294-5b; DEA / Biblioteca Ambrosiana 63bc, / Deagostini 61br; DigitalVision / Pixelchrome Inc 203tl; Education Images / UIG 149tr; EyeEm / Juergen Wallstabe 11t; Fine Art Images / Heritage Images 61cla, 61clb; Gallo Images / Shaen Adey 347t, / Peter Chadwick 82cla, 101crb, / Nigel Dennis 82cra, / Dereck Green 39tr, / Lefty Shivambu 54-5t, / Lee Warren 55cla; Godong 321ca; Jeff Greenberg 121tl; Roger de la Harpe 204-5b; Mark Edward Harris 314-5b; The Image Bank / Juergen Ritterbach 84b; Ryan Jack 362-3; Des Jacobs 352cla; Thomas Janisch 129crb; Rajesh Jantilal 293tl; Keystone-France / Gamma-Keystone 64bc; Andrew Lichtenstein 40tl; Benjamin Matthijs Lichtwerk 250-1t; The LIFE Images Collection / Margaret Bourke-White 64tl, / Terence Spencer 327b; Hougaard Malan 176-7t; Moment / LuismiX 236bl; Moment Open / Chiara Salvadori 268-9t; Nada Stankova Photography 198-9t; Jessica Notelovitz 42-3t; Photolibrary / Russell Burden 108br, / John Cancalosi 105tl, / Luis Davilla 56b; Print Collector 62bl; Chiara Salvadori 126-7b; Hannes Thirion 49cra; Tier Und Naturfotografie J und C Sohns 33tr.

**Gold Reef City /Tsogosun:** 311clb.

**Irma Stern Museum:** 164t.

**iStockphoto.com:** aaprophoto 217crb; Aberson 58bl; AndreaWillmore 230-1; Atypeek 262tr; Barichivich 156t; BirdImages 21tl,110tl, 332-3; Lukas Bischoff 32tl, 278-9t; Henk Bogaard 111clb, 343t; bradleyhebdon 12t, 58br; brytta 46tr, 225cr, 321tr; Ecophoto 94crb; EcoPic 47br; fbxx 34t; Firaxx 283tl; Freder 10-1b; Goddard_Photography 216bl; GroblerduPreez 252-3b; HannesThirion 194-5b; Ilonde 180-1t; IPGGutenbergUKLtd 53cla; jacobeukman 337crb; JacquesKloppers 35tr; Jan-Otto 181clb; jon11 210bl; kobuspeche 278br; Ktol 24cl; Maurizio Lanini 96br; LouisHiemstra 24cr, 166clb; ManoAfrica 4, 318t; mDumbleton 49clb; Eric Middelkoop 250br; E+ / Mlenny 12-13b; Marieke Peche 189b; Pil-Art 140bl; RapidEye 44-5t, 127cra, 165tl; Siegfried Schnepf 232-3b; sculpies 28t; SeymsBrugger 76-7; spooh 8-9b, 22cr; Sproetniek 11crb, 195cra; stobi_de 81tr; E+ / subman 300-1t; Sundariji 34-5t; THEGIFT777 6-7, 10clb, 112tl, 113tc, 122-3t, 159b, 198br, 238-9t, 267b, 346bl; timh222 274bc; Utopia_88 34-5ca,

**A NOTE FROM DK EYEWITNESS**

The rapid rate at which the world is changing is constantly keeping the DK Eyewitness team on our toes. While we've worked hard to ensure that this edition of South Africa is accurate and up-to-date, we know that opening hours alter, standards shift, prices fluctuate, places close and new ones pop up in their stead. So, if you notice we've got something wrong or left something out, we want to hear about it. Please get in touch at travelguides@dk.com

**This edition updated by**
**Contributor** Philip Briggs
**Authenticity Reviewer** Leanne Feris
**Senior Editor** Alison McGill
**Senior Designers** Ben Hinks, Stuti Tiwari
**Project Editors** Parnika Bagla, Elspeth Beidas
**Project Art Editor** Bharti Karakoti
**Editor** Chhavi Nagpal
**Picture Research Coordinator** Sumita Khatwani
**Assistant Picture Research Administrator** Vagisha Pushp
**Jacket Coordinator** Bella Talbot
**Jacket Designer** Laura O'Brien
**Senior Cartographer** Subhashree Bharti
**Cartography Manager** Suresh Kumar
**DTP Designer** Tanveer Zaidi
**Senior Production Editor** Jason Little
**Production Controller** Rebecca Parton
**Deputy Managing Editor** Beverly Smart
**Managing Editors** Shikha Kulkarni, Hollie Teague
**Managing Art Editor** Bess Daly
**Senior Managing Art Editor** Priyanka Thakur
**Art Director** Maxine Pedliham
**Publishing Director** Georgina Dee

First edition 1999

Published in Great Britain by Dorling Kindersley Limited, DK, One Embassy Gardens, 8 Viaduct Gardens, London SW11 7BW

The authorised representative in the EEA is Dorling Kindersley Verlag GmbH. Arnulfstr. 124, 80636 Munich, Germany

Published in the United States by DK Publishing, 1450 Broadway, Suite 801, New York, NY 10018

Copyright © 1999, 2021 Dorling Kindersley Limited
A Penguin Random House Company
21 22 23 24 10 9 8 7 6 5 4 3 2 1

A CIP catalog record for this book is available from the British Library.

A catalog record for this book is available from the Library of Congress.

ISSN: 1542 1554
ISBN: 978 0 2414 7403 7

Printed and bound in China.

www.dk.com